# ME AND MY

Lorna Luft was born in November 1952, the daughter of Judy Garland and noted producer Sid Luft. Her stage debut was as a young girl, when her mother brought her on stage during a performance at New York's Palace Theatre to sing to an ecstatic audience. She went on to make her professional showbusiness debut at 14, but it was when the world heard her powerful and soulful voice in the lead role of Bacharach and David's hit, *Promises, Promises*, that she was confirmed as a star in her own right. She has since appeared in many successful stage, film and television productions, winning superlatives for her inimitable Miss Adelaide in the recent world tour of *Guys and Dolls*, and has also toured nationally with Wayne Sleep in their hit show *Broadway and Hollywood*, including sell-out dates at the London Palladium. In June 1998, she co-hosted the remarkable *Celebration of the Music of Judy Garland* at New York's Carnegie Hall. The mother of two children, she is married to the musical director/arranger and composer Colin Freeman. They live in Los Angeles.

# ME AND MY SHADOWS

## SHADOWS

*A Family Story*

LIVING WITH THE LEGACY OF JUDY GARLAND

# LORNA LUFT

PAN BOOKS

First published 1998 by Sidgwick & Jackson

This edition published 2001 by Pan Books
an imprint of Pan Macmillan Ltd
Pan Macmillan, 20 New Wharf Road, London N1 9RR
Basingstoke and Oxford
Associated companies throughout the world
www.panmacmillan.com

ISBN 0 330 49135 0

1 3 5 7 9 8 6 4 2

A CIP catalogue record for this book is available from
the British Library.

Typeset by Intype London Ltd
Printed and bound in Great Britain by
Mackays of Chatham plc, Chatham, Kent

# Contents

Prologue  **xi**

Chapter One  Born in a Blender  1
Chapter Two  Judy, Judy, Judy  19
Chapter Three  A Star Is Born  41
Chapter Four  There's No Place Like Holmby Hills  61
Chapter Five  London Town  81
Chapter Six  East of Eden  103
Chapter Seven  Treading Water  120
Chapter Eight  Blue Hawaii  139
Chapter Nine  Rites of Passage  156
Chapter Ten  Spin-out  168
Chapter Eleven  Burn-out  185
Chapter Twelve  Goodbye  202
Chapter Thirteen  On My Own  220
Chapter Fourteen  Promises, Promises  246
Chapter Fifteen  Clueless  272
Chapter Sixteen  Wake-up Call  299
Chapter Seventeen  Liza  317
Chapter Eighteen  The Magic Lamp  339
Chapter Nineteen  My Own Back Yard  357

Epilogue  379
Index  383

# ACKNOWLEDGMENTS

I want to express my heartfelt thanks to all who have supported me on my journey in writing this book.

Alan Nevins: I couldn't have done this without you. Thank you from the bottom of my heart. I love you.

Ken Ross: Thank you for capturing, holding onto, and truly "getting me." I am forever grateful.

Mitch Ivers: Your never wavering support, love, laughter and focus kept me going.

Gordon Wise: Thank you for your caring friendship, wonderful dedication, and love for this book.

To all my friends who were there for me: Steven Rowley, Bob Duva, Elliot Weisman, Ronni Agress, Sonny (W.T.F.D.I.P.T.) Golden, Michael Goldburg, Gary (E.G.T.M.) Hecker, Barry Manilow, Vern Alves, Tony Oppedisano, Janet Fitzgerald, Gunnar Peterson, John Kelsch, John Minor and everyone at the Judy Garland Children's Museum, Dr. Joe Takamine, Nancy Conway, Alan and Arlene Lazar, Liz Derringer, Stacy Wood, Liz and Alan Wyatt, Trevor Jones, Joe Luft, Jered Barkley, Brian Aris, Jack Martin, Nikki Haskell, Maxine Messinger, Shirley and Raymon Greene.

And John (A.T.W.I.N.Y.) Fricke: Thanks for all your help.

## TO

MY PAST:
My mother and father

MY PRESENT:
My husband Colin for showing me the meaning of
unconditional love

MY FUTURE:
My children, Jesse Cole and
Vanessa Jade—you are my world

# PROLOGUE

There's a scene at the beginning of *Peter Pan* where Peter returns to Wendy's room in the middle of the night to find his shadow, which he accidentally left behind the night before. As Mary Martin played the role, Peter flinches painfully as Wendy sews his shadow back on with a needle and thread. Peter, it seems, isn't comfortable flying without his shadow.

Mine has been the opposite problem. I have spent much of my adult life flinching with pain as I tried to pull out the threads that bound the shadows of my past to me. The biggest shadow has been my mother. To this day, people come up to me as I leave the stage after a performance and tell me that they saw my mother onstage with me every time they heard me sing. I try to keep a sense of humor about it and pass off the remark with a wisecrack. "Was she up there again? You just can't drag Mama off a stage." But the truth is that it's difficult to live your life haunted by the ghosts of the past.

People are always asking me what it's like to be Judy Garland's daughter. How do you answer a question like that? For the most part, my answer is the same as that of anyone else with a parent: it's been wonderful, and terrible, and everything in between. But it's been different, too. Very different. Most daughters haven't attended a convention where most of the people there, male and female alike, are dressed like your mother, who died thirty years ago. From *Birdcage* to *Twister*, it seems like my mother's image pops up every time I turn around. If you don't believe me, type in my mother's name in your Internet search engine and see what comes up. You'll be flooded with web sites created by the Garland faithful.

My mother is a legend. It's hard to be a legend's child. Ask my brother or sister. Or ask my closest childhood friend, Leslie Bogart. Thirty years ago you could have asked my mom, who would have told you that it's even harder to be both a legend and a parent. I'm proud of my mother, fiercely proud, but I also know how tough it is when you give a human being the status of a legend. By definition, a legend is half fiction and larger than life. The same is true of my mother. My family has benefited from that reality, but it has also suffered from it.

Some of that suffering has been caused by the thirty-something books and countless articles written about our family. Most are about my mother, many about my sister, but all have one thing in common: none has been written by someone close to my family, unless you count what I've been told was a third-rate romance novel written by my mother's last husband, who knew her for only a few months.

My mom often toyed with the idea of writing an autobiography herself, but by the end of her life she was too sick and too frightened of the process to follow through. So our family story has been chronicled instead by a long list of people who don't know us and weren't present for any of the events, real or imaginary, they wrote about. Each of these writers has had an agenda, and they usually ended up either glorifying or vilifying a group of people they really knew little about. With one or two exceptions, the result has been a fairy tale that tells more about the writer than it does about my family.

I have an agenda, too, but it's a very different one. I don't want either to glorify or to vilify my family; I want to tell a much truer, much more interesting story about a group of people who grew up in the public eye and got through it all the best way they could. Mine is a story of family traditions, good and bad, traditions that began with my grandparents and survive in my children. Some of those traditions I carry on with pride; some I have spent a lifetime struggling to overcome. We're a complicated group, my family: funny, brash, talented, oddly naive, sometimes tragic, but seldom dull. I think you'll find our story an interesting one. Many of you will also find it familiar, not because of what you've heard about my mother, but because of what you've experienced in your own lives.

One last thing: this is my story. It's not my brother's or my sister's or my father's, though I've drawn on their experience in writing it. Joe and Liza and Dad each have their own story to tell. We all do. I wouldn't presume to tell it for them. I simply want to share with you the journey of my life, hoping that what I've learned along the way will have meaning for you, too.

# Chapter One

# BORN IN A BLENDER

All of my life people have asked me what it was like to grow up as Judy Garland's daughter. I don't have an answer to that question. How could I? It's not as if I started out in the typical American family of the 1950s and then got adopted by a movie star at age fourteen. I have nothing to compare my childhood to. I can only tell you what it was like to grow up as me. In many respects my life has been like everyone else's, filled with all the usual joys and sorrows. In other respects it has been as different from most people's as Ricky Ricardo in *I Love Lucy* was from Ward Cleaver in *Leave It to Beaver*. One thing it hasn't been, though, is boring.

When people refer to my family's life as a tragedy, they completely miss the point. My life wasn't a tragedy; it was a melodrama, and I was born into the cast. My life has been filled with exhilarating highs, terrifying lows, and more than its share of farce. But if I've learned anything along the way, it's that the show must go on, and it's up to me to make it a good one.

Born in a trunk? No, that was my mother. I was three years old before my mother packed me up and took the family on the road.

Me? I was born in a blender.

My aunt Jimmy (Mama's sister Virginia) used to tell a great story about my ancestors. She said that when she was about eleven, she asked my grandfather after church one day, "Dad, what are your forefathers?" (That had been the sermon topic of the day.) Before my grandfather could reply, my mother, who was only about five at the time, piped up with an answer. Interrupting her father, Mama proudly told her sister, "I know. The four fathers are the Father, the Son, the Holy Ghost, and the real one." Everyone laughed, but Mama couldn't understand why. It made perfect sense to her.

To understand how I've gotten to this place in my life, I have to go back into the past, back two generations to a couple of stagestruck kids – my grandparents.

From the day my grandfather ran off to join the circus, my family on Mama's side has been in show business. A talent for singing and dancing ties together four generations of us, from my grandmother and grandfather Gumm to my seven-year-old daughter Vanessa. Everyone has always said that my mother would sing if the refrigerator light came on. So will my daughter. And so would my grandparents.

I guess you could say my grandparents were destined to meet. My grandfather, Frank Gumm, seems to have been born loving music. He sang everywhere – at home, at school, as a soloist in the church choir. By the time his parents died, he already knew what he wanted to do. So when a minstrel troupe passed through his hometown near Nashville, Tennessee, Grandpa ran away with them for a while. After that he and his brother earned some money singing on the trains that ran from Murfreesboro to Chattanooga, my grandpa passing a hat among the passengers at the end of the act. There's a snapshot of Grandpa in blackface at thirteen dressed like Al Jolson, holding a ukulele and wearing a bowler hat, vest, and black string tie. In 1899 you couldn't get more dapper than that.

A summer or two later Grandpa returned home and went back to the life of a proper young Southern gentleman. He enrolled as a scholarship student at Sewanee Military Academy, a private prep school near home. A rich former suitor of his sister Mary (a young woman with a sweet soprano who eventually caused a family scandal by killing herself) paid for his tuition, and Grandpa's warm, mellow tenor voice made up for his mediocre grades. He led the choir as a soloist, enjoyed the leisurely Southern way of life, and developed the powerful Irish charm and sense of style that stayed with him for the rest of his life. My family has sometimes survived on charm alone.

At the University of the South he made a name for himself with his musical talent and his way with the ladies. He left the university two years before graduation to go back to his career in vaudeville, this time for real. He loved his school, but he loved show business more. I know how he felt. I spent most of my childhood hoping show business would get me out of school.

Some years later found him in Superior, Wisconsin. It was there, on a cold winter day in 1914, that he met my grandmother Ethel.

Somehow it seems fitting that my grandparents met in a movie theater – the Parlor Theater, as a matter of fact. Grandpa had gotten a job there as an "illustrator." Grandma was his accompanist. The rage during those years was the sing-along, where the audience would sing with the performers during the breaks between films. The lyrics were projected on the movie screen, and an "illustrator" would be hired to point at the lyrics with a long stick as he led the audience in singing. If the audience liked the song, they would buy the sheet music on the way out. It was tough to keep the audience's attention, but my grandfather, with his beautiful tenor and handsome looks, was a natural. He also got a chance to show off his talents with a song or two of his own choice.

Since this was many years before the arrival of recorded background music, a pianist had to be hired to accompany not only the performers but also the silent films that were the main draw. As fate would have it, the accompanist the day my grandfather rolled into town was my grandmother, Ethel

Marion Milne. She was twenty years old (though she later claimed, in a burst of vanity, that she was really only seventeen!). Grandma Ethel looked up from the orchestra pit with those piercing black eyes of hers, and my grandpa promptly fell head over heels in love. The song he was singing, according to family legend, was "You Made Me Love You." Less than a year later they were married.

Grandma Ethel came from a musical tradition of her own. One of seven children of a railroad engineer and his wife, she'd dropped out of school by the fifth grade to help the family make ends meet. Even so, she managed to get the musical education she'd always longed for. She played the piano by ear as a child and eventually took lessons, at a quarter a lesson, with money she earned herself. By the time she was a teenager, she was good enough to get a job in a five-and-dime store singing and playing sheet music for the customers, as her daughter (my mom) would someday do in *The Good Old Summertime*, with Van Johnson. Grandma Ethel had only an average contralto voice, which most people described as "pleasant" but my mother described as "terrible." Her brother John also sang, in later years performing as a soloist in my grandfather Gumm's act, and her little sister Norma was a singer and dancer too. My great-grandmother Eva spent years accompanying Aunt Norma on the road, even to Hollywood, as Norma tried unsuccessfully to dance and sing her way to fame. For a while she performed in Los Angeles as part of what was nicknamed "the beef trust," a chorus line of pudgy women dancers.

Yes, along with musical talent, a tendency to put on weight also runs in my family.

Once married, Grandma and Grandpa Gumm went on the road. They put together an act and called themselves "Jack and Virginia Lee, Sweet Southern Singers." I'm not sure which was the biggest stretch of the truth, calling Grandma's voice "sweet" or calling her Southern (fifty years later my Gumm relatives still called Grandma Ethel "that Northern girl").

Anyhow, "Jack and Virginia" did pretty well. As my mother later remembered it, the act always opened the same way. When the curtain came up, Grandpa would be standing next to Grandma where she sat on the piano bench. After introducing both of them in that Southern drawl of his, he would ask Grandma to show the audience how tiny her hands were. Straightening her small body, she would hold her hands up to the audience so they could see how tiny her fingers were. Then, turning back to the piano, she would launch into "Alexander's Ragtime Band," her fingers racing over the keys. That bit always earned a huge burst of applause.

A year later Grandma Ethel got sick while they were on a trip south. The flu turned out to be my aunt Susie, born in September 1915. Two years later my aunt Jimmy was born. With two babies to take care of, my grandparents decided to settle down. After looking around a little, they decided to invest their money in the only thing they knew much about: a theater. To raise cash Grandpa sold his "flasher," the big diamond ring he wore on his fourth finger when he played his ukulele onstage; and they invested everything they had in the New Grand, a motion picture house in Grand Rapids, Minnesota, where Grandpa was already the manager. Grandpa took tickets and ran the concession stand, Grandma played the piano for the films, and they both performed between pictures as "Jack and Virginia Lee" when Grandma wasn't too busy taking care of babies. All in all, they did well. The theater prospered along with the family, and soon they were directing the church choir (Grandma played the organ), running the local amateur show, and hosting a big percentage of the parties in town.

Loving a good party runs in my family too.

It wasn't long before "Jack and Virginia" became a family act – the Four Gumms. As soon as my aunts were old enough, my grandmother began putting together an act for them. Susie and Jimmy had been singing along with their parents at home for as long as they could remember, and when guests came to the house, as they frequently did, the girls would sing for them, too. So it was only natural that they soon joined their parents onstage. They'd grown up sitting in the New Grand every night while their parents performed, so the stage there was already a familiar part of their second home. By the time my aunt Susie was five, she and Aunt Jimmy were practicing along with the Duncan Sisters on their wind-up Victrola. Grandma Ethel coached their singing, taught them simple dance steps, and sewed them fancy costumes. What they lacked in harmony they made up for in volume and enthusiasm, and soon they were a popular part of the Friday night entertainments at the New Grand.

The Gumm family act seemed complete. My grandparents were happy with their little family and didn't intend to have any more children. Lucky for me, though, things didn't go as planned. Four years after my aunt Jimmy was born, Grandma Ethel discovered there'd been an accident. That little accident was Mama.

Once she came along, nothing was ever the same again.

Mama has always loved to make an entrance. When she did arrive, at dawn on June 10, 1922, she looked like a tiny version of Grandma Ethel. They named her Frances, after her father – Frances Ethel Gumm – but nobody ever called her Frances. They just called her "Baby." Once my grandfather got a look at her big dark eyes, he forgot that he'd been wanting a boy and fell hopelessly in love with Baby.

Mama would have that effect on people for the rest of her life.

The truth is, whatever Mama might say about it years later, everybody loved her. Even her big sisters, jealous as they were at times, found her irresistible. Every picture I have of her as a child shows this pixie-like creature with big black eyes, skinny legs, a tiny body, and enough life in her face for any ten people. Even in her baby pictures, her eyes draw you. And now, except for the color of her eyes, my daughter Vanessa looks exactly like her.

Mama's stage debut came at the tender age of two. She had grown up at home and in her parents' theater watching her family sing, and from the time she could toddle, she was running out onstage to try to join them. At home she would stand behind her sisters when they practiced their numbers and try to imitate them. At the theater on Friday nights she'd stand backstage in the wings, peeking out at Susie and Jimmy as they sang and danced. As soon as she could talk, she began begging to join them. When her parents said no, she'd scream and cry. Then one day, when she was just two, her father decided to teach her the words to "My Country, 'Tis of Thee," and she sang it right through to the end. Her father was her only audience at that first performance, and he was amazed. As Grandpa told Grandma when she got home, "Baby Gumm is good, she is." Years later Mama told me she still remembered those words of praise from Grandpa.

The time had clearly come to let Baby Gumm make her debut. As she sat in Great-grandma Eva's lap at her sisters' Christmas Eve performance that year, she did her best to sing along. After the performance, urged on by Grandma Eva, she edged up to her mother and whispered, "Mama, can I sing, too?" Grandma Ethel told her no, not that day, but promised she could sing at the performance on the 26th. "Not today, Baby – but in just two days."

Grandma kept her promise. Mama already knew some of the words to "Jingle Bells," so Grandma Ethel coached her until she knew it perfectly, and gave her a small bell to ring at the appropriate moment. Grandma also made her a little sleeveless dress out of white netting, with a white bodice underneath and sprigs of holly pinned on by Susie and Jimmy. With soft bangs and her hair curled into shoulder-length ringlets, Mama couldn't have looked sweeter. As I've heard it, when her turn came and her father gently pushed her onstage, she strode confidently downstage center. She was so tiny that she looked even younger than the two-year-old she was. The audience couldn't believe she was going to sing.

If my grandparents were worried about Mama as she stood there that night, they didn't need to be. Family legend has it that as Grandma Ethel began the first notes of "Jingle Bells" on the piano in the pit below, Mama launched into her number on perfect pitch, with astonishing volume, keeping time with her little bell. When she finished her song, to wildly enthusiastic applause, she looked down at Grandma Ethel and announced, "I wanna sing some more." And she did. Grandma hurried to catch up on the piano, doubled up with laughter the whole time, while Grandpa hissed to Mama from the wings, "Baby, come off! Come off!" Mama, of course, ignored him and kept on singing. (She'd be doing *that* the rest of her life!)

Each time she got to the end of the song, she'd pause, take a bow, and start all over again. By then the audience was applauding and cheering, and Grandma was too busy playing the piano to stop her. Finally, after the fifth chorus, Grandpa went on stage, picked Mama up, threw her over his shoulder, and carried her off – still singing and ringing her little bell as he took her into the wings. Friends in the audience that night swear they could still hear her when she got backstage.

The love affair between Mama and her audience started that night.

There were now three singing Gumm Sisters. If they'd stuck to Friday night performances in my grandfather Gumm's theater, nobody but me and my family would even remember them. But they didn't stay in Grand Rapids. When my mom was four years old, the whole family packed up and moved to sunny California, where I would be born over twenty-five years later. The Grand Rapids newspaper lists at least six going-away parties in their honor, one a big banquet at the Episcopal church where my grandfather was choirmaster. That move would change our family forever.

On a holiday trip to California that summer, my grandparents had touched up their old vaudeville act. They must have stopped in nearly every little town from Minnesota to Los Angeles. Whenever they passed through a town with a movie theater and a stage, they stopped and made their pitch to the manager. Most of the time, the manager made a deal for a percentage of the house. The whole family would run around town putting up posters on fences and posts, then go get dressed in the restroom at the nearest gas station. "Jack and Virginia" would perform that night, with the three girls sitting in the front row, applauding as loudly as possible. If they were lucky, they got offered a second night. Sometimes, to sweeten the pot, my grandparents would offer to let the Gumm Sisters perform, too. Since it was pretty hard to resist three little girls, especially my mother with her big black eyes, the managers often went for it. By the end of the evening the family usually had enough gas and food money to move on. It wasn't a very good way to get rich, but it was a lot of fun, and it paid enough to get them the two thousand miles to California when they decided to move there permanently in October 1926.

My mother never forgot those summer trips. Even though she was about four years old at the time, they remained one of her best childhood memories. And even then, Mama was a little clown. There's a very funny scene at the beginning of *Easter Parade* where my mother walks down Fifth Avenue making faces at the passing men so they'll turn around and look at her as she goes by. Well, Aunt Jimmy said that as they were driving around all those years ago, cars would sometimes swerve dangerously close to their car as they passed. Every time it happened, they'd notice that the people in the passing car would turn around to look at them, laughing and smiling. Finally my grandfather took a glance in the rear-view mirror at just the right time, and saw my mother kneeling on the back seat with her face against the rear window, making faces at passing cars, having the time of her life, crossing her eyes and pulling up the lids, sucking in her cheeks, wiggling her tongue. When Grandpa shouted at her, she stopped, but not for long.

Nothing could keep my mother from her audience – except my mother.

The family settled down in the little desert town of Lancaster, a place my mother would eventually come to hate as much as she'd loved Grand Rapids. Lancaster isn't exactly the entertainment capital of the world, but that didn't matter to my grandfather. There was a beautiful 500-seat movie theater for him to run, and Los Angeles was only a three-hour drive away. Transplanted from Minnesota to the movie mecca, Baby Gumm's performing opportunities soon skyrocketed. Besides, she was getting older, and the time had come to train in earnest for the profession her family – and her talent – had chosen for her.

Looking back on it, my mother always said that the move from Grand Rapids to Lancaster was the turning point in her life. In Grand Rapids, they were happy. In Lancaster, they weren't. In Grand Rapids, performing was a joy. In California it became a job, one that would consume my mother's entire life and eventually control mine. Mama used to say she started working at five and never got a chance to quit.

For a while performing was still fun. At first my grandparents sang together at the new theater in Lancaster, and the girls performed with them. Their first notices were good. According to a review in the *Antelope Valley Ledger-Gazette*, my grandparents were "accomplished musicians" whose "little daughters completely won the hearts of the audience with their songs and dances."

Slowly, though, things began to go downhill. As my grandparents' marriage started falling apart, they stopped performing together and began to go their separate ways. For my grandfather, running the theater and struggling to make a go of it took up most of his time. My grandmother coped with the stress by throwing herself heart and soul into her children, especially her children's careers. Every day after school now the girls had to come home and practice singing and dancing for at least an hour with their mother. Several afternoons a week they also went to dance lessons at the local studio. When things got really bad between my grandparents, my grandmother started taking the girls into Los Angeles every weekend for lessons and auditions. Eventually she would take an apartment there and live separate from her husband for long periods, keeping my mother with her most of the time.

My mother always blamed my grandmother for the strain in her parents' marriage. According to family friends, my mother believed that my grandmother was having an affair all that time with Will Gilmore, a family friend who became her second husband after my grandfather died.

There are other rumors, too, rumors that have been widely circulated since my grandfather's death. According to these rumors, Frank Gumm was a "latent homosexual," and the marriage collapsed when my grandmother found out. I don't know whether or not these rumors are true. My mother certainly never said anything to confirm this, even to my father, though she did once tell him she'd heard the stories. Marc Rabwin, a close family friend, believed the rumors. I respect his opinion, but since he wasn't speaking from direct knowledge, I take it as opinion, not fact. I'm suspicious of the widespread stories about my grandfather's orientation because none of them appeared in print until after his, his wife's and his children's death, when it was too late to verify them. Since everyone in my immediate family (including me) has been labeled "gay" in print at some point, I'm skeptical about the rumors surrounding my grandfather. As far as I know, the only gay member of my family was Peter Allen, my beloved former brother-in-law, who died of AIDS a few years ago. Not that sexuality matters to me anyway; family apart, I have friends who are gay, and friends who are straight, and I love them all.

One thing *is* certain: any stories of my grandfather having trouble with the authorities because of "unwelcome advances" to young men are false. A detective hired by the Children's Museum in Grand Rapids (formerly the Judy Garland Museum) spent months going through newspapers and public records in Minnesota for the eight years my grandparents lived in Grand Rapids, and he found no official complaints about Frank Gumm. If the police had ever been called about my grandfather, there would be a record buried somewhere. There isn't.

No one but my grandfather, and any men he may have had contact with, could possibly know the truth about the rumors. It's not for me to say what happened, because I don't know, and nor do I much care, either. What does matter is that Frank Gumm was a great father, and my mother adored him. I wish he could have been there for us when I was growing up.

Whatever the reasons for the rift, the tensions in my grand-parents' marriage created an atmosphere of anger and resentment at home. The result was that the family was together less and less. In a show business family, life on the road is the perfect cover-up for a dysfunctional, disintegrating family. It is a pattern that repeated itself in my own marriage.

So the Gumm family went back on the road again, this time on a part-time basis. Only now, instead of "Jack and Virginia" and the Gumm Sisters, it was just Grandma Ethel and the girls. Grandpa stayed in Lancaster, and Grandma took the girls to Los Angeles, where they enrolled in the famous Meglin School of Dance, which eventually produced Shirley Temple and a whole host of other child stars. The girls worked on their singing and dancing there and were soon appearing regularly in the *Meglin Kiddies Show* at Loew's State Theater in downtown Los Angeles. They also played an occasional booking at small theaters outside of town. As their popularity grew, they began doing bookings from Long Beach to San Francisco, eventually going out of state to Seattle. They also did radio appearances. They even made a few film shorts, and they eventually actually got paid for all this. For most kids it would have been a crazy way to grow up, but for a vaudeville family, it was no more unusual than a kid working in his parents' grocery store after school. It was just what they did.

Sometimes it was a lot of fun. Years later, after my mother's death, Aunt Jimmy told me stories about life as a child performer. On Saturday nights my grandmother would take the girls to see performances at all the best theaters in town – the State, the Paramount, or Warner's Hollywood. It was exciting and even glamorous. And although there were lots of long drives, the three girls would pass the time singing in the car together, everything from childhood favorites like "The Old Gray Mare" to the latest hits.

Even the performances could be great fun, especially when things didn't go as planned. My mother sometimes told us about the ridiculous things that happened to them on the road. One time when they were performing at a small rundown theater near L.A., the audience was filled with bored teenagers who had hidden cloves of garlic in the footlights before the show. When they turned on the footlights and Mama and my aunts came out to sing, the garlic started cooking. A few minutes into their act, the girls were overwhelmed with the odor of frying garlic. Giggling and choking on the fumes, they struggled on, but then a sandwich sailed onto the stage, hitting Aunt Susie in the stomach and strewing salami and cheese across the stage floor. Totally losing control, the girls looked at each other, linked arms, and danced sideways offstage where they fell down laughing.

That wasn't the only time the Gumm Sisters finished their number shaking with laughter and beat a fast retreat. On another occasion, when Mama was still very small, she got caught in the bangles on the pants of her harem costume while trying to do a quick change in the wings. When my aunts, who were right in the middle of a number onstage, glanced into the wings, there was Baby, stark naked, rolling around on the floor trying to kick the harem pants loose.

But mostly there was a lot of hard work. Being on the road meant living out of a suitcase, missing play time and school events, leaving their friends behind. While other children slept or played, my mother and her sisters worked. Every weekday there was practice after school. Weekends were taken up with lessons and performances. On Saturday mornings my mother had to get up at 7 a.m. and have her hair washed and set in tight curlers, then get in the car for a two-hour drive to the city. Lunch was often a quick sandwich between practice sessions. When the girls went on the road, they often had to perform in dirty little dives for next to no money. They were attending to business at a time when most children are busy just being children. That was something my mother tried hard to protect me from.

But worst of all, somewhere along the line Mama stopped feeling like a child and starting feeling like a commodity. She began to feel as if her only value was her ability to sing. As an adult she told friends that when she was a child, everyone was always "winding me up to sing, and then putting me back in the closet when they were finished with me." Even family friends introduced her as "Frances who can sing." Singing was her job, and she rarely got time off, even as a child. She used to tell me she'd been working all her life. The whole situation was complicated by the fact that my grandmother was her manager, and often her agent. My grandmother's motives in becoming Mama's manager were good ones – she wanted to protect Mama, carefully watching over her, but the fact remains that managers and agents promote "talent." And in Hollywood, talent is a product, not a person. When a child has a career, it's almost impossible for her parents to be parents first and managers second. And even if they find a way, it becomes impossible for their children to know whether they're loved for themselves or for what they can do.

The saving grace for Mama was my grandfather. Whatever the chaos of their daily lives, Mama and her sisters always went back home to their dad. The family album shows a picture of a handsome, stylish young man with a mustache, a derby, a jaunty suit, and a diamond ring on his fourth finger. My grandfather was very handsome, and very charming, too, but that wasn't why my mother loved him so much. She loved him because he was such a good father. He played with his girls, tossing them in the air, carrying them on his shoulders, romping in the snow with them. He sang and laughed with them. He held them on his lap at night and helped care for them when they were sick. Most of all, he was their advocate with their mother. He tried his best to give his girls a normal childhood, to see that they had time for school and play, time to be just kids. God knows he spoiled them, too.

Although the strife in my grandparents' marriage caused a breach between Mama and my grandmother, it seemed to bring Mama and my grandfather closer. She loved him so much that years later she once even listed her birthplace as Murfreesboro, Tennessee, because my grandfather was born there. The song she sang to close her TV show when I was a kid was one she said my grandfather performed. I never met my grandfather Gumm. He died years before I was born, yet in many ways he was one of the most important people in my life. He lived with us every day of my mother's life, in her memory and in her heart.

I wonder if she ever looked at my father without comparing him to hers.


When I drive with Jesse and Vanessa through the old Los Angeles theater district today, Baby Gumm and the Meglin Kiddie shows she was featured in seem like another century to me. What was once one of the most glamorous sections of Los Angeles is now a rundown street filled with seedy stores displaying gaudy gowns my mother's most ardent cross-dressing fans wouldn't be caught dead in. One five-block section of Broadway still houses the remains of the theaters my mother once performed in or went to on Saturday afternoons with her mother: the Orpheus is still in pretty decent shape, at time of writing its battered old marquee advertising Madonna in *Evita*. The Rialto is now a discount store (5 shirts for $10), and the letters that announce the State barely cling to the old brick building, its façade crumbled away under the shock of too many earthquakes.

Our parents' lives always seem so long ago, so far removed from our own. It's impossible to really comprehend that they were ever children, too. When I show Vanessa pictures of myself as a child, she smiles sweetly but uncomprehendingly. What does the little girl twirling in a television studio have to do with her mommy? The child in the picture is light years away from Vanessa's world.

But our parents were children, not so long ago, and their lives continue to interlock with ours until the day we die, as my life will always be a part of my son's and my daughter's. I am aware of that every time I look at my little girl and see my mother's face peering back at me, every time I see a picture from The Wizard of Oz or hear my mother's young voice on an MGM recording. It's remarkable, really, how much of our lives begins before we're even born. When I look at my mother's family, I'm amazed at the patterns that have been repeated in my life.

Generation after generation, we all seem to be born singing, to one degree or another. Childhood friends of my grandfather's say he was always whistling or singing. As for me, I could always sing better than my friends, and I could always follow the line of a melody and reproduce it on my own. Both of my children have the same innate musical talent, my daughter to a remarkable degree. It's strange indeed to consider how many of my mother's best-known moments in film were a replay of her parents' real-life experiences, from vaudeville to broken hearts.

Yet, in direct contradiction of each generation's advice, we all seem to be wedded to show business. My grandfather fought long and hard to keep my mother from becoming a "professional kid." Mama, in turn, always tried to talk us out of going into show business. "You'll break my heart," she'd tell us. "I don't want to watch you go through what I went through." Yet Liza and I both make our living singing, and like my mother did to me, I tell my own kids not to go into show business. But blessing or curse, we all seem driven to perform, in part because it's all we really know how to do. When I was a little girl, the only TV show I could relate to was *I Love Lucy* because Ricky was a performer. The "normal" families might as well have been from Mars. I used to ask myself what on earth I would do if I couldn't make a living in show business. I still don't have an answer.

I see other patterns, too: the women in our family can't seem to stay away from musicians. My sister married one; I married two. My grandmother married a musician. So did both my aunts, twice. So did my mother, the first time. I'm no different. My first great love as an adult was singer Barry Manilow, and I fell in love with him as much for his music as anything else. My ex-husband Jake was a rock guitarist. My husband Colin is an arranger-conductor.

There's also the pattern of family members serving as managers. Just as my grandmother managed her children's careers, and my father managed my mother's career, Jake managed mine. And just as it destroyed those relationships, it caused problems for Jake and me too. Somehow none of us seems able to keep family and business separate. Funny how that works.

Luckily, some good things got passed down, too. Just as my grandfather Frank was there for Mama, my father was always there for me, the port in every storm. Whether she realized it or not, my mother did just as well at picking a father for me as Grandma Ethel did picking a father for Mama.

Most important of all, my family passed on a lot of love. Whatever marital stuggles we may have, we love our children fiercely. My grandparents had a hard time later in their marriage, just as my parents did, but they gave their kids a lot of love. They may not always have done the right thing for their kids, but it wasn't because they didn't love them. I always knew my mother loved me, loved us, more than anything else in life. Everything I know about being a good mother to my children, I learned from her.

Did our parents love us? Damn right they did. That's another family tradition.


I wonder sometimes what would have happened to us all if Mama had just stayed Baby Frances Gumm, daughter of Frank and Ethel Gumm of Lancaster. But she didn't. She became Judy Garland. She became a legend.

# Chapter Two

# JUDY, JUDY, JUDY

Recently my seven-year-old daughter and I took an afternoon walk. It was one of those crisp, clear winter days that are so rare in Los Angeles, and we were enjoying the exercise after being cooped up in our house by the rain. As we strolled down Rodeo Drive, window-shopping as we went, we noticed a new shop – one of those Franklin Mint stores. I was looking in the window at one of the displays when I was startled by Vanessa's voice asking me, "Mama, isn't that Grandma?"

I turned to look where Vanessa's finger was pointing, and there to my right was a display of *Wizard of Oz* memorabilia, with my mother memorialized in a series of porcelain figures. Caught off guard, I thought, "Here we go again," as I told Vanessa that yes, that was her grandmother.

It is strange being the daughter of a screen icon, especially one who died so young. I am one of a very small group of celebrities' children who are reminded daily of a parent's life – and, of course, their death. When most people lose a loved parent, they go through a process of grief and bereavement and then move on with their lives. When your parent is a public idol, you never really have a chance to lay them to rest. I was painfully reminded of this only recently, with the tragic death of Diana, Princess of Wales, whom I felt honoured to be able to consider a friend. I understand as few people can what Prince William and Prince Harry will have to deal with for the rest of their lives. I'm still approached in public places by strangers who grab my hand or even my shoulders, sometimes with tears in their eyes, and offer their condolences as if my mother died last week instead of almost thirty years ago. To them, my mother will never really die. To them, my mother will always be a wide-eyed little girl in blue gingham holding her dog.

No child thinks of her mother as a legend. However famous parents may be in the eyes of the world, they remain "Mama" or "Daddy" to their children. My mother wasn't just my mom, though; she was Judy Garland – "our Judy" to legions of her fans. That reality affected my life long before I was old enough to understand it. It will affect my children's lives as well.

None of this might ever have happened if my grandfather had had his way. Much as he loved show business, he wasn't at all sure that becoming a "star" would be the best thing for my mother. For him, vaudeville was a family business, something the whole family could do together. After all, "Jack and Virginia Lee" had always been a family act. Until she was nearly twelve, my mother performed with her sisters, which was how she liked it. It was one thing to be "Baby Gumm," youngest and cutest of the three Gumm Sisters, strutting her stuff while her sisters harmonized in the background. It was quite another to climb up onstage alone, without her sisters next to her and her parents in the front row. Like it or not, though, my mother was headed for stardom.

A lot of things began pushing my mom into the limelight. The first was simply the effect of time. Mama's sisters grew up. Being so many years older, Aunt Susie and Aunt Jimmy inevitably grew out of the sister act. Like every other teenager, they wanted to date, go to dances with boys, and eventually to get married. Susie, the oldest, was the first to marry. Jimmy would soon follow.

Then there were the changes in the entertainment industry

itself. With talkies taking over the movies, "Jack and Virginia" were soon out of jobs as performers. Grandma Ethel was no longer needed to play the piano during the silent films, nobody was interested in "illustrators" to point out lyrics anymore, and fewer and fewer theaters wanted performers to entertain audiences between pictures. The result was that more and more vaudeville performers like my grandparents were out of work, even if for them it had become more of a sideline. Vaudeville was a dying art. If my mother hadn't made the change from vaudeville to film when she did, I might be teaching singing at the local junior high today instead of carrying on my own show business career.

But, of course, Mama did make the change. She stopped being Baby Frances Gumm and was rechristened Judy Garland. There are several stories about how my mother got her name, but they all involve George Jessel. It happened at the World's Fair in 1934. This fair wasn't in St. Louis like in Mama's movie, but in Chicago. That year the fair was billed as "The Century of Progress," and Grandma Ethel thought it would be a great experience for her girls to go. Grandma managed to book the Gumm Sisters in a vaudeville show hosted by George Jessel – a huge stroke of luck since Jessel was already popular.

When George Jessel introduced the sister act, though, everybody laughed. They thought the name "Gumm" was just another of Jessel's jokes. During the break following the second performance, Jessel told my grandmother she had to change the girls' name. It wasn't hard to convince her. All three girls and Grandma Ethel had been thoroughly sick of the name "Gumm Sisters" for quite some time. Over the years they'd been called everything from the Glum Sisters to the Dumb Sisters to the Spearmints (and every other brand of gum you can think of). Jessel told Grandma that he'd think of a new name for them before the next show, so when they went on again, he announced them as "The Garland Sisters." Jessel's version was that he got the idea from an old friend of his named Garland, who happened to call him between shows that day.

My mother had a different story, though. Mama always said Jessel chose it because she and her sisters were "as pretty as a garland of flowers." I like Mama's version better. Whatever the reason, everybody liked the new name, and it stuck.

Mama chose her new first name herself. She got the idea from the Hoagy Carmichael hit, "Judy." Mama said it was a "peppy name," and she liked the lyric it came from: "If you think she's a saint, and you find that she ain't, that's Judy." My mother never said so, but she obviously knew that the line described her perfectly. The result was that at twelve years old, my mother stopped being Frances Gumm and became Judy Garland. Not coincidentally, "Judy" became the most popular name for American girls for more than ten years after *The Wizard of Oz* was released. "Baby Frances" soon became a distant memory for my mother. Nothing made her madder when I was a kid than being called Frances. Gene Palumbo, her musical director on *The Judy Garland Show* years later, would do it occasionally to set her off. It worked.


With a new name that had considerable marquee appeal, all that remained was for Mama to be discovered. By this time Mama had her own agent, and it was clear that if any of the Gumms were going to be stars, it would be Mama. She was a stand-out in any group. Mama had started getting some serious attention around town, and it all came to a head one day in the autumn of 1935. There are several versions of what happened that day, but as I heard the story, my mom was playing outside in sneakers and dirty playclothes when her agent called. He said she had to come to Metro immediately for an audition. She'd auditioned once before, but it had all come to nothing. Mama protested, saying she was a mess and needed time to fix herself up, but my grandfather told her she looked fine and stuck her in the car, sneakers and all. (Grandma Ethel had a fit when she found out.) An hour or so later Mama was taken into the office of Mr. L. B. Mayer himself and told to sing. She did. When she finished, Mayer didn't say a word, so Grandpa took Mama home in a huff.

The next day, though, the agent called back. Could Mama sing for Mr. Mayer again, this time on a sound stage? This time around Grandma got the call, and you can bet that she fixed my mother up in her very best outfit. A short while later Mama was taken into a huge, empty sound studio to wait for Mr. Mayer. As usual, Mama rose to the occasion. When L.B. arrived, Mama sang again, this time ending with Mr. Mayer's favorite – the Jewish song "Eli, Eli." Legend has it that L.B. was moved to tears. Two weeks later Mr. Mayer signed my mother to a contract – no screen test, nothing. Judy Garland was on her way.

But on her way where? Metro wasn't really the lollipop land of the movies. It was a pretty overwhelming place to work, especially for a twelve-year-old kid. Ready or not, though, my mother was processed into the MGM studio system.


It's hard for us to imagine now what the system was like in the 1930s. Things are so different today – most actors would kill for a multi-picture deal. When my mother signed with MGM, though, that was the only kind of contract an actor could sign. There was no such thing as an independent agent. When you signed up with Metro, you weren't just signing up for a job – you were signing over yourself, body and soul, for the studio had an option on you every year.

In those days Metro was turning out a film per week. Doing this required incredible planning and organization, and Metro had it. They kept a large group of screenwriters, producers, and directors on staff year-round. All of them were assigned projects as part of their contracts, with little say-so in what projects they worked on during their six-day weeks.

The creative heads were just the tip of the iceberg, though.

Besides the seemingly endless costumers, musicians, and set painters, there were thousands of secretaries, nurses, doctors, teachers, and the like. And, of course, there were hundreds of actors and actresses, contract players who moved in and out of parts as the studio heads chose. Metro was not only a big company; it was a small city. Everything its "citizens" needed was right on the lot.

The school my mother attended was a storybook building right in the middle of the sound stages. It was a tiny replica of a one-room schoolhouse, complete with a front porch, a rocking chair, and a cobblestone lane leading to the front entrance. My mom's class included Mickey Rooney, Freddie Bartholomew, and Deanna Durbin. Mama had met Mickey before, when they'd both attended Mrs. Lawlor's Academy in Los Angeles, so they became instant best buddies. My mom was a good student, and she got plenty of attention in a classroom that averaged five students.

Traditional school subjects were only the beginning for these children. Every day there were voice lessons, of course, and dance lessons. There were also diction lessons, drama lessons, make-up lessons, charm and deportment lessons, and so forth. Mama was instructed in how to walk, talk, stand, and breathe – literally. She was also stripped down, measured, photographed, and analyzed, all in the most humiliating fashion, and all as puberty was first beginning for her. The studio was not pleased with what they saw. My mother was written up as too short and too chubby, with a round spine and no neck. She had a bad bite, and her nose turned up too much, they said. Her eyes were the only thing that got a good review from the MGM make-over artists. Nobody ever mentioned her lovely skin.

My mother was one of the most beautiful women I've ever seen. I always longed to look like her (instead of my dad!). But she wasn't good enough for Metro. They thought she should fit the movie star stereotype: slender, glamorous, and preferably blond. My mother was tiny, dark-haired, and barrel-chested. Not what MGM had in mind. They loved her voice, but they weren't crazy about her looks.

So they set to work to remake her. They put her on a diet. They squeezed her into corsets to make her middle look thinner, and they bound her chest to make her look younger. They inserted little rubber disks into her nose so it wouldn't turn up so much. They made caps for her teeth. To make her feel better about the caps, her musical mentor, Roger Edens, gave her a little music box shaped like a piano to keep the caps in. My aunt Jimmy still spent a lot of time with Mama in those days, and she told me my mom accidentally broke the tooth caps one afternoon when she shut the music box lid on them. My mom got so scared when she saw what she'd done that she begged Aunt Jimmy to tell L.B. Mayer that Jimmy had done it. Aunt Jimmy told me, "There was no way I was going to tell Mr. Mayer it was me because I could have gotten in big trouble." When it got right down to it, my mother and her sister were still just a couple of kids from Lancaster who didn't want to get in trouble with the grown-ups.

Overall, though, my mother loved being at the studio. People are always saying that my mother never had an adolescence. It's not true; she did have an adolescence. It just happened to be on a movie set. My mother never, ever told me she was unhappy growing up on the MGM lot. When I was a kid, she told me she liked it, that it was fun. It was exciting to work at the biggest movie studio in the world. Mama got to meet some of Hollywood's biggest stars, and she got to watch as Metro created the magic of films.

Besides, along with the unkind remarks from the make-up department, there was also the flattery. Mama got a lot of attention for her singing. She got a lot of attention, period. The studio aimed to please. And there was the money, lots of money, remarkable amounts for a kid her age. She was guaranteed $100 a week to start and $1,000 a week by her twentieth birthday, huge sums in the middle of the Depression. In reality, it turned out better than that, for MGM repeatedly raised her salary over the years, paying her far more than their contractual obligation. For the Gumm family, this was overwhelming prosperity after the years of struggling financially in Lancaster.

Even the money caused problems, though. When she signed her contract with MGM, Mama became the chief bread-winner for the family. Both of my grandparents continued to work, but their income couldn't compete with their daughter's. It's never healthy for one family member, especially a child, to support all the rest. My grandparents did their best to handle my mother's finances responsibly, but it was hard. My mom had never had any sense of discipline about money (her parents had never even made her stick to an allowance). None of the family was very good with money, and nobody was exactly sure where it all went – another family pattern. During her Metro years my mother got used to having money whenever she wanted it, and later in life this caused problems.

In the middle of all these changes, good and bad, came the biggest blow of my mother's childhood, maybe the biggest blow of her life. My grandfather Frank, the light of my mother's life, the source of all her emotional security, died suddenly of a massive hemorrhage. Four years later, on the anniversary of his death, my grandmother married another man. My mother never got over either event.

While my mom struggled to survive this personal loss, the studio was trying to figure out what to do with her professionally. She had reached what they call the awkward age. At thirteen she was too old to play the Shirley-Temple-style kiddie parts, but she wasn't old enough to play a teenage romance, either. She was rapidly developing the figure of a young woman, but her face still had the wide-eyed innocence of a little girl. She just didn't seem to fit in anywhere. Time was going by, and Mama was beginning to wonder if she was ever going to get a real part. And that's where Roger Edens came in.

Roger had started his career as a pianist for the Gershwins. He was the pit pianist when Ethel Merman did *Girl Crazy* on Broadway, the show my mom did as a movie years later. Roger was an incredibly gifted musician, and Metro soon became interested in hiring him. Shortly before MGM signed my mother, Roger had first gone to work for the studio himself. Professionally, Roger "created" Judy Garland. He recognized not only my mother's extraordinary musical gifts, but also her emotional sensitivity. It was his gifts as composer and arranger that gave my mother the chance to shine on camera. From the first time he heard her sing, he knew she was something very special. He also knew that if Mama was ever going to come into her own, she would have to stop using the inappropriate material of the popular singers of the day (the way Ethel had taught her) and learn to trust herself. He worked hard with my mom to get her to stop belting out numbers like a miniature Ethel Merman, which her vocal abilities could already cope with, and start singing like Judy, the fourteen-year-old girl who missed her father and longed for a boyfriend. It was Roger who gave Mama the courage to let the softness, the vulnerability that was a part of her into her singing. Without Roger we might never have had "Over the Rainbow," at least not the way we all remember it.

I loved Roger Edens when I was a little girl. Roger had an amazing speaking voice and a deep Southern accent; I loved to listen to him talk. He came into my mother's life at a time when she really needed him. Mama adored him, and he felt the same way about her. Roger was one of the very few people whom my mother completely respected. My mother learned young how to intimidate people when she wanted to, but it didn't work on Roger. Roger was the only man besides my father who could say no to my mom and get away with it. I think Roger knew my mother better than anyone in the world except us. He stayed with her to the very end. He even died very shortly after Mama did.

It was Roger who got my mother the break she needed. Clark Gable was having a birthday, and they were going to have a party for him on the Metro lot. My mom had a huge crush on him. So Roger got the idea to have Mama sing to

Clark Gable at the party and wrote "Dear Mr. Gable" for her. She sang it right to him, simple and sweet the way Roger had taught her. Clark Gable was completely taken by her, and so was everyone else. Mr. Mayer said they had to get my mother a property. In 1938 they got one. That property, of course, was *The Wizard of Oz*. My mother was cast as Dorothy, "Over the Rainbow" was written for her, and the rest, as they say, is history.

I don't think anybody knew at the time what a phenomenon *Oz* would turn out to be. How could they? That innocence is part of the charm of the movie. MGM knew it was special, and they hoped it would be a success. But they had no way of knowing it would become an annual television event, part of every American's childhood.

1939 was a huge turning point for my family. *The Wizard of Oz* premiered, and my mother became immortal. She was only seventeen, but she would never have a private life again. From then on she had to leave the U.S. if she wanted to be left alone in public. She couldn't go shopping anymore; she couldn't even walk down the street without being mobbed. She was no longer a girl; she had become an icon.

Mama and Mickey Rooney flew to New York to do promos for *Babes in Arms* and *Wizard*, and for the first time in her life my mother was literally mobbed. Thousands of people surged around her, screaming, wanting to touch her everywhere she went, to be near "Dorothy." It was both exciting and terrifying, and it never stopped. When she died thirty years later, it was still going on.

The crowds weren't the only things that started to overwhelm her. The money was pouring in, with MGM continually raising Mama's salary. That sounds wonderful on the surface, but what does a teenager know about handling such large amounts of money? My grandmother didn't know how to handle it, either, so both Mama and Grandma were surrounded by financial advisors who gave them conflicting advice. My mom gave Grandma money to build a house, and Ethel had a "movie star" house built on pricey Stone Canyon Drive, with a huge suite for Mama upstairs and plenty of room for Ethel's new husband, my aunt Jimmy (who was divorced from her first husband and back home by then), my cousin Judalein, and a whole staff of servants that neither my mom nor my grandmother knew how to manage. The number of servants, advisors, and managers of various types kept growing, and with them my mother's expenses. It was a pattern that continued for the rest of her life. She was never able to live within her income.

It was during this period that she encountered the monster that would eventually take her life. Much as she struggled with the pressures of finances, fame, and job demands all her life, she could have withstood these if she hadn't developed a dependency on what she later called her "crutches." The year *The Wizard of Oz* was made, the year she turned sweet sixteen, my mother was given her first dose of Benzedrine by the studio that had made her a star.

It seemed innocent enough at the time. No one in those days, certainly not those of the studio doctors prescribing them, had any idea what they were doing when they began administering amphetamines to their personnel. Nowadays we are all familiar with the dangers of these powerfully addictive stimulants, but nobody knew the risks in 1938. In those days Benzedrine was the new wonder drug, the brainchild of a Nobel Prize-winning scientist. Combined with phenobarbitol, also believed to be safe at first, these wildly popular little pills were considered small miracles in the diet industry. They curbed your appetite, made weight control painless, and filled you with energy, all at the same time. What could be better? Most of MGM was taking them, including a number of the creative heads. Monitored by studio doctors, the pills seemed to be a safe and efficient way to keep actors looking good and productions moving on schedule.

When studio doctors gave the new wonder drugs to my mother, my grandmother didn't object. After all, she reasoned, if the doctor said they were safe for Judy, they must be all right. At first everything seemed fine; Mama lost weight and had plenty of "pep" in the morning when she got up for an early shoot. But after a few weeks, it started getting hard for my mom to go to sleep at night, so it was back to the studio doctor for more advice – and more pills.

The second miracle drug of the late 1930s was the sleeping pill. It was also considered completely safe at prescribed levels, a harmless way to get "a good night of restful sleep," as the ads promised. Naturally, the studio doctor prescribed more "harmless" pills to help my mother get to sleep. Every night my grandmother would give her one at bedtime, and for a while they seemed to work beautifully.

It seems unbelievable now that it could all have been so innocent, but that's because we look back on those days with knowledge that makes the continual pill-popping seem sinister. It wasn't like that at the time. Even as late as the 1950s, family movies had characters played by actresses like squeaky-clean Doris Day casually suggesting a family member take a "diet pill" or "sleeping pill" to correct some minor problem.

Even back then, though, it was soon apparent that the pills weren't good for my mom. My mother had what we now call a genetic predisposition to chemical dependency. Almost from the beginning she craved more and more of "her medicine" to help her feel well. A few weeks into Mama's first course of weight-loss medicine, my grandmother became concerned and asked the doctors to stop giving my mom the pills. For a while they did stop, but my mom couldn't seem to do without them if she was going to suppress her appetite, so the doctors finally allowed her to take carefully regulated doses.

The problem was that they couldn't regulate her doses. No matter how careful everyone was, my mom always seemed to get her hands on more medicine than was good for her. My aunt Jimmy told me that later she used to catch my mom sewing pills into the seams of her dresses. Jimmy told my grandmother about it, and after that Grandma and Aunt Jimmy would go through Mama's clothes regularly, checking the seams and hems for pills. Later, her costumers had to do the same thing, too. My mom would hide Benzedrine pills in her costumes and behind the furniture in her dressing room. By the time she was seventeen, I wouldn't be surprised if my mom was already a seasoned pro at hiding medicine so she could stockpile it for later use. Mama didn't realize the seriousness of what she was doing; to her, it was as harmless as hiding candy, which she'd done when she first came to MGM.

It's no wonder that my mother suffered her first "nervous collapse" on the *Wizard* publicity tours. Her body must have been struggling to adjust to puberty, exhaustion, undernourishment and to what we'd now consider a chemical overload at the same time, and the result was an emotional roller-coaster. She was too exhausted and overwhelmed on the *Wizard of Oz* tour to enjoy her new star status. She was still just a kid, and too much was happening too soon.

Her age, of course, was the other problem. My mom was still a kid, but she wasn't a child, and everyone kept treating her like one. The Oscar she received for *Wizard* was a special "Juvenile Oscar" (like the one Shirley Temple got), yet by then my mother was past seventeen. In public she was supposed to look like "little Dorothy," even though they'd had to tape her breasts flat when they'd made the movie the year before. Back at the studio she was making pictures, usually with Mickey Rooney, where she always seemed to play a plain Jane girl-next-door several years younger than her real age. She hated it. My dad says my mother never completely got over feeling like that plain Jane kid she played on screen. There she was, surrounded by glamorous blond beauties like Lana Turner who were only a few years older than she was, yet my mom was costumed in little cotton dresses and given a scrubbed ingenue look. It was galling, and depressing.

So naturally she rebelled, first off the studio lot and eventually on it. My mother had always hated to be controlled. She was sick and tired of being Baby Gumm. With her hormones in high gear and an air of defiance, she began dating older men. Mama had been falling in love pretty regularly since she met Mickey Rooney at eight years old, but now she was dating men ten or fifteen years her senior like Artie Shaw. She fell madly in love at one stage with Joe Mankiewicz, the screen-writer, but the studio was very upset by the age difference between them, and broke up the romance. Joe's son, Tom Mankiewicz, is a friend of mine. A couple of years ago he jokingly said, "Just think, Lorna, you and I might have been brother and sister." My mother was still playing a kid on screen, but off the lot she was a woman.

Finally she took the ultimate step toward independence. In 1941, shortly after her nineteenth birthday, my mother married band leader and composer David Rose, who was already past thirty. They were together only about a year before my mom filed for divorce. I never met David Rose; he was ancient history to me, since he and my mom had separated a decade before I was born. Mama always spoke of him positively when his name did come up, though. She told me he was "a very nice man," but that she'd been too young when she married him, and they really weren't suited to each other. I've always thought she married David to assert her independence and escape my grandmother's control. I also suspect she was sick to death of being treated like "little Dorothy" by everyone around her. When you're nearly eighteen, it isn't much fun to be treated like you're twelve, even if everyone does think you're cute.

Marrying and divorcing so young did achieve one thing for my mom. For the first time in her life, she could make some decisions for herself. This included the chance to date anybody she wanted. My mother loved to go out – the fun, the flirting, the excitement of it all. It made her happy. And when a man started to make her unhappy, when she felt it was all falling apart, she learned how to "cut men off at the ankles," as our old friend Kay Thompson put it. My mother could dump a man with a vengeance when she wanted to. (I know; I watched her do it many times.) She wasn't little Dorothy anymore. For better or worse, she'd grown up, and she was ready to make her own decisions – and her own mistakes.

Meanwhile, her relationship with MGM had begun to resemble her love life – off and on, breaking up and getting back together, love and hate. Along with the personal changes in her life, Mama had gone through a lot of professional changes by then. In the old days she'd been shielded as a professional, first by her parents and later by trusted friends like Roger Edens who were her protectors as well as her mentors. By now, though, she'd taken her life into her own hands, and she didn't always show the best judgment. Over the years she put herself into the hands of "professionals," Hollywood agents and managers some of whom were often more interested in her financial worth than her well-being. She was now a valuable "property;" everyone had a lot riding on her success, and she couldn't afford to fail. She also couldn't afford to quit.

She felt the pressure. She would feel it for the rest of her life.

The result was disastrous where MGM was concerned. Each film became harder for her to do. Feeling insecure, she started missing studio calls (sometimes for a week at a time), having anxiety attacks, and hiding in her dressing room for hours, afraid to face a camera. There were problems with directors. The studio also became obsessed with her weight, which had always been hard for her to control. Now she panicked at the thought of gaining weight and not being able to lose it. The result was huge weight swings, from plump to anorexic, which began to destroy her health. No one understood eating disorders in those days, but Mama came dangerously close to developing one.

It wasn't only the pressure that had begun getting to her, either. By that time her "happy pills" were controlling much of her life. It had become apparent, even to her, that the pills were hurting her. When she realized this, Mama tried to quit taking them. She quit cold turkey several times and went through a series of hospitalizations, trying to get healthy and shake her dependence on her medicine. That was long before the Betty Ford Center, though, and no one really understood the detoxification process. So every time she put on too much weight, or couldn't make her morning make-up call because of exhaustion, or desperately needed sleep, she'd end up going back on the pills "just until this movie's finished." Eventually she became trapped in a vicious cycle, unable to function with or without her "medication." Looking back at her films, I can't believe the contrast between the glowing young ingenue on camera and the sick woman off camera. That she survived at all is remarkable.

Mama had worked with Vincente Minnelli a few times before he directed her in *Meet Me in St. Louis*, but it was then that they fell in love. Like David Rose, Vincente was a lot older than my mother. Also like David, Vincente was very talented in his own right. In 1945 Vincente and my mother got married, and a year later my sister Liza was born. For a while everything seemed okay. Mama was able to stay off pills for most of her pregnancy, and the thrill of becoming a mother kept her mind off her professional problems for a while. But soon enough things started falling apart again.

First there was the post-partum depression. My mom suffered severe post-partums with all of us. It didn't help that once again she'd married a kind but distant man who was absorbed in his work. Complicating everything were the pills. My mother had put on a lot of weight during the pregnancy and had to lose it rapidly so she could complete *The Pirate*, with Gene Kelly. Back on the pills she lost so much weight, so quickly, that she was sickly and bone thin for most of the shooting. She began making suicide threats, something Vincente had no idea how to handle. The result was another trip to a private sanatorium to "rest."

As usual, my mother bounced back. In fact, she used to tell us funny and ridiculous stories about her time in the sanatorium. She loved to tell the story of how she'd gone for a walk across the sanatorium lawn one dark night with a nurse. My mom kept tripping and falling down, but when she mentioned it to the nurse, the nurse told her she was just dizzy; there was nothing on the lawn. But when the sun came up the next morning and my mom looked out her bungalow window, she saw croquet hoops all over the grass where they'd been walking the night before. She'd been tripping over them in the dark. I don't know if the story was true, but it made us laugh when she told it, and my mother always laughed the hardest of us all. The nurse brought Liza to see Mama regularly at the sanatorium, and all in all my mom emerged in good enough health to make *Easter Parade* a few months later.

For a while everything seemed okay, but then the destructive cycle began all over, this time complicated by the fact that her marriage to Vincente was falling apart. Once again she had married a talented but unsuitable man, an intellectual and "artiste" who was wrapped up in his work and emotionally unavailable. My mother needed someone who would be wrapped up in her. Contrary to the stories that have been printed, the break-up had nothing to do with Vincente's sexual preference. I've often wondered where the stories that Vincente was bisexual got started, because men seemed to be the last thing on his mind when I knew him. The Vincente I remember had a roving eye and a weakness for beautiful women, several of whom he married. Granted, one marriage might be a cover, but three? I heard plenty of whispers about the women Vincente dated when I was growing up, but never a hint that he was bisexual. My sister Liza passionately resents the suggestion that her father had a secret gay life.

Whether or not it had anything to do with Vincente, my mother wanted a change. The question for my mom was, if not Vincente and MGM, then what? She'd been under contract to MGM since she was a child. For fifteen years her life had consisted of movies and publicity tours; MGM had been her workplace, her school, and in a sense her second home. Leaving was frightening, yet staying had become impossible.

The stress and exhaustion of the constant filming she'd been required to do since she was fourteen had taken their toll. By the time my mom was twenty-two, she had made nineteen films for MGM in a period of nine years. These days actors rarely make more than one film a year, even when they're in demand, because of the exhausting schedule. Filming means getting up at four every morning to be at the studio by 5 a.m. for make-up. My mom would shoot all day, rarely leaving the studio before 8 p.m. That meant a full fourteen hours of acting, singing, and dancing before she even left for home. By the time she ate and went to bed, there were only a few hours for her to sleep before the whole routine started all over again. Those were the days before child labor laws controlled conditions for child actors, so my mother had had to maintain a schedule few adults could survive. She was so sick and exhausted that they had to replace her with Betty Hutton in *Annie Get Your Gun*. In the old rushes of the film, which were never shown at the time, my mom is far too thin, with dark circles under her eyes. She was in such bad shape during *Summer Stock*, her last film at MGM (with Gene Kelly), that she had trouble standing up sometimes. No wonder she came to rely on her medication just to get out of bed in the morning.

As far as she was concerned, her marriage was also over in all but name. My mother and Vincente had tried and failed to make the relationship work, to the sadness of both. Only my sister held them together by that time. Privately, my mom had already told friends the marriage was finished. She and Vincente were deeply in debt; physically and emotionally, she was at a low ebb. Stress and medication had taken their toll.

There are several stories about what happened next. The common myth is that MGM simply fired my mother. The reality is considerably more complicated. MGM did suspend her for failing to appear on the set again; she got a telegram notifying her of the suspension on September 29, 1950. Two days later she locked herself in the bathroom at home, broke a decorative bottle, and scratched her throat. Then, according to Vincente, she unlocked the door and let him in. She hadn't cut herself deeply enough to cause serious injury, but there was a lot of blood because of the wound's location, and Vincente was terrified. Friends bundled her up, took her to another house (she and Vincente kept two homes), and met the doctor there. Vincente stayed behind with Liza and tried to keep the incident a secret. As usual, though, the story was leaked to the press, and in no time every paper in town carried headlines about my mother's "suicide" attempt.

My mother was in desperate need of a way out. She spoke privately to our old family friends, Marc and Marcella Rabwin, and asked Dr. Marc to help her. She'd always loved New York. She thought moving to New York and doing some Broadway shows might be the answer to her unhappiness. She and Dr. Marc talked the situation over, and at Mama's request, he went privately to L.B. Mayer and asked him to cancel my mother's contract, which legally had two years left. In a sense the request was only a formality, since both the studio and my mother knew her situation there had reached a stalemate. L.B. later agreed. He also later agreed to cancel my mom's debt to MGM ($9,000 she'd borrowed against her future salary to pay for her last rest cure).

Three months after her suspension and suicide attempt, on September 29, 1950, MGM officially terminated Judy Garland. It was a painful parting for everyone involved.

My mother rarely talked to me about her MGM years. Who could blame her? One thing I do know, though, is that she loved L.B. Mayer to the end of her life. Much has been made of the legend that MGM used my mother and tossed her aside. In the last years of her life, as chemical addiction ate away at her memory and her consciousness, she sometimes fed those rumors herself. In the decade after she left Metro, though, she never blamed L.B. for what had happened to her. She always spoke lovingly of him to us children, and to my father. It was L.B. Mayer who paid for my mother's real hospitalizations when she became ill during her years at MGM, even when it was clear she might never be able to make another movie for him. My father passionately asserts that L.B. loved my mother and wanted to help her get well, and that my mother always told him this herself. Years after my mother left Metro, my dad had breakfast with L.B. and an MGM attorney, and they still spoke of my mom with love and respect.

It's true that the studio started my mother on amphetamines, but they also provided her with doctors, therapists, and several "rest stays" in hospitals. Years afterward Aunt Jimmy told me that everybody at MGM tried to keep my mother's medication problem under control, from Mama's costumer to my grandmother to the police. It was useless. My mother sought escape in the pills, saw nothing wrong in them, and was determined to have them. After all, L.B. himself took the same kind of pills they gave my mother; as far as that goes, half the truck drivers in America took those pills to stay awake, and half their wives took them to lose weight. Ignorance, not evil, began the process that destroyed my mother's life. If she had been born two decades later, after the dangers of amphetamines were recognized, she would be alive today.

My mother wasn't Norma Desmond, endlessly rerunning her old movies. She rarely talked about the films she'd done when she was young. The one exception was *The Wizard of Oz.* Like everyone else in America, our family watched it on television every year. The only difference between our family and others is that, after the first time, we watched it with Dorothy.

I vividly remember my first encounter with the film. My parents were away, and we children were at home in Los Angeles with our nanny. I was seven at the time; my little brother Joey was only four. When our nanny learned *Wizard* was going to be shown on television that night, she thought Joey and I would want to see Mama's movie, so she let us stay up late. Unfortunately, it hadn't occurred to the nanny that the film can be frightening to young children. As Joe and I watched the monkeys fly across the TV screen, our nanny cheerfully pointed out to us that Dorothy, the girl on TV, was actually our mother wearing a costume.

Mama? That was Mama? We leaned closer. Sure enough, the girl on the screen had Mama's eyes. I panicked. Joey began to cry. Mama was being carried off by bad monkeys? Were the monkeys the ones who took her to New York? Joe and I both began to sob with terror. In spite of the nanny's best efforts to calm us, we became more and more distraught. At the height of all this hysteria, the phone rang. It was Mama. She'd just realized the movie was airing that night, and when it occurred to her we might be watching at home, she knew we'd be scared. She had the nanny put both Joe and me on the phone and kept reassuring us that she was all right, that the monkeys didn't take her to New York. I felt a little better, but Joe kept crying and asking Mama when she was coming home. We didn't really feel comfortable until she was home again so we could see for ourselves that the monkeys hadn't hurt her.

For years afterward, my mother wouldn't let us watch the movie without her. Instead, the annual televising of *The Wizard of Oz* became a special family occasion at our house. Mama would cuddle up on the couch with me and my brother and watch the film with us. When Liza was there (instead of at her father's), Mama would dress us up in matching "sister" dresses for the occasion. Then, while the whole family munched on popcorn, my mother would tell us about making the picture. She told us how they achieved effects like the tornado and the flying monkeys. She also told us what it was like to be on the set: how Jack Haley, Sr. had to lie on a board during breaks because he couldn't sit down in his tin man costume, how some of the male Munchkins were always leering at her, how bad Toto's breath was, and how nice Margaret Hamilton was. I remember her telling us that the studio served the cast lunch on the set after the first few weeks of filming. She said that when Jack Haley, Bert Lahr, and Ray Bolger went to eat in the studio commissary, they would pull off only enough of the prosthetics to eat comfortably. The problem was that the left-over adhesive still hung from their skin like strings of mucus, especially when Bert Lahr removed bits of the lion make-up. The result was so disgusting that everyone in the cafeteria complained. After enough complaints, lunch was served to them on the set.

Despite my original scare, I came to love the movie. It became my brother's and my favorite picture. It was an amazing achievement for its time, and I am very, very proud of it. I still watch it when it comes on television; only now I watch it with my children, just a few feet away from my mother's portrait, which sits on the shelf, along with a ruby slipper, in my living room. My daughter Vanessa calls the slipper the "Dorothy shoe." One of the original movie posters, with her grandmother's face, hangs in Vanessa's room. Vanessa has a pair of "Dorothy shoes" of her own. My mother would love it.

My mother entered the "magic gates" of MGM when she was only a child. She was twenty-eight when she walked out those studio gates the last time, but she'd already lived several lifetimes.

Leaving MGM wasn't her only parting in 1950. Although they remained legally married for another year, my mother and Vincente were parting too. They lived in the same house for a few more weeks that November, but they both knew the marriage was over. When she left Los Angeles for a few weeks in New York that fall, she already considered herself a free woman.

It's been forty-seven years since my mother walked out of her second marriage. She had no way of knowing when she left for New York that my dad would be there, and what that would mean in her life. One thing is certain. The day my father met Mama, he walked into a tornado of his own. Oh, they were a pair. Not exactly Romeo and Juliet or Tracy and Hepburn, but one of the great couples nevertheless.

Chapter Three

# A STAR IS BORN

Watching my father talk about my mother is like watching images on a Chinese lantern. My mother's presence fills his house. Almost thirty years after her death, he still speaks of her as if she might walk into the room at any minute. His expression changes from mischievous to tender to heartbreakingly sad, for my mother was all of those things. The emotions flit across his face like frames from a movie projector. Endlessly charming, occasionally belligerent, my dad, the self-styled "Hollywood tough guy," speaks of my mother with the humor and passion of the true romantic, Bogey's screen image come to life. In the midst of a sardonic little anecdote about Mama having "one of her fits," he will suddenly look directly into someone's eyes and say, "We loved each other, you know. I loved her, not the legend, the woman. Do you understand what that means?" And just as suddenly, the passion recedes, and he finishes his story. For him, the past is more a place than a time; his mind is the boundary that encloses a territory of the heart he can visit at will. For him, my mother is still alive inside that place.

My dad turned eighty in 1996 but he remembers the day he met my mother as if it were yesterday. She was eating dinner with a male friend in Billy Reed's Little Club in New York late one night when my dad walked in. She had just recently been terminated by MGM and was in New York to recover and have a good time. My dad knew my mom's friend, and when he went over to the table to say hello, the friend introduced Sid to my mother. My father's a good-looking man, and my mother was one to notice. That night she simply smiled sweetly and a bit absentmindedly said, "Hello." With that one word it was all over for my father.

He can still describe that moment with absolute clarity, as if it were frozen in time. My mother was wearing a gold coat, a black dress, and a little pillbox hat. Her hair was cut short, and her big dark eyes glowed in the dim light of the club. But it's my mother's voice he remembers the most. That voice, that wonderful voice of hers, unique even in speaking. That simple "Hello," as my father tells it, wasn't only Mama's voice speaking. "When you met her, she'd say, 'Hello,' and you'd fall down. The voice would kill you. In a sense, you would drop dead every time she talked to you. When she talked, the voice was Dorothy and *Meet Me in St. Louis* and *Easter Parade* and a whole string of movies going through your head. It was this mystique she had, like magic." All these years later, after eleven years of marriage, and a messy divorce, and all the pain, he still remembers the magic.

My mother was so beautiful, even more than you could see on the screen. She had the most incredible skin I've ever seen. Her skin was like delicate porcelain, so fine and translucent you could see the veins if you looked closely enough. When I was a kid, I longed to look like her instead of like my father. I used to sit on her dressing table when I was six or seven and watch her do her make-up. I would stare at her while she put on her lipstick, leaning in real close so I could see, and she'd try not to laugh at me because she didn't want to smear her lipstick. She had tiny little feet that were wide from dancing all those years, and great legs, and the most wonderfully expressive hands. My father loved her hands. My mother was just so beautiful. She was a movie star.

Dad had met her briefly many years ago, when he was working as an extra in a Nelson Eddy movie. He'd worn a soldier suit and been introduced to Mama on the set one day.

It wasn't until that night in New York, though, that the two of them really met. Dad had just separated from his second wife, and my mom had just separated from Vincente. The evening after they met at the club, the two of them went out, and the night after that, and so on.

If opposites attract, it's no wonder my parents fell for each other. God knows my dad was nothing like the other men my mother had known. Her first two husbands were gentle, artistic types, and most of the men she had dated before my dad were either musicians, directors, or performers. They all treated her like a lady. They were all gentlemen.

Sid Luft, on the other hand, was no gentleman. He was a weightlifter. He was a former test pilot. He was a gambler. He was a guy. He's still one of those old-time Hollywood guys.

When I was a kid, his best friend was Humphrey Bogart. Dad still loves to tell how he first met Bogey. It pretty much sums up both of them. When he and my mother first moved to Beverly Hills two years after they met – right after I was born – they went to a party together at Irving ("Swifty") Lazar's house. Nobody in the Beverly Hills A-crowd really knew my dad yet. Bogey liked to think of himself as the chief rooster in the neighborhood, and he wasn't happy when he learned my dad was moving in two doors down. Early that evening Bogey swaggered up to my dad and said, "So you're Sid Luft? I hear you're a tough guy."

Dad said, "You're right. I am."

They started talking, and after a few minutes Bogey said, "You know, you'd better behave yourself, Sid."

Dad replied, "Oh, I do, do I?" They were both squaring off like a couple of bucks by that time. Then Dad said, "Would you like to meet my wife?"

"Not really."

My dad turned and shouted across the room, "Hey, Judy! Over here."

As Mama walked toward them, my dad picked Bogey up and held him tightly in both arms, like you would carry a child to bed. Now keep in mind that Bogey was a small man, "a little shrimp of a guy," as my father describes him.

When my mom got there, Dad turned to her and said, "Honey, have you met our new neighbor?" He was still holding Bogey tightly. Bogart was so angry by then that he was purple, but all he could do was sputter and let out a string of swear words because try as he might, he couldn't get loose from my father's grip.

My mother said, poker-faced, "How are you, Mr. Bogart? I'm Judy." (They had, in fact, known each other for years.) She shook Bogart's hand and walked away again while my dad still stood there, holding Bogey in his arms. By then the whole room was watching and laughing. A minute or two later my dad gently set Bogart back down on his feet and just stood there, waiting to see what Bogart would do next. Bogey just stared up at my father for a moment, too angry to say a word; then all of a sudden Bogey started laughing, and Dad started laughing, too. After that they were the best of friends. Now there were two tough guys on the block, Humphrey Bogart and my father.

Dad had grown up in an upscale New York neighborhood where he and his sister were the only Jewish kids on the block, and he'd sometimes come home to anti-Semitic graffiti. Even though the family was well-off financially, my dad always had to fight to survive in the social scheme. He had an eccentric, strong-willed Russian mother who designed clothes but would rather spend her time at the track than in a tearoom. Dad had an eye for the ladies and for a good piece of horseflesh. He was a self-described "tough little son-of-a-bitch." He'd had to be. Nobody thought he was right for my mother – except Mama.

My dad was also a lady-killer, as charming as they come. Lady actors were nothing new to him, either, so when he met Mama, he had some idea of what he was taking on. He'd already gotten involved in producing "B" movies and he'd dated a lot of movie stars – Hedy Lamarr, Gene Tierney,

Eleanor Powell – a whole string of beauties. By the time he met my mother, he'd already been married twice, the second time to actress Lynn Bari. He hadn't just fallen off the potato truck when my mother came along. It wasn't as if he suddenly went from dating Rebecca of Sunnybrook Farm to dating a "star." He knew about actors – the egos, the neuroses. He'd also heard about my mother's track record with men. His heart might have heard Dorothy saying, "Hello," but his head knew exactly what he was getting into.

For my mother, though, Sid Luft was something else again. She'd never really known anyone like him. He was handsome, of course, a real hunk who knew how to carry himself. But it wasn't just that. Mama had known a lot of handsome men, and she'd usually had her pick of them. My dad was different. He was bluff and straightforward; he tackled problems head on. If somebody bothered my mother, if somebody said something about her that he didn't like, he'd turn around and just deck them. If too many Hollywood types hung around, bothering my mother, he'd tell them to get out.

Most amazing of all, he would say no to my mother. No one but my mother's mentor, Roger Edens, had ever really done that before, and Roger was a father-figure, not a lover. My mother was used to having everyone cater to her, including her sisters. She knew how to throw a tantrum. When my mom was little, according to my aunt Jimmy, she would lie on the floor and scream until she got her way. She wasn't neurotic back then, Jimmy said, just spoiled. But when Mama tried that kind of thing with my dad, he'd tell her to sit down and shut up. This was something completely new to my mother, and in a way, nice, and sort of charming. My father didn't flatter my mother the way everyone else did, and she liked it. You can't trust people who are always flattering you. They usually want something. My dad didn't want anything. She could trust him. He made her feel secure.

It was a good thing my dad could handle her, too, because

my mother drove most men crazy. Even for my father, being with my mother was a struggle.

Early in their relationship, my dad learned the hard way what could happen if he made my mom angry. A few months after he met my mother, my dad got a call from his old high school sweetheart. He hadn't seen her since she'd gotten married years before. Now she was divorced, and she wanted to see him again, to talk about old times and see if there was still anything between them. It meant flying to Denver, where she lived. Dad knew my mother would have a fit about his seeing an old girlfriend, so he decided not to tell her right away. His plan was to meet with his former girlfriend, see how it went, and tell my mother only if it looked like he wanted to pursue the old relationship. If it all came to nothing, there would be no reason to mention it. After all, he and my mother had made no real commitments at that point, and he didn't want to face her wrath for nothing.

His plan seemed foolproof. Dad had a business associate in Oklahoma, so he told my mom he was flying to Tulsa to talk to his associate about a horse, and he took a plane to Oklahoma. When he got to the airport there, he bought another ticket, this time to Denver, without telling anyone. His high school sweetheart met him at the airport, and they spent the evening together. So far, so good.

But when he returned to the hotel in the wee hours of the morning, there was a long distance call waiting for him. He was astonished, since no one but his old girlfriend knew where he was. He took the call, and it was Mama. She pleasantly reminded him that she was expecting him to attend a party in L.A. the next night to meet her California friends, and asked him what time his plane would arrive in Los Angeles, so she could pick him up at the airport. Floored, he managed to mumble the flight information before hanging up. How on earth had she known where he was? He hadn't told a soul.

Simple. The FBI had found him. When you're Judy Garland and you want something, you just pick up a phone and call somebody. Anybody. My mom wanted to find my dad, so she just picked up the phone and made a person-to-person call to J. Edgar Hoover (whom she'd never met) and asked him to find Sid Luft, right away. Mr. Hoover did. Years later she just picked up the phone and called President Kennedy to ask his advice on how to handle the personnel on her television show. None of this seemed unusual to her. That's simply what you did when you were Judy Garland.

The brush with the FBI was a real eye-opener for my father; part of his education as Judy Garland's "man." Lesson number one: never kid a kidder, especially when that kidder is one of the greatest actors who ever lived. My father was an amateur when it came to lying. He didn't do it often, and when he did, my mother always knew. My mom, on the other hand, was a professional. She'd been trained since childhood by the best directors in Hollywood. She could out-act – and out-lie – anyone she knew. You couldn't fool my mother because whatever you tried to do, she'd done before and done better. She hadn't believed my father's Tulsa story for a minute. My dad had tried to get one by her, and she'd busted him. He flew to Los Angeles that day a wiser man.

Clearly, my mother took their relationship seriously. From then on my parents were officially a couple. When my mother's separation from Vincente Minnelli became official about the same time, she went public about her relationship with my dad.

The press didn't like it one bit. Sid Luft? With Judy Garland? No, no, no. He didn't fit their image; he didn't fit anyone's image of who my mother should be with. The press didn't like him, and he sure didn't like them. He had no use for columnists, and he wouldn't cater to their demands. It was the beginning of a lot of bad press for my dad.

Meanwhile, my mother was trying to remake her career. With the help of her friends she'd done a few radio appearances with old friends like Bing Crosby, Dean Martin, and Frank Sinatra. But for the most part, she was feeling adrift in her career. Still, she had to keep performing. It was not only financially necessary; it was emotionally necessary for her. Performing was her life. She'd been doing it since she was two years old. She couldn't live without performing, didn't want to. If she went too long without working, she'd be climbing the walls, even though she did need this break.

So she continued to search for a way to keep doing what she loved best. Friends had suggested she try the concert circuit, but she was uncertain. Her vaudeville days as a Gumm Sister were long ago. The promotional tours she'd done for MGM had, for the most part, been nightmares. The huge crowds, the pushing and the screaming, the fear of failing before a live audience; all these things made her hesitate to tackle the concert circuit. But she had successfully managed countless shows for the armed forces in 1940–45. And she had to do something, and movies seemed neither possible nor desirable. So she wavered.

That's where my dad came in.

My dad was emphatic. He thought a concert tour was "a hell of a good idea." On a concert tour she could sleep all day if she wanted; she could get as chubby as she wanted, too, and no one would care. After all, weren't some of the greatest concert singers overweight? She wouldn't need to starve herself and live on diet pills as she had for her films, and she wouldn't have to drag herself out of bed at dawn, desperate for stimulants. Of course she should do it, he told her. It would be wonderful. She could reinvent herself in another country, another setting. She could put behind her all the unhappiness and bad press from her MGM days.

She took Dad's advice. Scared but excited, she went to England and prepared to open at the London Palladium. She wanted my dad to go with her for moral support, but at first he refused. He had business concerns of his own, and besides, he wasn't sure it was a good idea for him to be too closely involved in her business dealings. She had managers for that. That plan lasted about two weeks. A few days after Mama left, Dottie Ponedel, her make-up woman from the MGM days, called my dad and suggested that he come over to London because it "would mean a lot to Judy." Two days later Dottie called again from London.

My dad finally gave in. After all, the FBI might show up at his front door next! He flew to London, arriving the day before the Palladium opening. From then on, there was no going back for my father. Ready or not, he would be involved in "Judy's business" for the rest of her life.

A lot of people have criticized my dad for that. They have implied that he got involved in my mother's business because he wanted to ride on her coattails, take advantage of her fame. Nothing could be further from the truth. One of the results of her studio upbringing was that my mom got used to having everything done for her by the time she was a teenager, and she kept those habits in her adult life. My mother and Vincente were in debt when they separated; they hadn't been able to pay the taxes on their homes. According to Marc Rabwin, at the time my mom left MGM, she still owed the studio money they'd advanced her for hospitals and other expenses. Financially, my father was much better off before he married my mother. Dad came from an affluent family, and by the time he met my mom, he was not only something of a producer but had also invested in thoroughbred horses with Aly Khan.

There are hurtful accusations against my father that his gambling ruined my mother financially, but this is absolutely untrue. Once he married my mother and became a target for photographers and curiosity-seekers, Dad did stop going to the betting windows at the track himself. He wanted to remain anonymous, so he would give the money to his close friend and business partner, Vern Alves. Dad would write down the bets he wanted Vern to place, give the money to Vern in cash ahead of time, and have Vern place the bet at the track. Vern would also collect the cash if the horse won and give the money to my dad afterward. Dad would give him a percentage for placing the bet. This was the system Dad and Vern used during my childhood years in Beverly Hills. Vern still gets angry at the allegations that my dad gambled away all the family money. Vern says that he knows exactly what happened during those years because he handled the money personally, and that my dad used his winnings to pay the house mortgage and other expenses. According to Vern, Dad was always hoping his winnings would be enough to carry the family through the latest emergency.

My father was my mother's protector, financially and in every other way. He wanted to take care of Mama. He loved her, he wanted to help her, and in those days he was still under the illusion that he could solve all her problems if he just tried hard enough. As for managing her, he didn't really have much of a choice. Mama demanded it of him. All her life people had been managing things for her. To my mom, taking care of her was part of loving her.

Besides, nobody said no to my mother for long. What Mama wanted, Mama eventually got, especially where my dad was concerned.

So from then on, my parents were in it together – planning, traveling together through Scotland and then Europe. It was romantic, and they had the time of their lives. When she was happy, Mama was more fun than anybody. Onstage my mother was a phenomenon, and offstage she was almost as exciting. My father had fallen for her hook, line, and sinker. After Mama, everyone else was dull by comparison.

Once the Palladium opening was behind her, my mom knew that she'd found her place professionally once again. She loved being out under the lights, singing to all those people. At MGM she'd played to a sound stage full of crew members and recording machines. Now she was singing to a live audience once again, people who laughed and cried and were mesmerized by her presence. It was astonishing, like being two years old again and singing "Jingle Bells" to delighted applause. For my mother, it was more exciting, and more addictive, than any medicine. Mama loved her audiences; she came alive in front of them. And now, instead of her parents applauding wildly in the front row, there was my father, cheering her on from the wings.

It was wonderful. It was magic. It was the rebirth of a legend.

When they returned to the U.S. at the end of the tour, my dad searched for ways to keep the magic going. It was my dad who conceived the idea of my mom opening at the Palace. A vaudeville mecca in its heyday, New York's old Palace Theater was the ideal venue for a former Gumm sister. My dad found the building rundown and threadbare; he and the promoters refurbished the old landmark, restoring it once again to its former splendor. In 1951 my mother reopened the theater, restored, like the Palace, to her glory days. No one who was there that night has ever forgotten it. It became a part of theater history.

My dad got my mom booked at more concert halls and that same year the two of them formed Transcona Enterprises, their own corporation. My father had begun negotiating for the film rights to *A Star Is Born*. He planned to produce it himself, with the backing of Jack Warner and Warner Brothers. It was a perfect vehicle for my mother. The film would play into the public's perception of her crises, and by exploiting the rumors – the headlines about pills and suicide – put them to rest. More importantly, it would give my mother the great acting role she'd always longed for. Best of all, my parents would use their own production company. For the first time in her career, my mother would have control over one of her films. She was thrilled, hoping the trauma of her last years at MGM would soon be a thing of the past.

It seemed like the perfect plan, and it almost was. My father hired Vern Alves as his production assistant, and Dad and Mom's company Transcona started preproduction for the movie. Then something happened that put a kink in their perfect plan. A big kink.

My mother discovered she was pregnant with me.

Growing up, I had no idea that I was already on the way when my parents got married. It was just not the kind of thing your parents told you in the 1950s. I must have been seventeen or eighteen before the truth dawned on me. I knew when my parents' wedding anniversary was, and of course I knew when my birthday was, but I had never done the maths. It had never occurred to me.

I found out about my own conception years later from a book about my mother. By then I knew better than to believe most of what people wrote about my mother, so I decided to ask my dad. It was a memorable conversation. It went something like this:

Me:   Dad, can I ask you a question?
Sid:   What?
Me:   Was Mama pregnant with me when you got married?
Sid   (long pause): Where'd you hear that?
Me:   In this book.
Sid   (longer pause): Well, yeah, but that doesn't mean
        anything. I mean, well, you know, we were planning
        on getting married, anyway . . .

And that was the end of that conversation. My dad couldn't get out of the room fast enough. Just the fact that I'd asked the question scared him to death. Contrary to his image, my dad is a pretty traditional guy. He was embarrassed to tell his daughter that he'd gotten her mom pregnant before they were married. More importantly, he didn't want me to think that he and Mama had to get married. He didn't want me to be hurt, to feel that they didn't want me.

So my parents planned their wedding. They couldn't afford to wait very long, and they didn't want the press to find out and turn the wedding into a media circus. They decided to get married privately at a friend's ranch in Las Vegas. Using their real names, Frances Gumm Minnelli and Michael S. Luft, they had a friend get the license from a local justice of the peace. On June 8, 1952, they drove out to their friends' ranch and got married in a private ceremony. Not exactly the dream wedding most people would imagine for Judy Garland, but to my father, it may as well have been. Mama, he says, looked beautiful. His face still lights up when he talks about it.

A few days later Louella Parsons somehow got hold of the story and ran a headline reading "Judy's Secret Marriage Revealed." The bookmakers in Vegas sold odds on how long the marriage would last: six months was the guess, five years at the outside. It's not surprising. The press didn't like my dad, and my mother's marital track record wasn't that great, either. But my parents beat the odds. Maybe they didn't exactly live happily ever after, but they came closer than Mama did with anyone else. They truly loved each other. I'm not sure the world ever figured that out.

My poor sister found out about the marriage the hard way – on television. Liza already knew Sid. Since my mother traveled a lot, Liza lived with Vincente much of the time, but she and her nanny sometimes visited Mama and Sid. Liza liked my dad pretty well, but she didn't want our mother to marry him. A few weeks earlier my mom had asked Liza if she wanted her to marry Sid, and Liza had said, "But what about Daddy?" Like all kids of divorced parents, Liza still hoped her parents would get back together, even though that was clearly out of the question. When she and her father heard the news, Liza was hurt. Mama had married another man besides Daddy, and she'd done it without even telling Liza properly. It was a lot for a six-year-old to accept.

Things got better for everyone after the wedding. My parents moved into a house on Mapleton Drive in Beverly Hills and settled down to stay, at least for the time being. They hired a nurse and a full staff of servants, and Liza divided her time between my parents' home and Vincente's. They were a family now, and my mother was happy and excited about the pregnancy. All of this made up for a lot to my sister. So when Mama asked Liza to call my father "Papa Sid," Liza did it willingly. My dad, for his part, happily accepted the role of stepfather. Liza was a part of my mother, and that was enough for him.

Mama's relationship with my sister, in fact, was one of the things that had most attracted him to my mother. He knew by then that my mother was used to being the star, the center of attention. He also knew she had a daughter but hadn't seen her with Liza until my parents had been together for a while. When he finally got to see Mama and Liza together, he was amazed to see the change that came over my mother. Instead of the prima donna, with Liza my mother became the tender and loving parent. My sister was the center of Mama's universe; she looked at Liza with such love. When Liza was with her, my mother put her own needs second. My dad was surprised and touched. It was a good omen for him.

When Mama got pregnant with me, he pictured a little girl of his own, a little girl that Mama would look at the same way she looked at Liza. My dad already had a son, Johnny, from his marriage to Lynn Bari, so he hoped for a girl this time around. Johnny lived with his mother and visited now and then, but this baby would be special because Judy was her mother. Even if the timing was a little off, my dad was looking forward to my birth. After all, he teased my mother, any child of his was bound to be a "tough little son-of-a-bitch," even if she was a little shrimp of a girl like Mama. My mother just laughed at him.

Neither of my parents regretted having to postpone their movie. They were waiting for their own little star to be born – me, of course.

The biggest problem, though, wasn't the timing. It was my mother's medication. She was thirty and had been taking varying amounts of Benzedrine and sleeping pills since she was sixteen. Although the medicine was prescribed by physicians, my mother had never been able to limit herself to an appropriate dose for long. She always ended up taking more than was good for her. After fourteen years with chemicals in her bloodstream, her body had become dependent on them. To withdraw abruptly would be not only traumatic but dangerous for her. Worried about its effect on me, she had tried to cut back on her medication during pregnancy, but it was a constant struggle. Going off it completely wasn't an option, either, since the shock might even trigger a miscarriage.

With this in mind, Dr. Dietrich (the doctor who delivered me) decided to put Mama in the hospital three weeks before I was due to make sure she took care of herself. The doctor conferred with my dad and Vern Alves, and the three of them decided Vern would serve as my mother's companion at the hospital during her "incarceration," as Dr. Dietrich referred to it. Vern still chuckles when he recalls Dr. Dietrich's choice of words.

My mother agreed to the arrangement calmly enough, but instead of joyfully looking forward to my birth, she began systematically preparing for her own death. In spite of the doctor's assurances that she was perfectly healthy, my mom told Vern privately that she knew she was going to die giving birth. There was no medical reason to believe this, but as Vern says, "Judy was so fatalistic that she believed any plane she got on was doomed to crash." Convinced of her impending death, my mother decided to have one last party before she went into the hospital.

As soon as Dr. Dietrich gave her a date to enter the hospital, Mama began planning her "farewell party." She had a beautiful velvet dress made for the occasion, and invited the entire A-crowd to their home on Mapleton Drive the night before she went into hospital. Vern says my mom looked beautiful that night, in spite of her size (all the women in my family get huge with pregnancy). It was a glamorous, glittering evening. Roger Edens played the piano while my mother sang to all their assembled friends. Frank Sinatra sang, George Burns and Gracie Allen did a few jokes, and at the end of the evening my mother went from person to person, solemnly bidding them a "final farewell." Vern says he and my dad just looked at each other and rolled their eyes as the leavetaking ritual continued. Nobody had quite the flair for the dramatic my mom had.

Dad and Vern checked my mom into St. John's Hospital in Santa Monica the next day, and Vern settled in as full-time attendant. St. John's is a private Catholic hospital less than a mile from the beach in Santa Monica. They hoped my mother would have more privacy there than at Cedars Sinai, where Liza had been born. Mama did not enjoy her "incarceration." She was uncomfortable and irritable, especially without her usual medication to calm her nerves. She badgered Vern into bringing her "special ginger ale," a bottle of ginger ale with a drop of vodka. When he couldn't stand the nagging any longer, he would put a tiny amount of alcohol into the ginger ale and give it to her. He didn't like doing it, but he hoped it would appease her enough to keep her from trying to sneak in medication. She was irritable with my father, too. When he came to visit her, she would pick a fight and throw him out of her room, telling him she never wanted to see him again. Then half an hour later, she would turn to Vern and say, "Where's that Sid Luft? Where is that man?" Vern would have to call my dad to come back, and the whole routine would start over again. My mother, Vern says, was "very challenging."

My mother's moods weren't the only thing Vern had to deal with as they awaited my birth. He also had Louella Parsons on his back twenty-four hours a day. The Hollywood gossip columnists were all dying to get an exclusive on my birth, and my dad wouldn't give them the time of day. Louella Parsons turned to Vern and called the hospital until he took her calls. To get the press off their backs, Vern agreed to give Louella the exclusive "first word" of my birth, with all the particulars, if she would agree to "leave Judy alone." Louella jumped at the offer, and an open phone line was set up between Louella Parsons and St. John's Hospital so that Vern could keep her posted twenty-four hours a day.

In the midst of all this craziness, my mother's anxiety continued to increase as the day of my birth approached. I was to be delivered by Caesarean section, as my sister had been, and my mom remained convinced she would die in the process. She turned to Vern for comfort and reassurance. One afternoon as they sat alone in her hospital room, Mama asked Vern if he knew any prayers. He told her he did. My mom told him she didn't know any. Now this wasn't true – my grandfather Gumm had been choirmaster at the Episcopal church in Grand Rapids, and my mother had attended with her sisters every Sunday. Vern didn't know this, however, so when my mother asked him to teach her a prayer, he agreed. Vern is Catholic, so he taught my mother the Rosary and one or two other short prayers. My mom was a quick student; Vern said she had the prayers memorized after hearing them only once. That doesn't surprise me, since she could remember lyrics after hearing them only once too. Mama learned the prayers, and several times a day she would reach for Vern, and he would hold her hand while they prayed together. Vern was touched by these moments, even though he knew her fears were groundless.

Finally, on November 21, 1952, it was time for the main event. ME! Dad and Vern waited in the fathers' waiting room, with Vern on an open line to Louella Parsons the whole time. I was born by Caesarean section; six pounds, four ounces. Vern relayed this information to Louella, heaved a sigh of relief, and congratulated my father.

Dad was thrilled. He says I came out looking like I was six months old; small, but without a wrinkle or a bruise, with skin as white and pretty as my mother's. I had blue eyes and rosy cheeks and lots of curly blond hair. I was, in my father's words, just plain gorgeous. Who am I to disagree? Both my parents expected a girl (the obstetrician could tell, he said, by the fetal heartbeat), and Liza was excited to have a baby sister. My mother was happy, and my father was delighted to have "his own little Judy." He told me that every father wants a little girl. It was nice to be welcomed.

There are lots of myths about why they named me Lorna. One is that I was named after the Lorna Doone biscuits, which were very popular at the time. But I was most definitely not named after a cookie! My name wasn't chosen to look good on a marquee, either. Dad says that never crossed their minds. When I was small, they hoped I would never go into show business. They actually chose the name Lorna for several reasons. Mama liked the name because it was from one of her favorite plays, Clifford Odets' *Golden Boy*, and because it sounded good with Luft. Dad liked it because his mother's name was Leonora, and because he had a crush on a little girl named Lorna Doone when he was in grade school. (Years later in England my husband Colin bought me a copy of the classic book with that name.) Unlike my sister, and later my little brother, I wasn't given a middle name. My dad's only explanation is that I didn't need one. Personally, I think I got gypped.

No sooner was I born than my mother was sedated and put in intensive care to recover before being moved back to her room. Dad went back to the office, and Vern went home to get some much-needed sleep. He was exhausted from his weeks as attendant and unofficial "jail keeper." The next morning he returned to the hospital, refreshed, to find my mother back in her regular room and wide awake. They chatted about me for a while, and then my mother reached over and took Vern's hand. Since this was my mom's regular signal, Vern quietly said, "Do you want to say our prayer, Judy?"

Vern says that when he asked that, my mom just looked at him with surprise and said, "Of course not. Why would I want to say a prayer? I lived, didn't I?"

That was the end of my mother's special prayers with Vern. So much for religion!

The great event – my homecoming – was scheduled for a week later. The day before I was due to come home, my father had a horse running in a big race in San Francisco, and he was planning to fly up for the race and be back in time to take Mama and me home the next day. Besides being a terrific horse, the colt also had sentimental value for my dad. He and my mother had first seen it in Dublin during their European tour together. The colt was a beautiful chestnut. When Mama fell in love with it, my father bought it for her as a present and had it shipped back to the U.S. In fact, he and Mama had accidentally gotten locked in a stall with the horse the day it arrived in Long Island. Dad just couldn't pass up the chance to watch their colt in its first big race. With Mama and me still in the hospital, he thought, why not? When he told my mother he was planning to fly up for the race, she just smiled sweetly and said, "Fine."

Unfortunately for my dad, her cheerful mood didn't last. Unwilling to play second fiddle to a horse, Mama decided to stage one of her little scenes – to double-cross him, as Dad puts it. While my father was in San Francisco at the race, my mother announced it was time for me to come home. She managed to get herself released from the hospital a day early, and she made Vern take her home to Mapleton Drive. When my father got back from San Francisco and went to St. John's to visit her, he was astonished to discover that she'd already packed up and left with me.

Dad knew he was in for it then. He also knew how to handle my mother's moods. When he did arrive home, to find my mother propped up against the satin headboard of their bed in full pout, he was ready. He came armed to the teeth with flowers for Mama, toys for me, and fistfuls of his winnings. The colt had placed first at 15 to 1, and my dad had cleared over $5,000 that day. After the usual courting ritual, with Mama pouting and Dad begging, my mother "forgave" him, and all was well. In those days the games my mother played were still harmless, and my dad a champion player. Besides, he says, the making up was well worth it.

I undoubtedly slept through the entire scene. I needed all the rest I could get. I was one week old, and the family melodrama had already begun for me. I would later discover that, in the first six weeks of my life, my mother survived a severe post-partum depression, a suicide attempt, and her mother's death from a heart attack. Yet she would end 1952 by giving a dazzling performance at Jack Warner's coming-out party for his daughter in New York. Fortunately, I had the good sense to sleep through it all.

Chapter Four

# THERE'S NO PLACE LIKE HOLMBY HILLS

Driving through Bel Air on a spring morning is little different now from what it was thirty-five years ago. The streets are lined with beautifully kept houses with manicured lawns and lush borders of hothouse flowers. Most of the streets wind gently, the magnolia and eucalyptus trees shading the sidewalks. Nannies push well-dressed babies in carriages or strollers, stopping occasionally to chat with one another as they pass by in the warm Los Angeles sunshine. Often they have a well-groomed dog in tow, its leash looped over their arm as it sits patiently or sniffs the rear of a newcomer's equally well-groomed canine companion. Joggers trot by, most of them female, waving at the occasional neighbor as they pass. Now and then the silence is broken by the hum of a well-tuned Mercedes as it glides around the curves under the trees, deftly dodging both joggers and nannies, and continues on toward the city. It is a peaceful place, an idyllic place, a refuge for the privileged only ten miles from the heart of the city but light years away from the grime and noise of downtown Los Angeles. It is the sort of place many envy and few leave of their own will. About the only difference between the Bel Air of the 1990s and the Bel Air of my childhood is that now the nannies are Latina instead of European, and the cars European instead of American. For most people it is a place as far removed from reality as the MGM sound stages my mother danced on. For me, it was home.

Home for me was a large Tudor-style house covered with ivy on Mapleton Drive, just two blocks off Sunset Boulevard. It looked like it came straight out of England. There was a small yard in front enclosed by a wall, where old pictures in *McCalls* magazine show me playing and my brother Joe learning to walk. There was a huge back yard with a big trampoline that I jumped on with my dad. We didn't have a pool, but if I wanted to swim, I could just run across the front lawn to the Bogarts' house two doors down and jump in the pool with my best friend Leslie. I had an older sister who was off doing big girl things most of the day, and by the time I was two I had acquired a little brother along with a faithful dog to guard us. I could have done without the little brother, but I was crazy about the dog. It was all sort of Dick and Jane in Beverly Hills.

We lived on Mapleton Drive until I was eight years old, and all of my memories there are happy ones. My parents might have had their troubles at times, but I knew nothing about it. I lived in one wing of the house with my sister and my nanny, and my parents lived in another wing. If something bad happened in my parents' wing, I never knew anything about it.

Holmby Hills, the part of Beverly Hills we lived in, was the land of the toddler princesses, and I was Little Princess Lorna. I played with other princes and princesses like Steve and Leslie Bogart and Sammy Cahn's kids. I had a house filled with people hired to make our lives comfortable. There were usually thirteen people on staff at home during those early years. There was a cook and a butler and a gardener and a chauffeur to take me places. There were maids to clean up after me. And, of course, there was a nanny.

Most of the nannies were European in those days, fair-haired Irish or English women trained to the profession, who wore starched white uniforms. All of my memories of our nannies in those early years are good. It was their job to take the best possible care of the children in their charge. They fed us, bathed us, clothed us, and took us out to play. They made sure we were as healthy and safe as possible. I have a friend who says that the next time she has a baby, she's going to give birth to the nanny first. I ran into one of my former nannies just a few years ago. She's a red-haired woman, Irish, and very, very sweet. She's still in the profession. I believe she worked for Robert Stack's kids.

When the nanny had the day off or my parents had to be out of town for long, there was always Grandma, my father's mother Leonora, who lived down the canyon on Beverly Glen. What a grandmother she was! My brother and I always called her the mad Russian. She was a successful clothing designer when my dad was growing up, and she still had a stylish flair when I was small. She'd come to America by herself when she was twelve or thirteen, just a poor Jewish girl from Russia. But she worked hard and was very talented, so by the time she reached her twenties she'd worked her way up from the clothing mills back east to her own store. By an odd coincidence, one of her models in New York was Lucille Ball when Lucy was first starting out. Lucy became a friend of my mother's years later.

Grandma Leonora was a real piece of work. She was a tiny woman with gray hair, dark when she was younger, that she always wore swept up in the back. She always dressed well, really well, in beautifully designed clothing. Even after all the years in America, she still had a thick Russian accent. My grandmother Leonora was very dramatic and extremely domineering. By the time I knew her, she was as crazy for racehorses as my dad. If you wanted to find her, you paged the track. One time when I was a kid, I had her paged at Santa Anita Racetrack.

My dad used to tell us these amazing stories about her, about what it was like growing up with her and my grandfather. My dad had been a real little prince himself. He may have gotten into a lot of fist fights because he was Jewish, but afterward he had a chauffeur to take him home. His whole family went to Europe every summer on vacation, so the good life was nothing new to him.

My father's best story about his parents was one he didn't tell me until I was a teenager. It pretty much sums up my father's family. My grandfather Norbert, who passed away before I was born, was a jeweler. He was very good-looking. I have pictures of him from when he was young, and even in the old photos it's clear that he was an extremely attractive man. One summer my grandfather didn't want to go to Europe, so Grandma Leonora, my dad, and Aunt Perry (his sister) got on the boat and went to Europe without him. Of course, they had a grand time staying in all the best hotels and seeing the sights. My dad was about eighteen then, just ready to go off to college.

Meanwhile my grandfather was home alone, handsome and lonely, and at some point he got involved with a woman. I don't know that it was a real affair, but it was a something – maybe a midlife crisis. Anyway, he cheated on my grandmother while she was gone.

Some time afterward the "other woman" wrote a letter to my grandfather referring to their rendezvous, and like an idiot my grandfather put the letter in his sock drawer and kept it. When my grandma Leonora got back from Europe with the children, she found the letter. Naturally, she was furious; she started screaming and carrying on like a mad woman. Needless to say, my father and Aunt Perry overheard the argument. Dad was in high school at the time, so he asked my grandfather what was going on. What were they fighting about?

The next part of my father's story still amazes me. My grandfather had many talents, but he wasn't much of a liar. According to my grandfather, he'd just been driving through New York that day, and since the car was very stuffy, he'd been driving with the windows down to let the wind blow through. When he got home, it seemed really warm in the house after the nice breeze in the car, so he'd opened the windows to cool the house off. The wind came rushing in through the open windows, and all of a sudden, the strangest thing happened. A letter blew in through the open window and landed on the carpet, where my grandmother noticed it and picked it up. As it turned out, it was some sort of love letter. Just because the letter began with the words "Dear Norbert" (another coincidence), my grandmother had jumped to the conclusion that it was written to him. He finished the story by telling my father, "I just cannot understand why your mother does not understand this. Your mother is just being very, very . . . well, I just can't understand why she doesn't comprehend how this could happen."

My dad was dumbfounded. He just looked at his father and said, "Are you kidding me? It just blew in the window, with your name on it?"

Somehow my grandfather couldn't succeed in convincing my dad, or anybody else for that matter. Grandfather kept repeating, "I can't see why nobody seems to understand." Grandma Leonora never did understand. Shortly afterward, she divorced him.

By the time I knew her, Grandma had become more domineering than ever and very particular about the proper way to do things. (By the time she died, she was insisting that each knife, fork, and spoon be wrapped separately in cellophane before being put back in the drawer!) The staff at our house dreaded Grandma's visits. Each time she arrived to take care of me when I was small, she caused havoc. Everything had to be done her away. Of course, she was usually right about the best way to do something, but she drove the staff crazy saying, "What are you making? What are you doing? Why are you doing that? What are you opening tins for?" Oy!

She drove everyone around her stark raving mad, overseeing every move they made. She treated canned food like it was poison and had no intention of seeing it served to her grandchildren. She seemed to believe it would kill us. If she saw one of the staff opening a can of food to prepare for us kids, she would fly off the handle and say, "What do you think you are doing? You feed them this?" Then she would order the cook out of the kitchen and fix us something herself, from scratch. An afternoon with Leonora was a Russian food fest. I wasn't too crazy about the borscht, but the breads and cakes were wonderful.

Even when Grandma wasn't around, I was always well taken care of. I had a large suite at one end of the house, with my sister in a suite next to me and the nanny nearby. When I awoke in the morning, the nanny would always be there. When she'd been up late at a party or concert, Mama always slept until well into the afternoon unless she had an early call. The nanny would fix my breakfast, bathe me, and dress me, always in the latest fashions, and always in dresses. No pants or grubby clothes for me. When I was little, it was pinafores and kneesocks, and later it was always a lovely little frock, even for playing. I had long blond hair, which I always wore with the top half pulled back over the crown and fastened with a clip or a ribbon.

After feeding me breakfast and dressing me, the nanny would take me to Holmby Hills Park if the weather was nice, which it usually was. The chauffeur always drove us in my dad's big Mercedes or Cadillac, so I'd arrive in style like all the other little Beverly Hills princesses. Once we got to the park, my nanny would chat with the other nannies and keep an eye on me while I ran around or played on the slide and swings. An hour or two later I would be driven back home for an early lunch and a nap. My parents left instructions for the nanny to give me freshly prepared, healthy food, with milk or juice. I might have a peanut butter sandwich, but canned spaghetti was out of the question, and there were never any soft drinks in our house. My dad was almost as health-conscious as my grandmother, and no daughter of his was going to drink Coca-Cola.

After my nap I would play with my nanny or my dad until my mom woke up, usually about four in the afternoon. Someone would come and tell me, "Your mom's up," and I would run screaming down the hall to my parents' room to pile into bed with my mother. They had a big bed with a satin-covered headboard, and my mother would be propped up with a snack and the sleeping mask she always wore on the pillow beside her. I would try on the mask (I was always begging for one of my own) and play on the bed or explore the room while Mama got dressed. My daughter does exactly the same thing today, piling into bed with me first thing in the morning to ask, "What are you watching? What are you doing?"

My parents' room was a child's paradise. Their suite was really big. The bed seemed gigantic, and I loved jumping up and down on it. There were couches, too, and these tall lamps from the *Star Is Born* set – blackamoors they were called, big tall black men in Eastern clothing with curved swords and turbans. I remember that the turbans were lampshades. But my parents' room was never like a museum; it was a real bedroom, the kind you can play in. Nobody ever told me, "You can't touch this" or "You can't touch that." My mom would let me wander around and play with anything I wanted. It was heaven for a little girl because there was lipstick and perfume and clothes and everything else you can think of. There was also a bathroom, a dressing room, and a truly amazing closet.

My favorite thing was the closet. Mama had the best closet in the world for a kid to play in, a big movie star closet stuffed full of wonderful clothes and dozens and dozens of shoes. I spent hours in there looking around and trying things on. I loved putting on Mama's glamorous dresses and hats, and I especially liked trying on the shoes. My mom always wore those high spiked heels when she went out. I'd put my small feet into what seemed like big shoes to me (size, after all, is relative) and try to walk around in them. I thought they were just the coolest thing there was. Needless to say, I had very little success with the walking around part, and this frustrated me.

When I'd had my fill of trying on the goodies, I'd go over to the dressing table and watch Mama put on her make-up. It drives me crazy now when my seven-year-old wants to watch me in front of the mirror, but it never seemed to bother my mother. Maybe she was just used to it after all those years of make-up artists fussing over her at MGM, but I think it was more than that. I think she really enjoyed my company. I remember watching intently as she transformed her at-home face into her movie star face. She applied the make-up carefully, professionally, with the sureness and precision that come from good training and long practice. The eyebrow pencil and false eyelashes were essential; my mother didn't feel dressed without them. I would watch her carefully in the mirror, admiring the deftness with which she applied her lashes. In the light of the dressing table mirror, I would marvel at the whiteness of her skin, and trace the tiny blue veins with my eyes. I especially liked to watch her applying her lipstick. As she traced the perfect scarlet line around her lips, I would lean further and further forward so I could see better, so close to her face that she could feel my breath on her cheek. She would struggle to keep from laughing as I came close to her chin, and the scarlet line would waver as her lips trembled. Sometimes she gave up altogether and burst into uncontrollable laughter, and I would laugh with her. The make-up table was part of our special ritual together.

Some nights she and my father would stay home in the evenings, and we'd all play or watch television together, sometimes with my dad's son Johnny. Other times they went out in the evening, and every now and then they had grand parties at home. On those nights the nanny would put me in my nightgown and carry me in for a good-night kiss before I had to go to bed. I was still very small then, and my parents were strict about an early bedtime. My sister, who was lucky enough to be seven years older, always got to stay up later.

It was a good life, an untroubled life. I was Mama and Daddy's little princess, the center of attention, as was only right. And then one day, before I'd even reached the tender age of three, disaster struck.

My mother had another baby.

In March of 1955 my brother Joey was born at Cedars Sinai Hospital. Frank Sinatra and Lauren Bacall kept my father company in the hospital waiting room, along with ever-faithful Vern. Joe's birth was quite a media event – literally. In the interval between my birth and my brother's, *A Star Is Born* had been released, and my mother had been nominated for an Academy Award. She sorely wanted it. The juvenile Oscar she'd won for *Wizard* had always smacked of tokenism to her, and she longed for the validation a "real" Oscar would give her as an actress. She was in the hospital recovering from Joey's birth on the night the ceremonies were held; a swarm of television technicians were there to wire Mama's room – and Mama – for broadcast in case she won. She had wires running up her nightgown and all over the bed; her room was filled with sound equipment and other apparatus. It wasn't the ideal way to recover from a Caesarean section the day before, but somehow it all seemed normal for Mama.

Further complicating Joey's birth was the fact that my mom had taken more prescription drugs during her pregnancy with Joe than with Liza or me. In 1955 doctors still believed unborn children were at least partially protected from chemicals while still in the womb, so my mother didn't realize what a risk her medication was to the baby. The result was that my brother suffered some physical damage; Joe still struggles with the long term effects of our mother's intake of Benzedrine and barbiturates during pregnancy. Joe had only one functioning lung when he was born and barely survived the birth. The doctors told my parents that he was a high risk baby with a 50/50 chance of survival at best. My parents refused to believe that Joe wouldn't make it and tried to look calm in front of each other, but underneath the bravery they were both worried sick. Two days after birth Joe's second lung opened, and it was clear he was going to survive. My mother didn't win the Oscar, but Joe's recovery was the best consolation she could have gotten. Joey, my parents agreed, was my mother's award. He was going to be all right, and that was all that mattered.

At two and a half years old, I was oblivious to both the Oscar and Joe's birth. While all this drama was going on at the hospital, I was blissfully playing with my nanny and grandma at home on Mapleton. Finally, though, the worst happened. They brought my brother home.

Life would never be the same for me again.

To truly appreciate Joey's impact on me, you have to understand one thing: I didn't have the faintest idea he was coming. I hadn't noticed my mother's pregnancy. Nobody had told me there was a baby inside my mom, or let me feel the baby move. This was 1955, long before childraising experts published books on preparing siblings for a new baby in the family. My parents never sat down with me to say, "You're going to have a baby sister or brother," and even if they had, they would have told me that the stork had brought it. Then when Joe was born, no one told me about him at first because it was thought he might not survive, and they didn't want to upset me.

So all of a sudden, there he was, this tiny squirming creature. My mom and dad came in the door carrying this baby I had no idea even existed. To my horror, my mother, *my* mother, was cuddling this little creature and telling me that the stork had brought us a wonderful new baby, and wasn't that great?

A *new* baby? Being Mama's baby was my job. I took one look at my new brother and said, "Tell the stork to take him back."

That's typical of my early years with Joey.

Of course, my parents didn't take him back. Joe's arrival was deeply painful for me in the beginning. Everything was about "the baby," and that baby was no longer me. "But what about me?" I thought. I was meant to be the little princess. Who was this stranger on my mother's lap? Even worse, Joe was a boy, a boy who had nearly died. After two daughters, my mother finally had her son. The fact that Joey had come so close to dying made him doubly precious to my parents. From the beginning they saw Joe as a special gift, more fragile than their other children. This was especially true of my mother. The special bond between Joe and my mom is obvious in pictures taken when Joe was a baby. They adored each other; my brother's face still lights up with tenderness when Mama is mentioned. My father paid the same attention to me he always had, but it was different with my mom. She loved all her children, but Joe was her baby, her last child, her precious little son.

I was painfully jealous. I felt as if I had been replaced in my mother's affection, and I desperately wanted to return to the days before Joe was born. I had never been jealous of Liza; she was nearly seven years older, and she spent a lot of time at her father's house. Liza and I lived in separate worlds at that age. Her presence never threatened my position as my mother's baby. Joey was another story.

My jealousy led to a crisis when Joey was about a year old. I'd resented his presence in our home. I would stand next to his crib and stare at him when he cried, wondering why he didn't shut up, wondering why he was always crying and squawking. Eventually I just couldn't take it anymore. One night when he was crying, I crawled out of bed in the middle of the night and went over to his crib. The little intruder was lying there, making that awful racket again. I'd had enough of the noise and more than enough of Joe, so when he continued to cry, I decided to do something about it.

I climbed over the crib railing, into the crib with him. I still remember bending over him, staring at his face in the darkness. Joe was a beautiful baby, round and plump by that time, with a head full of blond curls. To me, though, he was the enemy, the creature who had stolen my parents. After staring at him for a moment, I suddenly lost control. Overcome with pain and anger, I began scratching at his face, gouging as deeply as I could with my fingernails until blood was running down Joey's face. His screams awakened the nanny, and the next thing I knew I was being pulled out of his crib, and all hell had broken loose.

I had really done it. I got the spanking of my life, and my mother was too angry to speak to me for days afterward. I don't blame her. At three I was too young to understand the seriousness of what I'd done, but I did when I grew up. I could have seriously injured my brother. Forty years later Joe still has a deep scar under his eye, about three-quarters of an inch long, where I scratched him that night. At the time I not only hurt my brother but made everything worse for myself because now everybody loved the baby even more and was angry with me. Life seemed barely worth living.

My father tried to help. A couple of days after the "incident" he took me out to breakfast at a diner. My mother had told him, "Take your daughter out of here," because she was still so angry with me. My dad thought it might help if we spent some time together, just the two of us. I think he knew how miserable I was.

Dad carried me into the diner and introduced me to Milton Berle, who was sitting with friends in a nearby booth. My dad vividly remembers how I looked that morning. I was dressed up in a little blue coat, white gloves, white stockings, and little pumps. Dad says I looked "cute as hell." He asked me what I wanted for breakfast. In full pout, I told him "Nothing." He went through the whole menu item by item: You want pancakes? No. You want eggs? No. And so on and so on. No matter what he named, I said I didn't want it. I wasn't going to be bought that easily.

Finally my dad gave up and ordered his own breakfast. He was furious with me by that point. I sat next to him and stared at him in angry silence as he polished off a large meal. Every now and then he'd offer me a bite, but I'd have none of it. I was miserable, and I was bound and determined to make everyone around me as miserable as I was. If my parents were going to keep Joey, I was going to make them suffer. My dad finished his breakfast and paid, and as we walked out, a woman approached us and asked if she could take our picture. I said, "No pictures, please," as I'd heard my mother do many times.

Dad glared at me and said, "Stand there and have your picture taken." I saw that picture once. I'm standing there, holding my father's hand, looking like I'd like to strangle someone.

It wasn't the last time I made my parents angry. Joey and I were in the living room one afternoon when he was a toddler; my dad had fallen asleep in the chair nearby. Somehow Joe got hold of a big pencil with soft brown lead, and he started drawing on the carpet. The carpet was very light, so the pencil marks stood out clearly. I was old enough to know better, but instead of trying to take the pencil away from Joey or waking up my dad, I just let my brother go on drawing. The whole time he scribbled, I kept thinking, "This is great. Boy, is he in for it. He's going to get in so much trouble when Dad wakes up." By the time Dad did wake up, the carpet was a mess. Unfortunately for me, though, my plan backfired. When my father saw the pencil marks and realized I had sat by the whole time and let Joe do it, he was angrier with me than with Joe.

"You're the oldest!" he told me. "What did you think you were doing? Joe's just a baby. He doesn't know any better!" Once again, I was in trouble. Life can be tough when you're the big sister.

I must have driven my father crazy, but he was remarkably patient with me. He was one of those dads who would throw you in the air and rough-house with you. We had a big trampoline in the back yard, and Dad and Liza and I (and Joe when he got big enough) would bounce around on it together. Leslie Bogart or Sammy Cahn's kids or Dean Martin's kids would come over and jump on the trampoline, too. It was great. I thought my dad was the strongest man in the world. I remember him chopping down a tree in the back yard at Mapleton. The tree was really big, a tall eucalyptus. One weekend a couple of guys came over with a electric saw, and my dad cut the tree down. I thought that was the coolest thing I had ever seen. My dad was a regular Davy Crockett.

It was always fun when my parents were around. When they had to go out of town for Mama's concerts, it seemed too quiet until they got back. Every now and then, Joey and I would be allowed to go to one of our mother's concerts, and that was the best of all.

Concert nights were very special occasions. Joey and I would be dressed up in our best clothes and driven to the theater a little while before the performance. Our nanny would take us backstage to our mother's dressing room, where Mama would give us a kiss and send us out front while she got ready to go on. Guards would escort us to our seats in the front row, and then the concerts would begin.

Those were amazing, magical evenings. My mother was electric onstage, and I vividly recall the extraordinary power she had over her audiences. They would laugh and cry and cheer for most of the evening. My mom would look down at us regularly as she sang, and sometimes she even sang to us. That was really special. At some point in the performance she would bring us up onstage and introduce us to the audience. There is a famous picture of her lifting me up to the microphone at one of her concerts to say hello to the audience. I couldn't have been more than three or four years old. The concerts never ended until way past our bedtime, and sometimes, in spite of the excitement, I would fall asleep before it was over. Joey, though, never fell asleep. Small as he was, our mother's concerts so enraptured him that he would sit wide-eyed through the whole thing, his little legs sticking out over the edge of the theater seat. He remembers those early concerts as the best moments of his life.

My parents went out a lot at night in those years, but they gave many parties at home as well. Sometimes we would hold a barbecue outside in the afternoon, but usually the parties would be at night, dress-up parties with lots of celebrities. Kay Thompson would come, and the Bogarts, and Roger Edens and Frank Sinatra. To me, of course, the people who came were just friends of my parents. At that age I hadn't seen their movies; I hadn't even seen most of my mother's movies. It's not like Frank Sinatra arrived in a sailor suit, ready to sing and dance for us. He was just Uncle Frank to me. The first one to arrive was always Roger Edens. I loved his deep voice and Southern accent, and I'd go running to meet him when he came through the door. He'd always pick me up and throw me in the air and carry me around. He was the kind of man you could climb on if you wanted to be held, and he would pick you up and give you a hug. Humphrey Bogart, on the other hand, was something else entirely. Climbing on Humphrey Bogart was unthinkable, even though he was my best friend's father. When he came in the door, it was always just "Hello, Mr. Bogart," and remembering my manners.

My parents felt very strongly about good manners. Liza and Joe and I were always told to be very polite, especially to adults. My mother was determined that we would be respectful and well-behaved. She detested what she called the "B.H. [Beverly Hills] Brats," and she would give us a sharp remark and a swat on the bum if we were rude. She had a way of looking at us with her big black eyes that made us straighten up. She was always the shortest adult in a room, but nobody crossed her, certainly not me.

. I had to go to bed before the parties got started, so the preparation was the best part for me. I got to stay up long enough to see my mom put on her party clothes and make-up. Then I would go in the other rooms and watch the staff get things ready for the guests. The big den next to the living room was the center of the festivities. Card tables would be set up near the bar because the men always played poker. I still remember the smell of cigarettes and cocktails in that room the next morning. My dad always made his famous clam dip, which was delicious, and I got to taste it. My mother always put on records, usually her own or Sinatra's, so the room would be filled with music when people arrived.

I'd get to greet the very first guests, but then it was time for Joe and me to leave. Just about the time everyone got there, I'd have to get ready for bed. My nanny would whisk me away, put me in my nightgown, and take me back to my parents only long enough for a good-night kiss. Then it was off to sleep for me and Joe. People like to imagine me lying on a couch taking it all in, but it's not true. (Frank Sinatra is the one who sometimes slept on the couch.) Liza got to stay up later because she was older. Sometimes she fell asleep under the piano, but I never knew anything about it because I was sound asleep myself. My mother usually sang at my parents' parties; it was one of her favorite things to do, and Roger Edens would accompany her on our piano.

It was at one of those parties at our house, in fact, that the idea of the Rat Pack got started. My parents would invite everyone on the Hollywood A-list to their parties, but they never invited the columnists. My parents didn't like the press, and they saw no reason why they should have to invite these people into their home. Some of those they excluded were very powerful people who were used to being treated with respect. Columnist Sheila Graham, angered by her exclusion from the guest list, referred to the guests at my parents' parties as "that rat pack" in her gossip column. Swifty Lazar thought the term was really funny. Instead of being offended by the reference, he suggested that they adopt it as their nickname. Swifty had little stick pins made, shaped like rats, with rubies for eyes, and he gave them to my parents and their friends. After that they would wear the rat pins when they came to our house, which must have made Sheila even madder.

The adults weren't the only ones who got to have parties. The kids got to have parties, too. It seemed like it was always someone's birthday. All the parties seemed to be catered by the same Beverly Hills rent-a-party company because every single one of us had the exact same format with the same cast of characters. I laughed when I saw Christina Crawford's birthday party in *Mommie Dearest* because I recognized it; I swear it was the same party. The parties were always held outside. This was Southern California, remember, after all. The caterers would arrive early and set up a carousel and some tables and chairs in the back yard. Then the children would arrive. There were usually fifteen or twenty of them, with their parents, so there were about forty people altogether. The kids always wore their best dress-up clothes. For the girls this meant party dresses and little white socks with black patent leather shoes. The boys wore little suits, and we all put on party hats. The celebrity mothers would all wear the same outfit, too: slacks with flats and those big, baggy blouses. I have a picture of me and my mom, with my best friend Leslie Bogart and her mom, all leaving one of the birthday parties together. My mom and Betty Bacall are wearing almost exactly the same thing, the uniform, as I like to call it. The only difference is that Leslie's mom is wearing a scarf.

They always served the same lunch, creamed chicken on toast, really disgusting and a very odd choice for kids. There were always clowns to entertain. We'd play games and ride on the carousel and blow out the candles on the cake, and finally we'd open the presents. Every year it was the same. It really was a case of "If you've been to one Beverly Hills party, you've been to them all." Joey didn't have many parties there because he was so young, but Liza did. The older kids had the same basic party, with the exact same caterer, just a slightly older version, which meant creamed chicken but no clowns. Liza's parties were with Candice Bergen, Mia Farrow, Gail Martin, and their celebrity parents. Same place, same thing, slightly older cast.

Not that I would have attended Liza's party, you understand. People always want to know what I remember about Liza when she was young, and the answer is, "Almost nothing." When you're little, seven years is a huge age difference. Liza was at school all day and was usually off doing things with her friends in the afternoons. A lot of the time she was at Vincente's. Even when she was home, she was busy with her own things. What preteen girl wants to play with her preschool siblings? Sometimes the generation gap was especially obvious. I remember sitting at the dinner table with the nanny one night when Liza came racing in late. My parents weren't there; I think they were out that night. Liza seemed nervous, and as she dived quickly into her food, I noticed a strong menthol smell coming from under the table. I leaned down to look and there were Liza's legs, all smeared with this awful smelling white stuff that was partly scraped off. I had no idea what it was. I straightened back up in my chair and was starting to say something when I saw Liza look daggers at me. She didn't say a word, but it was clear to me that if I said anything about what I'd seen, I was dead. I clammed up and ate my meatloaf the best I could amid the odor of soapy menthol. It wasn't until years later that I realized I'd witnessed my sister's first, failed attempt to shave her legs.

Most of the time, I played with Leslie Bogart. She's my oldest friend, my only real childhood friend because we moved around so much after I was eight. Leslie lived two doors down, and we were always running back and forth to each other's houses. Our parents were friends, too, and that made it easier. The Bogarts had a pool, and Leslie and I would go swimming there. My parents didn't want a pool when I was small because they were afraid Joey or I would fall in, so in the summer I would go to Leslie's house to swim. I remember that girls and women always wore rubber bathing caps in those days, and I didn't see why. They pinched my temples and hurt my head. I can still picture Betty Bacall, Leslie's mom, in her white bathing cap. In those days I still called her Mrs. Bogart. Leslie and her older brother Steve and their parents had put their hand- and footprints in the cement by the steps when they built the pool, and I thought that was really cool. I understand that the marks are still there, barely visible by the pool steps. It was great fun going swimming, though I was intimidated by Leslie's parents. Leslie's mom was nice to me, but she wasn't the kind of woman you'd want to make mad at you. Mr.

Bogart (it was *never* "Bogey" or anything informal) had this really deep, gravelly voice, and he scared me. Whenever I passed him in the house, I would just say, "Hi, Mr. Bogart," and he would say, "Oh, hello, hello," rather absentmindedly, and that was that. He was a lot older than most dads, and he had this way about him. You automatically knew not to jump around Leslie's father. Nobody had to tell you that.

In some ways we were the typical American family of the 1950s, only we were the upscale version.

We even had a dog. He wasn't Lassie, but he was close. He was half collie and half German shepherd. My mom brought him back from a party one night because he needed a home. His name was Sam. Out of everyone in the neighborhood when I was little, I remember Sam the most clearly. Sam used to get into fights with the Bogarts' two boxers pretty regularly, but with us he was always gentle. Joey learned to walk holding tightly onto Sam to keep his balance. Sam was very big and very, very protective. He would never let Joe or me leave the house without him. It was extraordinary. If it looked like we were going to leave the yard unattended, if we even got too near the front wall or the edge of the driveway, Sam would be there to growl and warn us back. I swear he'd frown at those moments. If my father called him when Sam was outside watching us, Sam would just ignore Dad. He had no intention of going off and leaving us alone. At night he'd stand guard outside the house. He never slept inside; he wouldn't. Instead he sat on the front porch of our house and kept watch every night of his life. No one came near our house without Sam's permission. Nobody was going to harm us as long as Sam was around. My whole family remembers him so clearly. He was a key member of it.

Even the disasters were fun in those days. The first fire I remember was at Mapleton. My mother had a tendency to fall asleep smoking. She would take a sleeping pill and then climb into bed with a book and a cigarette, and sometimes she fell asleep with the cigarette still burning. There were several close calls. One night she fell asleep and the mattress caught on fire. The smoke started spreading through my parents' end of the house. Sam started barking and woke my father up. My dad grabbed my mom and ran to make sure we children were all right while someone called the fire department. I vaguely remember being awakened and carried outside with Joey, both of us in our pajamas. The next thing I knew, we were on the front lawn with Mama and Liza and the whole staff. Dad had gone back into the house with the butler to try to put out the fire. I remember being very confused and not quite sure how we got there. I also recall thinking how odd it was to be on the front lawn in our pajamas in the middle of the night. The firemen came to put out the fire, and eventually somebody took us back to bed. The smoke had never even gotten to our end of the house. It wasn't what you'd call an inferno; it wasn't even scary. I remember being half-asleep but still thinking, "This is really exciting."

Everything was exciting in those days, or at least happy. I know now that there were problems behind the scenes, but I didn't know it then. I was loved and protected by both my parents. I was safe, and I was cherished.

I wish it could have lasted.

# Chapter Five

# LONDON TOWN

It's funny how time changes your perspective. When I was a little girl, the happiness of my life seemed a natural thing, as inevitable as the coming of spring. Like all happy children, I took life for granted, never questioning what was placed before me so lovingly each day. What I didn't know then was that my father had shouldered a tremendous burden, both financially and emotionally, when he and my mother created the pristine little nursery world of Mapleton Drive. My father was, in fact, the Atlas who carried our world firmly on his broad back. For a long time he was able to hold it steady. Eventually, though, even the strongest man begins to break down. My father was no exception.

One of my happiest memories of the Mapleton years comes near the very end of that time. It's a memory that has taken on symbolic value only in retrospect. Our whole family had gone to Las Vegas to spend time playing in the sun while my mom performed at the New Frontier Hotel. Vegas was still small then; in fact there were only two hotels, the Flamingo and the Frontier. We had a grand time, swimming and playing with my dad or the nanny all day long. The best part of the trip for me and Joey was the tumblers. My mom's opening act was two Egyptian tumblers named Yehad and Yaheed. They were brothers. Yehad was very muscular, and Yaheed was very light. They were amazing. Joey and I thought these acrobats were the greatest thing in the world, and since they were staying

at the same hotel we were, we got to play with them during
the afternoon. They were extremely nice to us. They'd flip us
in the air and show us how to do handstands, and we'd have
the time of our lives. Since my dad is very strong, too (after
all, he was the guy who'd grown up doing the Charles Atlas
weightlifting routine), Sid got in on the act. Dad could easily
press a 125-pound guy, so he learned how to lift Yaheed over
his head and hold him there in a handstand. After a while the
acrobats even worked Dad into the act, having him come up
on stage and lift Yaheed for the crowd. I can still picture Dad
standing there, holding Yaheed effortlessly over his head. What
I didn't know then was that he was holding us all up, Mama
included, and had been for years. Sadly for us all, the family
balancing act had begun to totter.

The problems had been escalating for a long time. My mother's
concerts during those years were very successful, but they didn't
provide the income necessary to maintain our standard of living
at Mapleton. Vern Alves says my dad kept trying to cut back
on the number of servants and other amenities, but my mother
was accustomed to having a large staff around and wouldn't
hear of it. She was also used to custom-made clothes, limou-
sines, and the finest restaurants. It was the only life she had
known since her early days at MGM. Those were the days
before the money earned by child stars was put in trust until
they were adults, so my mother had nothing to show for her
MGM years but a string of successful movies and an empty
bank account. Once she left Metro, she lost the luxuries provided for her at studio expense. My dad was also accustomed
to living well, but not at a movie star level. Dad was always
trying to put together new projects, constantly on the look-out
for new investments; he eventually worked with an inventor to
develop a new type of stereo sound system. He also owned
racehorses, but as expenses at Mapleton mounted, he began
selling them off. In addition, he was restricted by the need for

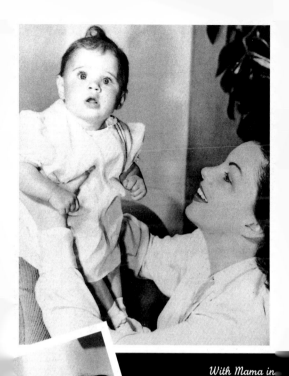

With Mama in

Proud parents: with Mama ar
in 1953 (below right) PAT CLARKE/

rrival: Liza, me and Mama
(above left) JOHN ENGSTEAD,
JOHN FRICKE

*Mama when she was still Baby Gumm* (left)
COURTESY JUDY GARLAND CHILDREN'S MUSEUM

*One of my favourite pictures of my mom, from the height of her studio years* (right)
COURTESY TURNER ENTERTAINMENT

*The Gumm Sisters: Frances (my Mom), Susie and Virginia (Aunt Jimmy)* (right) COURTESY JUDY GARLAND CHILDREN'S MUSEUM

*A study in curiousity: me and new arrival Joey, 1955* (below left)
© RICHARD AVEDON

*Lauren Bacall, Mama and me at a Beverly Hills western-theme birthday party* (below middle)

*Liza and me in our back yard on Mapleton Drive* (below right)
© GLOBE PHOTOS/PHIL STERN

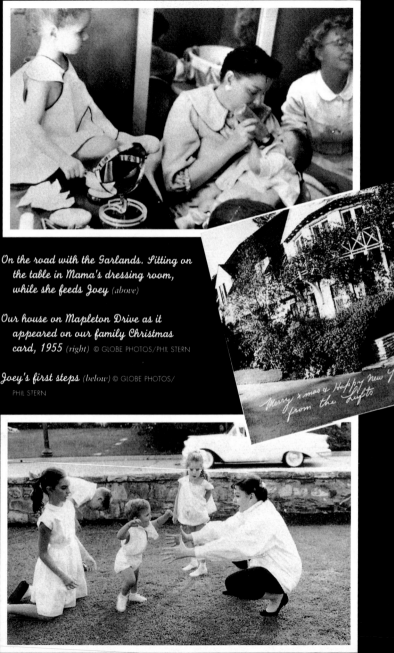

On the road with the Garlands. Sitting on the table in Mama's dressing room, while she feeds Joey *(above)*

Our house on Mapleton Drive as it appeared on our family Christmas card, 1955 *(right)* © GLOBE PHOTOS/PHIL STERN

Joey's first steps *(below)* © GLOBE PHOTOS/ PHIL STERN

Merry xmas & Happy New Year from the Lufts

Lorna Judy Liza Joe-Sid & John

*Consider yourself at home. The family in London, 1960. (above)* © BOB COLLINS

*Liza and me ice-skating at the Concord with the hotel's instructor (below)*

*Singing `Over the Rainbow' at the neighbourhood kids' show at the Marymount school (top)* © LEE SPORKIN

*In the pool with Mama at the Rockingham house (above)* COURTESY JOHN FRICKE

*Greeting Mama (right)*

*Mama and me, after I was
introduced at the end of her
famous Carnegie Hall concert
(above)*

*Liza, me and Joey at the
end of* The Judy Garland
Show *(right)* © CBS Inc.

*Joey, Mama, and me*

*The family home in London, 1960*

him to manage my mom's career. Both he and my mother thought Dad should manage her during those years, and in the beginning he did a wonderful job. It was time-consuming, though, and my mother was a very high maintenance woman in other respects. As the years passed, Dad took out a second and then a third mortgage on our Mapleton house as he and my mom sank further and further into debt. With debts piling up, taxes went unpaid as well. Eventually, the entire financial situation was hopeless.

I was about six years old when it all began to disintegrate. Until then Joe and I had been safely tucked away on the children's side of the house with our nanny, and since the Mapleton house was so large, we were unlikely to hear a fight between our parents even if there was one. At that age we already knew that although Dad might have been a foot taller than my mom, it was Mama who had the real power in the family. Mama always had, no matter which family it was. When Baby Gumm started belting out "Jingle Bells" at two years old and refused to leave the stage, she was already in charge of her parents and sisters. Luckily my mom was still small enough in those days for my grandfather to pick her up and carry her out. The situation was a little more complicated for my dad. As my aunt Jimmy once said, what Baby wanted, Baby usually got. Baby Gumm was sweet, but she was also spoiled. Louis Mayer eventually found out that even he had limited control over what my mother chose to do. She may have had a studio system running her life during her teens, but she also had an entourage of people on call twenty-four hours a day, whose job it was to keep her happy. Anybody who thinks my mother was powerless didn't know my mother. She learned young that if you scream long enough and loud enough, you get what you want.

Nobody said no to my mother. Joey and Liza and I knew it, and so did my father. Her whole generation of child stars was used to special treatment. Liz Taylor still gets that kind of attention every day of her life. When she celebrated her birthday a few years ago, they closed down Disneyland just for her. Mickey Rooney is still trying to figure out why no one does that for him anymore.

The other legacy for the child stars of my mother's generation was prescription drugs, health problems, and broken marriages. You don't take children and plant them in fantasyland, give them uppers and downers from the time they're sixteen, and expose them to constant adulation – and continual criticism – without the process taking a toll. The fact that nobody meant to hurt them is beside the point. By the time most studio children reached adulthood, the damage was considerable. There were some exceptions.

My mother was not one of those exceptions. She was funny and sweet and gifted beyond belief, but she was also damaged. When my father told her friends he was going to marry my mom all those years ago, they told him he was crazy. When he protested "But I love her," even her closest friends said, "We all love her, but you're still crazy." Maybe he was crazy; God knows he was crazy about her, but who could blame him? We all were.

Over the years the craziness of my mother's situation got harder to contain. In spite of her efforts to stay free of medication and my father's efforts to police her, she couldn't stay off it for long. She'd been physically dependent on the medicine from such a young age, and the doctors themselves were still so ignorant about its effects, that continued usage was almost certain. By 1959 she was powerfully addicted to amphetamines like Benzedrine, and barbiturates like Seconal and Tuinal. In emergencies she would be injected with Thorazine or paraldehyde, a powerful sedative designed to counteract the effects of Benzedrine. After twenty years of chemical bombardment, her body was beginning to break down. She was only thirty-seven years old, but her internal organs and nervous system had already taken a tremendous beating. A physician friend said it would take at least five years to get the chemicals out of her system even if she could remain drug-free, because amphetamines and barbiturates linger in body tissue. When she did try to go off the medicine, she became violently ill. With the physical symptoms came mood swings that gradually became more and more difficult to control.

Inevitably, my parents' marriage began to erode. As time went by, their arguments grew more frequent and serious. Their fights always seemed to come out of nowhere, as the chemicals peaked and ebbed in her body, and my father was her primary target. My mom began to insist on "separations" from my dad with increasing frequency. She filed, or threatened to file, for legal separation more times than my dad can remember. Sometimes she'd throw him out of the house for a while, and sometimes she'd pack up us kids and move us into the Beverly Hills Hotel for anywhere from a day to a couple of weeks. Liza may have realized what was going on, but Joey and I didn't. We were so used to hotels and to our parents coming and going that we never suspected a thing.

Meanwhile, the gossip columnists were having a field day. Years later I saw copies of newspaper headlines from this period claiming, "Luft Hits Judy; She Flees with Children." Although the stories make me angry, I also have to laugh. The thought of my father hitting my mother is so ridiculous that I can only shake my head. On one occasion my dad, who outweighed my mom by a good eighty pounds, told a reporter in frustration, "If I'd actually tried to strangle her, don't you think I'd have succeeded?" He was, after all, the guy who could do a military press with the Egyptian tumbler. On the other hand, my mother was more than capable of jumping all over my dad. She was a very physical person, and when she was angry, she'd come flying at him, all 4'11" of her. She hit him hard more than once. She even told me that one time she'd gotten so mad at Vincente Minnelli for snoring that she'd grabbed the phone receiver and smashed him over the head to make him be quiet. My father beat my mother? Not a chance.

It was not for nothing during this period that my mother was a great actress. She had a talent for staging scenes, and she always played the victim of the piece, never the bad guy. It also didn't hurt that she had press agents to publish "reports" whenever she wanted. Anyone under the influence of the medication my mother took becomes manipulative, but when you add to that the fact that my mom was a gifted performer, you can imagine the result. At our house a series of dramatic scenes was staged in the adults' quarters, and often leaked to the press by my mom's press agent the next day. My mother would periodically hire armed guards to "defend her and the children" from my father. These guys would be normal-looking men in suits that we kids assumed were just part of the usual huge Mapleton staff.

Emergencies were becoming more frequent at our house by then. One such emergency occurred when my dad was staying elsewhere after one of their bouts. My mother fell asleep smoking in bed again. This fire was extinguished almost immediately, but the result was that my mother burned her hip rather badly and needed medical attention. The funny thing about this episode is that the guards called my dad and asked him to come over and take care of my mom. The staff had been calling him privately for help all along. By then even the guards knew what the real story was and consulted with my dad several times about how to handle things at Mapleton while he was out of the house. So much for "Enraged Luft Attacks Judy."

After a few months of this chaos, my mom calmed down and the guards went home. Sid moved back in like nothing had happened, and as far as Joey and I knew, nothing had. By that time my mother was growing increasingly ill and had started putting on weight. No one realized it yet, but she was in liver failure, and the "weight" was actually severe edema. A physician friend recognized the symptoms just in time, or she might have died. At one point the doctors thought the problem might be alcohol-induced cirrhosis and ordered her to stop drinking, but alcohol wasn't the main problem. Contrary to rumors, my mother never drank heavily; for her a cocktail glass was more a prop than anything else. Prescription medicine was her problem. We now know that the liver failure was probably the result of the interaction of barbiturates and alcohol in her system. She also had a very bad case of hepatitis in 1959.

In spite of her tiny frame, my mother was amazingly strong physically. She came through her liver problems all right and returned home from the hospital. I was very relieved to see her, but not because I'd been afraid she'd die. We children hadn't been told about her liver failure. My secret terror was that she was pregnant again (to me "fat" meant "baby"), and that when they'd "taken Mama to the hospital to rest," she was going to come home with another little Joey. It had taken me four years to get used to the first Joey; I was horrified at the thought of another one! To my immense relief, though, she returned home alone. She also came home in a wheelchair, but my parents were careful never to let me or Joe see her in it. They didn't want to scare us. That was the other side of my mom's talent. Just as she made up stories when she was mad at my dad, she also made up stories to keep me and Joe from being frightened. She was careful to look happy and healthy whenever we were around. Both of my parents worked hard to protect us from the unpleasant truths, and for many years they succeeded.

Things were still difficult behind the scenes, though, and my parents needed a way out. My mom did some recordings and benefit appearances in the spring. Eventually, though, they did the same thing my grandparents had done when life overwhelmed them; they packed up the family act and took it on the road, first around the U.S. and eventually to England, leaving Mapleton Drive behind forever.

At the time I knew nothing of the real reasons for the move. As far as I knew then, we'd moved to London because my mother was going to appear at the Palladium. The reality was that the entourage my parents were maintaining on Mapleton Drive had grown beyond their means. The expensive property, the nineteen-room house and the large staff needed to maintain it, the cars and the Hollywood-style entertaining; all these were sinking my parents further and further into a morass of debt. In England my parents could live much less expensively, and my father hoped that selling the Mapleton house would clear most of their debts. The neighborhood itself was changing, too. Bogart had died, and Betty Bacall had sold their house and moved to New York, taking my best friend Leslie with her.

I didn't know it then, but Mapleton Drive would soon become for me what Grand Rapids had been for my mother. My mother spent the first five years of her life in Minnesota in a big white house, happy and protected, and she would have preferred to stay there forever. Life seemed perfect to her, but it had grown far from perfect for her parents. When Frank and Ethel Gumm's marriage began to fall apart, they tried to leave their problems behind in Grand Rapids and find peace in the Promised Land of California. My parents hoped for the same thing in England. Our journey was on a ship, not in the back seat of an old Buick, but otherwise it was pretty much the same.

I still remember our first trip to England in 1957. The ship was called the *United States*, and Joey and I had a wonderful time on board. There were all kinds of things for kids to do, games and movies and so forth, and a person to keep us busy all day. In the evenings we'd go walking around the decks with my mom and dad, and my dad would lift me up high so I could see the water. My mother would always say, "Don't drop her!" and my father would look at her as if to say, "Of course I'm not going to drop her." I would look down from the safety of my father's arms and marvel at what I saw. So much water.

Even though it was such a long way down, I was never afraid with my father holding me.

Ten days later we got to London, and not long after that my mom did a show at the Dominion. When she later did the Palladium I got to get up onstage one night in front of the whole audience with my brother and sister and my dad. I still remember looking down at that huge sea of faces. I wasn't nervous, just excited, and proud to be up there with my beautiful and glamorous mother. At those moments she wasn't the mother in the terrycloth bathrobe I knew from the kitchen; she was the movie star, and I was the movie star's daughter. Mama even made my dad sing "Swannee" with her at the Dominion one night, though I was in bed back at the hotel at the time. I wish I'd seen it. To say the least, my dad's singing is not what had attracted my mom to him.

The plan when we went in 1960 was to stay in England for at least a few months while my mom made records and did concert tours there and in Europe. We settled into a house on King's Road in Chelsea, and for a year or so my parents found the peace they were looking for. Our house had been built at the turn of the century by Ellen Terry, the actress George Bernard Shaw was in love with, and we'd rented it from the great director, Sir Carol Reed. I loved that old house. It was cold and drafty in the winter, but we had space heaters for the rooms and plenty of eiderdown quilts for the beds. I used to love cuddling down on the couch under a quilt to watch TV with Mama and Joey and my dad. Liza had joined us, but she was fifteen by then, so she wasn't really around that much. She was off being cool with her friends.

The school in England is the first school I really remember. It was called Lady Eden, and I liked it a lot. We wore uniforms like you see in the English movies, blue pinafores with white blouses, little blue coats, blue stocking caps with pompoms on the end, and white tights or kneesocks with black shoes. I still live in England part of each year, and I see the little girls go by on their way to Lady Eden wearing the exact outfit I used to wear. They still sell it at Harrods. The classes at Lady Eden were very small, only ten or fifteen students to a room. They gave us each a cigar box to keep our things in, and my cigar box had cardboard cutouts of shillings, tuppence, and other English coins so I could learn the British monetary system. I never did learn it because I hated arithmetic, and I knew that if I learned the coins, I'd have to do arithmetic with the rest of the class. The school day was carefully structured. Each morning they lined us up and took us to Hyde Park to play. We were taught good manners and the proper way to use a knife and fork, proper meaning British, which is very different from the American way. We'd have bangers and mash for lunch, with hot British mustard that made my nose run, and cake with runny custard for dessert. I still love that English custard. Most kids tried to give it away.

I also remember the eye patches I used to wear, which certainly were not part of the regulation uniform. One of the curses of my existence for much of my childhood was sties. I would get huge ones on both lids, and they were very painful. The doctors had my parents put medication on them and cover my eyes with wet packs for hours sometimes. My mom was always great when I got my sties. She'd sit for hours holding me, tickling me, and keeping me entertained during the long periods of darkness. She rarely sang to me, but she'd tell me stories. When I was well enough to go back to school, she decorated the eye patches I had to wear with glitter and sequins and eyelashes. In fact, they looked so good that the school asked her to stop doing it after a while because all of the other kids wanted an eye patch like mine to wear.

The year in Chelsea was a wonderful time. My mom was healthier than she'd been in years, and with some time off and less pressure from fans when she went out, she could do a lot of things with us she couldn't do at home. The British fans were much more polite in public than the American fans; they never approached you on the street or interrupted a family outing. At home my mother rarely went out in public with us, but in England she was much more relaxed. She would take us to Hyde Park to play and to Harrods to shop. She even walked us to school most days. Best of all, she took us to the theatre. It was my introduction to the West End theatre, and I got to see shows like *West Side Story* and *Oliver!* My mother would buy the cast albums and play them at home, so it was like taking the play home with us afterwards. Sometimes we really did get to take the show home because people like Georgia Brown and Lionel Bart would come over to visit. The whole year after I saw *Oliver!*, Georgia Brown was my favorite singer. I still remember watching the children dance onstage in *Oliver!* and thinking, "I want to do that."

One of my most vivid memories is going to see my first pantomime, a very old English theatre tradition. It was at the Palladium, and that day they were doing *Cinderella*. Some of the female parts were played by men, as is the custom. Halfway through the production the man who was playing one of the ugly stepsisters went behind a screen to change and suddenly burst into "Over the Rainbow" at the top of his lungs while he put on his gown for the Prince's ball. Apparently someone had told him my mother was in the audience that afternoon. The audience broke up (they all knew my mom was there too), and my mom nearly died laughing at this big ugly man in drag singing her song (not the last time that would happen!). I was sitting on my mom's lap, and I could feel her shaking with laughter. I was about eight at the time, and I didn't get it. "What's so funny?" I kept thinking.

The biggest theatrical event for me that year, though, wasn't the pantomime. It was my appendicitis attack. I had gotten very sick with a high fever, and no one knew what was wrong with me. My mother got worried and told my father to call a doctor; what she asked him, in fact, was to call one of the Queen's doctors. A regular doctor wasn't good enough for her little girl; she wanted a royal physician to see me.

My father thought she was being a bit dramatic. But my mother insisted that she wanted the best, and to her that meant going right to the top. After all, this was the woman who thought nothing of calling the President. So Queen Elizabeth's doctor was summoned, and he found nothing seriously wrong with me. For some reason, my mother wasn't so sure, and thank God she wasn't, or I wouldn't be here today. She wanted a second opinion. My dad had heard that Lenny Bruce knew a doctor in London, so he called Lenny. When this doctor arrived, he examined me briefly and said, "Get this child to a hospital *now*. Her appendix is about to rupture." So much for the Queen's physician.

My father wrapped me up in a blanket and carried me down to a waiting taxi. Everyone piled in, and they rushed me off to the hospital. My mom was trying to make an adventure of it so that I wouldn't be scared, and at first I was having the time of my life. All the attention was on me, and it was very exciting. For once I got to be the little drama queen, and I was enjoying every minute of it. Like mother, like daughter.

It wasn't quite so much fun when we got to the hospital. No one had warned me that when we got there, I was going to have an operation. My first hint was when my mother started crying. They were wheeling me down the hall, and I remember handing the doll I was holding to my mom and saying, "Take care of her for me, Mommie. She lost her shoe." My mother cradled the doll and started crying, and I began to notice that everybody looked pretty worried, even Dad and Liza. Maybe going to the hospital wasn't such a good idea. When they wheeled me into the operating room and took the white cloth off the instrument tray, I could see that it was covered with needles and other sharp instruments. I definitely wasn't having fun anymore; in fact, I was about to develop a lifelong phobia of needles. Finally, without any warning, they clapped a smelly mask over my face. I panicked and began struggling, scratching my face up pretty badly in the process. The mask was filled with ether, but nobody told me what was happening.

When I woke up in the hospital room, I was in a whole

lot of pain. My appendix had been wrapped inside a muscle, which was why no one had diagnosed the infection, and getting it out hadn't been easy. I remember opening my eyes and seeing my dad asleep in the chair by my bed. He and my mom had been taking turns sitting with me ever since the surgery. I was hot and miserable and threw up constantly from the effects of the ether. I would crawl down to the foot of the bed to comfort myself in my misery, and every time I did, the nurses would pick me up and put me back at the other end. Finally my dad lost his temper and said, "For God's sake, leave her alone! Let her sleep at the other end if she wants to!"

Mama and Sid visited me every day, bringing a little record player and my favorite records to listen to. My very favorite record at the time was Georgia Brown singing "Milord," and I played it over and over until Liza couldn't stand it anymore. One day she told me the record was gone. First she told me it had accidentally melted by the fireplace, and then she told me she'd dropped it down the elevator shaft at the hospital. I don't know which story, if either, is true. At any rate, the record was gone. (Years later, Liza recorded the song herself.)

Things started looking up again when I got to come home. My parents had house guests, Carolyn and Freddie Finklehoffe, and they made a big sign for me with glue and glitter that read, "Welcome home, Scarbelly," and hung it on the front door. I did have a scar, a whopping big one that I could show off. My mom and dad put me on the couch with quilts and dolls and warm slippers, and I got to watch TV all day long. I even got to make Joey stay off the couch because "Your sister is sick." Talk about power. It was great. My mother bought me *Madeline* to read while I got better. In the book Madeline goes to the hospital and has an appendectomy just like mine. I thought the story was really about me.

The whole adventure reached a climax on November 5. I had been home from the hospital just a few days, and my parents and the Finklehoffes had also gotten sick with food poisoning from a restaurant. Joey had a cold, so the only ones in the house who weren't sick were Liza and the staff. Since it was Guy Fawkes' Night, my mom dragged herself downstairs and asked the cook to get out the fireworks so we could have at least a small celebration, and the cook came back toting a big box.

The cook's name was Antonio, and he doubled as a butler. He had an Italian accent you could cut with a knife. He was one of the biggest klutzes I've ever seen, and just as nice as he was clumsy. My mom wanted him to light the fireworks for us kids to watch, so Antonio took the whole box of firecrackers outside into the courtyard garden. We kids sat down on the window ledge to watch, with the grown-ups all gathered behind us.

Antonio opened the box and took out a little sparkler, the kind that looks like a fairy wand when it's lit. He lighted the end with a match, and it started to sparkle. We thought it was beautiful, and everyone went "Wow!" But then one of the sparks hit Antonio's hand and burned him. He screamed "Ow!" and let go of the sparkler, dropping it into the firecracker box. The whole box exploded, and the entire collection of fireworks went off at the same time. It was astounding. Poor Antonio was backed up against a wall screaming and carrying on in Italian, with fireworks going off all around him and then sailing over the wall into the neighbors' yard. Meanwhile, we were all laughing hysterically. My mother said, "There goes the soufflé!" every time another round went off, and kept telling my father, "That's exactly how he cooks, too!"

Poor Antonio! Nobody tried to help him; we were all laughing too hard. My mom and dad and the Finklehoffes were all doubled over, roaring with laughter and clutching their sick stomachs. Liza and Joey and I were doing exactly the same thing. Each time a new round exploded, we'd explode with laughter. It hurt me badly to laugh because my wound hadn't healed yet, but I couldn't stop. The light show must have gone on for about five minutes before the box finally fizzled out. It's a wonder poor Antonio wasn't badly burned. He was pretty well singed around the edges. The poor man had been trapped in the middle of an explosion, and all we could do was laugh.

Life with Mama always meant plenty of fireworks.

It was exciting at our house a few days later, too, when John Kennedy was elected President. My mother had campaigned for him personally. I still remember her saying she didn't vote for Nixon because she could never vote for a grown man who would wear a propeller beanie hat during a campaign. When Kennedy won the election, he called my mother in England himself to give her the good news. My mother took the call in the living room where I was still resting on the couch from my surgery, and when she heard the news, she started jumping up and down and screaming with excitement like a little kid. It looked hilarious – she was so tiny, anyway, and there she was, jumping up and down like a six-year-old. I started laughing because she looked so funny, but it hurt when I laughed, so I begged her to stop. "Please don't do that, oh, please, please."

She kept on yelling, "He won! He won! He won! He's the President! He won!" still jumping up and down. Joey started laughing, too, and the more he laughed, the more I laughed. By the time it was all over, my side was killing me, but it was worth it because it was so funny.

I could have stayed in England forever. So could my father. It was the last time we were ever really happy as a family. Eventually, though, we had to return to the U.S. so my mother could work. In 1961, a few months after my ninth birthday, we went back home.


If you asked my father, he'd tell you that the turning point in my parents' marriage was the day he urged my mother to sign with Freddie Fields and David Begelman as her exclusive managers. One thing is certain: my dad was later convinced that signing that contract began a long process in which Fields and Begelman systematically excluded my father from my mother's life. In his view, they did it by manipulating my mother in the ways to which she was most vulnerable: by flattery and fear. And it worked.

First they dissolved my parents' management team and began to handle all of my mother's professional commitments themselves. In no time my mother had given them full power of attorney, including the ability to write checks and otherwise dispose of her money. My father objected to this arrangement, but by then he had been excluded from all contractual agreements and business decisions. Fields and Begelman said that was how my mother wanted it. But in my father's eyes, it was Fields and Begelman who were trying to remove him from my mother's life completely, including from their marriage, for "Judy's own good," of course. After the Mapleton house was sold (with the proceeds going entirely to debt), Fields and Begelman were careful to insist that any new real estate be acquired exclusively in my mother's name, whether my father lived on the property or not. They later said this was my mother's idea, but my father thought they were behind it.

My dad was put on his wife's payroll – humiliating for any man, and more so for a tough guy like my dad, and especially so as he'd made the introduction in the first place, wanting my mother to have good agency representation. Dad threw himself into promoting the new stereo system he'd invested in developing two years before, trying to make some money to pay off the family debts. His plan was to sell the new system to international airlines for in-flight music. Ultimately, the idea failed to catch on, but only after Dad had invested a huge amount of time developing and promoting it. He still has one of the systems sitting on a shelf in his living room. His face is a mixture of pride and regret as he shows it to visitors. For Dad, that stereo has become a symbol of what might have been.

For the first time, our family was beginning to splinter. Looking back on it now, the reasons are much clearer to me than they were then. I believe the biggest factor in the collapse of our family during those years was Fields and Begelman's entry into the picture. They committed my mother to a grueling concert tour that helped destroy her health. Three years later my mother discovered that Begelman had been embezzling from her the whole time. No wonder he wanted to take all financial control away from my dad. After giving a record number of concerts in an eighteen-month period, my mother ended up with nothing to show for it.

The other, more insidious reason for the break-up of our family was also linked to my mom's grueling schedule. To maintain the energy she needed to perform, my mother's intake of stimulants skyrocketed. Sometime in 1961 doctors started her on Ritalin, a powerful, then-new stimulant, now given for Attention Deficit Disorder. A normal dose of Ritalin is 20 mg. daily; 30 mg. is considered the maximum safe dosage. By late 1961 my mother was taking between 50 and 100 mg. of Ritalin a day – two to four times the maximum dosage – occasionally accompanied by Benzedrine capsules, and a heavy mix of barbiturates to make her sleep afterward. With this chemical time bomb inside her, she could go onstage night after night and perform at a frantic pace, but the toll on her health was frightening. In the early stages of overdose, Ritalin causes agitation, tremors, sweating, confusion, and paranoia. Within a year of our return from England, my mother had every one of those symptoms.

We lived in the East after our return to America. While my mom traveled and did her concerts, Joey and I stayed in New York with our nanny. Dad was traveling on business a lot of the time, but he saw me and Joe as much as he could. My parents separated repeatedly during this period as my mother's mood swings worsened. Vern toured with my mom for a while, but as her behavior got more erratic, she became estranged from Vern. Finally Vern said he'd had enough and returned to California to stay. It was years before I saw him again.

It was during this time that my mother was approached

about doing a cameo part in *Judgment at Nuremburg*, a powerful drama about the Nazi trials. She hadn't done a film since *A Star Is Born*, and in her state of mind the prospect of doing a movie again was frightening. She used that fear and vulnerability on camera, and the effect was riveting. When I saw the movie years later, I was proud and deeply moved by her performance.

My mom traveled a lot early in the year, so when summer came, she decided it would be a good thing for us to move to Hyannis Port and have some time together there. Liza had show business ambitions, so my mother arranged for her to work backstage at the Cape Cod Melody Tent, painting scenery for $15 a week. Mama thought it would be good for Liza to see what working in the theater was really like when you were starting out. My dad had gone back to California to deal with the debts they'd left behind, so we moved to Hyannis Port without him. I didn't think anything of it; after all, he was often away on business. I didn't yet realize that my parents' marriage was breaking up.

We settled into Hyannis Port for the summer; Mama, me, Joey, and Liza. The house we rented was right on the beach, just down the road from the Kennedy Compound. It seemed like everybody in Hyannis Port was either a Kennedy or working for the Kennedys. There were several houses on the compound, and a seemingly endless number of kids. Bobby Kennedy alone must have had four or five. Some of them were nice, and some were spoiled brats. John and Caroline were there, but they were very young, not nearly old enough to play with me and Joe. There were so many Kennedys, they just seemed to multiply as you watched. If you asked them who they were, they'd introduce themselves by saying, "I'm Ted's kid," or "I'm Eunice's child." It was a given that they were Kennedys. To this day I can't remember which one was which. There were also lots of mothers and their helpers, and every now and then a couple of dads. Joe and I just sort of blended in with the crowd of kids and enjoyed ourselves. Maria Shriver told me recently that she has a picture of the two of us in the bathtub from that summer. Apparently our mothers bathed us together. At the end of the day the parents just stuck us kids in the tub in groups, and rinsed us off.

Joe had a harder time fitting in on the compound than I did. He was small for his age and still somewhat frail, which was especially hard for a boy. My mother continued to dress him in short pants like boys wore in England. She also kept his hair very long while other American boys had crewcuts. The Kennedy kids were a rough-and-tumble crowd, and they gave Joe a really hard time. Sometimes he'd come home in tears because he couldn't do all the things the Kennedy boys could do. Whenever that happened, my mother would say, "Yeah, but I'll bet you they can't conduct *West Side Story*, either, like you can." Joe liked that idea. He even pointed it out to the other boys one day. Eventually he and Chris Lawford became friends, and since they turned out to have the exact same birthday, they celebrated together when we moved back to California (the Lawfords had a house on the Santa Monica beach).

Things did get out of hand at times. One of the Kennedy boys – I don't remember which – loved to play with matches. He was always lighting them. It scared my mother to death. One day my mom sat all the kids down and gave us a big safety lecture on why we shouldn't play with matches. She even lit one to demonstrate and burned herself in the process. She was something of an expert on fire safety by then; she had dozed off and started enough accidental fires of her own over the years to know what she was talking about. Most of the time, though, we kids just went swimming or sailing that summer. Nothing as exciting as a really big fire.

Although some of the Kennedy kids were rough and obnoxious, their parents were always nice. They spoke kindly to me and Joe and treated us well. Eunice and Ethel were there, and, of course, Jacqueline. I adored Jacqueline. She was wonderful with us children, always gentle and sweet, and careful and strict with her own kids. I remember being especially fascinated by her voice. I've never heard another one like it, before or since. It was soft and whispery and gentle, and I loved to listen to her speak. My mother was the one with the amazing singing voice, but Caroline and John's mother had the most remarkable speaking voice I'd ever heard. To this day, when I think of Jacqueline Kennedy, I remember that soft, wonderful voice.

Bobby and Jack Kennedy were around sometimes, too, though not as much as the moms. I knew Jack Kennedy was the President, but I didn't really understand what that meant. To me he was just somebody's dad or uncle, and my mother's friend. He had more hair than any man I'd ever seen, and I used to stare at it and marvel at how thick it was. He was great with us children, too, warm and friendly. You could run and play with him, but you couldn't climb on him because of his bad back. I remember one time when he stole the keys to the golf cart from the Secret Service and took us all for a ride. It was so much fun, even more so because the Secret Service came running after us like the Keystone Cops. The Secret Service was always around when he was there. The agents all seemed to look alike, as if somebody had cut them out with a cookie cutter: big men in suits and ties and dark glasses who never talked and never, ever smiled. They were always hovering around Jack Kennedy. It used to drive him crazy sometimes. That's why he stole the golf cart. I didn't understand who these big men were. I used to feel sorry for them because it was summer, and they were always wearing suits. I'd look at them and think, "Boy, I'll bet they're hot."

Eventually, summer ended, and we had to go back to school. We returned to New York and moved into the Dakota in New York City. I was thrilled because Betty Bacall lived there with Leslie and Steven, and once again I had my best friend almost in shouting distance, two floors up. I was happy in New York when I wasn't in school, and I loved going to the

Broadway shows with my mom. One of the most memorable was Ethel Merman in *Gypsy*.

Our trip to see *Gypsy* has become part of family lore. My mom always told us the plot and played the records for a few weeks before we went to see a musical, so Joey and I would know what was going on. *Gypsy* was a particular favorite of my brother's; he loved the music. By the time we reached the theater to watch an actual performance, Joe already knew all the words.

We sat front row center that night, with me next to Mama and Joey on her lap. Joe was only about four or five at the time. As the performance progressed, Joey got more and more excited, and when Ethel Merman launched into Joe's favorite song, he couldn't resist joining her. Several bars into the lyric, as Ethel took a breath, Joey sang out "Rose!" right on cue. Except that Joey couldn't pronounce his "R's yet, so what he actually sang was "Wose!" Everyone in the audience heard him, including Ethel Merman.

Mama, embarrassed, whispered, "Hush, Joey, Miss Merman's singing." My brother, completely oblivious to every-thing but the music, continued to chime in right on cue, belting out "Wose!" every few beats. I could see Ethel Merman shaking with laughter as she tried to get through the rest of the song. She knew perfectly well who the little voice in the front row was coming from. Mama and I were laughing by then too, tears streaming down Mama's face, but Joey remained blissfully unaware of the havoc he was causing. He just kept belting out his favorite song.

There would never be enough good times for us after that. By now my father was coming and going like we had a revolving door, and getting increasingly desperate. He couldn't get my mother away from Fields and Begelman, whom he perceived as a threat, and he was helpless to prevent our family from breaking up. He loved my mother as much as ever, but he knew her well, and he was terrified of what would happen to us all without him there to take care of us. The world as I knew it was about to topple off of my father's shoulders. When it fell, it made a crash that still reverberates.

# Chapter Six

# EAST OF EDEN

The Bay of Pigs and the Cuban missile crisis. All Americans of my generation remember it; our entire nation held its collective breath for weeks. As fate would have it, we were in Florida when the crisis reached its peak. I was almost ten years old, and my brother Joey was seven. Our whole family had gone to Florida on vacation while my parents reconciled for the umpteenth time. The vacation had started out beautifully, nothing but fun in the sun for me and Joey, and my parents getting along for a week or two. They flew up to the White House for a weekend to visit with the Jack and Jackie Kennedys while we children remained behind to swim and play.

Then the missile crisis broke. I'd never heard of the Bay of Pigs; all I knew was that my parents were suddenly very tense, and when I asked my mother an innocuous question one evening, she replied, "Don't you realize there are missiles pointed at us right now?"

I remember thinking, "In the living room?" I looked around. I didn't see any missiles.

The missiles were there, of course. The ones in our home were invisible but real. My parents were on the brink of war, and all four of us would soon be casualties.

Our ideal family holiday came to an abrupt end when Joe broke out with the measles. He was so sick that my parents got worried and decided to charter a small plane to fly Joe up to Miami. We packed quickly and got on the plane. My father proceeded to get into an argument with the pilot. He didn't think the pilot was flying the plane properly, so Dad insisted on taking the controls himself. He kept saying, "I'll fly the plane."

My mother kept saying, "Sid, stop being ridiculous. Let the pilot do it." For once, my mother lost the argument. My dad had been a crack pilot during the war, so he took over the controls and flew us to Miami. God only knows if he had a license.

Joey recovered, and two weeks later we went back to New York. Dad moved into the Dakota with us for a while.

To no one's surprise, I found a bump on the back of my neck right after we got back and showed it to my parents. Dad said, "Bingo! She's got them." The doctors in Florida had thought about inoculating me against Joe's measles, but my parents had decided to let me get them over with. Now it was my turn to have the measles. For what seemed like forever I lay in my darkened bedroom covered with Calamine lotion, itching and miserable. My eyes might have been damaged, so they had to keep me in the dark all the time. That was pretty much the story of my childhood.

Eventually Joey and I were both healthy again, and it was back to business as usual. For Dad that meant traveling around selling stereos and trying to patch things up with my mom. School was a nightmare. Our parents enrolled us in New York P.S. 6, the local public school. The difference between P.S. 6 and Lady Eden was, to say the least, dramatic. Comparatively speaking, the new school was huge, with big ugly buildings and thirty or more students per class. I had to enter the school year late, and I was terrified. I never got past the fear and discomfort of being the new kid in school. Making things even worse, by the end of the first day, everyone knew who my mother was. The rumor spread like wildfire that the new girl was "Dorothy's" daughter. Every kid in the school had seen *The Wizard of Oz*, so they all stared at me and asked questions. "Is it true? Is your mom really Judy Garland? Are you really her daughter? What is she like? Can we go to your house? Can we meet her?" And so on and so on. P.S. 6 wasn't like Los Angeles, where lots of celebrities' children go to local schools. These children had never seen a celebrity. I didn't have the faintest idea what to say when they asked me about my mother except, "Yes, she's my mom." What was she like? She was like my mom. What else could I say?

It didn't help that I wasn't very good at school subjects, either. I already knew I hated arithmetic, and it quickly became clear that I wasn't very good at reading, either. They put me in a special room for the "slow" readers and gave me a book called *A Big Ball of String* to read from every day. After that I had to read a whole series of Dr. Seuss books. I hated them. To this day just the sight of those books gives me a headache. What no one understood at the time is that I'm dyslexic. To this day I panic at cold readings. If I don't have a script at least five minutes ahead of time, I can barely get through it. I can go to a Broadway show and come out singing every song I hear, but I couldn't read those stupid little books. It was horrible. I was bored, frustrated, and humiliated.

Joey had the worst of it, though. Bad as public school was for me, it was worse for him. He was small for his age, and my mom sent him off to first grade in short pants, long hair, and kneesocks. Everyone teased him. We didn't find out until years later, but my brother has a learning disability that made school a struggle for him. As Joe describes it now, "Sometimes my brain just won't work like it should. I can see the pieces of ideas, but it takes me a long time to put them together." School was a miserable experience for both of us. We lived for the moment the bell rang at the end of the day and we could just go home. I'd run upstairs to find Leslie and try to forget about school until the next day. For Joey and me, P.S. 6 was childhood purgatory.

There was only one thing I did find interesting at that school. Until I went to P.S. 6, I'd never been around "special children," kids who were deaf or blind or otherwise physically disabled. One of these special students was in our class for part of each day. Her name was Helen, and she was blind. Each day a different child in our class was assigned to walk Helen back and forth to her special classes. One day it was my turn. As we walked down the hall together, I said, "Can I ask you a question?"

She said, "Sure."

"What happened to you so you can't see anymore?" Helen explained that because she was born early, they'd put her into an incubator. If there's too much oxygen in an incubator, she told me, the baby goes either deaf or blind.

I remember thinking, "Boy, I hope I never have to go into an incubator. I don't want to be blind." I never felt sorry for Helen, because she didn't feel sorry for herself. She was a pretty girl with dark hair and white eyes from being blinded. I thought she was an interesting person. Helen is one of the few good memories I have of P.S. 6.

I wasn't at P.S. 6 for very long. Soon we packed our bags and moved again, this time upstate to Scarsdale. Except for losing Leslie, it made little difference to me. By that time I was used to change; we were constantly changing houses, hotels, schools, staff, everything. Only the family – Mama, me, Joey, and sometimes Liza and Dad – stayed the same. As long as we had each other, everything was okay. A move to Scarsdale was nothing. Staying in the same place for a long time – that would have seemed odd by then.

We moved into a house in Scarsdale, and my mother enrolled us in yet another public school, once again a faceless place with big buildings, large classes, and lots of strangers who asked, "Is your mom really Judy Garland?" Liza enrolled in the local high school, where she got her first lead role in her school production of *The Diary of Anne Frank*. I remember watching the Nazis and being scared, but that's the only thing I recall. We all went to see Liza, even my dad, and my mom was very proud of Liza's performance. My dad didn't move into the house with us, but he still came around regularly.

Joey and I liked the house in Scarsdale. It was a suburban area a little like Mapleton Drive had been, with lovely country all around. When my mom wasn't touring she cut back on her medication, so there were still good times when she was home. That fall the four of us went trick-or-treating together through our neighborhood – Mama, me, Joey, and our nanny. My mom dressed up like the clown in *The Pirate* and went door to door with us asking for candy. I wondered if people realized who she was, or if they just thought she was another Judy Garland impersonator. We giggled and ran and had a wonderful time.

The high point of the year for my mother professionally was the concert at Carnegie Hall. Of the hundreds of concerts she gave, this was one of her most brilliant performances. Joey and Liza and I were all there, in the front row, and when she brought us up onstage to introduce us to the audience, I was brimming over with pride. When my mother was onstage at moments like that, it was magic, and we were a part of it.

In December my mom left for Europe to promote *Judgment at Nuremburg*, which was just being released, while Joey and I stayed in Scarsdale with our nanny. When Mama got to Paris, she got really sick with bronchitis. She was afraid she was going to die. In her panic she called my dad and asked him to come to Paris right away. My dad virtually commandeered the next plane and raced overseas to rescue her. When Mama recovered, my parents came back to Scarsdale together, and Dad moved in full-time. For a while everything was wonderful. It wasn't exactly Mapleton Drive, but it was close.

They began having people come over again for small parties in the evening. One morning I went outside to find George Hamilton still asleep in a chaise by our pool, recovering from my parents' party the night before. Dad played with Joe and me like he had in the old days, tossing us in the air and carrying us on his shoulders. He was so relieved to be home with us again.

Christmas was wonderful. My parents got along better than they had in years. My mother staged a little holiday pageant in our living room just for the family, with Christmas songs and little parts for each of us, and tape-recorded it all. My dad still has the tape, with my childish voice saying, "Hi, I'm Lorna!" We all sound very happy. In a sense, I think my mom was playing a part that Christmas, the part of the happy suburban wife and mother. I didn't mind; Mama was never happier than when she was performing. Her happiness was all that mattered to us.

My mother tried so hard to do the things with us that other mothers did. While we were living in Scarsdale, my teacher planned a class trip to the zoo. She asked for mothers to come on the bus to help with the children, and my mother decided to go. At first everything went fine. We looked at the animals, and my mom was treated like any other mother. Then we went for ice cream, and as we sat there eating, bees surrounded us, attracted by the sugar. A little boy in my class named Simon was allergic to bees, so he began to panic when they swarmed around. My mother had been swatting bees away from him all day, but now there was a cloud of bees, and my mother was trying to keep them from Simon. All her swatting attracted attention, and someone recognized my mom. A crowd immediately swarmed around us, asking for autographs. "Can I have your autograph, Miss Garland? Will you sign this, Miss Garland?"

My mom tried to be polite but kept saying, "Look, please, I'm just trying to help this little boy. Please, I'm here with my children's class today . . ." Of course, it was hopeless. In no time we were overrun with my mother's fans, and we had to end our day early.

It was always that way when my mother went out in public. Most of the time it didn't bother me. As my mother always reminded me, I was a very fortunate young lady. I had beautiful clothes, and went to great restaurants, and had the best seats at plays and concerts. When fans approached our table at a restaurant, my mother always smiled pleasantly and signed whatever they held out to her. As soon as she finished, we went on eating. It was a normal part of our lives. The only time it ever bothered me was when the crowds got out of control.

I remember one time in particular. It was at the concert my mom did at Forest Hills. Joey and I were with her. As we got into the limo after the performance, hundreds of people surrounded us, pressing up against the windows, banging on the sides of the car and chanting, "Judy, Judy, Judy!" Flashbulbs were going off from every direction. The crowd was hysterical, completely out of control, and the driver couldn't move the car. As the fans surged around us, trying to get to my mother, the car began to rock back and forth so hard I was afraid it would turn over. Joey sat next to me white as a sheet, scared to death. My mother kept shouting "thank you" and waving, hoping the crowd would move back, but they didn't. Mama seemed perfectly calm, but I was terrified. The driver kept trying to move forward through the crush of people as my mother repeated, "Be careful. Don't hurt them. Don't hurt anybody." Finally the police came to escort us, but even then we had trouble moving out. It seemed like an eternity before we pulled free of the crowd.

The whole experience was frightening for me, and for Joey too. I still can't be in a crowd like that without panicking. My mother reacted with panic when it first happened to her on the MGM tour for *Wizard* twenty years earlier, but she got used to all the hysteria. I never did.

Not long after our Christmas in Scarsdale, my mom was signed to do *A Child Is Waiting* with Burt Lancaster, and a CBS Special with her old pals Frank Sinatra and Dean Martin. That meant moving back to California. Once again we all packed up and moved into a rented house in Bel Air.

My mom was gone a lot during that time, working first on the special and then on the film. I remember her making the movie very clearly. Mama would take me to the set with her sometimes, where I promptly developed a huge crush on the boy who played the lead in the film. Mostly, though, I remember the children.

*A Child Is Waiting* was about retarded children, as they called them then, and except for the boy who played the lead, most of the children in the film were mentally handicapped. Most had Down's syndrome, which was called "mongolism" in those days. I remember the first time my mother took me to the set. Before we left, she sat me down and had a long talk with me about what I would see there. She explained that many of the children looked different from the children I was used to. She told me it was very important that I not point or stare at them because it might make them feel uncomfortable. I thought to myself, "I've been pointed at, so I know how that feels. Sometimes people stare at me and think I'm different because of my mom." I took my mother's advice to heart. I promised myself I wouldn't stare at them no matter what they looked like.

When we got to the set, I was introduced to some of them as "Judy's daughter." I couldn't tell if they understood what that meant, but they tried to talk to me, and some of them hugged me the way little children would. I had trouble under-standing them because they couldn't pronounce their words clearly, and some of them looked a little odd, but I pretended not to notice. Instead I listened carefully and told myself over and over, "They just look different, but inside they're like me. I mustn't hurt their feelings or make them feel uncomfortable." These children made me sad. Apart from Helen, the blind girl in my class in New York, they were the only disabled children I'd ever met. The difference was that I'd never felt sorry for Helen, but I felt sorry for them. For a while I thought about becoming a teacher so I could help children like that. Years later, when I saw *A Child Is Waiting*, it made me cry. My mother gave a wonderful performance. I was proud of her.

Things were bad between my parents by then. A few weeks after we moved back to California, my mother moved us into the Beverly Hills Hotel. Joey and I accepted it as just another move, but in reality it was the most serious separation yet. My mother filed for legal separation for the first time, citing "extreme mental cruelty" as the grounds.

Later that spring she went back to New York to do some recordings. Joe and I stayed behind in California. Not long after she arrived, she got very ill again and had to be hospitalized. My godfather, Dr. Lester Coleman, called my father from New York and said, "Judy's really sick. She wants you to bring Lorna and Joe and come to New York immediately."

My dad just told us, "We're going to New York to see your mom," packed everything up, took us to New York, and moved us into a hotel. Joe and I enrolled in another new school. We didn't find out until much later that we'd moved there because my mother was sick.

My mother's sicknesses were getting more and more frequent. She had been in and out of the hospitals when we were in Hyannis Port and New York. Almost every time she was away from my father for any length of time, she got sick. It wasn't psychosomatic; the sickness was real. When my dad wasn't around, nobody monitored her medication or made sure she got enough food and rest. She was evidently taking a large quantity of Ritalin a day by then. At night she would try to counteract it with barbiturates like Seconal, Tuinal, and Valium. Her liver and kidneys were breaking down, and her health had begun to decline alarmingly. The mood swings continued to worsen, as did the other psychological symptoms of Ritalin toxicity. Like her health, her relationships, especially the one with my father, suffered under the strain.

It was at this crucial point that Fields and Begelman decided to book my mother in England again, this time for the film *I Could Go On Singing*. In an escalating crisis, my mother decided not only to go to Europe without my father, but to take Joe and me with her. It was a deliberate attempt to remove us from his reach. My parents were already separated again; Mama and Joe and I were living at the Stanhope, and my dad had taken a room on another floor. In her growing paranoia, my mom had developed a fear that my father would kidnap me and Joe. She had repeatedly hired guards since our return from England to make certain my dad didn't take us, though Joe and I knew nothing about it. As far as we knew, the men in suits who came and went were just more of my mother's staff.

My father had reached his limit. It was one thing for my mother to move into a neighboring hotel, but it was another to take us to a different continent. He'd already lost control of his house and his finances; he wasn't about to give up control of his children. The result was a fight that made the headlines.

I remember the day vividly. My parents were arguing again, so my mom had sent me and Joey to Central Park with the nanny to play. At some point my mom left the hotel for an hour or two, and someone told my dad that Joey and I were at the park. Dad came and got us and took us back to his suite. I was wearing white kneesocks and black patent leather shoes, and I remember sitting down and taking one shoe off. About that time there was a knock on the door of my father's room. It was my mother. She came into the living room and told my father, "I just want to say goodbye to the children before I leave for England." My father told me and Joe to leave the room. We went into the next room and turned on the TV.

As Joey and I sat there watching television, it was very quiet in the other room. Then, all of a sudden, we heard my mother yell, "He hit me! He hit me!" Joe and I nearly jumped out of our skins.

I thought, "What is going on?" I'd never seen my father hit my mother. What could have happened? I was completely confused. Joey and I crept into the other room to see what was going on.

All hell had broken loose. My mom had bodyguards waiting just outside the door, and her yell was their entrance cue. The guards rushed in, grabbed my father, and picked up Joey and me. Some of the guards pinned my dad down by both arms as others carried me and Joe toward the door. I remember Dad struggling to get to us, screaming, "No! You can't! I'm calling a lawyer! You're not taking those children away from me! You're not taking them to England!" I think he was afraid that once my mother got us to another continent, he'd never get us back.

Joey and I looked at our mother. She was perfectly calm. I remember thinking, "Mama's not upset, so I guess everything's all right."

She told me, "Put your shoes on; we're leaving now," but I couldn't remember where my other shoe was in all the confusion. Finally the guard carried me to the elevator with my mom and Joey, still wearing just one shoe.

My mom seemed completely relaxed, so I wasn't that scared. I just asked her, "Where are we going?"

"We're going to England now," she replied. "Isn't this exciting?"

It was exciting. When we got in the elevator, I remembered her yelling earlier, so I asked her, "Mama, why did you say Dad hit you?"

She said, "Oh, I was only joking. He didn't really hit me."

"Oh." It never occurred to me to question her. Whatever my mother said, I accepted. As long as Mama was there, everything would be fine.

Only one thing worried me. I didn't have my other shoe. So I said to my mother, "But I can't go to London, Mama. I only have one shoe." My mother told me not to worry, that she'd buy me more shoes in London; in fact, she'd buy me all new clothes. Then we got in a cab, where Liza was waiting for us, looking like she'd just thrown on some clothes, and we went to the airport. I still remember climbing the steps up into the airplane with one shoe on.

Mama, me, Joey, Liza, the nanny, my mother's hairdresser, and all thirty-odd pieces of my mother's luggage set off for

London. I was still excited by the events of the day. When the stewardess served dinner, I tried to open the little carton of milk she gave me, but I'd never seen that kind of carton before. I lost my grip, and the carton went flying through the air. I found myself sitting in the plane seat with milk streaming down my face and clothes. My mom took one look at me and burst out laughing. My dress was soaked, but I couldn't change because I didn't have any clothes to change into. Everything I owned was back in New York.

The other thing I remember about that flight is turning to the stewardess and saying, "Do you know who my mom is?"

Liza overheard me and was furious. She turned around, fixed me with those dark eyes of hers, and said, "Don't you ever say that again."

I shut up immediately, but I didn't understand what I'd done wrong. Other kids could brag about their mothers. Why couldn't I?

Somewhere over the Atlantic I fell sound asleep. When I woke up, we were in London.

Once we got to England, we moved into the Savoy Hotel, and my mother hired a proper British nanny for us – Mrs. Elizabeth Ann Colledge. Mrs. Colledge was very sweet, young and attractive, with a little boy my age. I liked her immediately. I saw her son recently, and he gave me a picture of Mrs. Colledge and me together with a note I wrote at the time, saying, "To the nicest person in the world. Love, Lorna." Mrs. Colledge took wonderful care of us, and we were perfectly content.

Joey and I had no idea that we were actually in hiding from our father. Mama was afraid that Dad would fly over and try to find us, which of course he did. With her usual flair for the dramatic, she had us declared Wards of the High Court of Britain so that my father couldn't take us back to America. It's a wonder my mom didn't have the guards from Buckingham Palace guarding our hotel.

It didn't take my father long to track us down. He flew

to London and moved into a small, cheap flat with sloping ceilings on the top floor of a building. My mother couldn't keep him away completely, but she wouldn't let him see us often. When he missed us, he would write us letters, wonderful letters. I wish I still had some of them. My dad is a talented artist, and he would illustrate our letters with hilarious cartoons of Joe and me. Sometimes my mom would let Mrs. Colledge take us over to his flat to visit, and we'd beg him to draw more cartoons for us while we sat next to him, his tall frame hunched under the slanted roof. He always did.

Incredible as it seems, I still had no idea my parents were on the brink of divorce. With the exception of the incident at the Plaza, they'd never fought in front of us, and they'd never criticized each other to us, either. That would come later. Joe and I were still well protected from all the trauma. As long as we were with one parent or the other, we were content. We actually enjoyed our time in England. My mother made her movie and Joe and I got to be extras on the ship featured in the film. It was our movie debut.

Years later I learned that the time in England was anything but peaceful for my parents. Mama was in and out of the hospital with overdoses and related health problems the entire time we were in London, but I was never aware of it. Mrs. Colledge took care of us when my mother was gone; as far as I knew, Mama was just working. It was a heartbreaking time for my father, but the pain had yet to touch me or Joey.

My false sense of security didn't last. A few months later, my safe little world began to crumble.

As soon as Mama finished shooting her movie, we went home to the U.S. My father returned, too, separately. By then we were living from hotel to hotel, and we saw my father less frequently.

Shortly after our return, we all went to Las Vegas for my mother's appearance at the Sahara. Not long afterward my aunts, Jimmy and Suzy, joined us there. For the first time in a very long while, all three Gumm Sisters were together. I knew their names, but I barely remembered them. While they got reacquainted, Joey and I played.

My mom was worried about leaving me and Joey at the hotel all day. Apparently she was afraid that my dad would try to take us away while she wasn't watching. My mother had developed almost an obsession about losing us to him by then. Thinking we'd be safer there, she had Mrs. Colledge take us to a friend's ranch for a little while.

The ranch was in the middle of the desert, somewhere near Las Vegas. It had a main house, three guest houses, and a big fence all around it. The only way in or out was by the main gate. The whole place was a cross between a resort and a fortress. Joey and Mrs. Colledge and I stayed in one of the guest houses. The rooms were pretty rustic; I remember Mrs. Colledge making us shake out our shoes every morning before we put them on. She was afraid there might be scorpions in them. It wasn't an idle fear on her part; there were plenty of scorpions on the ranch. Mrs. Colledge trapped one with a water glass one day.

What I remember most about the place, though, is the dogs. There were two white German shepherds named Saber and Whitey. Whitey and Saber were guard dogs, and they were dangerous, really dangerous. My brother was bitten one day when he bent down to pick up their ball and throw it. Joey was only seven, and when he bent over, Saber bit him in the side. We were both terrified of the shepherds.

Apart from the dogs, the ranch was pretty nice. There was a swimming pool and plenty of room to play. No matter where we went, though, there were always those two big dogs watching. When we went swimming, they'd sit on two chaise lounges and growl every time someone walked by. They gave me the creeps.

We were staying at the ranch in November 1962, the day I turned ten. I don't remember celebrating my birthday that year, but I vividly remember my dad coming to see me the next day. That particular moment is etched in my memory. Apparently he'd asked to see me for my birthday the day before, but my mother had refused. Naturally, Dad was hurt and angry. Never one to give up easily, he collected a friend of his, a guy named Bullets Durgom (honestly, that was his name), and they came out to the ranch to take me and Joey back with them. My father hadn't been allowed to see us in weeks, so he'd decided to take matters into his own hands.

When Sid and Bullets drove up to the main gate in Bullets' convertible, Joe and I saw them coming. We were completely taken by surprise, so when we saw Dad, Joe and I got very excited. We ran to meet him before the convertible even stopped, yelling, "Dad! Dad! Dad!" and jumped into his arms the minute he got out. He scooped us up and gave us a huge hug. We were so happy to see him.

But when he started to put us in the car, all hell broke loose. Guards came running from everywhere, some of them with guns, and lunged at my dad. There was a lot of pushing and shoving; I remember someone telling my father he wasn't going to take us. Bullets was trying to calm my dad down, but when the guards grabbed me and Joey too, Dad completely lost control. Desperate to get to us, he kept screaming, "Don't touch those children! Those are my children! Don't touch my children!" It was one of the worst moments of my life.

I was absolutely terrified. Those men were hurting my dad, and I couldn't stop them. I didn't know why he was trying to take me and Joe, or why the men were hurting him, and this time there was no Mama there to turn it into an exciting game. Joey and I were sobbing uncontrollably by then in fear and confusion. Mrs. Colledge managed to pull us away and get us back inside the guest house. Joey was hysterical, so I started trying to calm him down, but all he would say over and over to Mrs. Colledge was, "Please call my mom. Please call my mom. Where's my mom?"

It was terrible. I wanted my mother desperately. I wanted her to explain what was going on and to tell us that everything was going to be all right. Because if she said it was all right, it would be true.

After a while the shouting stopped, and it grew very quiet outside. We heard a car drive away. Mrs. Colledge went to the main house to call my mother, and eventually she got a call through. When Joe and I finally got to talk to her on the phone, she told us that everything was all right, that nothing really bad had happened, and tried to calm us down. She told us Dad was really upset, and that she didn't want us to see him right then because he might try to take us away from her.

Take us away from Mama? That idea frightened us more than anything else that had happened that day. Take us where? Why? "We don't want him to take us away from you, Mama," we kept telling her. That was our biggest fear, that someone would take us away from our mother. It was also her biggest fear. Until that day, she'd never said anything like that to me or Joe.

Later that night Mrs. Colledge took us to the Sahara to be with my mother for a little while, and then we were taken back to the ranch and put to bed. I couldn't sleep. At ten years and one day old, I'd come face to face with disaster. It was also one of the biggest turning points of my life. The bubble of protection surrounding me and Joey had finally burst. I couldn't ignore the reality of what was happening to our family any longer.

The painful irony of that day is that my father wasn't taking us away from our mother. She was taking us away from him, and he was helpless to stop it. Strangers had taken his children and locked us away from him. My father was succumbing to despair and to sheer terror as the inevitability of it all sank in on him. He had no job, money or place to live. Our safe little world was crumbling around him, and my father, the strongest man in the world, couldn't do anything about it.

# Chapter Seven

# TREADING WATER

After the incident at the ranch, there was no turning back for
my parents. There were several more attempts at reconciliation,
but the situation was clearly hopeless. If it had been up to my
father, they would have kept on trying, but my mother's condition made a lasting reunion impossible. The illness that would
take her life six years later was too far advanced. The prescription drugs had taken their toll. First they take over your body,
then your mind, and eventually your whole life. The family is
one of the first casualties. My mother had been handed her
first dose of medication when she was just a kid herself. That
same medication was slowly but surely beginning to destroy
my childhood as well.

The years of sheltering and protection were over for Joey
and me. We returned to Los Angeles with our mother and lived
in a brief series of rentals, the most memorable being a creepy
little house on the beach in Malibu with an ugly wooden tiki
out front like some sort of household god. Somehow the grisly
look on his face seemed all too appropriate. Joey and I were
pulled in and out of various schools with each move (I had
attended more than seventeen schools by the time I gave up)
before we finally landed on Rockingham Drive. Nobody but
the locals had heard of the street back then, but it wasn't far
different from what it is today. Even then it was a refuge of
the elite, nestled in the hills above Sunset Boulevard only a

mile or two from the Pacific Ocean. My mother's management team made sure my father's name wasn't on the mortgage.

Most of the time, though, life was still good that first year at Rockingham. My mother had just started her TV show, and that was a wonderful period for Joe and me. Mama was thrilled to be doing the show, and we got to spend time at the studio with her after school. The network had fixed everything up beautifully for her, even painting a yellow brick road from her dressing room to the stage. There were a lot of interesting people around, too; Bob Mackie and Ray Aghayan did my mother's costumes, and Carol Burnett was taping next door. Joe and I got to watch a lot of the rehearsals, and we were always in the audience on the nights Mama taped, in the front row where the lighted ramps met. You can see our small shadows on the show tapes, just a foot or two from the stage.

The most memorable moment for Mama and us was the Christmas show in 1963, since the whole family got to participate. Eight-year-old Joey wore a little suit and tie and sang "Where Is Love?" to my mother in a sweet, small, frightened voice. He'd loved the song ever since we saw *Oliver* in London. I wore a velvet dress and a ribbon in my hair and sang "Santa Claus Is Coming To Town." Liza got to do the most numbers because she was the oldest (at seventeen she was already a veteran performer), and all four of us did a little chorus line number right out of the Gumm Sisters' old routine. I was scared to death and very, very excited. I'd have done it every week if someone had let me.

The most memorable moment of *The Judy Garland Show* for me personally, though, was the night my mother pulled me out of the audience and sang to me onstage. She sang my song "Lorna." The lyrics had been written by Johnny Mercer, and the music by Mort Lindsey (years later Johnny gave me the lyrics, which I have framed on the wall in my house). I didn't know she was going to do it, and I was so surprised. She sat down on the edge of the ramp near Joe and me, reached down her hand, and pulled me out of my seat and up onto the stage next to her. I still have the tape of me sitting there in my little velvet dress and white tights. She held my hand and sang a love song just for me, looking into my eyes the whole time. She looked beautiful sitting there that night in a long, sequined, cream-colored top with pants and diamond and pearl earrings. I gazed into her face and forgot all about the audience; it was just me and Mama and her voice, a pinpoint of light in the darkness. When she touched my face, I instinctively reached out and took hold of the arm she used to hold the microphone. When she finished the last note, she put down the microphone and reached out her arms, and I crawled into her lap while she held me close. I could dimly hear the applause from the audience as she rubbed my back and kissed me gently on the top of my head.

Sunday nights were the high point of the week during those months. There was always a party. The *Judy Garland Show* aired on Sunday evenings right opposite *Bonanza*, and every Sunday night a big group of people would come to our house to watch with Mama and Joe and me. The regular cast and crew would be there, and usually that week's guests would come, too. Mickey Rooney lived down the street from us then, and he would come and entertain us on the piano during the breaks, with his four daughters along. It was so much fun. Sometimes the cast would also come to our house to rehearse, and there were a lot of parties on the set as well.

Even the famous off-camera disagreements were often funny. The musical director loved to call my mother Miss Gumm just to infuriate her. My mom would get angry and start yelling if things didn't go well during rehearsal sometimes, and when she wouldn't stop, someone put flatulence noises on the intercom and played them back at her so everyone could hear. Mama would always start laughing. Another time, when she was rehearsing at home, George Schlatter, the producer, got so mad at her that he threatened to drown her if she didn't stop yelling. He pulled a chair up under the emergency sprinkler in our kitchen, struck a match, and threatened to set off the whole system if she didn't shut up. My mother, taken completely aback, said, "What are you, crazy?"

He said, "Stop yelling."

She did.

Another time I came home from school and found Ray Aghayan sitting in a chair with a towel wrapped around his head and blood running down his neck. He had come to our house to fit a new dress for my mother. I asked him what had happened, and he told me that he'd accidentally walked through the plate glass window in our dining room. The big bay window overlooking the patio was shattered, and glass was all over the room. I wasn't really frightened by the blood, just interested, but then the thought crossed my mind, "I wonder if that's what really happened." Years later, looking back on the incident, I thought, "Geez, how bad could that dress really have been?" Poor Ray. What a sweet man.

I had no way of knowing it at the time, but my 1963 birthday would be another crisis point in my life. On November 21 of that year, I turned eleven. The next day someone assassinated John F. Kennedy. My life was never the same again.

I was in class at Brentwood Elementary School the day it happened. One of the teachers came running into the room and said, "The President's been shot!" My first reaction was terror. This was my friends' Uncle Jack, someone I knew. I felt as if someone had been pulled out of my own living room and gunned down. How could this be? Everybody started crying, even our teacher. The nanny came and took Joe and me home, and the next thing I remember is seeing my mother. She was white as a sheet. She told us she was going over to the Lawfords to see if she could do anything to help, and then she left. A short while later the television announcer said the President was dead. I just sat there, crying, thinking about Uncle Jack, and the golf cart, and the big men in suits, and most of all, about how Caroline and John didn't have a dad now. I couldn't get over that. Someone had killed their dad.

My mother came back, and all three of us sat very close

together and watched the news on television, Joe on one side and me on the other, with our mother's arms around us. I couldn't tell if she was comforting us or clinging to us for support. Maybe a little of both. Over and over we watched the news footage from Dallas of the President being shot. Every television in the house was on; even if you went into another room, you saw it. I had never seen anyone shot before, even on television, and what made it even worse was that I knew this person.

It was a terrible time. One of the things that made it so terrible was that you could never get away from the fear and the sadness. Everywhere you went, people were talking about it. Even if you got out of your own house and went to a friend's house, her parents were talking about it, too. There was no escape. It was all-encompassing, like a shroud of sadness surrounding us twenty-four hours a day. There was silence everywhere, too, like an episode of *The Twilight Zone*. It was terrifying.

I vividly remember the day of the funeral. All the businesses closed down that day, and all over America people were home watching the funeral on television. Mama and Joey and I watched it on TV like everyone else. We sat in the den together, with Joey and me cuddled up on my mother's lap, and we were all crying. My mother explained to me why the horse's saddle had backwards-facing boots in the stirrups. I remember Walter Cronkite crying, and how I'd never seen a newscaster cry. I kept wanting to pretend that it was just a TV show, that it wasn't really happening. I kept remembering the summer at Hyannis Port, and Jackie Kennedy's gentle voice when she spoke to me. I started crying when I thought of that familiar voice. It felt as though everything that had made me feel safe in the world died that day. If something so terrible could happen to the President, how could any of us be safe?

My mother desperately wanted to fly east for the funeral, to be there for Bobby and Pat and the others. But she couldn't because she had the television show to do, and CBS wouldn't give her the time off. With incredible callousness, they told her that she didn't need to go, that in a month the nation would have forgotten about the whole thing. The only thing my mother could do to help was to say goodbye to Jack Kennedy the only way she knew how. She decided to sing "The Battle Hymn of the Republic" at the taping as a tribute to Kennedy. The network told her she couldn't because they didn't want the show to be "too political." She did it anyway. She never said a word about it ahead of time; she just did it. It was the last number on the show that night, and it was one of the most memorable things I've ever seen. Joe and I watched from the audience as she sang, and it took our breath away.

Mama didn't cry; instead, she put all of her love and sorrow into that song. Her face on the tape of that night is a mask of pain. The audience was stunned. All around us people were crying. I'd never seen anything like it. When the last note quivered into silence, the entire audience got to their feet and started cheering for what seemed like forever. What could the network do? They couldn't very well cut a performance like that. The best they could do was cut the words she whispered into the camera during dress rehearsal just before she began the first note of "Mine eyes have seen the glory . . ." – "This is for you, Jack." Six years later Joe and Liza and I sang that same song at my mother's funeral.

A few days later, Jack Ruby shot Oswald. We saw that on TV, too. It was the first time I had seen my mother smile since Jack Kennedy's murder. For me, though, the execution was almost as terrifying as the assassination. It was the second time I had watched someone gunned down on TV. It seemed as if the whole world was going mad. I wondered if anything would ever be the same again.

When I look back at *The Judy Garland Show*, I have such mixed feelings. It was a difficult time in our lives, but I had not yet given up hope back then that everything would still be okay someday, that Mama would be well and that we'd all be happy. When the show first started, she was happy, but as the season wore on and things began to fall apart, she seemed to age overnight. You can see it on the tapes. In the early shows she looks fit and healthy, in good voice. By the end she is still in good voice, but her weight has dropped alarmingly and her face has aged ten years. One of the most ironic moments for me is when she sang "As Long As He Needs Me," the show stopper my English idol Georgia Brown sang in *Oliver!* My mother's voice is full and rich, and she looks lovely as she leans up against her trademark trunk, but her eyes are as empty as glass as she sings about staying with her man. I can only imagine what my dad must have felt, watching her sing it.

I didn't want the show to end. It broke my mother's heart when they canceled it. She took it very, very personally. I still remember the last show. Joe and I were sitting in our usual place in the audience, and the last number Mama was scheduled to do was a song from *Little Me* called "Here's to Us." It wasn't going well, so my mother had to keep doing the number over and over. After a while she lost her temper. She did it in one take, then overcome by emotion, took her bows and walked offstage. I was so depressed on the way home. What would we do without Mama's show? I feared what would happen to Mama, to all of us, with nothing to fill the vacuum.

My dad stayed with us occasionally when we first moved into the Rockingham house, but he never really lived there. He was more a visitor than a resident in our lives by then. The fighting between my parents had become unbearable. As my mother's anger grew, so did the stories she told about my father. By that time she was blaming everything on my dad. One time the gardeners put rat poison around our house, and Joey's dog ate some of it and died. The next day she told Joe and me that my father had climbed the fence during the night and poisoned the dog. Joe and I just looked at each other. We knew it wasn't true. Other times she'd show us these terrible bruises on her arms and say my father had hit her. By then she was so under the influence of Ritalin that she was injuring herself on purpose, then saying that my father had done it to her. One time I watched her go to the stucco wall that ran behind the garage at Rockingham and throw herself against it repeatedly in a fit of rage. She even put her bare arm against the rough stucco and scraped it until she was bleeding. Two hours later she showed me the bloody scrapes on her body and said, "Look what your father did to me!" I'd just watched her do it to herself.

The stories she told us got increasingly fantastic. She said my father had scaled the wall, vandalized the house, beaten her up, and escaped without notice, all in the course of an hour or two. Mama had always told us stories – everyone knew my mother told real whoppers – but it had never been this bad before. Joe and I kept our mouths shut and tried to calm her down. Contradicting her would have been pointless. All we wanted was a little peace.

I didn't mind when my parents finally divorced. I just wanted all the fighting to be over. I still clung to the hope that when the divorce became final, everything would calm down again. As long as Mama was happy and we could see Dad on the weekends, Joey and I were content. We were used to the separations by then, so it wasn't traumatic for us not to see our father every day.

What we didn't know about were the custody disputes that come with divorce. Both Joe and I had already decided to live with our mother; there was never any question about that. Dad would miss us, but he would be okay either way. My mother, on the other hand, couldn't get along without us. Besides, most of our emotional security was tied up in Mama.

Over the years people have seen our decision as an indictment of our father, which is absolutely untrue. Mama was sick by then and she would get sicker, with profound consequences for us all. Even at her sickest, though, the one thing Joey and I never questioned was whether our mother loved us. We knew she did. She loved just looking at us, and she never went to bed on tour without our pictures lined up on the bed table next to her, where she could look at them as she fell asleep.

She was the most affectionate of mothers. There are hundreds of candid photos of our mother with us at home, at the airport, backstage during breaks – and she is almost always touching us in those pictures. She was always happiest when one of us was sitting on her lap or cradled in her arms; she loved to cuddle up on the couch with us in the evenings when we watched TV. When we went to bed, she would sit next to us and gently run her fingertips up and down our arms and over our faces until we fell asleep. She held our hands everywhere we went until we got too old. One of my most vivid memories is the way she drummed her fingers lightly on my palm when she held my hand. I asked her once why she did that, and she told me she was tapping out the music in her head. Mama was our whole world. My father understood that. She was his whole world, too.

Even the custody fights wouldn't have been that bad for us if the professionals hadn't gotten involved. Unfortunately, my mother's greatest fear by then was that she would lose me and Joey, either because my father would take us or because we would choose to live with him. She was terrified that we'd choose Dad and not her. She convinced herself that we were afraid of our father and might give in to him out of fear. When she took us to the court-appointed psychiatrist, her greatest fear was that we'd tell him we wanted to live with our father. If she had known what was happening in that office, my dad would have been the least of her fears.

I can't imagine how such a sadistic therapist stayed in practice, much less qualified to testify in custody cases. His office was in Culver City, near the old MGM lot. During my first session he asked me what I was most afraid of. I told him, "Needles." I'd been phobic about hypodermic needles ever since my appendectomy in England. The next time I went to see him, he asked me to take my clothes off and lie down on the table in his office. It was covered with a white sheet, with a small pillow at one end. I took off everything but my little knickers and lay down on my back. Next he told me that he gotten permission from my pediatrician to do something. Then he picked up a kleenex box and, holding it in front of me, took out a hypodermic needle. He held the needle an inch or two from my face. I panicked and started saying, "No, no, no," as he slowly moved the needle down toward my bare chest.

In an odd, rhythmic voice, he asked me, "How frightened are you of your dad?"

"What do you mean?" I answered, terrified.

"How frightened are you of your dad, Lorna?"

"I'm . . . I'm not . . . I don't know."

"You're frightened, very frightened, aren't you, Lorna?" he chanted hypnotically, moving the needle a hair's breadth above my naked body.

By then I was crying. "Yes, yes," I sobbed.

"Good girl. Good, Lorna." The needle moved away. He made a note on his notepad. Then he picked up the needle again.

Week after week, these "sessions" went on. Each time I went there, the doctor made me take my clothes off and lie on my back while he moved the needle near my body. To this day, I can remember how it felt lying on that white sheet, naked and completely vulnerable. It was frightening beyond description. He never actually put a needle into me; he didn't have to. That's the nature of psychological torture. The fear is more than enough. After a while I knew what he wanted to hear and would have said anything to please him.

"Do you want to be with your dad?"

"No."

"Do you love your dad?"

"No."

I didn't tell my parents. I didn't tell anyone. I was too afraid. Joey never said anything, either, so I assumed he was all right.

These "therapy sessions" went on for a couple of months, but it seemed like a lifetime. Finally, as Joe and I were climbing the stairs to the doctor's office one afternoon, I accidentally found a way to bring it to an end. The outdoor staircase leading up to the doctor's door was very steep. Joey was in front of me, and as we climbed, Joe shouted, "Watch this!" and slid down the banister to the ground. It looked like fun, so of course I had to do it, too. The only problem was that I shoved my arm underneath the banister as I slid and forgot to pull it out when I hit the bottom rung. My arm got caught at the bottom and took the full force of my descent. There was a loud crack as I landed, and a shattering pain shot through my forearm. The nanny was right behind me, and she took me upstairs to the doctor's office. He put some ice on my arm and told the nanny, "I think she's broken it. We'd better cancel this session so you can take her to the emergency room."

I had never been in so much pain in my life, yet I had rarely been so happy. All I could think was, "I don't have to stay with that doctor!" I would gladly have broken the other arm and both legs if it meant not seeing him again.

The nanny drove me home, where my mother took one look at me, said, "Oh, my God!" and rushed me to the emergency room. When they showed me the x-rays of my arm, I couldn't believe what it looked like. I'd shattered my whole forearm. They called it a green stick fracture because if you take green wood and bend it hard enough, it splinters. That's exactly what had happened to my bone. It had splintered lengthwise. To this day I get a shock sometimes when I touch that arm. The doctor couldn't set it because of the way it was shattered, so he wrapped my arm in gauze and put a cast on it.

That evening I sat out by the pool with my brother. We had a big basket chair hanging from ropes near the pool that you could swing in. With my newly broken arm carefully propped on the edge of the chair, I was gently twirling the chair around and around, then letting it spin back. Joey had wedged into the chair next to me. At eight years old, his tiny frame didn't take up much room. As we sat quietly together in the dusk, Joe touched my good hand.

"Lorna?"

"Yes?"

There was a small silence. "Lorna, I don't want to go to see the doctor anymore. Please don't let them make me."

I glanced down at his sober little face and then looked at the cast on my arm. "Don't worry, Joey. I've taken care of it. You don't have to go there anymore." Joe sighed and leaned against me in quiet contentment, safe in the knowledge that his big sister would take care of him. It was thirty years before I found out how terrifying Joe's trips to the doctor really were. If either of my parents had known what that doctor did to Joe, they would have killed the man. I would have helped them.

Just as with my appendicitis attack, Mama took wonderful care of my arm. When it was time for me to go back to school, my mom decorated my cast with glitter and feathers and glue, just as she'd decorated my eye patches years before. She got out one of her glamorous scarves for a sling, and I thought I looked really cool. Since I couldn't write with my broken arm, I didn't even have to do my homework when I returned to school. All my classmates signed my cast, and I was a celebrity. Each time the doctors changed my cast, Mama decorated the new one. Finally, just like at Lady Eden, the teacher sent a note home to my mother, asking her not to decorate my cast anymore because everyone in my class now wanted a broken arm. Apparently this presented a safety hazard.

The only down side was that nobody had told me what weeks in a cast does to your muscles, so when the doctor removed the cast permanently and I saw my shriveled forearm, I was horrified. My arm was skinny enough to begin with, but now it looked downright withered. It didn't help that my mom seemed equally concerned. She told me how Peter Lawford (her old friend and *Easter Parade* costar) had injured his arm when he was a kid and how, as a result, his arm had never developed properly. I was convinced that I was going to grow up with a freak arm. Fortunately, my arm was back to normal in a few weeks.

Eventually the courts awarded my mother full custody of me and Joe, with my father given visitation rights on the weekends and every other Wednesday. After the visitation issues were resolved, things calmed down between my parents. The doctor testified that living with our mother would be in Joey's and my "best interest" at the hearings. Mama never found out what he'd done to Joe and me. Another person who testified on my mother's behalf was our nanny. Her name was Mrs. Chapman.

I never found out where my mother found Mrs. Chapman. She just showed up at our house one day. She was a short, squat Southern lady with graying hair, a face that would freeze water, and two grown daughters who lived nearby. I don't think she was a career nanny; she never wore a uniform like our other nannies, and she certainly never behaved like any of them. A workman put up a partition in the bedroom Joey and I shared, and Mrs. Chapman moved in with us. She stayed with us all day, and at night she slept just a few feet away. There was no escaping her. It was like sleeping in a cave, just a few feet away from a slumbering bear.

My mom was touring again, and Mrs. Chapman took care of me and Joey in her absence. I use the phrase "took care of" very loosely. As soon as my mother left town, Mrs. Chapman would bring over her three-year-old granddaughter and let the little monster run wild. The child's name was Dawn, and she had every ounce of her grandmother's charm. Dawn was a brat, running all over the house and climbing on everything. She'd even get into my mother's belongings. If I ever said so much as "Don't do that" to Dawn, Mrs. Chapman would punish me. She never punished Dawn, even when Dawn broke things.

Mrs. Chapman seemed to hate me almost as much as I hated her. I never understood why. Maybe it was because I'd speak up if I thought something was wrong, and Joey wouldn't. I was older, and I thought it was my job to watch out for things. When somebody got hit, it was usually me.

Mrs. Chapman knew how to make me wish I'd kept my mouth shut. She usually hit me with a wooden ruler, sometimes raising big welts. She would always hit me on the back of my legs, the tender skin right below my bum. That way the hem of my dress covered the marks, and they didn't show. She hit me often. My mother had spanked me with her bare hands occasionally when I deserved it, but never anything close to this.

I didn't tell either of my parents. Every time Mrs. Chapman hit me, she threatened me with something worse if I told anyone. Sometimes she'd say, "Don't ever tell your mother or I'll leave, and then you'll be all alone with her, and you know what will happen." I was terrified of being left alone in the house, without anyone else to take care of Mama. I knew by then that something was very wrong with my mother, though I didn't yet understand the nature of her illness. I was scared something bad might happen to Mama without another grown-up around. I never even told my father. Mrs. Chapman stayed, and the punishment went on.

Christmas that year was an appropriate ending to a turbulent year: the infamous Garland children kidnapping. The headlines read "Luft Steals Judy's Kids," but it wasn't much of a kidnapping. It was more like a dysfunctional family Christmas.

Joe and I were supposed to fly to New York that Christmas to spend the holidays with my mom (who had just returned from London) and Liza, but my dad was really upset about not getting to spend Christmas with us. He was also unhappy about Joe and me being left at the house with one of the staff my mother had hired, a real piece of work. He moved into the pool house for a while when we first lived on Rockingham. Huge, tall and heavy, he was also, as we found out, a flasher. Joe and I discovered this the hard way one day when this guy tapped on the window as we walked by the pool house. When we turned to look, there he was, fresh from the shower and naked. We looked away and ran into the house, giggling uncomfortably. A few days later he tried it again when some of our friends came over for the evening. Not knowing what else to do, we told my dad what was going on, and he had a fit. He couldn't fire the guy, but he wasn't about to leave us alone with a pervert while Mama was in New York, so he did the next best thing. He got us out of there.

Shortly before Christmas Day, Dad showed up at our house and told me and Joey we were going to Disneyland with him. It sounded like a great idea to us. Mrs. Chapman reminded him that we had to be home in time to fly to New York; Dad said okay, and a few days later put us in the car, and drove down to Anaheim. On the way there he stopped to make a phone call. When he came back to the car, he seemed very upset. We asked him what was the matter, and he said he'd called a friend who lived nearby because we were going to spend Christmas there. But when he'd called his friend's house just then, his friend's wife had told him that the friend had had a sudden heart attack and died an hour or two earlier.

At first I said, "Oh, how awful." Then I thought, "Wait a minute. Aren't we supposed to go to New York to meet Mama for Christmas? Something's not right here."

So much for Disneyland. We drove over to the friend's house and sat around the living room with his kids for what seemed like forever. It was a very strange few hours. Their father had just died, yet everyone was trying to act like nothing was wrong. I kept thinking, "I don't want to be here. I want to go to New York and be with my mom." I asked my dad when we were going home.

We left then and drove to a house at the top of Tower Road, near Sunset, where my dad dropped us off with some friends and left again. By that time I knew something was fishy. Dad was supposed to be taking us home so we could catch our plane. Joe and I went out in the front yard to play, and when we looked down the street, I realized that I knew where we were. Mrs. Chapman's daughter lived just a block or so away. I took Joe, and we walked down to her house and knocked on the door. I was planning to ask her to call my mom and have someone pick us up and take us to the airport, so we could catch our flight. The door opened; I started to say, "Hi, remember me? I'm Lorna," when the woman gasped and said, "Oh, my God! They're looking all over for you!"

She grabbed me and Joey and pulled us into the house, asking us where we'd been. We told her. Then we went back to Dad's friend's house. A few minutes later my dad pulled into the driveway. Just as he did so, we heard the loud wailing of sirens, and police cars came racing into view and surrounded the house. The next thing we knew, someone was taking Joey and me to a car, and then to the airport to put us on a plane to New York. We later found out that all the television stations were broadcasting the news that Joe and I had been kidnapped. Kidnapped? The police were kind and reassuring, but we hadn't been scared in the first place. We had never been in any danger. We'd just had a boring time with our dad. I was actually quite pleased with myself for the way I'd handled the whole thing. Now Mama wouldn't worry, and we could celebrate New Year in New York with Mama and Liza like we'd planned.

"Have Yourself a Merry Little Christmas." Yep, just another Christmas special at the Garland house.


By this time my mother had started dating the man she would marry next, Mark Herron. He was a nice man, always very kind to Joe and me. In some ways it was a relief when he came into her life. Everybody wonders if Joe and I resented Mark because of my father, but we really didn't. The thing we wanted most at that point was for Mama to be okay, and if Mark made her happy, then he was all right with us. Mark gave us a respite from all the chaos, and for a while life settled into something of a routine.

Meanwhile, my dad had found a girlfriend of his own. He never called her that, of course. Dad was still waiting for

Mama to come back to him, so he didn't want me and Joe to know he was dating. He certainly didn't want my mother to know. He always introduced the woman with him as his "friend, Bridget." We liked her; she was lively and fun, and on the weekends Dad and Bridget and Joe and I would go out and do all the things my mother couldn't do with us in public. We'd go horseback riding or to Pacific Ocean Park, and it was wonderful because we were a normal family; without Mama along, no one paid any attention to us.

There was just one catch. "Bridget" wasn't really Bridget. As a matter of fact, the Bridget I knew didn't exist. In our continuing family farce, my father had decided to hide Bridget's real identity from Joe and me because he didn't want to upset my mother. I might never have found out who she really was if I hadn't turned on the TV one boring afternoon. There was a game show on, and the actress on the show was a woman named Mariana Hill – except that it wasn't Mariana Hill. It was Bridget. I was dumbfounded. How could this be possible? Did Bridget have a twin sister? Why hadn't anyone ever mentioned her? Maybe it wasn't Bridget. I looked closer. No, it was definitely her. I couldn't figure it out, and I didn't dare ask.

A few weeks later I went to see *Blue Hawaii*, starring Elvis Presley, and there was this woman again! Sure enough, the credits listed her as Mariana Hill. It just wasn't possible. Bridget wasn't an actress; she'd told me so herself. She was just a regular person, a secretary or something. Now I was really confused. Who was this person with my father? Did Bridget have a double – you know, one of those exact duplicates they always tell children everybody has? I didn't say a word to anyone, not even Joey. I didn't want to upset him.

At the time, I never did figure out what was going on. I was a teenager before I finally asked my dad about Bridget. One day, years later, I said to him, "Dad, who's Mariana Hill?"

I thought he was going to have a heart attack.

"Who? Why?" Eventually he calmed down and explained

to me what had happened. He told me that he'd decided not to tell us who Bridget really was because he didn't want my mother to know about her. My mom might have known who Mariana Hill was, but "Bridget" was just some nobody, some friend that Mama never saw. He explained that he hadn't told me before because at eleven I had a big mouth, and I might have said something to my mother. That, he said, was too dangerous. There was no telling what my mom would have done to get back at him. The fact that they were divorced and that Mama was seeing Mark Herron had nothing to do with it as far as Mama was concerned.

Dad's fears had been justified. I didn't hear the story at the time, but a couple of years later my dad brought Bridget to a large party that my mother attended. Every time my father tried to dance with Bridget, my mother cut in, and when he finally sat down and refused to dance at all, my mom had the hotel switchboard page him every five minutes so he couldn't talk to Bridget. If you'd pointed out to my mother that she'd already been through another husband, a couple of fiancés, and was about to marry again by that time, she would have said, "What's your point?" The fact that she'd divorced my father didn't mean he wasn't still hers. Unfortunately for my dad, she was right.

A few months later my mom asked Joe and me if she should marry Mark. Of course, we said that was fine with us. We couldn't very well say no. By then Joe and I would have done nearly anything to keep our mother happy. Mama also asked me if I wanted to change my name to Lorna Herron when she married Mark. I didn't know what to say, so I asked her, "Do you want me to?" She told me to think about it. Fortunately for me, she never mentioned it again.

Our only real disagreement was when she tried to get us to call Mark "Dad" after they were married. We told her, "But we already have a dad."

She exploded, shouting, "No, you don't!" During that period of our lives, our dad existed only if our mother wanted him to. Eventually we ended up calling Mark either "Mark" or "Marko." Mark was easy to be around, and for a while everything was relatively peaceful. Inevitably, it didn't last.

In the spring of 1965 Mama decided we all needed some family vacation time in Hawaii to relax. We would go together: Mama, Mark, Joey, and me. Those two weeks in paradise turned out to be the end of my childhood.

## Chapter Eight

# BLUE HAWAII

Like most things with my mother, it started out fine. Mama and Mark packed up me and Joey and a few dozen of my mother's outfits, and we all took off for Waikiki.

At first we had a grand time. We rented a house beneath Diamond Head, right on the beach, next door to Steve McQueen and his wife. It was like a scene from Elvis's *Blue Hawaii*. My mother hired a female personal assistant for the trip to take care of her various daily needs, so Joe and I were free to do whatever we wanted. I got to take surfing lessons with an instructor at the Royal Hawaiian Hotel down the beach from us, which was pretty exciting for a twelve-year-old. Every morning I'd walk down the beach to the bright pink hotel and go surfing with my instructor. In the evenings I'd fall asleep with the tropical breeze blowing gently through the window.

One night a few days after our arrival, I woke up to the sound of angry shouting. Joe and I shared a bedroom next to my mother and Mark, and since the bungalow wasn't very big, I could hear the voices clearly. The noise seemed to be coming from the living room. I heard screaming and cursing, and the sound of things being thrown. When I got out of bed to listen, I heard my mother screaming for help. I was so frightened, I didn't know what to do. I crept to the door in my bare feet and peered into the living room to see what was going on.

I'll never forget the scene before me. There stood my

mother and Mark. My mother was wearing her nightclothes. She was deathly white, and one of her eyes was blackened and swollen like an egg. Mark was completely naked. He was very drunk, and my mother was far from sober. Both of them were covered with blood. They were screaming at each other; my mother was shaking with anger. Some of the furniture had been knocked over, and there was blood spattered around the room. I held onto the doorjamb, staring at them in shock. I stood there frozen, unable to move. I don't know what frightened me more, the blood or the sight of a grown man standing naked and aroused in the dim light of the room. Mark's blood was streaming down his bare white skin. My mother was twitching from anger and whatever she'd taken.

One of them threw something at the other. There was a loud crash; I flinched and pulled back. A moment later I felt Joey come padding up behind me and tug on my nightgown.

"Lorna? What's wrong?"

Instinctively, I moved to block the scene from his vision with my body, yelling at him to get back to bed. I heard him scurry back under the covers. He was only nine years old. I didn't want him to see what I was seeing.

Mark must have heard me. Turning to look, he pulled himself together, rushed into the bedroom, grabbed some clothes, and ran out into the night.

Meanwhile, the assistant my mother had hired came into the living room. She forced my mom into a chair; my mother was shaking violently, and the woman had to hold her down. The lady told me to get some ice for my mother's eye, which was bloody and swollen. She kept trying to make my mom sit still, holding the ice against her face and talking to her. After a while she got Mama to take some pills, and the shaking began to lessen. My mother had no idea I was in the room. She was still conscious; her good eye was wide open, but mentally she was absent.

As soon as Mama calmed down, the woman turned to me and said, "We can't let anyone see the room like this. You've got to clean it up while I take care of your mother. Get some soap and water and start wiping up the blood."

I looked around the room. There was blood everywhere – on the floor, the furniture, everything. The half-darkened room had an overwhelming smell of cigarettes and liquor and blood, all mixed together. I'll never forget that smell.

I started cleaning. There was no bucket or mop, so I went into the bathroom, soaked some towels and washcloths, and began mopping up the blood. I wiped it off the coffee table, and off the floor. I wiped it off the chairs. I went back into the bathroom over and over, to rinse the cloths and wash the bloody water down the drain. And all the time there was that smell filling my mouth and lungs. When the floor and the furniture at last were clean, I started scrubbing the throw rug. It was one of those woven cotton rugs, with a deep bloodstain I couldn't get out. I got down on my hands and knees and scrubbed it over and over with soap and water, going back and forth to the bathroom, but I couldn't get the blood out. Even in the dim light, I could still see dark red color in the carpet fibers. Like a small Lady Macbeth, I desperately scrubbed away at the final reminder of what had happened that night.

I kept trying not to look at my mother, propped listless in the chair nearby. I was terrified she was dying; she looked so white, and her eye was unnaturally wide open. After what seemed like forever, the woman who was taking care of my mother said, "I'll clean up the rest of it. You go to bed." My mother was calmer by then. Still conscious, but calmer.

I climbed back to my feet in my damp nightgown and gathered up the last of the cloths. I went back in the bathroom to rinse out the cloths one last time. The bloody water ran down the drain in the graying light. I noticed a bottle of Pepto-Bismol sitting on the sink, a sickly pink in the yellow bathroom light. I felt so ill. I reached for the Pepto-Bismol, took a sip or two out of the bottle, and sat down on the damp bathroom linoleum to rest. Almost immediately, I began to vomit. I couldn't purge myself of the images that filled my mind, or rid my nose of the smell of blood. The linoleum hurt my knees as I clung wearily to the toilet bowl. Finally the vomiting stopped. I rested my head on the edge of the toilet for a few moments, and then I pulled myself to my feet.

Still in my bare feet, I crept back down the hall to the bedroom. Joey was still half-awake, huddled in the corner of the bed. As I crawled in next to him, he asked me if everything was all right. I told him to go back to sleep, that everything was okay now. I lay down next to him, my body aching and my feet cold. He closed his eyes and was soon breathing regularly.

Only then did I begin to shake. My body trembled so hard that the bed shook, and I was afraid I'd wake my brother. I tried to control the trembling, telling myself over and over, "You mustn't wake Joey. You mustn't wake Joey." As I lay there, I could feel the ocean breeze blowing gently over our bed. Sometime in the gray hours of morning, I drifted off to sleep.

When I woke up, it was light, and I was a lifetime older.

Joe and I got out of there early the next morning. My mother's traveling companion had finished straightening up the living room and put my mother to bed. It was quiet in the bungalow. We walked down the sand to the Royal Hawaiian and ordered breakfast, but I couldn't eat. Joey kept saying, "What do you think is going to happen?" and I kept saying, "I don't know."

"Do you think we're going to go home to L.A.?"

"I don't know."

"What do you think happened to Mark? Do you think he left? Do you think he's okay?"

I didn't know. I didn't have anyone to ask. My father was thousands of miles away in Los Angeles. We were just children, and no one told us anything. After a while, we got up and walked back down the beach to the bungalow. I was afraid of what we might see when we got there.

It was at that moment that the gothic family tragedy I'd

just witnessed turned into a farce. A black farce, but a farce nonetheless, with my mother writing the script.

I'll never forget the scene as we walked the last few yards to the beach house. It was a beautiful summer morning, straight out of a movie, with white sand and sparkling blue waters off Diamond Head. Our cottage lay directly in front of us. In front of the cottage sat my mother. But instead of the bruised and bloodied woman I'd seen just a few hours before, there sat Miss Garland herself, sunning her legs in a beach chair (which was amazing in itself, since my mother never went in the sun if she could help it). Mama had on a huge hat and movie star glasses, and she was looking out over the ocean. Behind her, through the open door of our beach house, smoke was billowing into the air. When she noticed our approach, my mother turned to us and said casually, "Don't go inside. The house is on fire."

"What?" I said blankly.

"The house is on fire," Miss Garland repeated calmly. Then she explained, "I'm burning Mark's clothes," as if that was the most natural thing in the world. Joey and I looked at each other in disbelief. There she sat, lucid, dressed, and wearing her hat. Not knowing what else to do, we sat down on the sand next to her.

Then right on cue, just when it seemed things couldn't get any more bizarre, they did. As I mentioned, Steve McQueen had rented the cottage next door, so naturally he saw the smoke. The next thing we knew, Steve McQueen came hurtling over the wall (much as he would do later in *The Towering Inferno*), running toward us shouting, "Get some wet towels!" He was all ready to charge inside and start putting out the fire himself.

But my mother did not want him to put the fire out. On the contrary, she wanted to make sure all Mark's things burned. So she languidly replied, "Don't be a hero, Steve. This isn't the movies. Just sit down and wait for the fire department like everyone else."

I don't know what in the world Steve must have thought. He looked at me and Joe, and we just shrugged. He didn't know what to do next, so he asked us if everyone was out of the house and if we were all right. Finally he sat down on the sand next to me and Joey and waited for the fire department with us. He was very sweet. It was nice to have the company.

Eventually the fire truck did come and put out the fire. Our rooms were okay, but the closets were damaged and the clothes ruined. Ironically, it turned out that there was a shaft running between Mark's closet and my mom's, so the smoke was sucked through to her side and had ruined all her clothes. She was furious when she found out her plan had backfired. That was the end of her calm demeanor. When the firemen finally emerged with the news that the fire was extinguished, she told them that it had been started by "something electrical," which was patently ridiculous since the clothes had obviously burned first. The firemen, though, didn't ask a single question. Instead, they all lined up to get Mama's autograph. Somehow, it seemed appropriate. A perfectly ridiculous ending to a perfectly ridiculous day.

By that time I was too tired to worry much about anything. My only concern was Mark and what would happen if, and when, he came back. I needn't have worried. He and Mama made up as quickly as they'd parted. That night Joey and I found ourselves on a plane back to L.A. while my mother and Mark spent a few days alone. I came home careworn but otherwise all right. I had survived my first major crisis, but I had only begun learning the same hard lessons my father was still struggling to master.

Until that week in Hawaii I'd never seen one of my mother's crises first-hand. Up until then I had been pretty well protected. I'd known for a long time that my father hadn't let my mother sleep in a room with a lock on the door, but I'd really never thought about why. It wasn't until years later that I learned that my dad had originally removed the locks from her rooms when I was only a few weeks old. In the grip of her post-partum depression following my birth, my mom had made a suicide attempt, and my father had broken down the door to get to her, injuring his shoulder in the process. After that, there were no more locks. My father knew that it wasn't her first attempt to harm herself.

It wasn't her last attempt, either. She'd overdosed with barbiturates after Joey's birth, again in the grip of a deep post-partum depression. Two years later she'd slit her wrists in a Washington hotel with me and Joey asleep in the next room, oblivious to the whole episode. She'd also tried to throw herself out a hotel window; poor Vern Alves had to drag her back in and hold her down until she quit thrashing. Later she'd been hospitalized with an intentional drug overdose. By the time she died she'd had her stomach pumped so many times, it's a wonder she had one left.

Those of us who were close to her don't believe that Mama ever had any real intention of killing herself. When you really want die, you don't call someone first and say, "You'd better get right over here; I'm going to commit suicide now," and then take a fistful of sleeping pills, which is what she usually did. If you really want to die, you get a gun and blow your head off. Even when she used a razor, she never cut herself deeply enough to bleed to death. My mother used her suicide attempts as a way to release anxiety and get attention. Some of the attempts were drug reactions that she didn't even remember later on.

There was, however, a family history of suicide. At least one of my great-aunts killed herself. I also didn't know until later that the oldest of the Gumm Sisters, Susie, killed herself with an overdose of barbiturates that first year we were on Rockingham. She had tried to kill herself the year we saw her in Vegas too, and almost succeeded, but my mother only told me at the time that "Aunt Susie is very, very sick." Aunt Susie's second attempt succeeded, but again I wasn't told the truth. I was only told that my aunt Susie had died. The official story was that she'd had cancer. Even my grandma Ethel had tried to kill herself, when my mother had excluded her from her life shortly before I was born, and she nearly succeeded. But if my mother's suicide attempts weren't genuine, the moods that produced them were. When my mother was low, she was frighteningly low. She went down deep, to the very depths.

No one, least of all my mother, knew when the descents would begin. It wasn't as if she decided to plunge into a severe depression. They hit her hard, usually as the result of a drug interaction, and once they started, they spun quickly out of control. When my father was in the house, her mood swings were fairly well controlled because he monitored her medication, saw that she got enough rest, and tried to protect her from pressure. Dad consulted regularly with Mama's doctors about the proper dosage levels for her medicine – which her body now required to function – and tried to see that Mama followed their instructions. He locked up the medicine as soon as each prescription was filled and counted out the pills himself for each dose. If he suspected she'd found a way to increase the dosage, he tried to reduce their potency. With Benzedrine and other medicines that came in capsules, he would carefully cut them open, pour out half the powder, replace it with sugar, and seal the capsules again. No matter what he did, though, my mother always managed to get her hands on more medicine than was good for her. Her address book was filled with page after page of doctors, and she knew how to manipulate many of them into giving her what she wanted. Anyone that drug dependent, especially someone as convincing as my mother, can find ways to get more medicine.

When she did fall apart, Dad saw that someone took care of Joey and me while he took care of her. As children on Mapleton Drive, we never saw our mother sick or seriously upset. My father made certain of that. Once my parents had divorced, though, there was no one to protect either my mother or us. Mark Herron tried for a while, but he was in way over his head. He couldn't begin to compete with an old pro like my mother.

Until that spring in Honolulu, I had seen only one of my mother's "sick spells." I was really little at the time. We were staying at a hotel, and my mother came into the room in her nightgown. She had just woken up after sleeping many hours. She seemed disoriented. She walked around the living room in a circle a time or two, looked up at the ceiling, and then fell over and passed out cold on the floor. The minute it happened, the nanny had grabbed hold of Joey and me and guided us into the other room, saying, "Your mom's fine. She's just real tired, but she'll be okay." When we saw her a little later, she was okay. What I didn't understand at the time was that I had just witnessed a form of withdrawal. My mother had slept so long that she was several hours overdue for her usual dose of medication. The result was a seizure. Once the medicine got into her bloodstream again, she recovered. Years later I was to see this reaction several times, and sometimes it became my responsibility to nurse her through it. At twelve years old, I would become my mother's keeper.

When *The Judy Garland Show* was cancelled and she went back on the road, her medication intake skyrocketed and her mood swings rapidly worsened. The most frightening symptom for Joe and me was the outbursts of rage that would suddenly grip her. In the months following her marriage to Mark, these outbursts worsened dramatically. Complicating my mother's unhappiness about her career and financial situation was Mark's sexual orientation. I didn't understand the implications at the time, but guys came to the house regularly to see him, and Mark and my mother had many fights about it. Jealousy and suspicion of other men began eating my mother up. The odd thing about their relationship is that Mark really cared about her. But he couldn't change his orientation, and the result was a disaster. The fights between them grew worse and worse.

My mom was in bad shape by then. With the TV show canceled, she hadn't been able to pay off her debts. She and my father owed a fortune from the Mapleton Drive days, and the IRS was after both of my parents for back taxes. Dad had scaled down his lifestyle dramatically, but my mother resisted. In her movie star world, where someone else had always taken care of her, reality was simply unacceptable, unintelligible. How could this be happening to her? After she'd worked so hard, and made so much money?

She was about to get another profound financial shock. It was while we were living on Rockingham that she found out one of her managers, David Begelman, had been embezzling her money. My brother was home with Mama and his best friend the day she found out. Joe was outside by the pool when the chaos started. He could hear my mother screaming and yelling, and a short while later he heard the crashing of furniture and of objects being thrown. Joe and his friend took refuge in the pool house while the ranting and raving went on. About dusk Joe heard a loud splash. My mother had jumped in the pool.

Joe looked at his friend and said, "Good. Maybe this will cool her off."

But when Joe crept out to look a few minutes later, he was just in time to see a trail of wet footprints and my mother's form disappearing into the house. A moment or two later the crashing and screaming started all over again.

Joe's friend looked at him and said, "Gee, your mom's really mad. Do you want to sleep at my house?"

Joe said no, he'd sleep in the pool house until Mama calmed down, and his friend went home.

Things were very bad with Mark by then, too. She wasn't working much, either, and my mother was always miserable when she couldn't perform for long periods of time; apart from the money, she desperately needed the creative outlet. She felt truly alive only in front of an audience. It was a very, very low period in her life. By then she had been on prescription medication for more than twenty-five years, much of the time at toxic doses. Her nervous system had begun to deteriorate under the strain. Sometimes she would simply lose control, and it always seemed to be in the middle of the night.

It was about that time that the nightly raids started. They always seemed to happen in the small hours of the morning. Mama would come into the room where Joe and I were sleeping, with Mrs. Chapman on the other side of the partition, and wake us up, saying that she couldn't see. She would be hysterical and temporarily blind, hallucinating from the medication. I would get up to calm her down and then go and take care of her in the next room so Joey wouldn't be frightened. Other times there would be fights during the night between her and Mark. I would lie in bed listening to the yelling and screaming, pull the covers over my head, and think, "Please don't come closer; please don't come closer. Please don't come in the kitchen." And I would remember Hawaii and think, "Please don't let that happen again." I'd curl up and put the pillow over my ears and tell myself repeatedly, "It will stop. It will stop." For years afterward I slept with the covers over my head that way. Usually, though, the outbursts didn't stop.

When the fights got really bad, I'd go to Mama's nurse for help. Snowda-Wu, or Snowy as we called her, had come back with my mom and Mark from Hong Kong after my mother's concert tour in the Far East the year before. Mama had the bad luck to arrive in Hong Kong the day before the worst typhoon in the colony's history. Terrified, she'd taken too many sedatives; Mark found her unconscious on the floor in the middle of the night, barely breathing. Panic-stricken, Mark managed to get her to a hospital in spite of the storm, where they pumped her stomach – unsuccessfully – and put her into an oxygen tent. The doctors had no hope she would recover and told Mark so. One nurse actually pronounced my mother dead the next morning, and the news was leaked to the press. Poor Mark tried to stop the story and continued to insist that Mama was not dead, that doctors should continue trying to revive her. Thankfully, he was right. Mama recovered, but not without serious damage to her heart, liver, and throat.

Doctors told her she would never sing again. Instead of frightening her, the prediction infuriated her. A few days later she proved them wrong by serenading guests at a Hong Kong night club. My mother had more endurance than anyone I've ever known.

Mark had hired a nurse to take care of Mama when she came home from the hospital in Hong Kong. The nurse was Snowy, and my mother liked her so much that she hired her and brought her back to the U.S. to live with us at Rockingham. Snowy moved into the pool house as my mother's live-in nurse. I was never completely clear about whose orders Snowy was working under; I was told it was "one of Mama's doctors." I don't know what Snowy was told, either. I only knew that she was the one who gave my mother shots when Mama felt bad or got upset, and that the shots seemed to make Mama feel better. The injections were most likely Thorazine or paraldehyde, powerful anti-psychotic and anti-convulsants that were prescribed for alcoholic seizures during the 1960s. I didn't understand yet that the shots were feeding my mother's addiction, and I don't think Snowy knew it, either. In those days the process of addiction wasn't nearly so well understood as it is now.

Mark was rarely around by that time, so when things got out of hand in the house, it was my job either to calm Mama myself or to go get Snowy. Mrs. Chapman pointedly ignored every emergency, and I didn't want Joey to have to deal with our mother's crises. He was still so young. He would wake up every time our mother had one of her night spells, but I'd always go over to him and say, "Joe, stay there and pretend you're asleep."

And he'd say, "What are you going to do?"

I'd tell him not to worry, that "Everything will be all right," and then I'd go for Snowy. I'd race around the pool to the pool house in the middle of the night to wake her up. Snowy would grab her medical supplies and come running in to wherever Mama was. She would gently but firmly restrain

Mama and begin talking to her while she prepared the injection. Then she'd look up at me as if to say, "It's okay; I'll take over now," and I'd think, "Thank God." After a while my mother would calm down, and I would go back to bed, relieved that Mama would be all right now. She wouldn't hurt herself. I was never afraid for myself in those moments; I was always afraid for her. Really afraid.

In the long run, of course, the injections didn't make things better; they made things worse. As my mother's chemical intake escalated and her body deteriorated, her outbursts became increasingly frightening. I didn't always see them, but I sure heard them. There would be screaming and the sounds of things crashing in nearby rooms, and the next day there would be lots of broken lamps and missing breakables. The furniture took a terrible beating. When my mother was in a rage, she would throw herself against things – walls, furniture, anything – until she was black and blue. Snowy would have to give her another shot of whatever the doctors has prescribed to calm her down. Nothing else stopped her.

The self-inflicted injuries, and the stories that accompanied them, followed the same pattern they had with my father. One night my mother called Peter Lawford and claimed that Mark had attacked her and sliced her face with a razor. The truth was that she had gotten a razor and cut herself. Lionel, our butler, knew what had really happened – we all did – so Mark was never charged with assault. Peter Lawford called a doctor, who came over and took care of Mama in the middle of the night. By the time I saw her the next morning, she was all wrapped up in bandages, with most of her body black and blue. Mark didn't come around again after that. He couldn't take it anymore.

Mark Herron wasn't the only one to disappear from our lives about this time. People seemed to be leaving on a daily basis. Grandma Leonora had been thrown out along with our father, and we knew better than to ask Mama to see her. Grandma was also in the early stages of Alzheimer's by that time and deteriorating rapidly. Our other grandparents were dead, and our only remaining aunts were in Texas and Florida, completely unaware of what was going on. Joey and I barely knew them, so it never occurred to us to turn to them for help. My father visited me and Joe whenever my mother let him, but we didn't dare tell him the truth about what went on at Rockingham. We were afraid it would only cause more trouble. As the weeks went by, the staff dwindled away. As my mother grew worse, even Snowy couldn't take it anymore and went back to Hong Kong. The next thing we knew there was no one left but the cook; Lionel, our beloved and long-suffering butler; and the nanny, Mrs. Chapman.

The only real refuge for Joey and me during this terrible time was the Englunds' house down the street. Cloris Leachman lived there with her husband George Englund and their four children. I adored Cloris Leachman, or Mrs. Englund as I called her then. She wasn't anything like most of the actresses I knew; she was the kind of mom I'd only seen on TV. She got up early every morning and cooked a big breakfast for everyone, and when Joe and I came over, she cooked for us, too. We'd go there in the afternoons whenever we could, as soon as school was out, and sit around the kitchen eating snacks and chatting with Cloris. Cloris must have suspected what was going on at our house, but she never said anything to Joe or me; instead, she let us know that we were always welcome in her home. The Englunds' house became our safe place, the only place we could go and be all right.

Apart from the Englunds, Joe and I had little social life. Even on the days my mother was okay, it was hard to bring a friend home because my mom always slept in the afternoon. She was often up most of the night, either because she was performing or because of insomnia, so what sleep she got was usually during the day. We couldn't go swimming because the splashing would wake her, and we had to be quiet around the house. Besides, we never knew what shape she'd be in, and people were always curious about my mother because she was Judy Garland. Joe and I always called to ask permission before bringing a friend home, and even then we couldn't be certain she would be all right when we got there. Most of the time, we just went over to the Englunds.

Eventually even that haven began to crumble. Years later I found out that George Englund was having an affair with Joan Collins during that time, and the strain on the Englunds' marriage became severe. Something else upset me at the time, though. I had a big crush on their son Brian – he gave me my first real kiss when I was twelve. One night Brian got drunk at a neighbor's party and fell through a shower door. The police brought him home in a squad car. Brian was only thirteen at the time. I couldn't understand it – why would a boy with such a wonderful mom do something so stupid? It scared me to death. His parents handled the whole incident as well as could be expected, but to me it meant that even at the Englund house, bad things could happen. Maybe no place was really safe.

Mrs. Chapman was one of the last to leave the house on Rockingham Drive. I'm not sure why she stayed as long as she did. It certainly wasn't out of concern for Joe and me. Mrs. Chapman was the one person I wasn't sorry to see go. The day she left our house was one of the best days I'd had in quite some time.

Her departure was truly spectacular. One night my mother went into a rage, but this time Mrs. Chapman was the target. Mama had argued with her, fired her on the spot and told her to get out of the house that very night. Instead of leaving, though, Mrs. Chapman locked herself in our bedroom and wouldn't come out. My mom was livid. She decided that if Mrs. Chapman wouldn't leave willingly, she'd have to burn her out. As Joe and I watched from the safety of the hall, my mom got a book of matches and started striking them one by one, pushing them under the bedroom door as she did, to set the threshold rug on fire. All the time she was doing it, she shouted at Mrs. Chapman that she was going to burn her out of the room.

Meanwhile, Mrs. Chapman had managed to find an escape route through the sliding door leading to the pool. She grabbed a bag of clothes and left the bedroom the back way, running around to the garage where her car was parked. When my mom saw her race across the back yard, she screamed with fury. Once she realized where Mrs. Chapman was heading, Mama ran toward the front of the house to try to intercept her, with me and Joey in hot pursuit. We were scared to death, but we were also very excited that Mrs. Chapman was finally going to get what she deserved. On her way through the kitchen, my mom grabbed a large butcher's knife from the counter and sprinted for the front door. You can't imagine how fast that little body of hers could move. By the time we reached the front porch, Mrs. Chapman had started the car and was backing down the driveway as fast as she could go. In a thundering voice, my mother screamed, "If you ever come near me or my children again, I'll kill you!" and hurled the butcher's knife with all her might, right at Mrs. Chapman's face behind the car window. The knife hit the window dead on target, shattering the windshield on the driver's side. I still remember the sound of splintering glass and the knife clattering off the hood of the car onto the driveway. I also remember the look of terror on our nanny's fat face.

Mrs. Chapman drove away at high speed, with the three of us still on the porch. Joey and I were clinging to our mother with excitement. We didn't say a word; we just looked at each other, but inside I was cheering, thinking, "Go, Mom! Get rid of the old bat!" The next morning when we got up for school, Lionel arrived, looked at the scorched carpet, and asked me, "What happened here?"

"All hell broke loose," I told him.

Pause. "Where's Mrs. Chapman?" he asked next.

"Gone," I replied succinctly.

"Ah," he replied, equally succinct. At that point Lionel was all we had left. The rest of the staff had disappeared. Even if their nerves could have survived it, my mother could no longer pay them. Loyal, long-suffering Lionel. We loved him whole-heartedly.

Soon even Lionel was gone, and it was just me and Mama and Joey in that house. That was the really bad time. With the staff gone and Mama often unable to function, I was now in charge. Secret-keeping is the first rule in addictive families, and I knew instinctively that I couldn't tell anyone else what was going on. Liza had been out on her own for years, and telling Dad meant more court hearing and custody battles. I wasn't much more than twelve, but it was up to me to take care of Mama and Joey. We'd started running out of food and money regularly. Sometimes I would call Marc Rabwin late at night, and he would bring us hamburgers and groceries and food money. Marc was a doctor, our oldest family friend, and he had known my mother since Grandma Ethel was pregnant with Mama forty-four years before. He was the closest thing to a grandfather I had left; I knew he'd keep our secrets. Besides, I needed help. I needed it desperately. Mama and Joey were depending on me.

# Chapter Nine

# RITES OF PASSAGE

Help arrived from an unlikely quarter. His name was Tom Green, and early in 1966 he became my mother's "personal publicist," which was Garland code for somebody my mother wanted to have around all the time. A few months after Mark Herron's departure, Tom bought my mother an engagement ring. That didn't surprise me. My mother had always needed a man in her life on pretty much a daily basis. People have called my mother promiscuous in the last few years of her life, but I never thought of her that way. She was tired, increasingly sick, and insecure about the toll her illness was taking on her looks. She was also lonely, and she needed someone to give her constant affection and emotional support. My mother held onto me and Joey a lot during those years, literally and figuratively. She needed to be physically close, to be touched. This part of her nature fed the later rumors that my mother was bisexual, which is patently ridiculous. There were never any gray boundaries for her sexually, except with men. With men, she had trouble separating friendship and sex, at least near the end. Many of her male admirers had the same problem.

I never understood why my mother and Tom Green got together. Maybe it was just because he wasn't a "macho-type guy" like my dad and Mark Herron had been. Mark was gay, but I hadn't realized it when he married my mother. I'm equally certain my mother didn't realize it, either, not until after she married him. Mark was handsome in a traditional masculine sense; there was nothing to mark him as homosexual. He was not effeminate, and he didn't flaunt his sexual orientation. In the 1960s it didn't occur to any of us to wonder whether he preferred men to women, just as it didn't occur to Liza when she married Peter Allen. We didn't even talk about those things in those days.

Tom wasn't like Mark, though. Tom wasn't traditional at all. For starters, he wore green eyeshadow. It was discreetly applied along the edges of his lashes, but it was visible. He also wore lip gloss a decade before American men even used hair spray. It didn't take a genius to figure out that Tom was different. I had grown up with a "regular guy" for a father. I knew what they looked like. Tom was something else again. At thirteen I looked at him with skepticism and suspicion.

Meanwhile, as they say, life goes on. At thirteen your primary interest is not in your mother's sex life. If my mother's boyfriends made her happy, at least for a while, that was all I really cared about. I was a whole lot more interested in my own "sex" life, even if that just meant going to the school dance or watching *Peyton Place* on television. I was no different. In between family crises I was as anxious as the next girl to find out what growing up was all about. And like most teenagers, I found out it wasn't very easy.

To me, being grown-up meant smoking cigarettes, drinking cocktails, and dressing up in high heels and glamorous outfits like I'd tried on in my mother's closet when I was small. Drinking cocktails wasn't much of a temptation for me, since I hated the taste of liquor and felt sick after the smallest sip. So experimenting with liquor was never really a part of my life, even though it would have been easy enough to raid the bar at home while my mother was sleeping. Smoking was another matter. My mother had always smoked like a chimney, several packs a day, so of course I had to try it for myself.

My best girlfriend at the time was Katy Sagal, who lived a couple of blocks away from our house on Rockingham. Long before she became Peg Bundy on the popular TV show *Married with Children*, she was just the girl down the street. She was sweet, and we got along really well. Katy's mom smoked, too, and one afternoon after school we decided to sample one of her mom's cigarettes. We were in the eighth grade at the time. We went to Katy's house, and Katy managed to filch a cigarette and some matches from her mother's purse without getting caught. We went out in the back yard behind some bushes, and Katy lit up the cigarette, took a drag, and handed it to me. We passed it back and forth between us, coughing and choking the whole time, with tears running down our faces. Rocket scientists that we were, we finished the whole thing anyway. By the time we'd finished, I was so sick that I could hardly stand up. Mrs. Sagal was starting to wonder where we'd gone, and Katy was madly trying to fan the smoke away before her mom caught us. I wasn't much help. I was too busy throwing up behind the bushes. A few minutes later we went back in the house, me white-faced and nauseated. I told Katy's mom that I thought I was getting the flu and that I'd better go home. Katy and I must have smelled like a couple of chimneys, but Mrs. Sagal didn't say anything. Maybe she thought our green faces were punishment enough.

Being thirteen, though, I was naturally a slow learner. Sick as it made me, smoking was still a brave and cool thing to do in junior high school, and a few weeks later I got caught smoking in the girls' bathroom. They called my mom and sent me home. My mother was really good about it. She wasn't exactly pleased, but she sat down and discussed it with me, pointing out how foolishly I had acted and saying that next time I wanted to try something like that, I should tell her. She would have let me try a cigarette at home if I was just curious. Every now and then I did have a cigarette at home with her, but I gave up smoking in the girls' bathroom. Fortunately for me, the smoking never really caught on. I never had problems with the socially acceptable addictions. I waited for the big stuff later on.

Boys were another matter. I'd already had my first

romance with Brian Englund in the seventh grade. He'd given me my first kiss and my first charm bracelet, which I'd hidden from my mother (she would have thought I was too young to go steady). Our time together had all the poignant innocence typical of childhood sweethearts. Things didn't always go so smoothly with boys, though, in part because of the problems at home.

My first grown-up dance was all too typical of what life is like when your parent is sick. I was in the eighth grade at the time. There was going to be a formal dance at school one Friday night, and I was very excited about going. My girlfriends and I had talked about it at school for days, planning exactly how we'd do our hair and who we'd try to dance with. I had bought a new outfit for the occasion and carefully picked out every accessory so I would look just perfect. On the afternoon of the dance I spent hours getting ready and arrived at the school gym that evening with my friends, giddy with excitement. This was to be our big night.

I'd already gotten my mother's permission to go days before, and I'd left the house without incident. But like all children in families like mine, I wanted to call and make sure that my mother was all right before I felt comfortable going into the gym and enjoying myself for the evening. So I sent my friends ahead, promising to meet them inside in a minute, and went to the phone booth on the side of the gym to call my mom. I thought she might be asleep, but I wanted to check with Lionel and be sure.

Unfortunately for me, she wasn't asleep. She was awake, and she was over-medicated, and she was in a bad mood. When she found out it was me calling, she got on the phone and began yelling at me, accusing me of sneaking out without her permission. I tearfully reminded her that she'd said I could go, that we'd been planning for the dance all week. Logic made no difference when she was in that frame of mind. She continued yelling at me for several minutes and then told me that she forbade me to go to that dance. I was not even to go into the gym. I was to stay outside by the curb and not to move until Lionel came by and picked me up to take me home.

I hung up the phone, found my friends, and told them I couldn't go to the dance after all because something had come up at home. I didn't tell them why, and they didn't ask. One of the oddities about being Judy Garland's daughter was that everyone, even my friends, treated my mother with such awe that they would never have asked me the normal questions kids get about their moms. And I would certainly never have told them the truth, anyway. I could not, must not, tell. Not ever.

I went back outside and sat down on the curb to wait for Lionel. I could hear the music playing in the gym behind me. The Beatles, I think. It got darker and darker, but no one came. I didn't dare move. Finally, just as the dance was about to end, our car pulled up and I got in. When I got home and went in the house a few minutes later, my mother was sound asleep. She'd been asleep ever since she'd hung up the phone. The next day she had no memory of the conversation, or of the dance. I remembered, though. It was my first dance, and I would never forget it.

It hurts when your parent is too sick to be a full-time parent. That's true for any child. But my situation held some particular cruelties, for my mother was not only sick but famous, and some people exploited that. Children can be incredibly vicious toward the families of the famous, whom they inevitably perceive as privileged and snobby. Painful as my first dance was, the last junior high dance of that year was even more humiliating. An older boy invited me to go to the "Senior Prom," as they called the ninth grade graduation dance, and I was thrilled. To be asked by a ninth grader was a great honor, and this boy was very cute. Once again I bought a special outfit and got all dressed up for the big night. The boy was going to pick me up at my house, and I waited on pins and needles for his arrival. Only he never came. And he never called. I was crushed. When I got to school the following

Monday, I found out why. The rumor had already gone all around the school that he'd bet a bunch of his friends that he could stand up Judy Garland's daughter. The "date" had been a joke designed to embarrass me and make him look like a big man at school. Everyone but my friends seemed to think it was very funny, and for days I was stared and pointed at, and people would giggle when I went by. It was funny, all right. So funny that thirty years later the tears still sting my eyes when I remember.

Fortunately, when my mom was well – well for Mama meaning healthy and properly medicated – she still came through for me when it really counted. When it was time to tell me the "facts of life," my mother did it in a wonderfully straightforward and caring manner. And when it came to "women's matters," she was careful to make sure that I knew what to expect so that I wouldn't be frightened the way she had been as a girl when her body had started to change. Like most women of her generation, my grandmother Ethel had discreetly avoided talking with her daughters about bodily matters, so that when my mother's first period began, she thought something was horribly wrong with her. She explained these things to me just as she had explained them to my sister seven years earlier, and on the day my first menstrual period began at thirteen, my mother congratulated me on becoming a woman, and we toasted with a glass of wine. She made it seem like a wonderful thing, a blessing – instead of the usual view of the menstrual cycle as "the curse." She was great, and I loved her for it.

She didn't do quite so well with the other hormonal changes I was going through during those early teen years, though. By that time I was beginning to understand the connection between my mother's mood swings and her pill intake, and my view of her "medication" gradually began to change with this new understanding. It was becoming clear to me that "Mama's pills" were a problem, and I didn't like it. I was also beginning to rebel against the chaos of our lives. I resented the loss of stability and peace I had known as a little girl. I was also getting old enough to recognize when my mother was behaving inconsistently or irrationally, and since I was no longer an adoring child, my mom was beginning to get on my nerves. When she acted irrationally, I would roll my eyes as if to say, "Please! This is nuts!" I was still keeping my mouth shut, but I would glare at her defiantly with "Look who's talking!" written all over my face. I would still go to bed at night and quiver after one of our fights, and sometimes I would think bad things about my mother, like "I wish you weren't even here!" Later I'd feel frightened and guilty for having even thought it. My mother couldn't understand what had happened to her little Lorna (after all, Mama thought, there was nothing wrong with *her*, so it must be me). Her solution was to take me to the doctor for a check-up.

The doctor looked me over and told my mother that I was a perfectly healthy young girl experiencing the normal changes associated with the hormonal shifts of puberty. My mother asked him if that meant I was retaining water, and the doctor said that might be happening periodically. For reasons I'll never understand, my mother interpreted this to mean that I had water on the brain. She even went so far as to explain to me that she now understood why I had been acting so irrationally lately; I had water on my brain! In another belief that defies explanation, she also decided that the solution to my hormonal madness was for me to take birth control pills, and she persuaded the doctor to put me on them. At that age I needed birth control pills like a lizard needs skates, but for some reason my mother was convinced the pills would make me more rational. Maybe she thought they would drain off all that water in my head!

From her point of view I guess I did seem pretty crazy at times. The Beatles were a case in point. In spite of watching her own generation go crazy over Frank Sinatra (and going pretty crazy herself the night she met Elvis Presley), she simply could not understand my virtual obsession with the Beatles.

Mama herself had first described them two years before when she'd returned from a concert in England and she'd met the Beatles. When she came home she told me about these four boys from Liverpool with long hair who had sung that night. When the Beatles hit big and came to America on their first tour, I naturally had to see them.

I was one of the chosen few who actually got to see the Fab Four during their famous concerts at the Hollywood Bowl. Not only that; I got to see them twice, and from the best seats in the house. The first time, Leslie's mom, Betty Bacall, took me. She and Leslie were in Los Angeles that summer, and she took Leslie and me to the concert to see our idols. It was incredible. Even with all my mother's concerts, I had never seen people go crazy the way they did over the Beatles that night. They were completely out of control, screaming hysterically, sobbing, and fainting. I was almost as fascinated by the crowd as I was by the performance onstage. Leslie and I were so excited we were about to burst, but we sat quietly and took it all in without a peep. We didn't dare peep. The only mom I've ever known who could be as intimidating as my mother was Leslie's mother. When Lauren Bacall gave you *that look*, you shut up and minded your manners. And she gave us the look that night, the one that said, "Just because these other people are acting like lunatics doesn't mean you can. You're going to act like little ladies." We did. The next night I was back again, this time with my father and Bridget. My father didn't glare; he just looked around at the hysterical teenagers like they were all insane, and as usual I minded my manners. He and my mother had been pounding those manners into me from the time I could toddle.

The high point of my entire junior high school career was going backstage after the concert to meet the Beatles. Leslie's mom took us back. She had been to a party with them the night before, so they said, "Ah, Lauren Bacall," and came over to greet us. I even got to shake hands with them. I had a huge crush on George Harrison at the time, having inherited my family's passion for skinny musicians, and I was simply awe-struck to be meeting the Fab Four in person. I was so awestruck I didn't even ask for their autographs; instead I just said what I thought was polite and even asked John Lennon cour-teously about his wife. As we got ready to leave, Leslie and I said, "Nice meeting you," and then Paul asked us if we didn't want them to autograph our programs. I told him we hadn't wanted to trouble them, but then John smiled and said, "That's what we're here for" and proceeded to write "Love, John Lennon" on both our programs. George, Paul, and Ringo did the same. Leslie and I returned home in a state of altered consciousness, and I spent months afterward listening to their records every waking moment and staring at the Beatles posters on my bedroom wall. My mother thought I'd completely lost my mind. I don't know what happened to those programs. They must have got lost in one of our countless moves. I hate to think what they'd be worth today.

Whatever my mother thought, in many ways the Beatles kept me alive during those difficult days. I think adults forget how passionate those first celebrity crushes are, and how important they are to a child who is just beginning to grow up. The Beatles helped me define who I was, what I found attractive in a man, and how my generation fit into the world. And when things were dark on Rockingham Drive, I could get lost in their music and forget about the darkness and the silence for a while.

Even in the darkest days, though, there were moments of light. My mother had a wonderful sense of fun, and it never left her completely, even when things were bad. She loved a funny story more than anything, especially when she got to tell it, and she could be silly in ways that were truly inspired. When Mama was feeling well, she was still Joe's and my favorite playmate. I remember one night Tom Green had a whole lot of money from somewhere, and he and my mother went to the supermarket and bought the place out. They stocked the kitchen up on food, and then my mother decided she was going to make a shepherd's pie, which was one of her specialties. We were all in the kitchen. My mother noticed that Tom was rolling the meat into balls, and grabbed a big spoon, leaned forward, and started shouting, "Hey, Batter! Batter! Batter!" The next thing we knew she'd tossed a meatball into the air and whacked it across the kitchen like a baseball. Then she whacked another one, and someone caught it. The next thing I knew we had a full-fledged baseball game going on, with the spoon for a bat, hitting meatballs all over the kitchen and running bases. We never did get our shepherd's pie, but no one cared because we were exhausted from laughing ourselves silly. Lionel, on the other hand, was not nearly as amused when he saw the kitchen the next morning. There was minced meat everywhere, even on the ceiling.

Though Lionel was still getting stuck with much of the clean-up, in many ways I was becoming the adult in our little family. Tom Green and other friends helped out when they could, but when everyone went home and it was just me and Mama and Joey, I was often the grown-up in charge. The pills knocked my mother out of commission regularly, and my survival instincts told me that I'd better make sure everything was all right because no one else would. I kept an eye on the food supply, and when there were no groceries in the house, it was my job to figure out a way to get some. One night in New York she ran out of Ritalin, and I ended up calling her friend John Carlyle in California in the middle of the night to see if he could find us some. John Carlyle and his partner Charlie Cochran were good friends to my mother, unlike so many of the other men in her life, but they didn't yet understand the real implications of her medication problem and thought nothing of the request for Ritalin. Half the musicians they knew took Ritalin and other stimulants to keep themselves alert for late night performances, so John called Charlie, who eventually showed up in the wee hours of the morning with a couple of Ritalin for my mom and a man he introduced as "Dr. Deans". I was thankful to see them. It meant that my mother had her medication and I could go back to bed. What I didn't know was that "Dr. Deans" was disco manager Mickey Deans, who two years later would become my mother's last husband. To this day John regrets what he did. He is still a good friend.

The happiest event in our lives in 1967 had nothing to do with Mama, though; it had to do with Liza. Liza and Peter Allen got married. My mother was thrilled because she really liked Peter, and I thought he was wonderful, too. My mom had introduced Liza to Peter herself, so I think that made the marriage even more gratifying for Mama. Peter was sweet and warm and very talented, and I already thought of him as a big brother. I still do.

We flew back to New York for the wedding. It was at Stevie Phillips' apartment, the reception at another. The apartment was beautiful, and everything had been done up very elegantly for the ceremony. Liza wore a victorian wedding dress, looking pretty and happy. My mother wore a rainbow-colored coat over a yellow sheath dress, and a pillbox hat. She looked as bright as a daffodil, and almost as happy as Liza. The wedding was small, just the families and a few friends. Liza's father Vincente was there, and so was mine. He and my mother were back on speaking terms by then, and he still thought of himself as Liza's stepdad. Liza and Peter said their vows, and it was all very lovely and very romantic. I was fourteen by then, naive and starry-eyed about the whole thing. Besides, for the first time in quite a while my parents and Joe and Liza and I were all together as a family, and no one was fighting. It was almost like old times.

Almost, but not quite. At least my parents were talking again, instead of staying away or screaming at each other, and that was good for all of us. My dad had always provided what stability there was in our lives, and with him around a little more, things seemed slightly less chaotic.

Shortly after Liza and Peter's wedding, my mother started filming on *Valley of the Dolls*. She was desperate to do a good job, to find her way back to peace and sanity. But for my mother a movie meant early make-up calls, staying thin, and facing the ghosts of a whole string of past failures. It also meant more medication. A few weeks into production she was up to twenty or more Ritalin a day, with more Seconal to bring her down, and the strain on her health became unbearable. Eventually the film company had to let her go, and she plunged into utter despair. It was heartbreaking to watch.

After the *Valley* fiasco, my mother was desperate to start working again, and once more she turned to Sid. Whatever their personal problems, she still trusted him more, professionally, than she did anyone else, and she asked him to begin putting together another concert series for her. My dad, ever the rescuer, and still carrying the world's biggest torch for my mother, agreed. Vern Alves also returned to the fold, a new management contract was drawn up, and the old team was back in business. The plan was to go east again, find a place in New York where we could see Peter and Liza more often, and book a series of concerts on the East Coast. The Rockingham house was to be sold to meet IRS back tax demands, and Vern agreed to stay there and clean up the business details while we went ahead to New York. So once again, in the finest Gumm family tradition, we packed up those same old trunks, tried to leave our troubles behind us, and took our act back on the road.

## Chapter Ten

# SPIN-OUT

When I think of those last two years of my mother's life, I always think of a ball of yarn unwinding. When yarn unwinds, it does so slowly at first. Because of the ball's size, the unraveling process has little visible effect in the beginning. But as the ball continues to unravel, it gradually becomes smaller until one day, you suddenly notice that it has shrunk to an alarming degree. At that point the uncoiling seems to pick up momentum, and you realize that you are helpless to stop it. It was like that for my mother. Her sickness was a slow unwinding. For more than ten years our family had slowly spun out as we lost our center. It was only near the end, though, that we realized we were all spinning out of control.

We arrived in New York in the middle of 1967. I was fourteen and a half by then, five inches taller than my mother and rapidly growing up in other ways as well. After a few hotels, we moved into a huge three-level brownstone on 62nd Street that looked like a cross between a French bordello and a mausoleum. No expense had been spared by its owner in making it truly hideous. It was the ugliest place I've ever seen in my life, and it gave everyone who came through the door a shudder.

That building still haunts my dreams on occasion, or at least my nightmares. It was a tri-level monstrosity. Downstairs was a maid's room and a small service area with a washer and dryer. On the main floor were the entrance area, the dining room, the living room, and a small kitchen. The dining room was Louis XIV on a bad day, with everything done in pale blue – blue carpeting, blue wallpaper with a gilt pattern, matching drapes, and highly formal, intricately carved furniture. Adjoining the formal dining room was a huge living room decorated with smoked glass, dark wood, and orange drapes and carpets. Everything in the room was ponderous and ornate; even the big pool table at the far end was made of heavy mahogany. In the middle of the living room was a staircase leading to the upper level. The banister was constructed of fancy glass rods and mirrors. When you came down the stairs at night, the reflection in the glass gave a ghostly effect.

It wasn't any better when you reached the top floor. My room had red carpet and was done entirely in black, white, and red. Joe's room, which was kind of a converted library, was done entirely in lime green. My mother's room was an ornate Oriental affair. One of the brownstone's former occupants, I was later told, was a lecturer with an interest in sado-masochistic sex. Apparently my mom ran across his cache of whips, chains, and other implements shortly after we moved in and nearly moved us all out again. A friend of hers came and disposed of the collection. I never saw it myself, but somehow it doesn't surprise me that it was there. The whole place smacked of the Marquis de Sade. Mapleton Drive it wasn't.

Fortunately, we didn't spend much time there that summer. We spent most of our time on the road in New York and New England, playing the Westbury, the Tent, and other summer concert venues. My dad decided it might be fun to have Joe and me do a couple of bits onstage with our mom, so we tried out some routines in New England. I got to go to a store called Splendiferous in New York and pick out a hip outfit to wear for my number: long white shorts with shells around them and a mini dress that came down over the top – very 1960s. I would sing, and Joe would play his drums. We were a huge hit, and the next thing I knew we were appearing with Mama at every performance. It was really exciting.

Rip Taylor was usually the opener. My mother would stand in the wings watching as the orchestra went into the overture, pumping herself up by singing along in the wings. Then she would go bursting onstage, and the audience inevitably went crazy, standing and cheering. About forty-five minutes later, just before intermission, she would introduce me and Joe and bring us out onstage with her to do a sort of family segment. I sang Petula Clark's "Don't Sleep in the Subway, Darling," which was a big hit on the radio at the time, and then we later all did "Bob White" together, a Johnny Mercer song my mom had taught us. Finally we'd do "Together" from *Gypsy*, Joe's old favorite.

The crowning glory of the tour for all of us was the famous run at the Palace. My mother had gotten pregnant with me during her first Palace run, and now, fifteen years later, my dad booked us in for four weeks. It was amazing. By then Joe and I had gotten a lot more professional than we'd been in the beginning of the tour, and we worked hard to prepare for the opening. I got to work with some of the best in the business, people like Harold Arlen, who had written "Over the Rainbow" for my mother all those years ago; and John Bubbles, the dancer who had done numbers with my mother in concerts when I was small. John taught me to soft-shoe, and Dick Barstow, who had choreographed the numbers for *A Star Is Born*, did the choreography. I wore a yellow dress, and Mama, Joe and I all had on burnt orange bowler hats.

Opening night was truly extraordinary. Jackie Vernon opened for us, followed by my mother, and a little later it was my turn. As I stood in the wings waiting to go on, I could actually hear my knees knocking together from fear. My heart was pounding so loud I could hardly hear the orchestra. When my cue finally came, I entered to join singing "Me and My Shadow," which my mother had already joined John Bubbles in singing. Soon after the line "All alone and feeling blue" I would jump out and fall into step, and finally Joe would jump out and fall into step behind me. We were all wearing our bowler hats which had been worked into the choreography, and as we strutted our stuff, the audience went crazy. Mama then left me alone on stage saying the line "This is it kid" (from *A Star is Born*) and I sang a solo of special material put together for me by Harold Arlen, such as "Singing in the Rain" and "Happy Days are Here Again". It was so much fun being out on that stage, dizzyingly exciting. And it felt so good to be doing it together. I can understand how my mom must have felt when she was singing with her sisters and parents on the vaudeville stages all those years ago, before the pain and trauma that destroyed "Jack and Virginia Lee." They say the family that prays together, stays together. For my family, performing together had pretty much the same effect. After the performance we went to the opening night party at the El Morocco, and that was thrilling, too. I was almost fifteen, and I got to bring a real date, a boy from the Splendiferous dress shop that had supplied my costumes. I felt that at long last, I'd arrived. I was up there with my mother the way my older sister had been at the Palladium three years before.

When the summer was over, we settled into the mausoleum on 62nd Street. Tom Green had come to New York with us, and my dad had moved into a hotel. He would soon meet Patricia Potts, the woman he eventually married. Patty was a singer (Sid had met her when my mom went to open Caesar's Palace in Las Vegas), and since neither she nor my dad thought "Potts" was much of a name for an actress, my father rechristened her Patty Hemingway. The family wasn't exactly together again, but we managed. Joe and I got to see our father often, and it was comforting to know that he was usually only a few miles away. Liza and Peter were nearby, too, so for the first time in a long while we were functioning more like a family. A dysfunctional family, but a family nonetheless. Soon Vern Alves joined us in New York, and life seemed almost normal.

That fall my parents enrolled me in school, but thankfully it wasn't one of the tough New York public schools I remembered from our last stay in the East. This was the Professional

Children's School, designed for kids who performed for a living. What that meant was that you could show up in the morning, sign out to go to work or an audition, and be excused. For a girl who hated school as much as I did, it was heaven. I hardly ever went to class. I showed up most mornings just long enough to sign myself out and take the day off. Every now and then I really did go on an audition, but most of the time I was just playing legal hooky. I spent my days with Tony Sales, Soupy Sales' son, and his girlfriend Nancy Allen, who went on to be a movie star in her own right years later. We'd all check out of class together and go off and do whatever we wanted.

Whatever her reasons, the summer of touring had changed the way my mother treated me. Somewhere along the line she had come to regard me as a peer, a fellow performer. I wasn't her baby girl anymore. I was her best friend. We wore each other's clothes and consulted one another about hair and make-up. In the evenings when she didn't have a concert and wanted to get out, we would usually go to a night club. I never drank there; my mother wouldn't have allowed it, and besides, I didn't want to. It was being there that I wanted, dancing and talking and laughing and sharing in all the excitement. Both of my parents always loved parties, and I had inherited the same social nature. Most important, though, at least in the beginning, was that it meant I was growing up. I wasn't little Lorna anymore, the girl who had to be carried to bed in her pajamas just when the party was getting started, the kid who had to be left behind with her baby brother and the nanny. At long last, I was a grown-up.

The first night club I ever went to was Arthur's, the hippest club in New York in the 1960s. It was owned by Sybil Burton, Richard Burton's ex. My mom took us there the first time after her Forest Hills concert. Mama and Liza and Joe and I went in the limo, with Roddy McDowall, who was an old friend of my mom's. There was a big fuss over us when we arrived, and we sat at a table in the back with the A-crowd. Everybody in the place was coming and going from our table; we were the center of attention. I was very dressed up and feeling glamorous, and everybody paid a lot of attention to me, too, talking to me and asking me to dance. All I could think was, "I want to stay here for the rest of my life and never go home. I don't ever want this to end." For a long time it didn't. After that first night at Arthur's, I kept going back for more. At first I went with Mama or Liza, later with friends I'd met there. Years later, after Arthur's had changed management and been renamed Hippopotamus, I was still going there. Soon I was making the club circuit all over Manhattan with people like Salvador Dali, and Mia Farrow and Sinatra; and hanging out at the Salvation in the Village with the Rolling Stones when they were in town. I even got to party there with the Beatles, my old idols. Clubbing became a kind of addiction. I lived for the nights I could go out to my favorite club. School? Please! Who wanted to go to school when you could be out partying with Mick Jagger?

Meanwhile, I was growing up in other ways as well. I knew by then that my mother couldn't always function, and I also knew that she was used to having someone take care of her. Someone always had. Most significantly, shortly after the move to New York, my father began my formal education in the care and protection of my mother. What that meant was monitoring her medication intake. I learned to go through all of her clothes and the drapes – all the places she'd hide it – whenever she left the house. It was my job to keep the pills locked up and give her a certain number on schedule. I would count out the pills, so many of each color, and bring them to her with a glass of water. When my father was not around, it was my job to dilute the ones I gave her with sugar.

I also had to learn to take care of her when the medication became badly imbalanced, or she overslept and went into withdrawal. When that happened she'd sometimes pass out, or worse yet, have seizures. I learned how to put a stick in her mouth to keep her from choking on her own tongue and suffocating, and how to get her in a safe position until the seizure passed. I also learned who I could and couldn't call for help. When your mother is Judy Garland, you don't just dial 911. It isn't that simple. I had been introduced to that painful reality years before in Hawaii. Now I wasn't just cleaning up the mess in the room, though; I was also making sure my mother made it through the night. I became expert at who to call for help and when to call them. I might not have spent much time in school during those years, but I learned a great deal more than most teenagers ever have to know.

Her declining health continued to take a toll on her career. They were recasting the lead in *Mame* and my mother wanted the role so badly she could taste it, and composer Jerry Herman really wanted her to do it. She would have been wonderful in it, too. She went all out to get the part, even staging a tryout at home. But the company wouldn't sign her because no company would sign a performance bond on my mother with her history. She told me she was uninsurable, and she was desperately hurt by that. Everyone else understood why, but she didn't. It was incomprehensible to her that no one would hire her. After all, she was Judy Garland, the biggest star MGM had ever produced. Now nobody would give her a job. How could such a thing have happened?

The same problems were creating havoc with her concert schedule. At the end of 1967, a month after I turned fifteen, we were scheduled to do Christmas week performances at Madison Square Garden. Joe and I were in the show with my mom. Andy Williams' brother was the choral director. We'd rehearsed a big production number, and I even had my own back-up chorus. We had red Christmas costumes and did all the traditional Christmas numbers. I think my dad had in mind sort of a reprise of the Christmas episode of *The Judy Garland Show* – the whole family holiday thing. To say the least, it didn't quite work out that way. We rehearsed until late Christmas Eve and returned to open the next night, Christmas Day. By the time that first performance was over, my mother was exhausted and strung out. The usual explosion occurred, and soon my mom refused to go on, ending up in hospital with bronchitis. My dad had to cancel the last three shows, and we forfeited the money, not to mention having to pay off all the production expenses. Nobody got kidnapped that year, but let's just say we should have stuck to doing Christmas on TV. In real life it didn't work out quite as well. Christmas with Judy Garland was not exactly *Meet Me in St. Louis* by that point. "Have yourself a merry little Christmas," she'd once sung. Little Margaret O'Brien had the right idea in that movie. You needed a good grip on that wooden sword at Christmas time. You just might need to whack a few snow people.

Madison Square Garden was just the tip of the iceberg, of course. As my mother's health continued to degenerate over the next few years, a vicious cycle developed. Concerts were canceled, revenues lost, and production expenses were left to pay. So she had to keep on working to deal with the debt. Working meant expending more energy than she had left, and that in turn meant more amphetamines to carry her through. As the cycle continued, her anger and despair mounted.

The concerts continued, alternating triumphs and fiascos. The disasters were frightening to watch. She did a concert with Tony Bennett where she was badly over-medicated. Joe and Dad and I were all there that night, sitting in the audience. Tony went on first, and when no one was watching her, my mom apparently got her hands on some medication backstage. By the time she went on for her part of the show, she could barely walk. The minute I saw her come onstage, I knew what had happened. We all went rushing backstage in a panic. We kept pacing up and down, trying to figure out what to do. Should we get her offstage? Ring down the curtain? Call an ambulance? Tony went out onstage once to try to help her through a number, but after that he wouldn't go out there with her again, and I don't blame him. She could barely talk, much less sing, and she was completely incoherent. She just sort of staggered through a few numbers, and the minute it was over, we put her in a cab and got her back to New York. The press release for that night said she had been suffering from food poisoning. I lost track of how many times my mom was in and out of hospitals before it was all over.

That particular night was frightening. Sometimes, though, my mother wasn't frightening; she was just plain infuriating. The Boston concert in 1968 is a famous example. We'd gone to the Chelsea Naval Hospital the afternoon before opening night, and my mother had spent a lot of time with the disabled veterans there. My mom had always been wonderful with people with disabilities. That night at the Chelsea hospital, Mama was at her best. She went from room to room, bed to bed, talking to each of the men, alternately charming and comforting them, and signing autographs. Gene Palumbo, her music director, came along to play the piano so she could sing for them. Before she left for the theater, she invited all the vets to the concert the next night as her guests. She was still at her best when she arrived at the theater. She had the audience on their feet throughout the performance. She was electrifying.

By closing night the situation had changed. That night she decided not to go on. She was mad at Sid, had been locked out of her suite at the St. Moritz because the bill hadn't been paid, and her personal effects had been impounded. Joe and I went on over to the theater to talk to my dad, and there he was, sitting in this tiny little office with the head of the theater. My dad had already been on the phone to her with no luck, so he decided to let Joe – the "baby" – give it a try.

My brother got on the phone and said, "Mama? I really want you to come and do the show."

"I'm not coming." Click. She had hung up the phone.

Joe tried again. "Mama?"

"Don't you get it? I'm not coming." Click.

Joe dialed the phone one last time. "Mama, I . . ."

Loudly, "Don't – you – speak – English? I'm – not – com – ing!" Bang!

Joe looked at Dad. "I'm sorry."

Dad said, "Don't worry about it." Then he looked at me and said, "Your turn to give it a try."

I said, "What should I say?"

He sighed and said, "Anything that will get her here."

So I squeezed into the little office with the rest of them and called my mother. "Hello, Mom."

"What?" she snapped. Then, "Are you there with your father and Joe?"

"Oh no, Mama," I lied, "he's not here. Mama, please come and do the show. I really wish you would."

"I'm not doing that God-damned show!"

Then she was off and running, "I want all the money up front . . . I want . . ." Ranting and raving, I want, I want, I want.

Finally I said, "But Mama . . . Mama, remember when we went to the hospital yesterday and you invited all those Vietnam veterans to come see you? Well, they're all here, Mama."

Silence.

"They're all here waiting to see you. They rolled them all in here in their wheelchairs."

Another silence. And finally the big line. "Well, if they can wheel them in, they can wheel them out again, can't they?" And she hung up.

I looked at my father. I was crying with anger and frustration.

"What did she say?"

I told him. He sank back in the chair and put his hands to his temples. Another migraine. "Well, that's that." He was furious. I knew how he felt, but I was also worried. I knew my mother needed the money. But when she got like that, there was no talking to her. She never did show up that night, or the nights after. I tried not to look while they took all the vets out in their wheelchairs.

Sad to say, those episodes were getting more and more frequent. I don't know how many concerts she eventually canceled. I couldn't begin to count them. Sometimes she never even made opening night. A night at Caesar's Palace went down the drain when she refused to go on but demanded her money anyway. Bert Lahr, the Cowardly Lion from *The Wizard of Oz*, died that day, and she said she was too upset by his death to sing. It might also have had something to do with the fact that my dad had Patty Hemingway with him that night, and my mom was livid. She could put up with a theoretical woman, but a real flesh and blood female on my dad's arm was another matter entirely. She might not want him back as a husband, but that didn't mean anyone else could have him. He was *hers*. (In actual fact, of course, he was. To this day, two wives and thirty years later, he's still waiting to get back together with her.) The result was another huge blow-up, and another concert down the drain. It was an endless, hopeless, downward spiral.

For a long time during this period, my dad still clung to the illusion that he could fix things, that he could make it better. He still thought he was Atlas. Even with all the professional disasters, he tried to maintain some semblance of a normal family life – normal for us, anyway. The Christmas concert fiasco was a classic example. When we finished rehearsing that December 24, it was about 5 p.m., and we were all exhausted from the run-through. My mom had already left, and it was just me, Joe, Sid, and his girlfriend Patty. We'd all been so busy we'd completely forgotten it was Christmas Eve. My dad looked at his watch and suddenly said, "Oh my God, it's Christmas tomorrow! Come on, everybody; the stores are about to close!"

And off we all went. In the midst of all the trauma, none of us had thought about the holidays, but my dad was bound and determined that we'd have some kind of Christmas. We took a taxi to Bloomingdale's and got there just before closing. We literally took off running, Joe and Patty and I racing along behind Dad, and ran down the aisles of the store as Dad shouted, "Grab this! Grab that! Grab one of those!" It was like a scene from a Marx Brothers movie. At one point Dad grabbed a fishing rod. I remember saying, "What are we going to do with that?"

"I don't know. Hang it out the hotel window and see what we catch? We'll wrap it up!" By then we were all laughing so hard we were crying, our arms loaded down with useless gifts. We made it to the counter just in time to pay for all the stuff before the store closed, and when we got back to the Plaza, we wrapped up some of the things to take back to the "mausoleum" for Mama. The next morning, when we got to the hotel, Dad and Patty had wrapped up the rest of the things and put them under a tree my dad had found and managed to decorate. My dad. Sid Luft might not have been Ward Cleaver, but he was pretty remarkable in his own way. Not exactly a traditional Christmas, but Christmas nonetheless. The memory still makes me smile. It helped carry both Joe and me through the disaster of the concert cancelation the next week.

The concert failures were just the most public symptom of my mother's problems. The personal toll was actually much more serious. It was becoming harder and harder for her to get along with anyone for long. She went through one relationship after another because she just wore everyone out. By then there were regular outbursts almost everywhere – at home, in restaurants, you name it. One of the more spectacular outbursts did make the papers. She was supposed to go to London with Ray Filiberti (a business partner of my dad) and his wife Sharon, and Sharon didn't like my mother one little bit. Most people catered to my mom, but not Sharon. She wasn't impressed. Dorothy Schmorothy. Big deal. Once, on a flight to London together, an argument blew up over a game of cards. Sharon thought my mom was cheating. They had been drinking, so this soon led to screaming and yelling, throwing drinks at each other, and what sounded like a free-for-all. It was horrendous, and the papers had a field day with it. My mother turned right around and took the next plane home, canceling her planned engagements in London. Twenty-four hours later those red suitcases of hers were back in the house, and Joe and I thought, "Oh God. Here we go again."

With every month that passed and the pressures mounted, she kept getting harder and harder to live with. The problem with addiction, especially in that advanced stage, is that it isn't a static condition. Either you get help and get better, or you get worse. My mother was getting worse. More and more often, she would simply lose control of her emotions. She was taking huge amounts of Ritalin and amphetamines by then, twenty or more times the maximum recommended dose. Her brain was literally shorting out. No amount of narcotics at night could counteract such a load of stimulants, and the more she took, the more she craved. Her intake of stimulants was complicated by the fact that she drank, never in large amounts, but enough to throw another chemical into the mix. To top it all off, she was consuming huge amounts of nicotine, two or three packs of Salem menthol cigarettes a day. The combination of chemicals was explosive.

And what explosions. Daily, sometimes several times daily, she would become randomly enraged by almost anything that came in her path. Some of the incidents were triggered by the small, normal stresses of everyday family living. If I forgot to make my bed, or just threw it together carelessly, she'd explode with fury. Something that hadn't bothered her an hour before – or five minutes before – suddenly became intolerable to her. Anything could set her off, anything was possible when she was overdosing, and we knew it. I tried to protect Joe as much as possible, to keep him out of it if I could and absorb the brunt of her anger myself. I was older, and besides, I could take it. Joe had a gentler nature, and I worried about how it would affect him. I also think it was harder for him because he'd always been her baby boy, and she'd treated him with a special tenderness. It's funny; the little brother I'd so bitterly resented years before had somehow become my partner in survival, someone I protected against all comers, even our mother. Still, the situation was hard on both of us. Joe and I lived with tension twenty-four hours a day.

Sometimes the outbursts went far beyond the yelling and screaming that could result from a dropped jacket or an unmade bed. She would break things. She broke all the glass rods on the staircase in one outburst, and she broke just about everything else in the apartment that would break before we finally moved out. When the chemicals hit her bloodstream, she would just pick up anything within reach and throw it. She was amazingly strong under any circumstances, but when she was in the grip of an amphetamine-nicotine mix, the adrenaline rush made her even more powerful. Even at 4'11" and ninety pounds, she could hurl almost anything across a room with deadly accuracy: big ashtrays, heavy books, lamps, anything handy. She was one powerful little lady. There's a scene in *The Pirate* where she hurls most of the props in the room, including several large vases and an array of pirate weapons, ten or fifteen feet across the room at Gene Kelly. She never misses. I've got a pretty good idea where Vincente Minnelli got the inspiration to direct that scene. He was married to Mama at the time.

As the months went by, these outbursts increasingly occurred in the middle of the night, about 3 a.m., like the old night raids on Rockingham Drive. Two or three times she actually threw me and Joey out of the house. The first time it happened, I was really upset. She kept screaming at me and telling me to get out. I was afraid to leave Joe alone with her in that condition, so I took him with me. We showed up at Liza and Peter's house at about 4 a.m., and they were wonderful. Thank God, Liza was just as protective of me as I was of Joe, and Peter was like my big brother. We all took care of each other. They took us in and calmed us down. But just about the time I began to feel better, my mom started calling Liza's house demanding they bring us back home. She kept calling and calling, screaming at Liza. Finally Peter took the phone. He was furious; it was the first time I'd ever heard him raise his voice to my mother. He shouted, "I am not bringing these children home while you're behaving this way. Now stop calling my house!" And he slammed down the receiver.

There was a huge silence, and we all sat there looking at each other. I knew in my gut I had to go back home. She was in bad shape and I loved her. I had to go. I finally said, "Take us home, Peter." So he did, reluctantly. When we got there, it was like nothing had happened. My mother just thanked Peter for dropping us off and told us to go to bed. Later on, when she realized what she'd done and the guilt set in, she'd get angry at Peter. She couldn't bear to face the way she was treating us, so she'd always look around for someone else to blame. On nights like that, it was Peter.

All in all, there were three or four of these late night escapes to Liza and Peter's. After the first time, I really didn't mind. Their apartment became a place of refuge. Joe and I came to look forward to going over there, even if we had to get thrown out of the house to do it. It was so peaceful there.

I adored Peter Allen. He was one of the most gifted performers I've ever seen, and the best of brothers to me and Joe. I was never angry with him for marrying my sister, or for their divorce, either. I was just sad, for both of them. I don't believe Peter intended to mislead Liza about his sexuality. I think he misled himself. Maybe he thought he could put his lifestyle behind him permanently when he married her. He couldn't, and I admired his courage in going public about his sexuality years later. Peter truly loved my sister, but he was confused about the kind of love he felt for her. We were all pretty confused during those years.

In the last two years of her life, my mother never seemed to sleep. How could she, with dozens of Ritalin and Benzedrine capsules in her system? If someone didn't watch her constantly, she would wander around the house half the night like a restless spirit. One night when I couldn't stay awake any longer, she wandered into Joey's room. He was lying curled up on his side, facing the door. Joe and I were both light sleepers by then. He heard her, but he kept his eyes closed, hoping she'd go back out and let him sleep. Peering through his closed eyelashes, he could just see her outline, eerie in the darkened room. As she bent over his still form, Joe could hear her breathing oddly. She was taking heavy, wheezing breaths – in, out, in, out – a heavy, unnatural sound in the silent room. Joe began to panic, thinking, "Oh God, Mama's possessed!" He lay perfectly still, scared to death something evil was going to get him. A minute or two later Mama turned and made her way back toward the open door as Joe watched. Still in the grip of an overstimulated imagination, Joe felt that my mother was floating, her feet moving silently through the air a few inches above the floor. Afraid to go back to sleep, Joe lay awake all night, fearing the ghostly form would return. When he tells the story now, we both laugh at the fear that gripped his twelve-year-old's imagination. At the time, though, it wasn't so funny.

I tried to keep an eye on her at night, but after a while I became almost obsessed with the need for sleep. When my mother didn't sleep, I couldn't sleep, either. I didn't dare. I had to make sure she was all right. As the medication took its toll on my mother's system, it indirectly began to take its toll on my body, too. People talk about twenty-four-hour-a-day jobs; I had a seventy-two-hour-a-day job. During that year at the brownstone, and later at the St. Moritz when we moved out, I rarely slept more than every second or third night.

The nightly ritual went something like this. My mother would go to bed, usually sometime after midnight, with the TV and radio going to provide white noise in the background. At some point, if we were lucky, she'd drift off to sleep. Joe would already be in bed, but I'd still be up checking on her until she finally dozed off. When that happened, I'd go back to my own room and go to bed, hoping for the best. An hour or two later she would wake up, either excited or agitated, and needing company. She'd come into our rooms and wake up me and Joe, and we'd go back to her room and crawl into bed with her. And she'd start talking. She'd talk and she'd talk and she'd talk, for hours at a time, with me curled up beside her and Joe dozing on the pillow next to me. For a while I'd talk with her, but after an hour or two the best I could manage was, "Uh huh. Uh huh." And she'd keep talking. Every now and then she'd doze for a few minutes, and when she did I'd nudge Joe and whisper to him to go back to bed. He'd stagger back down the hall to his room in his pajamas and go back to bed while I stayed with Mama. Sometimes she'd wake up and start talking again, and sometimes she'd sleep for a few hours. Not daring to get up, and too weary to move anyway, I'd stay in the bed next to her, alternately dozing and listening as she needed me to. If I was lucky, we'd both fall asleep next to each other by dawn.

Two years later, when she died, I came to treasure some of those moments of closeness. It was usually then, in the middle of the night, that we shared our secrets the way best friends do. But at the time, it was grueling. I was fifteen, growing rapidly and badly in need of rest and a healthy way of living. My life at Mapleton as a little girl, with its carefully regulated hours for play, naptime, sleep, and healthy home cooked meals – never anything from a can – seemed like a dim and distant dream. More than anything in life, I wanted my mother to be healthy, to get well and become once again the woman I remembered from those early years. I would have done anything to make that possible. But no matter how much my heart and spirit wanted to bring that about, my body was beginning to give out under the strain. Quite simply, I was about to spin out.

# Chapter Eleven

# BURN-OUT

Few things make me angrier, or cause me more pain, than listening to the drivel in countless books and interviews about how my mother spent her life unloved, neglected, and betrayed. Even her obituaries routinely talked about how she "never found love" or how "everyone she loved betrayed her," leaving her alone and abandoned in her times of need. Near the end she fed that belief herself because she was too sick, too far gone, to face what was really happening. Didn't love her? Neglected her? We, my brother and sister and I, loved her more than anything else in life. So did my father. My dad has taken so much abuse from the press over the years, but none of the people who condemn him was there to watch as he struggled to rescue a woman who was beyond rescue. There wasn't enough love in the world, enough attention in the world, to save my mother. No one could have saved her but herself, and at the end it was far too late even for that.

I should know. I nearly killed myself trying.

The months and eventually years of stress and of physical exhaustion had begun to take their toll on me, too. From the time I'd walked through the door of that beach house in Waikiki with wet washcloths to clean up the blood, I'd been struggling to clean up my mom's disasters. I am my father's daughter, and when the world toppled off his shoulders, I tried to hold it up with my own skinny arms.

For five years I'd kept on trying. But I wasn't my father;

I was just a kid, and my body was trying to remind me that I had shouldered a burden far beyond my strength. When I continued to ignore what my body kept telling me, it finally took its revenge. One day, it just quit.

Most of that day is gone from my memory. The one thing I do remember clearly is walking down the staircase that afternoon. I had come down that ugly glass staircase into the living room after being up with my mother for one of our marathon nights. I don't remember thinking about anything in particular that day; I was too tired for feeling or thought. I only remember descending the last stair, stepping into the living room, and for some unfathomable reason, looking up at the ceiling. I remember standing there for a few seconds, looking straight up, and then raising my hands overhead and beginning to spin. I spun and spun, right there by the staircase, my hands reaching for the dim recesses above my head. That's all I remember. The next thing I knew, everything went black.

I later learned that I had lost consciousness and passed out on the floor at the bottom of the steps. Joe saw me fall, and, terrified, he called my father, who sent for a cab (an ambulance would attract too much attention). I vaguely recall coming to for a moment as my dad carried me out. That's the last thing I remember for seven days.

They took me to the hospital and examined me. The doctors determined that I was suffering from severe emotional and physical exhaustion. They said it was a type of mental breakdown, in the sense that my brain had simply shut down from prolonged stress. I had been staying up with my mother until 7 a.m. every morning, then pulling on some clothes and trying to get me and Joe to school. When I got back home in the afternoon, the whole routine would start all over again, day in and day out. My father talked to the doctors and confirmed that I hadn't been getting enough sleep and had been under terrible emotional strain. He didn't want me sent home to my mom's until I was better, so after three days in the hospital they transferred me to the hotel where my dad was living at the time, for further rest. I don't even remember the move. All together, I slept for seven days straight. My dad and Vern Alves took turns watching over me while I slept. They would make sure I got water periodically and try to get some soup or juice down me every few hours. I don't remember any of it. When I woke up four days later, it was night, and Vern was sitting next to my bed. He told me I'd been asleep for a very long time. I had no idea where I was or what had happened. That week of my life is still a complete blank.

I stayed there at my dad's a few days longer. I was too exhausted to leave, and I was also terribly confused. I didn't know what I wanted to do. Part of me was so relieved to be with my father, where it was safe and I could sleep. Part of me never wanted to leave, wanted to stay in that safe place forever. But the other part of me said, "You have to go back. You have to take care of Mama. She needs you. You have to make sure she's all right." That part of me was still the strongest, and after a few days of rest, I decided to go back home to my mother. My father didn't try to stop me. He knew it was useless, that this was a decision I would have to make for myself, and that I was still determined to return. He was in so much pain about it all. He had watched my mother destroy herself for years, and now he was watching his daughter fall apart, too, and he felt completely helpless.

So a few days later I moved back home with my mother and had to deal with her regrets. She was overwhelmed with guilt about what had happened to me, and she kept saying over and over, "I'm sorry I was such a bad mother. I'm so, so sorry." And over and over I had to say, "It's okay, Mom. Don't worry, Mama. No, Mom, of course you weren't a bad mother." And on and on and on. Somehow, it always ended up being about her feelings. I had to comfort her, endlessly comfort her, so that she wouldn't feel bad about what had happened to me, when all I really wanted to do was go back to bed.

She was rapidly running out of resources. Not long after my hospital stay, we had to move out of the old brownstone and into the St. Moritz. Nobody told me why, but I suspect it was because we couldn't pay the rent anymore. By that time Joe and I could pack in our sleep, so it was no big deal to move into yet another hotel. Besides, we didn't exactly have fond memories of that hideous old mausoleum.

We left behind more than the brownstone. My mom was also going through friends and lovers at a dizzying pace as her condition worsened. One of the casualties was Tom Green. Things had been going downhill with him for quite a while, anyway. They fought constantly about sex.

By that time she and Tom were fighting about money, too. My mother accused Tom of hocking two of her rings during one of her frequent stints in the hospital. I heard several stories about this. At one point my mother said he'd sold them to buy birthday presents for Joe's twelfth birthday; another time he said he sold them to pay my mother's hospital bill. He said she'd told him to; she denied it. Whatever the truth, the jewelry ended up in a pawnshop. The rings were beautiful: an emerald set with diamonds and another ring set with diamonds and pearls. I loved that emerald. We never got it back. I don't have any of my mother's jewelry. By the time she died, it had all been sold.

Apparently the incident with the rings was the last straw in a relationship that was already very strained. Not long afterward, my mother decided to get rid of Tom Green in true Garland style. One night she looked at me and said, "I know how to get back at that son-of-a-bitch."

She picked up the phone and called Bellevue Hospital, telling whoever answered that it was an emergency, and proceeded to give an Oscar-worthy performance.

"You have to help me," she sobbed into the phone. "My husband's taken an overdose, and he's going to kill himself!"

I could hear the person on the other end say something, and then my mom replied, "His name's Tom Green . . . No, no, he's not here. He's at the Alrae Hotel. You have to help him. Please! He's just taken an overdose of sleeping pills, and I'm afraid he's going to die. You have to help him before the pills get into his system!"

More sobbing, more talking on the other end, and then, "Please, please save his life. He's had a breakdown. He needs help." Sob, sob.

I sat in the chair by the phone, eyeballs popping, watching her. A moment later I heard her say, "Yes, yes. Oh, thank you, thank you. Yes, right away." And then, "Oh, by the way. He's got a Judy Garland fixation. Please be kind." My jaw dropped.

Then she hung up, turned to me, and said, "That ought to do it."

Sure enough, as I found out later, an ambulance went screaming over to the Alrae Hotel in the middle of the night, two big attendants took poor Tom Green to the hospital by force, and they pumped his stomach. All the time they were dragging him down the hall to pump his stomach, he was shouting, "I know who did this! It was Judy Garland! I tell you, it was Judy Garland!" And the emergency team said, "There, there, now, it'll be all right. We're going to take good care of you."

My mother knew how to get rid of a man.

The same dramatic flair she'd used to get rid of Tom Green got us in and out of quite a few other fixes, too. By that time Joe and I had been in and out of more hotels than you could count. We might not have been born in a trunk, but we were more or less living out of one. It was kind of like, "If this is Tuesday, it must be the Plaza." There was one little catch: we were out of money, but the hotels still insisted on getting paid eventually. By that time nobody seemed to know where the money had gone; between the IRS, some crooked agents, my parents' old debts, and a string of canceled concerts, my mom was flat broke. My dad was, too. For years afterward there would be IRS agents knocking on the door in the middle of the night.

None of this deterred my mother from going first class. She had been going first class since she was thirteen, and she didn't know any other way to live. She had no idea what things cost or how to keep track of her money. Someone else had always done that for her, ever since she was a kid, and the result was that no matter how much she worked those last years, there was never any money. Either she spent it, or somebody else took it (she was a sitting duck for unscrupulous managers), yet she continued to live like we were in the land of Oz, first class all the way.

Every now and then, though, reality caught up with us in the form of an eviction notice.

One day I got a call at school to come home right away, and when I got to the hotel, I was told that my mother was trying to kill herself and that she wanted to see me. So I went up to her room, and there she was sitting on the window ledge with a horde of reporters with cameras gathered in the street below. I looked at her and said, "Mama, what's going on? Are you all right?"

And she looked at me and said, "I'm fine, honey. We can't pay the bill, so I'm threatening to jump out the window." Then she had me call the manager, the same guy who'd been threatening to evict us for nonpayment, and say, "How's it going to look for you when Dorothy jumps out your fucking window, huh?" My mother had a pretty rich vocabulary when she was angry. Of course, the manager caved in and let us stay. As soon as he did, my mother calmly climbed back into the room.

Sometimes she'd use the stunt as a diversion to give me and Joe time to pack up the suitcases and get our stuff out of the hotel so they wouldn't hold our things as collateral. One time a frustrated manager, afraid to evict her, refused to clean our room. After several days of this treatment, she was furious, so she stripped all the sheets off the bed and soaked them in the bathtub. Then she hung them all out the windows of this first class hotel and shut the windows to hold them in place, flapping in the wind like a tenement clothesline. In less than a minute our room was overrun with hotel personnel armed with fresh sheets and cleaning equipment, accompanied by the manager, who said, "Okay, okay, you win. I give up." Then she called her lawyer, told him she'd taken care of the problem, hung up, and said, "Haven't had this kind of service in years" (or something less printable) and screamed with laughter. She'd won again. She always did. It was astonishing. She most definitely didn't take no for an answer.

Meanwhile, she was going through people faster than hotels. And the sicker she got, the stranger the people surrounding her became. These were far more than fans: I called them the "Garland Freaks" because they worshiped my mother like a goddess, but they also poisoned her with that worship, catering to her every whim in the sickest possible ways. They didn't really care about her as a human being; to them she was a celluloid legend, and they wanted to be around her and soak up some of the aura so they could say, "Oh, yes, Judy is a close personal friend." If anything, they encouraged her sickness because they could identify with it, because it made them feel better about themselves, and because, to be blunt, they could profit from it. These hangers-on were invariably male and usually gay. Sometimes she found them, and sometimes they found her. For a long time she used them primarily for late night support. She would meet them practically anywhere after her concerts, and they would give her their phone numbers.

Late at night, when she couldn't sleep, she would start calling them and talk for hours. It was fine with me, because it meant I could get a little sleep now and then. When I got desperate for rest, I would call one of the less crazy ones and say, "Get over here now. She needs to talk." I learned to talk on the phone so that nobody could hear what I was saying, even someone standing right next to me. The person would come over to keep my mom company, and I would go to bed. My mother had to have someone with her all the time by then; if she was alone for even an hour, she would fall apart. She'd always had a fear of being alone, but by this time it had developed into a full-blown phobia.

I wasn't very tolerant of the people who surrounded my mother during those last years. A decade later I partied at Studio 54 with people who looked just like them, but I was in my mid-twenties by then. In 1965, long before the underground culture "came out," the press called these people the "Garland Freaks," and some of them really were bizarre. When some of them came through the door, Joe and I would just look at each other and roll our eyes as if to say, "Where does she find these guys?"

I didn't mind the late night visitors; in fact, I was grateful for the help. After a while, though, she started hiring some of these people. That was really a mistake since they had no credentials except admiration for my mother. By then my mom's health had degenerated so much that she was easy prey for anyone who came along. She would announce these people as "my new managers" and put them on salary. When the inevitable business disaster followed, she'd always end up calling my father and saying, "Please, Sid, you've got to help me straighten this out." Since he was still trying to rescue her, he'd always get sucked back into the whole mess. Sometimes, when my dad arrived in the middle of one of the ongoing disasters and found her surrounded by her newest "staff," he looked like he'd walked into a zoo. These weird-looking strangers would tell my father, "Look, Sid, this is what Judy wants." My father would swallow his resentment and try to fix the problem. Even Dad was wary of a personal relationship with my mom at that point, but he kept trying to bail her out professionally. When it came to work, he was always the one she ended up turning to, to "fix things." Somehow, though, things never seemed to stay fixed.

The male groupies who came and went from our apartment became the support system my mother depended on. Although most of them were gay, some of them made sexual advances to my mother. It was an odd situation, one that I never understood and sometimes resented. I didn't mind their being gay; they had every right to live their lives as they chose.

What I objected to was their trying to be something to my mother they never could be. In my opinion, a gay man has no business leading on a heterosexual woman. It seemed to me these "suitors" were lying to her, both explicitly and implicitly. These men owed it to my mother to be honest with her. They weren't.

Part of the fault lay with my mother. She had a powerful and often unhealthy ability to make-believe that things were what she wanted them to be, instead of what they were. She had been the heroine of too many romantic movies. In real life this meant that if a man told her she was beautiful and that he loved her, she immediately cast him as the romantic hero of some MGM musical. These men flattered her continually: "Judy, you're beautiful. Judy, you're the best. Don't ever let anybody tell you you're not." My mother had always needed a lot of praise, but by then, with her health declining and her fortieth birthday long past, her need for reassurance had grown enormously. The groupies surrounding her catered to that need, flattering her shamelessly when it wasn't good for her. She had always been willing to listen to the lie she wanted to hear, so it came as no surprise to me that she accepted whatever these men told her, however outrageous. I would look at some of the men who professed to be eligible bachelors, ready to fulfill all my mother's romantic fantasies, and think, "Please! You've got to be kidding!" Anyone with less need to believe them would have seen the obvious in a New York minute. Yet my mom, one of the most intelligent women I've ever known, was determined to be blind.

She actually thought she could find true love with these men, and my mom's definition of true love certainly never included bisexuality. Contrary to what's been written, she neither understood nor accepted her lovers' often ambivalent sexual orientations. I remember all too clearly the screaming accusations that filled our house in the middle of the night when she encountered one of their "indiscretions." I didn't hear the word "fag" from the kids at school: I heard it from my mother. When she was over-medicated and wanted to hurt me, she'd tell me that a boy I liked was a fag, too. To her, homosexuality within a relationship with her was a kind of betrayal.

My mother's attitude wasn't simple homophobia. Perhaps the reality of my mom's attraction to these men, and of her sense of betrayal when confronted with their lifestyle, went much deeper than she ever acknowledged. She certainly had powerful emotional ties to some gay and bisexual men. It is no coincidence that several of her relationships were with gay men. Some of the appeal is obvious: many gay men offer a sensitivity, an artistic passion, and an emotional openness that can be hard to find in straight men. Also, gay men have always been drawn to the arts, and thus my mother had been around them all her life. Part of their attraction for her was simply their availability and their common interests.

Another factor may have been her closeness to her beloved mentor, Roger Edens, who was already living a discreet gay life by the time my mother met him. Roger was an extraordinarily gifted musician, and the only man who ever came close to qualifying as a second father to my mom. He came into her life when she was only thirteen and remained in it until the day she died. Roger had my grandfather's handsome charm, soft Southern accent, and great warmth. After my grandfather died, Roger was the only person in my mother's life whom Mama completely trusted. Some of my happiest childhood memories are of Roger sweeping me up into his arms at social gatherings. Small wonder then that for my mother, some gay men became symbols of love and trust.

Of course, the catch was that it's one thing to have a gay man for a father-figure or best friend, and another thing entirely to try to make one into a husband. It took a long time for Liza to figure that out. My mother never figured it out, and the result was inevitably disastrous.

It was about this time that I got sick again. This time it wasn't just the exhaustion, though; I kept getting strep throat,

*Mama and me on stage together
at the Palace Theatre, 1967*
COURTESY JOHN FRICKE

*Backstage at the Palace Theatre (left)*
COURTESY JOHN FRICKE

*Joey, Mama, and me out on the town
(below left)*

Joey, me, Mama and John Bubbles sing 'Me and My Shadow' at the Palace Theatre, New York, 1967 COURTESY JOHN FRICKE

*Francesco Scavullo's cover
photo for* Interview
magazine *(right)* © FRANCESCO
SCAVULLO

*On assignment: modelling
Norma Kamali clothes
in New York (below)*
© DICK HALSTEAD

*A 'Girl For All Seasons' in*
Grease 2 *(above)*

*Another Francesco Scavullo
photo for* Interview magazine
*(opposite)* © FRANCESCO SCAVULLO

*Working with Sammy Davis, Jr., in Lake Tahoe* (right)

*Maureen Keefy (left), me and Allison (Muffy) Becker (right) as the Pink Ladies in* Grease 2. *Francesco Scavullo took the photo.* (below)

Joey, Liza and me at the Director's Guild re-release of the uncut version of A Star is Born *(opposite top)* © MICHAEL JACOBS

Jake, left, and me on our wedding day, London, 1977. Bill Wyman and Astrid Lundstrom sit behind us. *(opposite middle)*

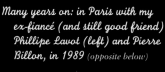

Many years on: in Paris with my ex-fiancé (and still good friend) Phillipe Lavot (left) and Pierre Billon, in 1989 *(opposite below)*

All grown up: Leslie Bogart, Lauren Bacall, me and Steve Bogart *(above)*

With Uncle Frank - my favourite male singer - backstage at the Royal Albert Hall in London, 1992. Maria Weisman took the photo *(below)*

*Visiting my dear friend Ryan White. Ryan was a true hero.*

and I couldn't seem to get well. I was sick all the time, and I was getting sicker. My dad was taking me to see Lester Coleman, my godfather, who was also a well-known ear, nose, and throat specialist. Lester kept telling me that I would never get well until I had my tonsils out, because they were seriously inflamed, but I steadfastly refused to have it done. I still had nightmare flashbacks of that doctor's needles and of my bout with appendicitis in England. Finally Lester refused to see me again unless I had the surgery, so my dad sat me down and talked to me until I reluctantly agreed.

When he took me to the hospital for the procedure, Lester met us there, and he was wonderful with me. He'd written a popular children's book about going to the hospital, and he was a strong believer in making kids feel involved in the medical process, so he did everything he could to make me comfortable. After I put on the hospital gown for the surgery, he took me by the hand and led me down the corridor to the operating room himself, hand in hand with me all the way. Then, still holding my hand, he led me around the operating room and showed me everything there, explaining exactly how they would do the procedure and what to expect. And when the technician came to give me the ether, he held my hand and talked to me while they put the mask over my face and I slowly drifted off.

So far, so good. It was a huge improvement over my appendectomy. But then I woke up. I'll never forget the sensation. I was alone in the recovery room, and the pain in my head and neck was overwhelming. I was shocked; no one had prepared me for that level of pain. My father was gone; my mother had had another of her crises, and he'd gone back to the hotel to take care of her. Lester was gone. It was just me. There was a child screaming down the hall, and when a nurse finally came to check on me, I whispered to ask what was wrong with the child. She said he'd just had his tonsils out. Then she explained that the reason I felt so bad was that I was fifteen, much older than the average tonsillectomy patient, and that the pain was just that much worse as a result. I was so hurt that Lester and my dad hadn't told me what to expect. They'd kept telling me that I would be fine, that it wouldn't hurt very much. I felt betrayed.

When they took me back to my dad's hotel four days later to recuperate, I continued to feel abandoned. Someone checked on me regularly, but everyone was too busy with my mom's latest crisis to pay very much attention to me. I remembered the way my parents had cared for me when I had the operation in England, and I bitterly reflected that getting older was a pretty lousy deal. The only funny part of the experience was that *Laugh In* was on TV my first night out of the hospital. I'd never seen anything like it, and in my half-drugged state I thought I was really losing it as I watched the actors popping their heads in and out of boxes while some silly blonde giggled. It was all very confusing. The only good thing about it all was that I got to sleep most of the time for two weeks. Sleep, blessed sleep. Most teenagers beg to stay out all night. I begged to go to bed. When I'd recovered completely, I reluctantly returned home to my mother.

In June 1968, just before my mother's forty-sixth birthday, the world fell apart again. Sirhan Sirhan shot Bobby Kennedy. Joe and I had gone down to Boston for my mother's concert, so we were with her when we found out. I remember my mom waking me up and saying, "Bobby passed away. He died." It was like Jack Kennedy all over again. I remembered Hyannis Port, and I thought, "Poor Ethel. Ten children and one on the way. What will they do?" My mother was beside herself with grief and with anger. She couldn't understand it. Why were people shooting all the Kennedys? Had the country gone mad? This time it was even worse for her because she was so unwell by then. I was worried sick about her. I couldn't help thinking, "This is going to be bad, really bad. I'm going to be up for days. There won't be any sleep."

I had no way of knowing that just over one year from that day, my mother would be dead, too.

There is a time of reckoning in all our lives, and for me the time had come to begin facing facts. The situation at home had become intolerable. I no longer had a home in the true sense of the word. We couldn't go on much longer the way we were. Even my mother knew that, at some level. Not long after Bobby Kennedy's death, she began to talk about going into a hospital to get well, if she could only get the money together. Mickey Rooney and some of her other friends started trying to raise enough money to help her. Mickey had seen her picture and been horrified by how bad she looked. She was only forty-six, but her body was wearing out.

My dad was trying to find a way to make sure Joe and I would be okay while things were being worked out. He'd decided by then that the best thing for him to do would be to move back to California with Patty, but he was broke, too, and he didn't have a home to take me and Joe to right then. My sister had recently come back to New York from a tour of Australia, so he asked her if Joe and I could stay with her and Peter for a while until he could work out something more permanent. They were glad to help, so Joe and I moved in with them while my mom made plans to go to the hospital and Dad tried to settle matters in the East. I still had a little hope left that if my mom just went into the hospital and stayed for a while, she would get better. After all, she had gotten better so many times before, even when everyone thought it was impossible. So I kept hoping. We all did.

That particular hope didn't last long. My mother never went into the hospital. Instead she moved in with various friends for a while, signed yet another team of managers, and tried to carry on.

Shortly after that my dad and Patty moved back to California. Joe went with him. Much as he loved our mother, he simply couldn't take it anymore. It had come to a head for him late one night when he was home alone with my mom. I don't remember why I wasn't there. Joe, who was thirteen at the time, was sitting in the living room in his pyjama bottoms, longing to go to bed, when Mama flew into one of her rages. She went way over the edge this time, and since Joe was the only one there, he became the target. She started chasing him around the apartment until, terrified, he bolted for the front door and out into the hall. Once there he raced for the stairs leading down to the lower stories. As he neared the landing, he glanced back and saw my mother standing in the doorway with a butcher's knife. When she raised her arm, Joe instinctively threw himself flat onto the landing. As he hit the ground, he felt the knife blade graze the top of his hair before it landed quivering in the wall next to him. Not pausing to look back, he hurtled down the remaining stairs and out into the night. It was 3 a.m., winter in New York, and he wasn't wearing either a shirt or shoes. Shaking with cold and shock, he picked his way barefooted through the snow to the hotel where my father was staying. It was only three or four blocks, but Joe said they were the longest three or four blocks of his life. Once there, my dad let him in without asking any questions. Joe didn't tell him why he'd come. The safety and warmth of Dad's room were all he wanted.

Joey was our mother's precious son. For most of his life my mother would have killed anyone who hurt a hair on his head. That night, she'd almost killed him herself, but she didn't know what she was doing. I don't think she even knew the phantom she was chasing that night was Joe. By then her brain was so seriously damaged that she lived part of the time in a nightmare where nothing made sense to her anymore.

I didn't go with my dad and Joe. I knew my mother would be coming back to the East from L.A., where she'd been staying most recently, and she would need someone to take care of her. I kept thinking, "In case she comes back to New York, in case she needs me here, I have to stay." I couldn't leave her by herself. So I stayed in New York alone, the sole survivor of our battered little family group. Even my father had given up, consumed by migraine headaches and crippling neuralgia. He'd taken his son and gone back to California to make a new home for us all. But I wasn't ready to go. Not quite yet.

My mom returned to the East, though not to New York, and did another concert. Remarkably enough, she had pulled herself together one more time and managed to give a truly remarkable performance. None of this meant much to me by then, though. I was simply trying to survive.

I decided to move in with a friend on Long Island named Joan Lee. I had got to know her at the Professional Children's School. She was a very sweet person with a wonderful family, and her parents (her father was the Marvel Comics artist Stan Lee) said I would be welcome to stay with them so I could have a little stability until I decided what to do next. My dad got me settled in with Joan before he left, and for a few weeks I got to live the life of a normal teenager. Joan's mother cooked our meals, and I ate and slept on a regular schedule. It had been years since I'd had anything like a structured family life. Except for brief stayovers at the Englund house with Cloris Leachman on Rockingham, I hadn't been part of a normal family since I was nine. It felt luxurious to keep regular hours, be free of the constant fear and chaos, and just act like a kid. I no longer jumped every time the phone rang. I could go to bed and sleep straight through the night. Those weeks at Joan's house were a real eye-opener. I'd forgotten what it was like to live like a normal person. I knew it wouldn't last forever, but I tried not to think about it. My moment of decision would come soon enough.

In a sense, my mother forced that decision on me herself. She didn't come back to New York; instead she called me at Joan's house one night and told me she wanted me to come up to Boston and be with her there. She was in bad shape on the phone, drugged and abusive. And somehow, the sound of her voice on the phone that day made something in me snap. I'd had nearly two months of food and sleep and peace, and when I heard that familiar voice raging at me over the phone, I just couldn't take it anymore. I couldn't face it one more time –

the rage, the fear, the chaos, the exhaustion. I couldn't do it. Something inside of me just shut down, and for the first time in my life, I said no to my mother. No, Mama, I'm not coming. No, Mama, I can't do it. Not this time. Not anymore. No, Mama. No.

My mother was beside herself with rage. She kept screaming and screaming at me, and I just stood there and held the phone, sobbing and shaking. Finally Mrs. Lee, who had come in and was standing next to me, couldn't take it any longer. She took the phone away from me and said to my mother, "Please don't scream at this child anymore. She's having a real tough time. Leave her alone." She stood up for me. God knows I needed someone to stand up for me at that moment.

Mrs. Lee hung up the phone, and as soon as she did, I called my dad in California and said, "Dad, I have to come live with you in California. I have to come to you right now, today, tonight. Please, Dad. Please send me a ticket. I have to come right now." I was crying so hard I could hardly talk. I was terrified and guilty about leaving my mom; but something deep inside, some survival instinct, told me that I had to leave, and I had to leave *now*, or I wasn't going to make it. I had to be with my dad and my brother, and I had to be safe. My father was wonderful; he kept trying to calm me down and said, "Of course, baby, of course you can live with me. I'll send you a ticket tonight. I'll have them leave it at Kennedy Airport. Mrs. Lee can take you to the plane, and I'll pick you up when you get here. You can come home tonight." So in the middle of a hot August night, Mrs. Lee drove me to the airport and put me on a plane for Los Angeles. On the way to the airport, I begged Mrs. Lee, "Please don't tell my mother where I am. Promise me you won't tell her." She promised.

A few hours later I landed at Los Angeles Airport and began a new life with my father and brother. One by one, my mother had worn us all out. She would soon wear herself out, too. Dad and Joey and I were a sad and emotionally ragged little band of refugees, and we held onto each other for dear life, but my father was determined to make a life for us. He was nearly as sick and exhausted as I was, but he thought, "I have these two children, and somebody has to take care of them. We have no other choice. Somebody has to be sane."

For all practical purposes, my mother wasn't herself anymore. God knows she was no longer the woman we all loved and remembered. I was almost sixteen years old by then, the same age my mother was when she first began taking the drugs that would eventually claim her life. For thirty years those chemicals had ravaged her body, gradually robbing her of her health, her dignity, her family, and finally her life.

A lot of very uncharitable things have been written about my mother's behavior in the last years before she died. I have no desire to add to them. What people don't realize is that the brain is an organ, too, and when the body is dying of the disease we call chemical dependency, the mind slowly dies with it. Drugs are a slow-acting poison, a thief that steals your life away piece by piece.

My mother wasn't rational those last years; if she had been, she would have been horrified by her own behavior. If we'd loved her less, we could have seen her fall from grace with infinitely less pain. If she'd loved *us* less, she couldn't have held onto the remnants of our relationship as long as she did. I've questioned many things about my mother over the years. The one thing I never questioned was whether or not she loved me. I knew she did. I knew that if she were well, she would want me to do whatever was necessary to keep myself safe.

Ten months later she would be gone. I would never see my mother alive again.

Chapter Twelve

# GOODBYE

A few months ago in London, I took a cab across town for an appointment. Shortly after we pulled into traffic, I noticed that the cabbie was looking at me carefully in the rear-view mirror. "Excuse me, miss," he said, "but aren't you Lorna Luft?" "Yes," I said, smiling pleasantly and thinking, "He must recognize me from one of my concerts." But then his expression changed in the old familiar way, and I thought, "Oh, no." His face contorted, and he actually began to cry. "Your mother, oh, your mother, miss. Such a tragedy, her death. What a tragic life she had." And he was off. For more than twenty minutes, as we inched our way through the London traffic, I remained trapped in the back seat listening for the umpteenth time as he retold the tabloid version of my mother's life. All I could think was, "Oh God, get me out of here." Several lifetimes later, when we reached my publicist's office, I shot out of the back seat, mumbled something polite to the cabbie, and tried to make my escape. No luck. He grabbed my hand, kissed it tearfully, and told me he'd wait and take me wherever I needed to go next. No amount of polite dissuasion on my part could make him leave.

I have no doubt that the poor cabbie meant to be kind and sympathetic. So do the endless number of my mother's fans who still approach me almost daily to remind me of her death. People are always telling me that I should appreciate the fans' devotion, that I must understand how much my mother means to them even thirty years after she died. On one level, I do. But there is a special cruelty to such devotion for the survivors of that death, for Joe and Liza and I lost a mother, not a legend. We had to deal not only with the overwhelming grief, but with the public exposure of that grief and the belief of thousands that they felt the same pain we did. They did not. They certainly did feel loss, but not the loss of a beloved parent.

For years we also lived with the peculiar and fearful vulnerability that comes from learning the most heart-wrenching family news from the public media. Those who live private lives are, at the very least, given the news of a parent's death privately by the authorities before the loved one's name is released publicly. Celebrities' children don't enjoy even that basic courtesy. Tracy Nelson learned about the unexpected death of her father, former teen idol Rick Nelson, from a television broadcast while she waited at an airport. Years before, when I was eleven and we were still living on Rockingham Drive, Joey and I heard a false report of our mother's death in Hong Kong as we were listening to music on the car radio. Our governess, Mrs. Chapman, had abruptly snapped off the radio and told us that we'd heard wrong, and fortunately, it turned out not to be true. But the anxiety remained. What will we hear next? And will it be true this time? The press goes on about the "people's right to know," and loyal fans line up offering condolences, but the reality is that all this attention simply multiplies the pain endlessly. Thirty years later, people still resent the fact that I needed to bury my mother to survive and get on with my own life. My sister would be a much healthier and happier person if people could look at her even once today and not see my mother's face looking back at them.

At fifteen, though, I understood none of this. At fifteen, the biggest part of me thought my mother would live forever.


When I landed at LAX on that hot August night in 1968, I began a whole new life. My father and Patty met me at the airport and took me home to my dad's apartment in Westwood for some R & R. I needed it. I was an emotional wreck, barely able to function. For the first few days I holed up and did almost nothing but cry and sleep. I was overwhelmed with guilt and grief and fear and anger. I had left my mother, my greatest childhood fear, the one thing I'd always said I would never do. "Oh no, Mama, we won't leave you. We would never leave you," my brother and I had told her that night in Vegas after my father had tried to take us. Six years later Joey and I were both gone, driven to leave by despair and a survival instinct that told us if we didn't leave, none of us was going to make it. The truth was, as I now realize, we hadn't left her. She had left us, taken away by an illness that first seduced her and then left her to die. None of us could have stopped it.

It didn't take long for my mother to find out where I'd gone, and at first it was horrendous. She called my father's apartment constantly, demanding to talk to me and my dad, alternately enraged and guilt-stricken. My dad knew I didn't need any more of this insanity, but he couldn't stop her from calling. Poor Patty was answering the phone: "No, Judy, he's not here right now. Not now, Judy, Lorna's in the shower . . . Lorna's asleep . . . Lorna's not here." After a week or two of this, my dad said, "Lorna, you're going to have to talk to her. She won't accept it from anyone else." I finally did. I told her I loved her but that I needed to live with Daddy for a while. I was just worn out.

After a time, the phone calls grew less frequent. She still called regularly, but no longer several times a day. And sometimes I called her. I missed her terribly, yet I dreaded those phone calls. She'd given up screaming and yelling at me. Instead she made me feel guilty. My mother could teach a class in guilt. She should have been Jewish. She was a brilliant actress, the master of the finely tuned emotion, and she could play you like a fiddle when she chose to. She knew exactly how to play me. "I understand what you've done. I understand that I'm not a good mother. It's no wonder you left me to live with your father. I deserve to be all alone." And on and on until I was sick to my stomach and in tears. It was really hard. Still, I couldn't go back. Every time I thought of the craziness and the rage and the days and weeks without sleep, my brain would just shut down. I couldn't live that way anymore.

Meanwhile, my mother was managing to survive. She did another benefit or two and some talk shows, and spent her nights clubbing so she wouldn't have to be home alone. In December she flew to London for a series of shows at the Talk of the Town and stayed to tour Europe for a while. In January of 1969, four months after I left, we got the news that she'd married a man named Mickey Deans in London. He was her fifth husband. Like everyone else in America, we heard about it on the evening news. I remember thinking, "Who the hell is Mickey Deans?" She hadn't said a word about him to Joe or me – none of the "I'm going to marry Uncle Mark" discussion that had preceded her marriage to Mark Herron – and we didn't have the faintest idea who he was. We found out later that he had been the manager at Arthur's, the first night club I'd gone to, three years before. He was younger than Mama. More than anything else, he was someone who happened to be there to fill the vacuum created by Joe's and my departure. My mom announced to the press assembled in London that at last, she'd found true love, someone who could just love her for who she really was. I just sighed and wondered how long this one would last. Mickey, of course, had no idea what he was getting into, and he certainly wasn't up to the task. He thought he'd married Dorothy, or at least Dorothy after the tornado, and he'd bought into my mother's recurring optimism that her life would still turn out like an MGM musical. He had no idea how to cope with a woman in the final stages of addiction. She was dying in front of his eyes, but he never realized it. He started planning a string of Judy Garland Theaters and hoped they'd have a successful partnership.

In late May Mickey and my mom returned to New York briefly to try to sell the Judy Garland Theaters idea. They stayed with Mama's old friend Charlie Cochran at his apartment there. My mother was feeling really sick by then, and Charlie was worried. He wanted to put her in the hospital, but she didn't want to go, and Mickey didn't think it was necessary. He took her to a doctor who suggested they switch her from Seconal to Thorazine, hoping her system would tolerate the Thorazine better. A few days later she celebrated her forty-seventh birthday resting in bed at Charlie Cochran's apartment.

Joe and Liza and I all called her for her birthday. She sounded tired, but otherwise she seemed better than she'd been in a while. She was always happy when she first had a new man in her life; it seemed to renew her optimism, and she usually cut back on her medication for a while after she began a new relationship. And it was her birthday, so she was getting lots of attention, and that always had a therapeutic effect. Ironically, the fact that her body was now failing rapidly had calmed her and temporarily reduced her need for stimulants. Her body was giving up on her, and she was content just to rest for a while. I was so relieved to find her sounding happy for a change. We had a good conversation – no guilt, no making me feel bad because I wasn't with her. She told me that she and Mickey were going back to London in a few days, and that she wanted me and Joe to come over for summer vacation there. We could stay with her all summer and come back to California when school started in the fall. We talked about making plans to fly over when school ended in two weeks, and then I wished her a happy birthday and said goodbye.

That was the last time I ever talked to her. Five days later she and Mickey flew back to London, and four days after that, some time early in the morning of Sunday, June 22, 1969, she died. Later I would be glad that our final conversation had been such a good one.

I got the news of her death from a friend's mother. I had gone to a concert that night with a good friend from school,

Jody Henderson. We'd gone to see the Young Rascals, a rock group from England that was popular at the time, and afterward I spent the night at Jody's house. We'd had a great time and come home exhausted shortly after midnight and gone to bed. I was sound asleep in the twin bed in Jody's room when, for no apparent reason, I woke up. It must have been about 3 a.m., the time of my mother's old night raids. I sat up in bed, wide awake, and looked around the room. It was dark and quiet. Everything seemed fine. I felt a little odd, as though I'd had a dream that I couldn't remember. Finally I thought, "Oh, well," and lay back down again. A few minutes later I drifted back to sleep.

The next morning I woke up at about nine and went into the kitchen. Jody and her sister and her mom were all in there, sitting around the kitchen table, and when I walked in, the room got very quiet. I was still excited about the concert the night before, so I just said, "Wasn't the concert fun?" and started talking about it, but nobody answered. Finally there was a silence, and then Jody's mother said, "Lorna, I have to tell you something very important." As soon as she said it, Jody and her sister both burst into tears, and I thought, "No. Whatever it is, I don't want to hear this." Then Jody's mom came over to me, took both of my hands in hers, and looking gently into my face, said, "Lorna, your mom passed away last night." I later found out Jody's mother had heard the news on the radio and tried to call my dad to find out if it was true. After a couple of hours of failing to reach him, she became worried that I'd hear the news on the radio when I got up. She wanted to spare me that, so she told me herself.

I felt like someone had kicked me in the stomach. I couldn't breathe. I began to shake my head. "No, no, it isn't true. You're wrong. It isn't true." I was shuddering like a leaf, but I kept remembering Mrs. Chapman turning off the radio when they said my mother had died in Hong Kong, so I said, "You've got it wrong." And then, "Where's my dad? I want to talk to my dad."

I went straight to the phone and started calling, but no one answered. I later found out that he'd taken the phone off the hook the day before because he was getting so many calls from collection agents. I dialed and dialed, but I couldn't get through. Meanwhile, my mind was racing. Where was Joey? I knew he'd gone to spend the night with a friend, too. What friend? Where was he? Had he heard? I thought about my sister and called her in New York, but there was no answer there, either. I later found out that Liza was trying to get a hold of my dad, too, to make sure that Joe and I didn't get the news on TV. Mickey Deans had called her from London to tell her, and she'd been calling us ever since. It felt like an ongoing bad dream. None of us could find each other.

I called and called and called, for over an hour, all the while fearing someone would turn on the radio or TV. I didn't want to hear what they might say. By this time panic was overwhelming me, and I couldn't control it. Finally I got through to my dad. Someone had just gotten a hold of him to tell him the news. The first thing I said was, "Dad, is it true?"

Instead of answering, he just very quietly said, "Honey, you'd better come home." Then I knew. I was still trying to deny it, but I knew. Jody's mom put me in the car and took me home.

I ran through the front door, where Joey and my dad were waiting for me. By then I'd convinced myself that I shouldn't get hysterical, that it was probably all a mistake, that she'd overdosed again but they'd been able to revive her by now, like they always had in the past. One look at my father's face destroyed that last bit of hope. There was such pain in his face, and in his voice when he spoke to me. Then, at last, I knew.

From that moment on it was one long, endless nightmare. Liza finally got through to us and said that they were flying Mama's body back over to New York for the funeral as soon as the autopsy was complete in London. She and Mickey and Kay Thompson, the performer and songwriter, who was one of our oldest friends, were already making plans for the funeral. Nobody ever asked me or Joe what we wanted. I don't think they meant to be cruel; we were just "the kids," and I'm sure they were trying to spare us pain. But it hurt nonetheless. We felt so left out, as though we didn't really belong – Judy Garland's "other daughter" and Sid Luft's son, as the press referred to us. We probably would have agreed to whatever Liza and the others thought best, but we just wanted to be asked.

The phone rang incessantly – Liza and Kay with funeral arrangements, friends and relatives, the sympathetic and the curious. And of course, the press, who descended like vultures around the body, all hoping for a scoop or some juicy details. They camped at our front door. My mother had died of an apparent overdose, and the rumor had already started to circulate that it was a suicide. I felt like some of them hoped it was suicide; after all, it would make such a great headline – you know, "Has-Been Singer Dies of Overdose" or "Little Judy Ends It All," like she was still twelve years old. It infuriated me. She wasn't twelve years old, she sure never thought of herself as a has-been, and most important of all, she hadn't committed suicide. I knew it, even before the autopsy reports confirmed it.

My mother would never, ever have killed herself, certainly not in that way. The only people who thought she might were the people who didn't know her very well. Liza and Joe and my dad and I, we knew she hadn't. She wouldn't. In spite of her well-publicized reputation for suicide attempts, we never considered her a suicide risk. All of her previous "attempts" had been accidental overdoses, cries for help and attention, or, on occasion, simply ploys to get us all out of a fix. If she had really wanted to die, she would certainly have succeeded many times over. She simply wasn't the type. People who kill themselves succumb to despair, desperation, or self-hatred. In sharp contrast, my mother remained the eternal optimist at heart, in spite of her binges of self-pity, and I have no doubt that she died fully expecting yet another miraculous comeback and triumph. My mom was a phoenix who always expected to rise again from the ashes of her latest disaster. And in spite of her self-doubts, she had a very strong sense of who she was. She had self-worth. She loved being Judy Garland. Did she secretly long to be Frances Gumm Somebody, Minnesota housewife? Are you kidding? She'd have run off with a vaudeville troupe just like my grandfather did.

Most important of all, though, she would never, ever have committed suicide because she had us – me and Joe and Liza. Maybe she wasn't much of a mother to us those last few years, but it wasn't because she didn't try, and it certainly wasn't because she didn't care. People sometimes look at us incredulously when we say that, but it's true. We knew she would never willingly leave us. The fact that all three of us dismissed that possibility without a second thought speaks volumes.

For a long time after I learned what killed her, I blamed Mickey Deans. Everyone close to my mother knew that she required careful watching. I'd been monitoring her medication myself since I was thirteen, and everybody knew to check on her regularly to make sure she was all right. Later, after the coroner had found Seconal in her bloodstream and determined that an accidental overdose had killed her, we found out that a prescription for Seconal had been filled out for her the day she died. She'd apparently taken her normal dose, then sometime during the night she'd gotten up, half asleep, gone to the bathroom, and swallowed several more of the capsules. She passed out there in the bathroom and never woke up. It took me a very long time to stop blaming anyone in particular and to realize that if it hadn't been that night, it would have been another one. It was inevitable. Mostly, though, I blamed myself – not because I wasn't there that night, but because I wasn't there that year. Why wasn't I with her? Why hadn't I gone over sooner? I could have saved her; I know I could. I kept on thinking of all the things I had learned to do and hadn't done those final months. I remembered the countless times my father or I had searched her clothes, unlocked doors, doled out medicine, sugared pills, and watched over her to make sure she stayed safely in bed all night. I'd learned to take a thousand precautions; I knew an endless number of ways to avoid disaster. If I'd been with her, she never would have had access to the Seconals. If I'd been there, I would never have let her wander around alone at night. I wouldn't have let her lock the bathroom door. I should have been there. All the hard lessons of survival I'd learned in the last year vanished in the face of my mother's death. Somewhere deep in my heart, I'd expected her to get by somehow. Somehow, I hadn't really thought she'd die.

It was still hard to believe. Everything around me had collapsed into chaos: the funeral arrangements, the visitors, the reporters, and I couldn't accept what was happening. When things got out of hand, I'd think, "I know; I'll call Mama and ask her what she wants us to do," and then it would hit me all over again. I was in shock. I kept wanting to pick up the phone and call her, but she wasn't there. There would be no voice at the other end of the line. There never would be. I almost welcomed the chaos after a while. When it stopped for a moment, in the quiet times, the pain would overwhelm me. My dad was struggling to hold himself together, to cope with all the details and keep me and Joe from falling apart. Liza and Kay were giving him orders over the phone, and he had to accept whatever they told him because he no longer had any right to make decisions. He was just "the ex-husband." Mickey Deans, a comparative stranger to whom my mother had only been married five months, got to decide everything, although Liza and Kay made suggestions. It was bitterly painful for my father. Every little while, I'd say, "Are you okay, Dad?" and he'd try to act as though he were.

Two days later we flew to New York and were taken to someone's apartment. Liza and Peter and the others were all there. That's when we were told that it would be an open casket funeral. I kept thinking, "What are you doing? Mama would hate everybody staring at her like that. You can't do that!" But they could. A huge event had been planned, one that over thirty-five thousand people eventually showed up for, and an endless procession of onlookers would file past that open casket. I was horrified. It seemed like a kind of violation. Before things went any further, before those thousands of people lined up to see my mother's body, I wanted to see her first. So I said, "I want to go see her." And everyone objected all at once, saying, "No, you don't; you don't want to do that." And I got really angry then. I was sick and tired of being told what to do. I said, "Don't tell me what I want. I want to go. I want to see Mama." Nobody was going to tell me I couldn't see my mother one last time.

Then my dad said, "If you're going to go, I'm going with you." And Liza said, "I'd better go, too." And then Joey said, "I just, I just can't." I was glad he didn't want to, but I couldn't believe the others would let Mama be buried without seeing her one more time. We called ahead to Frank E. Campbell Funeral Chapel to tell them we were coming so they'd close the place off, and then Dad and Liza and I got in the limo that took us to the funeral home. As we approached the mortuary, I looked up and saw thousands of people jamming the streets. I panicked at the sight of them and said, "Please, there's got to be another door. I don't want to go in there." The funeral director led us through a private entrance and into the main room. The place was empty. He had cleared it out for us.

When I saw my mother's coffin there in the center of the room, I got really scared. I backed up, and for a moment I wanted to turn around and go out again. But I couldn't. I had to see her one more time.

After a moment's hesitation, I began inching slowly toward the open casket. I had never seen a deceased person before, except on television, and I didn't know what to expect. My dad followed along next to me. My sister followed behind, even more slowly. We all three crept to the side of the coffin and looked inside. There lay a tiny person in a gray dress on a bed of yellow roses. The first thing that went through my mind when I saw her was, "Oh, they've made a mistake. That's not her." I didn't recognize her. I could find no trace of the beautiful face I had watched in the make-up mirror as a child. I looked at the tiny, emaciated body, and then I noticed her hands. When I saw her hands, I knew. Those were my mother's hands. And looking down at them, it hit me at last.

My father was standing next to me on one side, and as I started to cry, he put his arms around me. And then he started to cry, too. He stood there looking at her, sobbing as if his heart would break, and I was stunned. I had never seen my father cry. We kept trying to comfort each other, but we were both too caught up in our own pain to do the other much good. We must have stayed there together about ten minutes, and then suddenly I wanted to go. I had to get out of there. It was all becoming surreal.

The three of us went back out through the private entrance and climbed into the rear seat of the limo, Liza first and then me in the middle between her and my dad. The driver pulled away from the curb, and when he did, my dad just disintegrated. I don't know exactly why it happened at that particular moment; maybe it was leaving her behind that final time, but he said, "She always did break me up" and he gave way to convulsive sobs. I'd never seen that kind of grief before, and I felt helpless. I put my arms around him and held him like a child as he collapsed into them. It was the worst moment of my life. My mother lay in a box in that terrible place, and my father, the strongest man in the world, the one person who'd always kept me safe, was beside himself with grief in my arms. Liza started to sob, too, and I kept thinking, "What will happen to me now? Who will take care of me?" I was so scared. We all three put our arms around each other and cried uncontrollably. We were beyond comfort; the only thing we could share with each other was our grief. We'd been holding ourselves together for days, years really, and in that moment it all came crashing down on us.

We went back to the apartment, and it was like going back to the circus, with phones ringing off the hook and the press everywhere. We pulled ourselves together and carried on. What else was there to do?

The funeral was the next day. I remember that I didn't have anything appropriate to wear, so someone went out and bought me a long navy blue dress and a big hat. It was a hot New York day at the end of June, and the limo could hardly get through the streets to the funeral parlor because there were so many thousands of people there. I was used to crowds; I'd gone to my mother's biggest outdoor concerts, but I'd never seen anything like the crowds that day. They were everywhere; some of them had even brought along little record players and were playing my mother's recordings. Everywhere I looked out the windows of the limo, there were faces, thousands of them. We pulled up to the side door, and I was the first one out of the car. I took Liza's hand to lead the way in, and she grabbed hold of Joey, but halfway up the entrance carpet I lost hold of Liza's hand when she slowed down for Joe. There's a clip of me on an old newsreel turning around at that moment to wait for Liza, then grabbing her firmly by the hand and waiting for her to get a good grip on Joe. Joey, his sweet little face sober and pinched, turns around to take hold of my father's hand, and then I turn back to the entrance door and lead us all in, hand in hand like a human chain. We all look pale as ghosts and determined to be brave.

Once inside, someone led us into the "family section," the private area reserved for family and close friends. I remember wanting to turn around and look at the audience to see who was there, but I didn't. It would have seemed rude. The service itself was small and private and didn't last long. Father Peter Delaney, my mother's old friend, officiated, and James Mason, Mama's costar in A Star Is Born, gave the eulogy. Liza had originally wanted Mickey Rooney, but we were all afraid

Mickey would fall apart and never make it through the eulogy. The family sat in the front row – me and Liza and Joe and Sid, and I think Mickey Deans at the other end of the row; and Kay Thompson sat behind us with my godparents, Lester and Felicia Coleman. It was so hot, and I was getting dizzy. The coffin had been closed and covered with a huge blanket of the most beautiful yellow roses I'd ever seen, and the smell of the flowers only made me dizzier. After the eulogy they made us all sing "The Battle Hymn of the Republic," just as my mother had sung it when Jack Kennedy died. Kay Thompson nudged us and whispered, "Sing! Sing!" I suppose she thought my mother would have wanted us to. All I remember thinking was, "Why are they making us do this?" Then they had us all stand up as they lifted the coffin under its veil of yellow roses to carry it back down the aisle. Suddenly, I was afraid I was going to faint. The stress and the heat overwhelmed me, and I felt my knees buckle. Kay Thompson caught me from behind and literally held me up as they carried the coffin down the aisle.

Then they took us back into a side room, and I was shaking uncontrollably. I couldn't stop. Felicia Coleman had helped me out, and I remember saying to her, "Please, I have to have something. Please, I can't stand it. You have to give me something."

Felicia turned to her husband and said, "Lester, can't we give this child some medicine to calm her down? I really think she needs something."

But Lester said, "She'll be all right. I don't want to give her anything." At the time I thought he was being cold-hearted, but in retrospect, I know he was probably right. I think that, considering my genetics, he was really afraid to give me anything. And I did manage to pull myself together again and put on a brave face for the crowds outside. That's the odd part of losing such a famous parent. I spent much of my time that week trying to make total strangers feel better.

I didn't go to the graveside. We all went back to Liza's

apartment. But not directly to the apartment. First Mickey Deans had a little errand to do. In a move that takes my breath away to this very day, Mickey had scheduled a meeting and wanted me to go along. I hardly knew the man, but Liza had said, "Why don't you go with Mickey, then, and we'll all meet back at my apartment." I said "Okay," and we got in a car and drove to a nearby office building and went up a few floors and into a big office. I was too emotionally exhausted to pay any attention to where we were. A few minutes later a man came in, and Mickey introduced me to him: "I wanted you to meet Lorna. Lorna, this is Mr. So and So." I mechanically shook hands and said something polite and then just sat there in a daze in my funeral dress and hat while Mickey and the other man discussed some sort of business deal. I didn't pay attention. Then we left. Months later someone told me the other man may have been a publisher, and that Mickey might have arranged to stop by on the way back from my mother's funeral to cut a deal on a Judy Garland biography. I don't know if it was true, but his book did come out a couple of years later under the title *Weep No More, My Lady*. Needless to say, I didn't buy a copy.

Mickey Deans. What a putz.

After our meeting with the publisher and Mickey's five minutes of fame, we went back to Liza's apartment and the revolving door. The TV and radio were on all day, and every station seemed to be playing my mom's music. They kept showing clips from *The Wizard of Oz* on television, and several of the newscasters did tributes to her. All in all, the news handled it very nicely. They showed the clip of the coffin being carried in over and over, and of us arriving at the funeral, but they were all very kind and respectful. I didn't mind that part, but the radio really bothered me. All day long and into the evening they kept playing her songs over and over until I could hardly stand it. Everywhere I went, I could hear her voice. Late in the day Peter Allen's sister Lynne put on my mother's Carnegie Hall record, and I remember shouting, "Take it off. Please, just take it off. I can't keep listening to that."

But for some reason I still don't understand, she said, "No, I won't take it off. You must listen to this."

When she said that, I really went off and started screaming at her, "Why is everyone doing this? Why do you keep forcing me to listen to her? Why can't you just leave me alone?" But instead of taking the record off, Lynne just turned the volume up so we could hear it above my shouting. Angry and desperate to escape the sound, I went into the other room and slammed the door.

That night Liza came to me and asked me if I'd go with her and Mickey to see a friend of his out on Long Island and go swimming. It was hot, and Mickey didn't want to go alone, and she thought it might be nice to get out of the apartment for a while. My dad had already gone back to another apartment with Joe. By then I was more than glad to get away from the crowd, even with Mickey Deans, so I said I'd go, and the three of us climbed in Mickey's car and headed for the country. It was a beautiful night, the sky filled with stars, and the air felt good on my face. As we drove, Liza pointed out the window at a particularly bright star and said, "Look, Lorna, it's Mama." I looked where she was pointing, and for the first time that day, I felt a moment of peace. I was longing for some silence by then, but there was still no escaping the sound of my mother's voice. Mickey kept the radio tuned to it all the way out.

When we got to the friend's house, we all sort of went our separate ways for a while. I was out in the back yard for a few minutes when suddenly I heard the strangest sound, like kids screaming, except not quite. It sounded so odd that I began to think the strain of the last few days was getting to me and that I was hearing things. But when the sound continued, I finally went to the owner and asked him, "What's that noise?" Liza had heard it, too, and she couldn't identify it, either. He said that he'd been an animal trainer for the circus when he was younger, and that he still had some of his favorite animals living there in the basement of his house. Would we like to see them?

Liza and I looked at each other and said, "Sure."

So he led us down the basement stairs and turned on the light, and there in cages all over the room sat these chimps. Their cages were roomy and clean, not like something out of a horror movie, and the chimps looked up cheerfully as we came into the room. They were incredibly cute. Liza and I took one look at each other and burst out laughing. We laughed so hard we nearly fell down. All I could think was, "This is perfect, just perfect," and Liza said, "Wouldn't Mama just love this?" Nobody ever had a better sense of the ridiculous, or enjoyed a good story more, than my mother. The chimps were just the cherry on the sundae of that strangest of days. We laughed until we were sick and then, wiping tears of laughter from our eyes, told Mickey it was time to go home. We all got in the car and drove back to the city.

It wasn't until we reached Manhattan and someone took me back to my dad and Joe that I finally escaped all the chaos of that endless day. The silence was blessed, and it felt so good to settle down in the sanity of my father and brother's presence. We were all exhausted. I didn't tell my dad about the chimps. That could wait until another time.

It was very late by the time I got to bed. For hours the only thing I had wanted was to be alone in a safe place. It's hard to explain, but I knew that only by being alone could I be with my mother again, just for a moment. Only once during that terrible twenty-four hours had I felt her presence. I'd gone out into the darkness of the back yard at Long Island to be by myself for a moment and escape into the silence. It was a beautiful warm evening, and as I looked up at the stars I began talking to my mother. It was so hard. And as I started to cry, suddenly I could feel her presence there next to me in the dark, comforting me. And it felt so good. I needed her so much. I remember that moment when I read those horrendous tabloid stories about my mother's ghost haunting my sister, taunting her and pushing her to collapse. I have felt my mother's presence more than once since her death. So have my brother and sister. If my mother were really haunting Liza, it would only be to remind her of how very much she loves her. That night, in the darkness of the back yard at that ridiculous house, I felt her soothing me the same way she'd held me in her arms when I was a little girl.

I cried myself to sleep that night and for many weeks after. I missed my mother so much. I was sixteen years old, the same age my mom had been when she played Dorothy Gale, and I would never see her again.

Goodbye, Mama. I will miss you for the rest of my life.

# Chapter Thirteen

# ON MY OWN

There's an old proverb that says you should be careful what you wish for, because you just might get it. I was about to discover how true that was.

We stayed in New York for a week or two after my mother's funeral, and then we returned home – me, Sid, Joey, and Patty – and settled into my dad's apartment in West Los Angeles for good. At long last, I began the life I had longed for since I was eleven years old. I enrolled in Palisades High as a junior and began the normal teenage routine of school, homework, and dances in the gym on Friday nights. Patty, who for all practical purposes was already my stepmother (though my dad took his time about marrying her), took me and Joe to school every morning and picked us up every afternoon. We had regular meals, an orderly house, and eight hours of sleep every night. Life couldn't have been more normal. We were practically the Brady Bunch. Peace, at long last.

I hated it.

I spent every hour planning my escape.

That's the problem with continual chaos. It's exhausting, sometimes frightening, like riding on a roller-coaster blind-folded. The catch is that it's also very exciting and very addictive. I had grown accustomed to a life of high drama, or at least melodrama. For years I had survived on the daily adrenaline rush that came from coping with my mother, never knowing when the next crisis would break. I had also become accustomed to the life of a celebrity, always being in the big middle of everything, clubbing with the rich and famous every night, staying up until all hours. The quiet domestic life in which I now found myself was as foreign to me as the old *Leave It To Beaver* reruns that still aired on afternoon television. It seemed old-fashioned and deadly dull. School? School was the place you met your friends, signed out for auditions, and then took off for the day. Study? You must be kidding.

And, of course, I was sixteen years old, drowning in hormones, trying to cope with life in the slow lane and a stepmother who was only ten years older than I was. It didn't help that Patty was beautiful – tall, blond, and gorgeous, with a full bust and hips that were still just a distant dream for me. At sixteen I was all legs, skinny as a rail, with barely a ripple under the bodice of my trendy clothes and hips that wouldn't hold up my hot pants unless they were skin tight. Just looking at Patty made me feel inadequate. One day I got so frustrated that I decided to pad my chest and hips before I went out so I would look more "womanly." I can still remember my father's face when I walked out with my new curves stuffed into place. Far from being impressed, he looked at me incredulously and said, "Are you kidding?" I, of course, burst into tears and went running back to my room. No one understood me. No one ever does understand you when you're sixteen.

Worst of all, of course, I missed my mother. Sometimes I missed her so much I could hardly stand it, and the fact that I couldn't let my feelings show made everything that much worse. At school everyone stared at me for weeks after her death, and I felt like some kind of freak. They would point and whisper everywhere I went. I used to think, "They stared at me when she was alive, and now they stare at me because she's dead. Isn't it ever going to stop?" I couldn't cry at home because it would upset my brother. Besides, I didn't want to upset Dad, who looked as sad as I felt most of the time.

When I went out in public, strangers would come up to me almost daily, fall on my shoulder crying, and say things like, "We know how you feel. We loved her, too." And a lot of times, it would make me mad. I'd say to myself, "You don't know how I feel. You have no idea how I feel. You didn't lose *your* mother. You didn't even know her." But then I would feel guilty and say to myself, "What are you thinking? God, you're such a bitch," and I would try to make them feel better. After months of that kind of thing, though, I got to the point I could hardly stand it, and I just sort of shut down. I wouldn't talk about it, to anyone; I didn't want even to think about it. I was like that Simon and Garfunkel lyric, "I am a rock; I am an island." When someone tried to talk to me about my mother's death, I would turn stone cold. Sometimes I'd even walk away. I can imagine what people must have thought of me: "Strange girl. Hard as a rock. Doesn't even care about her own mother's death." But it was the only way I could survive. I was a kid, and emotionally I was on overload.

The death of my friends, Princess Diana and Dodi Fayed, brought a sense of some of that pain back. Prince William and Prince Harry are almost the same ages Joe and I were when our mother died, and the sight of their solemn young faces seemed eerily familiar – my mother's death, the flowers, the processions, the international television coverage. My mother's death wasn't as public as their mother's, but the similarities are striking. I understand some of the pain they must feel, for everywhere they look, they see their mother's image; everywhere they go, someone is watching for their reaction. It is an endless, agonizing process. It is always a terrible thing for a child to lose a mother. It is even harder when you're never left alone to grieve.

I could never get away from my mother's passing. Every time I walked into a drug store for months afterward, I would see Mama's face staring back at me from a magazine cover. When I went home and turned on the TV for escape, one of her movies would be playing. In the months following her death, every station in LA ran her movies as a tribute, everything from the Andy Hardy series to *Judgment at Nuremburg*.

For a long time it seemed like *The Million Dollar Movie* on TV was always one of my mom's. It was endless. I soon came to dread the sight of her on television, cringe at the sound of her voice on tape. It was years before I could listen to her sing again without pain. I just wanted to be left alone to heal.

The only time I had any sense of privacy was at night. Out of sight of staring strangers and the sympathetic but often obtrusive gaze of my new stepmother, I could crawl under the covers and be a little girl again. For weeks after the funeral I cried myself to sleep. I missed my mother's touch, I missed the laughter and the insanely funny stories she used to tell, and most of all I missed the fact that I couldn't just pick up a phone and hear her voice on the other end. At the same time I was still shell-shocked from my years of combat duty at my mother's side. I didn't sleep well, especially in the early hours of the morning, and when the phone rang unexpectedly I still jumped as though I'd been shot, expecting to hear her screaming at me from the receiver because I'd let her down again. That reaction went on for years. I used to wonder if I'd ever hear the phone ring without twitching. It was all very confusing.

Sometimes, though, I would feel her presence with me when I was alone at night, and in those moments she was never screaming at me. She was just loving me, holding me close to comfort me the way she had when I was small. Those were the precious moments. I hung onto them with all my might.

Inevitably, the target of all this pent-up frustration and resentment was Patty Hemingway. Poor Patty. My father had half-heartedly tried to make her a star, but her career never really got off the ground. For one thing, my dad was still too caught up in my mom's career (not to mention her personal life) to have much energy left over for anyone else. Patty was a good soul, kind-hearted and loyal to my father in spite of the fact that he would have dropped her in a second if he and my mother had gotten back together.

She was good to all three of us from the beginning, and

after my mother's death she heroically launched into the task of taking care of my dad and two very confused stepchildren. Naturally, I didn't appreciate any of her good qualities at the time; I just wanted her to go away so I could have my father all to myself. (Remember baby Joey? I was never very good at sharing my parents!) As far as I was concerned, I had just lost my mother, and now Patty was trying to take away my dad. I was bound and determined to drive her out of the house, and it's a miracle I didn't. For a long time my every waking moment was devoted to driving her crazy. If something annoyed her, I made sure to do it. She didn't like me to wear her clothes, especially without asking, so every time she left the house, I put on something of hers. When she'd ask me about it, I'd look her in the face and say, "So what? It was hanging in the closet. It's not like *you* were wearing it." If she said to me, "Please put that away," I'd throw it on the floor, point at it, and say, "What, this?" In those days I'd have set my hair on fire just to irritate her. I never did anything really drastic, although I thought about it. I was more like dripping water with attitude, twenty-four hours a day.

One evening I intentionally baited her until she completely lost her temper, purposely staging the scene for my father's benefit. I went flying at her, and by the time my father walked in the kitchen door, Patty had me pinned to the floor, trying to subdue me. It was a real picture for my father, just as I'd intended. I used it as a photo op to say, "See, Dad? She's so mean to me. You have to make her go away!" (I hadn't watched my mother stage scenes all those years for nothing!) One night at dinner Patty and I screamed at each other until my father burst out in exasperation, "I can't stand any more of this! One of you has to go!" And Patty and I both yelled in unison, "It's not going to be me!" We were equally stubborn.

Luckily for all of us, Patty never tried to take my mother's place with me and Joe. For one thing, she was too young, and for another, she knew better. The truly absurd part of the situation is that throughout those early months of living together, my dad tried to keep up the pretense that he and Patty were "just friends." He even made up a bed on the couch every night and pretended that they slept separately. When I'd get up early and see Patty coming out of his room, I'd think, "Oh right, Dad, just friends. Give me a break!" I thought the whole charade was ridiculous, but my dad was still the old-fashioned father who didn't want his little girl to know he was sleeping with someone he wasn't married to. After all that time, and everything we'd been through, there was a part of him that still wanted to shelter me.

I spent every waking moment fantasizing about leaving California and going back to New York, to my friends, to the clubs, to my sister, to the lifestyle I'd grown accustomed to. I thought my schoolmates in California were so out of it, so "unhip." I wanted to be back in the Village with the cool people. I wanted to be anywhere but in school.

Ironically, though, it turned out to be school that eventually got me out of LA for good. Patty was tired of the long drive twice daily from Los Angeles to my school in Pacific Palisades (when I didn't play hooky and refuse to go), so my dad decided to transfer me to the local school, University High in West Los Angeles. The new school was slightly more interesting than Pali High – a little less white bread, a little more ethnic and hip – but more importantly, it had an excellent music program. By that time I hadn't sung in a long while, not since my days performing in my mom's show, but at Uni High I started singing again. The music teacher there was Mr. McGruter, and he got me started singing with the band. I would come in a couple of hours a day and practice with the band, and it was fun. I liked it, and I started learning more about music and working on my performing skills. Somebody heard me singing with the band, and this led to an offer to sing on the *Merv Griffin Show*, which was taped in LA at the time. Mr. McGruter did some arrangements for me and helped me rehearse, and my dad took me to Beverly Hills and got me a pink and burgundy velvet pants outfit, and I got to sing on

TV. Now this was more like it. For the first time in a long while, I was starting to enjoy myself again.

The *Merv Griffin Show* turned out to be only the beginning. Michael Butler, who was producing the road company of *Hair*, called and asked me to audition for the show. Auditions were being held in LA for the San Francisco production, so I went down to the Aquarius Theater on Hollywood and Vine and tried out, along with several hundred other girls. Some of the girls were really good, especially one girl named Delores, but I was happy with my own audition, too. I sang well, and I had a great time. Afterward I went back to school and pretty much forgot about the whole thing. I wasn't expecting to get the role, and I had another TV singing appearance lined up, so I felt fine about the way things were going. What I didn't know until many years later was that I had, in fact, gotten the part in *Hair*. Sid eventually told me that the producers had called to tell him I had the part, but he hadn't told me because he didn't want me leaving home at sixteen to perform, especially in a show that required me to do nude scenes onstage. I wasn't mad at him; I wouldn't have wanted to do the nude scenes, either, but I did wish he'd told me. It would have been a real boost to my self-confidence just to know that I'd gotten the role.

It was only six months later, during the beginning of senior year at Uni High, that I got what seemed like my big break. I was asked to audition for *Lolita, My Love*, a new Broadway musical based on the Nabokov novel. The show, produced by Norman Twain, featured a score by Alan Jay Lerner and lyrics by John Barry. Tito Capobianco, a crazy opera director, staged it. I auditioned in LA for the part of Lolita's best friend (I was a skinny brunette, not the buxom little blonde they needed for the title role). When they called to tell me I'd gotten the part, I was so excited I could hardly contain myself. I couldn't believe it – Broadway! My dream come true.

My dad agreed to let me take the part, booked me into the Barbizon Hotel for Women in New York, and helped me make all the arrangements. My moment had finally come. I was escaping Los Angeles and the prison of school and home-work, and I was leaving for New York and the lights of Broadway. Like two generations before me, I was packing my bags and heading across a continent to find my destiny in show business. I wasn't afraid. After all, what could go wrong?

I don't know what was in my father's mind as he drove me to L.A. airport for my flight to New York. He was happy for me; this was my dream, and he knew it. But looking back, I know it must also have been very hard for him. His little girl was leaving home alone, facing all the challenges of the toughest of businesses in the toughest of cities, and somewhere in the back of his mind, he must have been remembering all the things my mother had gone through walking down this same path. With the ignorant optimism of youth, though, I was blissfully confident, certain I wouldn't be repeating my parents' mistakes, exhilarated by the prospect of what lay before me. My family and friends saw me off at the airport terminal, and I boarded the plane clutching my rehearsal schedule and counting the minutes until I landed in the city of my dreams. When the plane touched down in New York, I was eighteen, not much older than my mom had been when she went there with Mickey Rooney on her first publicity tour. It was the most exciting day of my life.

Norman Twain, the producer, was waiting to greet me at the terminal and took me over to baggage claim to wait for my luggage. As we waited, he chatted about the show and then casually mentioned that one of the *Lolita* cast members had been fired earlier that day. He said it off-handedly, as if it were just another bit of gossip. For the first time a tiny warning bell rang in the back of my mind, and I said anxiously, "But that couldn't happen to me, could it?"

He replied, "Oh, no. I mean, I don't think so. Why would it?" Temporarily reassured, I claimed my luggage, and he saw me safely to the hotel. The next morning I was up bright and early, taking a cab to the first rehearsal of my Broadway career.

At first everything was fine. I met John Barry, Alan Jay Lerner, the great John Neville, Leonard Frey, and the rest of the creative team. The musical director spent a lot of time with me teaching me my numbers, and everything went great. The next day I worked a while with the director, whom we'd nick-named the crazy Ukrainian, and that went great, too. Then the third day something rather odd happened, though I didn't register it at the time. A rather unattractive girl showed up at rehearsal. No one introduced her to me, but it seemed like everywhere I went, she was right behind me. I thought she must be a production assistant and didn't think too much about it. Every day for two weeks it was the same routine – show up and work with the cast and directors while this girl hung around me for no apparent reason.

Then one evening after rehearsal, about two weeks after I arrived, the producer stopped by and casually asked me if I'd like to go to dinner. I said, "Sure," and went off to the res-taurant with him. Who knew that I was about to become the main course? About halfway through the meal conversation came to a standstill, and I noticed he looked very uncomfort-able. Finally he cleared his throat and said, "You know, Lorna, I'm afraid I've got some bad news for you."

My stomach clutched, and I immediately said, "Oh, no. I'm not fired, am I?" One look at his face told me it was true, even before he replied. I burst into tears and said, "But why? Aren't I doing a good job?"

He mumbled something about it being hard for him to say why, that they'd just decided to go a different direction, yadda yadda yadda – classic show biz double-talk that meant nothing, as we both knew. Then he told me that the homely girl who'd been hanging around me all that time was replacing me in the part. I felt even sicker at this news. You mean they'd been planning to replace me all along? I asked him to please take me home, and he did. He couldn't get out of there fast enough.

I called my dad with the news, sobbing so hard I could

barely talk, and then I cried all night. The next day Sid called up the producers to give them a piece of his mind. I don't know what they told him, but they apparently gave him the impression that I'd been a real screw-up because the next day a letter arrived from my dad that made me feel even worse. It was a truly horrible letter telling me that I couldn't just expect to tuck my tail between my legs and come crying back home. I suppose he was trying to make me keep a stiff upper lip (my mother had written Liza a similar letter after her first show business failure as a teen), but the effect on me was disastrous. I was devastated. I was all alone in New York, I'd just been fired from my dream job, and now my own dad thought it was all my fault and told me I couldn't come home. Seventeen years old, and already a failure. I was in the depths.

Thank God for my sister. If she'd done nothing else for me, I'd be forever grateful for her help at that moment. Liza was in Europe filming *Cabaret*, and she called me the minute she heard what had happened. She comforted me, telling me those things happened to everybody, and she told me she'd take care of me until I was on my feet. And she did. She hooked me up with her business manager, enrolled me in the Herbert Berghof Studio and paid the fees, and supported me financially so I could stay in New York. She was wonderful.

Even so, I was depressed about the whole episode for a long time. Your feelings are tender at that age. I thought about the day four years before when I'd told my mother I wanted a career in show business. I was about thirteen at the time, and she sat me down, looked very earnestly into my face, and said, "Look at me, baby. Is this the way you want to look in thirty years?" Her face was white and pinched, hollow-cheeked with illness, with wells of sadness hidden in the depths of her dark eyes. At forty-three years old, she already looked sixty, and she knew it. All my life she'd talked about how hard it had been for her to work throughout her childhood, how exhausting and lonely it was to live out of suitcases, how painful it was to be fired, to read those nasty reviews. Show business is, after all, one of the few businesses fueled almost entirely by rejection. It's an actor's job to be rejected, to go to dozens or even hundreds of auditions knowing you'll be told you're not wanted. But like everyone else in my mom's family, I was already hooked. I didn't have that killer instinct some actors have, but I did have the single-minded notion that performing was what my family did.

So I signed up for classes with Uta Hagen at the Berghof Studio, took voice and dance lessons, and a few months later moved out of the Barbizon Hotel for Women and into a cute little studio apartment on the East Side with two kittens named Fred and Ginger. Life was beginning to be good again. At eighteen, you can only be depressed for so long. It didn't hurt that *Lolita* was a colossal flop. It opened in Boston to disastrous reviews and never even made it to New Jersey, much less New York. Along the way almost everybody in the cast got fired at some point, including the director himself. More than a year later I finally found out why I'd been fired. A friend of mine who worked for William Morris found out that the wife of one of the big shots had suspected her husband was interested in me and had insisted on having me fired. No wonder they'd given me all that double-talk about "going a different way." Finding out the reason for my dismissal was a huge relief. I hadn't done anything wrong after all. I called Sid and told him what had happened. It was then he finally told me that the producers had implied to him that I'd been unreliable, coming late to rehearsal and acting irresponsibly in general. In retrospect, I think he wrote me that horrible letter in part because he was afraid I'd follow my mother's pattern in her later years. Whatever the reason, he was almost as relieved as I was at the news. Everything considered, I was probably lucky to get fired when I did.

Meanwhile, I had settled back into the night life of New York all too happily. During the day I went to class, but at night I hit the clubs with my friends, and with my sister when she was in town. Once again it was the Hippopotamus (formerly Arthur's) or Adam's Apple every night, partying with the rich and famous. One night, in that oddly tight little circle, I ran into the most unlikely of all clubbers, Jacqueline Kennedy Onassis, there at the Hippopotamus. She was there with Aristotle Onassis, sitting in a back booth. I went to greet her and was very pleased to find that she remembered me. She invited me to sit with her, and I remember being next to her in the booth, hearing that same soft beautiful voice, and feeling like a little girl again. I also remember noticing that her husband was oddly inattentive. He seemed almost unaware that she was even there. I had just moved into my first apartment at the time, and Mrs. Onassis sat there with me and discussed the relative merits of various kinds of sheets. It was nice, kind of a mother–daughter style discussion, and I remember thinking how odd but wonderful it was to sit with her again after all those years. She was such a sweet lady, and that night she seemed very much alone. Her husband seemed completely isolated from her, in his own little world.

Things were definitely looking up for me. I was beginning to feel like I might get a bite of that big apple after all. About a year after I arrived in New York, I got a call to audition for *Sugar*, a musical version of *Some Like It Hot*, about to open on Broadway. The director was Gower Champion, an old friend of my mother's from her MGM days, and he greeted me warmly when I showed up to read. When I received a call-back for a second audition, I was surprised. I knew I wasn't right for the Marilyn Monroe role, but I went back a second time, and soon for a third. Finally Gower invited me to his house one evening to inform me, with gentle anxiety, that he wouldn't be able to cast me in the role. I took the news calmly and told him that I already knew that I was wrong for the part, that I'd been surprised to be called back in the first place. Gower was very sweet, and very relieved to find I was taking the news so well. It seems that he'd heard about the *Lolita* fiasco and thought I'd been treated very badly. He hadn't wanted to hurt my feelings again. I reassured him that I was just fine. Before he said goodbye to me that day, he told me that I was very special and that he would find a part for me because I deserved one. I was touched.

Soon afterward I got a call from an acquaintance of mine, a girl who worked in David Merrick's office. David Merrick had been my dream producer ever since I'd seen his production of *Oliver!* in London when I was a kid and decided I wanted to dance and sing like that. My friend Fran told me that something was about to happen to me, but she couldn't tell me what. Naturally, my curiosity was piqued. A short while later she called me again and said that Mr. Merrick wanted me to come down to the Shubert Theater and meet with someone named Samuel "Biff" Liff. By now I was really curious. I went down to the theater to meet Mr. Liff, who told me that they were interested in having me audition for *Promises, Promises*, a hit musical written by Neil Simon, with music by Hal David and Burt Bacharach. The show had already been running on Broadway for some time and was a big hit. I sang something for them and went home, not really expecting much from the audition. A little while after I got home, Fran called me again. After some pointless chitchat, she finally said, "I can't stand it. I've got to tell you this, but you've got to promise not to say anything yet." I promised. Then she told me that David Merrick had decided to cast me in the lead for *Promises*, but that no one was supposed to know it because the girl currently playing the lead hadn't been told yet.

My heart stopped. Part of me felt bad for the girl who already had the part, thinking, "Oh no, they're going to fire her just like they fired me." But the bigger part of me was turning cartwheels with excitement, thinking, "Oh, my God! Oh, my God! I wonder if it's true!" It was true. A couple of weeks later Merrick called to offer me the part. I was euphoric. I would not only be opening on Broadway; I would be opening in the lead role of a major musical. It was incredible. I called everyone I knew with the news.

After that my life became a happy whirlwind of activity.

I had only two weeks to learn the role. They turned me over to Charlie Blackwell, the brilliant stage manager who taught me the part and rehearsed me until I had it down cold. From morning to night I rehearsed my songs, walked through my blocking, practiced my lines, and worked with the choreographer. At night I fell into bed, exhausted. I was giddy with it all. Pictures of me from that period show a skinny kid, all legs and eyes, my face glowing with excitement and the sheer joy of living. I was eighteen years old, and New York was mine. One of the great moments of my life was the morning I stood in front of the William Morris office, between Fifth and Sixth Avenue, gazing up at it like a scene straight out of the titles for the television series *That Girl*. I was about to walk in and sign with William Morris, the king of the theatrical agents, when who should appear but the *Lolita* producer who had fired me the year before! Apparently he hadn't heard the news about *Promises* because he looked at me sympathetically, as if to say, "You poor thing," and said, "How are you?"

"Just fine!" I replied. "The best day of my life. I open on Broadway tonight!" And I ran into the Morris building. That moment, that encounter, is still etched in my memory. It was a moment of triumph, and of sweet, sweet revenge. Like a scene from a 1940s movie, it couldn't have been better if I'd staged it myself.

Opening night was the Palace all over again for me, except worse. As I stood in the wings waiting to go on, I could feel my legs trembling and the blood rushing through my temples. My mind was a blank. I hadn't even done a full technical run-through yet, for the intricate set pieces were moved around only in performance (the expense of the technicians made rehearsing with the sets prohibitive). The front row was filled with my friends and my godparents, Lester and Felicia Coleman, though my family hadn't been able to come. I was so excited I could hardly breathe. When I finally came bursting onstage, my friends began clapping and cheering wildly, and somehow I got through that first performance without disgracing myself. Most of it is a blur now; the one thing that sticks out in my memory is my fellow actors making sure I didn't get knocked unconscious by a flying set piece. Afterwards the audience applauded enthusiastically, and seemingly everyone drowned me in flowers. Best of all, the attention was for me, not for my family. Mr. Merrick hadn't publicized the fact that I was Judy Garland's daughter, though most people undoubtedly knew it. After the performance there was a party, and once again I was showered with praise and attention. Little Lorna had finally arrived. For the first time in my life, I was the center of attention – not Mama, not Liza – me. It was glorious.

After that night it seemed as if my whole life fast-forwarded into high gear. 1971 was a watershed for me. Besides performing every night in *Promises* (twice on matinee days), I appeared in eight television shows that year, with David Frost, Mike Douglas, and a host of others. I even had my own fan club, founded by a woman who lived downstairs from my sister, complete with my own fan club newsletters. Now I was the one giving autographs at the stage door and reading my own fan letters. It was heady. Liza was back in town by then, and I got to party with my big sister and her new steady, Desi Arnaz (her marriage to Peter had dissolved by then). I even wore Liza's clothes, inheriting some of her best hand-me-downs, like her unsheared sheepskin coat. It was very exciting. Sid and Joe and Patty came to visit when they could, always for the holidays, and life was about as good as it could get.

I did *Promises* for nearly a year before it closed. I have wonderful memories of that time. One of the funniest is the first day I remember Michael Bennett came to see the show (he was the brilliant choreographer who went on to create *A Chorus Line*). Michael was the new kid on the block; he'd just finished doing *Company* and *Follies* to rave reviews, and his star was rising rapidly. About six months after I started *Promises*, we were told that Michael would be coming in to work on the show again. We were all very excited to get him back. The day he arrived, I had just gone up to my dressing room after the performance when a strange man (Michael, as it turned out) came bursting in without knocking and pointed at me, saying, "You two [meaning me and my leading man] have a case of the cutes. Get downstairs right now!" And he swept out again. I just stood there and thought, "Hello, Mr. Bennett, it's nice to meet you, too." I was floored, but realizing who he was, I went downstairs immediately and lined up obediently with the rest of the hastily assembled cast. The only thing going through my head was, "The choreographer can't fire me, can he? Only the director or producer can do that."

As soon as I walked onstage, Michael pointed at me and said, "You! Who the fuck put that hair piece on you?" He was referring to the long hair fall I wore for the part.

I stammered blankly, "Uh, I don't know. They just did."

At which Michael turned away and exclaimed, "James Congdon [who romanced me in the play] looks like a child molester! She looks like she's twelve in that thing. Cut that goddam fucking hair off of her!" Someone did. The next day, Michael changed all my blocking. Welcome to show business! Later, Michael and I became good friends. His mercurial moods didn't bother me. I was honored to work with him, and always loved and respected his work.

By that time I was something of a veteran, and I took the changes in stride. A few months later *Promises* closed, but this time I had help deciding what to do next. Marty Bregman, Liza's manager, was managing me, too, and he and the Morris office decided that the next step for me should be a night club act. They wanted me to do the circuit like Liza had done years before. It had worked for her, so why not for me? The Morris office set me up with Larry Grossman and Hal Hackaday, a couple of talented lyricists who'd done some good work on Broadway shows but wanted the opportunity to put together a night club act. They did some arrangements for me, mainly Cole Porter and Gershwin tunes, and a choreographer planned some numbers for me and two male dancers. We got some Halston gowns, and I was ready to go.

When I say that my night club debut was one for the books, I'm not exaggerating. Memorable doesn't begin to describe it. I'd grown up on road stories of the Gumm Sisters and the vaudeville venues from hell, but in all modesty I'll put my debut up against any of theirs. If you want to talk about the bottom of the performance barrel, try the Steel Pier in Atlantic City. On Memorial Day weekend, 1972, I made a truly – uh – memorable debut.

It was the William Morris agency's bright idea to have me try out my act in New Jersey before my big opening in Houston the following month. It was a big occasion for me; my dad even flew out from California so he could be there. My road manager, Steve Vandow, had gone on ahead with my agent and the rest of the group, and I took the train down to meet everyone there.

The marquee in front of the theater was my first hint that all was not well. In huge letters across the theater it read, "JUDY GARLAND'S DAUGHTER! LIZA MINNELLI'S SISTER!" And then, in tiny letters down in the corner you needed a magnifying glass to read, came my name, "MISS LORNA LUFT."

Now contrary to rumor, I've never been jealous of either my mother's or my sister's success. I've always been proud of them and hoped I could someday be even half as good. One of the best things about my family is that we've always supported one another's careers, from the days way back when the Gumm Sisters sat in the front row to applaud madly for Jack and Virginia Lee, and vice versa. My mother was always proud of us. And Liza and I have always been proud of each other. But let me tell you, there's a limit to family pride. No matter how much I loved them, nobody wants to start her professional career billed as the other daughter and the baby sister!

Nevertheless, I tried to be optimistic as I greeted my dad and my crew and made my way to the tiny dressing room reserved for me in the back. My dad and my friend from the

Hippopotamus, Jody Russell, crammed themselves in with me and chatted cheerfully as I tried to apply my make-up in the small mirror. I had to hand it to them for even trying to talk to me; the waves were crashing against the wall of my dressing room with such force that they had to shout to be heard. After a particularly loud wave, my dad turned to me and shouted, "So, when do we dock?" As I squinted into the mirror, I asked Steve to find out when I went on. There were several acts, and I wasn't sure where I fit into the line-up.

A few minutes later he came back with a perplexed look on his face, and I said, "What?"

He shook his head and said, "Never mind. You'll find out soon enough." A pause. "Okay," he said, "it's like this. The chimpanzees go on first. Then the adagio act. Then Wanda. Then it's you."

"The chimpanzees?" I responded blankly.

"Yeah," he replied. "They're opening for you."

Right then, as if on cue, the door across the hall opened, and five chimps wearing gold lamé tuxedos and blond wigs waddled out followed by their trainer in a matching gold suit. I smiled weakly at him from the doorway. "Gee, they're really cute," I said, trying to be friendly.

He just looked at me with no expression. "They'll tear your fucking arms off, lady."

I backed away a couple of steps. "Okey dokey," I replied, and looked at my dad. He was staring at the chimps incredulously. I waited for the chimpanzees to clear the hall and then stepped out. A little way down the hall I ran into the adagio "ballet" act, a nice older couple who introduced themselves as Joy and Ron Holiday. As I shook hands, I couldn't help but notice that Joy's hair was actually a wig held on by a chin strap that didn't match her make-up. The chin strap was supposed to hold her wig in place while she was upside down in their balancing act. Well, at least Joy and Ron didn't bite. By the time I got backstage, the chimpanzees were already on, and I could get a good look at the audience. As the saying goes, just when you think it can't get worse, it does.

I was expecting to see a crowd of vacationers ready for some casino-style entertainment, but instead what I saw was a crowd of eight-year-old children eating hot dogs and running up and down the aisles. I looked at Steve in astonishment and said, "What the . . .?"

Steve cringed. "That's the part I didn't want to tell you. It's the Philadelphia Safety Patrol. They bussed in four hundred grade-school kids for the shows today."

There I stood in my Halston gown, ready to do a little Cole Porter, with several hundred hyperactive fourth-graders playing keep-away with their hot dog buns. I couldn't believe it. But it was too late to back out. The adagio dancers were just finishing up, and it was almost my turn to launch into the fray. But not quite. First, Wanda the Wonder Horse had to dive into the water from a platform at the end of the pier. The chimpanzees, the geriatric Joy and Ron, and finally Wanda the Wonder Horse – ain't show business great!

Finally, the emcee went to the microphone to introduce me. The emcee was a former boxer who looked like he was so punch-drunk he could hardly walk. Staggering up to the microphone, he waved for the kids' attention and then announced dramatically, "And now here she is! Judy's daughter! Liza's little sister! The scintillating Miss Erna Lust!" Erna Lust? He made me sound like a porn star! Those children could not have cared less whose daughter I was. But there was nothing to do but sweep onstage with my two male dancers in tow and launch into my act. For fifty endless minutes I belted out Gershwin and Porter, and finally, seated on a stool downstage, I crooned a tender rendition of "Mama, a Rainbow" as a group of little boys kicked open the side doors. When it was all over, I just wanted to go back to the hotel with my friends and take a long, long nap, but I couldn't. I still had four more shows to do that day.

That Memorial Day holiday was one of the longest weekends of my life. For three days in a row, five times a day, from ten in the morning until midnight, I trooped out on that stage after the chimps, the adagio act, and Wanda, and sang through all my numbers. It was endless. The emcee never did get my name right. It was the Gumm (Rum, Bum) Sisters all over again – Erna Lust, Lorena Tuft, Lana Ruft – until I threatened to strangle him if he didn't get it right just once. One night while my friends laughed helplessly backstage as he mangled my name yet again, I turned to Steve and shouted, "Get him!" The whole thing was sheer lunacy. My only comfort was that I wasn't alone.

The Steel Pier might not have been the most elegant kick-off for my illustrious singing career, but it was pretty good preparation for what was to come. God knows things did get better after that, and the Morris agency booked me into some of the best clubs around. Still, I never knew what I was getting into. When I opened at the Sands for my Vegas debut a few months later, I was in for an education of another kind.

I was to be the opening act for Danny Thomas. Danny was a successful singer and comedian who had one of the most popular television shows in America in the early 1960s. He was also actress Marlo Thomas's father – and eventually Phil Donohue's father-in-law. Danny was famous for his work raising money for St. Jude's Children's Hospital, and for his wholesome family image. Opening for him seemed like a great opportunity; Danny was still very popular at the time. When Danny offered to introduce my act, I was flattered.

That first night at the Sands, I waited nervously in the wings as Danny stepped up to the microphone. I was wearing a Bob Mackie gown, dripping with sequins and bugle beads, and feeling quite sophisticated. Danny began by saying, "Ladies and gentlemen, I'm going to tell you about a baby."

"What baby? What's he talking about?" I wondered.

Danny continued by talking about his "old friend, Sid Luft," and it gradually dawned on me that *I* was the baby in question. Then he began to talk about the "legendary Judy

Garland," and I continued standing in the wings as he went on and on about my mother. By this time nearly fifteen minutes had passed, and I was climbing the walls. Finally he said, "Now, ladies and gentlemen, don't expect a young Judy Garland to walk out here because you'll be disappointed. Nobody could fill her shoes. But here she is, anyway. Miss Lorna Luft." And he walked offstage with the spotlight trained on him as he'd instructed the technician to do. Thoroughly demoralized, I walked onstage and found my place in total darkness.

Night after night this miserable process continued. I couldn't understand why Danny was doing it. I tried to talk to his personal assistant, an odd man who seemed to be a combination butler and valet – a bad imitation of Alistair Cooke, complete with a fake English accent. The valet stuffily replied that "Mr. Thomas is doing you a favor." Some favor! I called everyone for help – Sid, the Morris agency – but no one seemed able or willing to do anything about it. Finally I called my old friend Maxine Messenger (now my son's godmother) and asked her what to do. Maxine's a columnist with the *Houston Chronicle* and had been a big supporter of mine from the beginning. Bless her; she hopped on the next plane to Vegas, caught my act, and walked straight into Danny's dressing room after the show and said, "What the hell do you think you're doing to Lorna? Cut it out!"

He replied, "I don't know what you mean."

She said, "You know exactly what I mean. The truth is that she's wiping up the floor with you, and you don't like it."

Danny didn't like it, but he didn't dare ignore her, either; she was too powerful a columnist. So he quit introducing me. Instead, when I finished my act the next night, he walked onstage right behind me and said, "You know, ladies and gentlemen, Vegas is such a hot, dry town, and the winds have been so bad lately. Miss Luft just hasn't been feeling her best. Even Robert Goulet, who's playing just down the street, is having trouble with his voice, and just think, he's a *trained* singer." I couldn't believe it. I kept right on walking, through the wings and out the back. I don't know whether he made that speech every night after that. I didn't hang around to listen.

What a guy. *Make Room for Daddy* was the name of his TV show. The only problem with "Daddy" was that he had a lapful of sexy young things in his dressing room every night. When I asked someone if they worked for Mr. Thomas, she laughed at me. I decided they must be his girlfriends, but then I heard him onstage one night talking about his "lovely wife." Wife? I wondered if he made the girls get off his knee before he called home at night. I doubt it.

One thing about the life of a night club entertainer; you get to know a very – uh – diverse group of people. Vegas may be known for some less than upstanding citizens, but it doesn't hold a candle to Chicago. Two months after my Sands appearance, my sister introduced me to one of the oldest "families" in that toddlin' town.

I'd just opened at the Palmer House in Chicago, and I hadn't seen Liza in a few months. She'd been in Paris since the Fall with Marisa Berenson and the cream of European society – including, it seemed, all the Rothschilds. Liza's introduction to the European high life had followed closely on the heels of her success in *Cabaret*, and for the past several months I'd seen pictures of my sister in newspapers and magazines as she hobnobbed with the classiest of the high class. That November, however, she apparently got tired of the high life, for she flew in from Paris to Chicago to catch my show and try a change of pace. A big change of pace.

When I looked down into the audience at the Palmer House one night, there was my sister, surrounded by the most amazing group of human beings I'd ever seen. Liza was seated at a table near the stage; next to her sat a little guy with a strikingly Italian face; and seated around them was a group of gorillas – no, not primates, tough-looking. All four of them were huge, hulking men in shiny suits and white ties. Grinning up at me from the midst of them all sat my sister, with "Isn't this a trip?" written all over her face. I couldn't believe it. I almost choked with astonishment.

After the show Liza brought the whole gang backstage to introduce them to me. "This is my friend Nick," she said with no further explanation, and then invited me to go out to dinner with the five of them. I said, "Sure," and off we went. I remember thinking, "My sister thinks she's in a movie."

We all piled into a car together – me, Liza, the "little guy", and all four gorillas – and went speeding off to a nearby restaurant. Once inside, Nick led us upstairs to a private room with a long table lined on both sides by Italian men who looked vaguely alike, all wearing suits straight out of *Guys and Dolls*. It was like walking into a scene from *The Godfather*. Nick told me they were his "family" and then seated me and Liza at the head of the table. Various people introduced themselves, and finally someone leaned over to me and, nodding at Nick, said, "That's Nick Nitti, you know."

I just looked back at him and said, "Nick *Nitti*. Nitti as in Frank Nitti, as in *The Untouchables*? You're kidding." And then, just because I couldn't resist, I turned to Nick and said, "So, Nick, there's something I've always wanted to know. Is there really such a thing as the Mafia?"

Suddenly, there was total silence. You could have heard a pin drop. Everybody looked at me. And then Nick looked into my face and said, very seriously, "Absolutely not. There is absolutely no such thing."

"That's exactly what I thought," I replied, and turned to order a drink. Everyone relaxed, and conversation resumed.

Then, a moment later, the waitress entered, carrying a big tray of shrimp cocktails, and tripped over the edge of the rug as she neared the long table. The reaction was instantaneous; nearly all the men in the room leaped to their feet and reached under their coats as they whirled to face the noise. The poor waitress froze in her tracks and looked like she was going to pass out. There was total silence, and I thought, "Now this isn't funny." Finally I said, "Jumpy, boys?" They looked around the room, realized it was just the waitress, and all sat back down again. I heaved a huge sigh of relief. Everyone was very nice and extremely polite for the rest of the evening, and afterwards Liza and I went to the ladies' room and howled with laughter. I told her that I couldn't believe that she'd gone from the Rothschilds to *The Untouchables* in what seemed like twenty minutes! I've seen Nick many times since that encounter, and he's always been a perfect gentleman and a successful legitimate businessman.

The most memorable moment of those early years on the night club circuit, though, is one I still treasure. I was playing the Fairmont Hotel in Dallas. The last time I'd heard, my mother's sister Jimmy was living somewhere in Dallas and I wanted to see her again. I hadn't seen her since I was ten or eleven, when Mama and Aunt Jimmy had had a falling out. I didn't know exactly what had happened; I only knew that my mom wouldn't talk about it, and that my aunt hadn't felt comfortable enough to attend my mother's funeral. I did know the name of Jimmy's husband, so when I arrived in Dallas for the show, I looked him up in a phone book and gave them a call, not knowing quite what to expect. I needn't have worried; both my aunt and uncle were thrilled to hear from me. I invited Aunt Jimmy to see my show, and she asked if she could please come early so we'd have time to talk for a while. I told her, "Of course," and we made plans to meet late that afternoon.

About 5 p.m. someone knocked on my dressing room door. I felt my stomach clutch nervously, wondering if it was her. Opening the door, I saw a woman standing on the other side, and at first glance I felt like someone had knocked the wind out of me. It was four years since Mama had died, and here in front of me stood a tiny woman with dark hair, those familiar hands, and my mother's face. I started to shake, and Aunt Jimmy teared up.

I invited her in and, still unable to take my eyes off of her, asked her if she'd like something to eat. She thanked me, and when I asked her what she wanted to order, she said, "A chicken sandwich with extra mayo, please." It was the same thing my mother always used to order. I watched with fascination as she ate her sandwich. She sat like my mother; she chatted with me in my mother's voice. She even chewed like my mother did. Looking at her was the eeriest – and the most wonderful – sensation I'd ever felt. It was almost like being with my mother again, in her healthy days, if only for a moment.

That evening, at the end of my act, I told the audience a story. "Once upon a time," I said, "there were three little girls named Suzy, Virginia, and Frances. When Suzy grew up, she was still Suzy, but Virginia grew up to be Jimmy, and Baby Frances grew up to be Judy Garland – my mother." The audience laughed and applauded appreciatively. And then I added, "And one of those little girls is here with me tonight. Ladies and gentlemen, I'd like you to meet the last of the Gumm Sisters, my aunt Jimmy." They brought up the lights; Aunt Jimmy stood up and took a bow, looking shy but delighted, and the audience went completely wild. They crowded around her after the show, asking for her autograph, and she signed everything they gave her like she was an excited child.

Afterward, unwilling to let her go, I invited her and her husband, John Thompson, to stay a while. We went into the bar area after nearly everyone was gone, and sat and talked for hours. After a while someone said to my aunt, "Please, won't you sing something for us?"

I don't know if she'd done much singing since her vaudeville days, and she said, "Gee, I don't know. I don't know if I still know anything." My conductor, Gene Palumbo (who'd directed Mother too), immediately volunteered to accompany her, and she said she'd try. She sat down next to him on the piano bench, they conferred a moment, she hummed a little and then said, "Okay, let's try." And Gene began to play.

I don't remember what she sang. It didn't matter. What did matter was the voice – my mother's voice, rich and full like it had been so many years before. I looked at Gene. His face was filled with emotion, and his hands began to shake so hard he could barely play. I stood next to her, transfixed, listening to that familiar voice, and as I did so I began trembling. I never wanted it to end. It was terrifying, and at the same time, it was the sweetest thing I'd ever heard.

Afterward she and my uncle went home, but not before we made plans to see each other again. I was traveling constantly in those days, but we kept in touch by phone, and I went to visit her at her home in Dallas. The first time I stayed several days and got to meet my cousin Judalein again, as well as all of Aunt Jimmy's friends and neighbors. It was on those trips that I got to hear first-hand about the early years of my mother's life, before fame and ill health had begun to eat away at her existence. Even after my aunt died, I kept in touch with her husband, a dear man.

Aunt Jimmy died in the early 1980s, shortly before my son Jesse was born. I wish she could have seen him. Jimmy was the last of the Gumm sisters, and the healthiest in every sense of the word. She developed heart problems late in life, much like my grandmother Ethel had done, and died in recovery after heart bypass surgery. Her death marked the end of an era. She was a wonderful woman; sweet and warm and funny, with her feet planted firmly on the ground. She'd had the good luck and the good sense to get out of Hollywood as a young woman, before the problems that haunted her sisters had a chance to consume her life, too. When I looked at my aunt, I saw the woman my mother might have become if destiny hadn't sent her down a different road, and I wondered what would have happened to my life if my mother had been able to walk away from it all. It's a question I'll never be able to answer.

Chapter Fourteen

# PROMISES, PROMISES

A career is all very well, but woman does not live by work alone. What's the point of having an exciting career in the big city if there's no one to share it with? I'd been falling in love at regular intervals from the day I'd met Brian Englund in the seventh grade, but it wasn't until I was out on my own that I got seriously involved. At home with Sid, I was Daddy's little girl. But from the time I touched down in New York, I was prepared to become a woman.

One afternoon not long after the *Lolita* fiasco, I went into a hip Eastside eatery across from Bloomingdale's called Yellow Fingers. I was going to have my usual salad and potato lunch before I went to class at Berghof's. I found a table, and a moment later the waiter came over and asked if I wanted to order something. I looked up at him and nearly passed out. Did I want something? Oh, yeah. I wanted *him*.

His name, I soon learned, was Philippe Lavot. He was an actor from Paris, trying to make it on the New York stage. I couldn't take my eyes off him. He was the handsomest man I'd ever seen in my life. He had dark hair, bedroom eyes, and an authentic French accent. He looked exactly like the French heart-throb Alain Delon. I just stared at him, my eyes nearly popping out of my head. Fortunately, he was staring back at me with the identical expression I could feel on my own face. It was the most extraordinary moment I'd ever experienced, like something out of a French movie. Needless to say, we exchanged names and phone numbers before I left that day. Lunch? Who could eat?

We began dating and were instantly inseparable. As a teenager you think that if you're not together twenty-four hours a day, you'll simply die. I told him I was an actress, but I didn't tell him who my parents were. After a lifetime of people staring and pointing at me, I wasn't sure I wanted him to know, at least not yet. Then one day he came to singing class with me. He'd never heard me sing at the time – after all, contrary to those MGM movies, people don't *really* sing on dates! I was taking a musical comedy class from Rita Gardner, who was in the original cast of *The Fantasticks* (the longest running musical in American theater history) and Philippe sat and watched. I noticed him watching me intensely while I sang, and I couldn't quite read his expression.

After class he asked me an odd question: "Who are you?" I wasn't sure what he meant. Then he explained that there was something special about the way I sang, a quality he couldn't put his finger on. "You can't just learn to sing like that. There's something different about you." There was nothing for it but to take the plunge at that point, so I told him who my mother was. He'd heard me talk about my dad, but he hadn't put it all together until then. He wasn't really that surprised. He just told me that it explained a lot of things about me. For my part, I was relieved to have the "family secret" out in the open. By that time it was clear that Philippe was in love with *me*, not with my name, so it didn't matter who my parents were. He loved me, and that was that.

In record time we got engaged and moved in together. He couldn't afford a real engagement ring, so he bought me a slender gold wedding band which I never took off. We started planning the wedding at some vague, unforeseeable date. It didn't matter when we got married; what mattered was that we were in love. It was all wonderfully romantic. Even when we found out a few months later that Philippe would have to return to France because his visa had expired, we weren't heartbroken. True love would win out. By then I was doing *Promises*, but we planned for me to visit him during my week off, and once the show closed, for me to move to Paris so we could be married. It would all work out in the end.

When you're nineteen, forever is a long time away. Philippe went back to Paris, and at first I missed him terribly, but after a while I got used to his absence. We still wrote and called each other, and I did go over for a week in Paris, but meanwhile life was exciting in New York, and I was never very good at staying home night after night. By the time *Promises* closed I'd found reasons to postpone my move to Paris. Philippe was busy with his new life too, and although we still talked about getting married "someday," someday was getting further and further away for both of us. Eventually, "someday" disappeared altogether. I never did become Madame Lavot. The affection lasted, though, and so did the friendship. We kept in touch over the years, and when I remarried in 1996, Philippe met me and Colin on our vacation in France. He's just a wonderful friend now, who enjoyed teasing me about my "younger man" and my new hair color. Philippe was my first love. I chose well.

Back in New York, life went on. *Promises* was over, so I had more opportunity to visit the clubs in town. One night a friend of mine called and told me I had to go to a tiny one in the Village called Downstairs at the Upstairs, because there was a woman singer there with an incredible act. So I went, and in that little place, I saw the most remarkable club performance I'd ever seen in my life. The lead singer called herself "The Divine Miss M," and her back-up group of three women (Merle Miller, Gail Cantor, and Melissa Manchester) was called "The Harlettes." The divine one was, of course, Bette Midler, but this was long before anyone outside of the Village had heard of her, or of Melissa Manchester. (When she left the Harlettes a few years later, Melissa went on to a successful career of her own with big early 1980s hits like "Midnight Blue" and "Don't Cry Out Loud".) As great as the Harlettes were, though, it was

Bette who was the stand-out. I had never seen anything like her. Bette was a complete original, and all of us sat mesmerized by what we were watching. I went back to that club the next night, and the next, and the next. I couldn't get enough of it. Eventually we became great friends. But Bette, brilliant though she was, was by no means the only reason.

Before Bette even walked out on the stage that first night, I was hooked. As the audience waited for her entrance, her musical conductor came onstage and seated himself at the piano. He was a skinny young man in his twenties with a shock of blond hair and shy, soulful eyes. I took one look and kaboom! It was Philippe all over again, except that this time instead of a handsome Frenchman, it was a threadbare young musician named Barry Manilow. Nobody had heard of him in those days, of course, but none of that mattered to me. I watched with fascination as he played the piano that first evening. Once again, I was head over heels in love.

That night, after the show was over, I went backstage and introduced myself to Barry. To my surprise he recognized me immediately from my work in *Promises*, which was flattering, and was as excited to meet me as I was to meet him. He introduced me to Bette and the "girls," and after that I went backstage after the show every night and hung out with Barry and Bette. I was becoming a regular groupie.

Once Barry and I met, things faded fast with Philippe. We were still engaged, but I hadn't seen him in a long time, and I wasn't really ready to settle down yet. Paris was rapidly fading into a distant dream. Meanwhile, Barry and I had begun dating. We were swept up almost immediately into a furious, passionate relationship. I don't know quite where Barry ended and his music began, but his phenomenal musical talent was like an aphrodisiac for me. He was so gifted. He was also funny and tender and shy and romantic. Before long I was spending most of my time at his Westside apartment with his piano and his sad-eyed beagle named Bagel. He would play and sing love songs – all his songs – for me in that little apartment of his.

How much more romantic can you get? After about six months of this, I called Philippe in Paris and said, "You know, maybe we shouldn't go through with this marriage plan." You think?

I was barely twenty and Barry was twenty-four, and the world had scarcely heard of either one of us. It was a wonderful time, a precious time. Barry introduced me to a whole range of music that was new to me. At night in his apartment he would play his songs for me, and I would say, "Barry, you've got to start recording these. They're good – very good." In those days, though, he still thought of himself as a back-up person, not exactly the wind beneath Bette's wings, but still not a solo act. By then Bette was beginning to make a name for herself, and it wasn't long before she and her group were touring nationally. *Promises* had closed and I was touring too, so my nights in Barry's New York apartment gradually became fewer and fewer. We tried hard to keep the romance going. We called each other from every city in the U.S., and when we couldn't see one another, we tried to see each other's friends. My drummer, Lee Gerst, was a good friend of Barry's, and whenever we played a city with mutual friends, we went out together and caught up on Barry. It was a way of keeping touch when geography made it impossible to be together. After a while, inevitably, the romance evolved into a friendship.

It's a friendship that has endured. Barry has gone from being the love of my life to being a friend for life. Our relationship has always been close and tender and, in a sense, pure. I've been fortunate in holding on to the best of the good relationships in my life. Barry and I have kept in touch for over twenty years, and to this day I can call him anywhere in the world and know he'll call me back in twenty-four hours. We still share the things that close friends share, and when we need someone we can say anything to, we call each other. He tells me he doesn't see how I manage to walk and chew gum at the same time, much less dance *and* sing. I also love to tease him. Barry certainly never thought of himself as a "hunk" when we were dating, so if I want to embarrass him, I can just talk about how sexy he was. Not long ago we were talking on the phone, and I said, "Do you have any idea how in love with you I was?" He just laughed, so I said, "Oh come on, Barry, let's have phone sex right now. It'll be just like the old days when we were in different cities."

He nearly choked and said, "Do you have any idea how much I'm blushing? Cut it out – for crying out loud, you're a married woman!" Which, of course, is half the fun – knowing neither of us would ever follow through on any of the romantic threats. When Colin and I got engaged a few years ago, Barry was the first person to be really happy for me. He and Colin, in fact, get along great.

Barry and I continue to talk about singing together someday, and he still gives me the star treatment when we're together. When I went to see him in concert a few years ago, I was amused to watch thousands of women throw themselves at him onstage. Afterward, when I went backstage to say hello and was confronted by a horde of hysterical women surrounding him, I was very flattered to find that the flood of females parted like the Red Sea when my name was sent over to Barry. His "people" instantly cleared a path straight to him, and when I got close enough, he swept me up, put his arms around me, and said, "You are coming to dinner with me tonight!" It was like a scene out of *Funny Girl*. When we got to the restaurant, he ignored all the excited fans to take me aside, and we had a wonderful conversation just like old times. Somehow whenever we're together, we're both twenty-something again. (That illusion is shattered, however, whenever he calls me at home. My teenage son Jesse answers and shouts, "Hey, Mom, that guy Barry's on the phone!" Barry Manilow is "just one of Mom's friends." Come to think of it, I thought the same thing about Sinatra.)

I suppose that being serenaded by Barry Manilow sounds like the most romantic date possible to many women, but I have to admit that when it comes to romantic, the best date I ever had was a completely different kind – and completely unexpected. It was what you could call a one-night stand to remember.

I had decided to settle in Los Angeles for a while with my sister and her new husband, Jack Haley, after traveling around the U.S. with my night club act for a couple of years. Liza wanted me to come, and it sounded like a nice change, so I went. To my surprise, however, I was barely off the airplane from New York when my sister informed me that we (Liza and Jack and I) were going to Chita Rivera's opening at a great night club, Studio One, that evening, and Liza had lined up a blind date for me. I was exhausted from the long flight and not really up for being charming to a total stranger all evening, but I knew Chita would put on a brilliant performance, and I wanted to be a good sport. So I said, "Sure, great. Who's my date?"

Liza just said, "You'll see," and the next thing I knew, Jack was guiding me to the limo. I settled into the back seat while we made the rounds to pick up Sammy Davis and his wife, Alouise.

Liza still hadn't told me anything about my date except that "You'll like him. I promise." I started chatting with Alouise and paid little attention as the limo pulled up in front of a strange house. The driver went to the door, and a few minutes later out of the corner of my eye I saw a man approaching the limo.

The door across from me opened, and I sat up straight and put on my company smile as I turned to greet the new-comer. Liza giggled as I found myself face to face with Fred Astaire, dressed to the nines and sporting that magical smile. I hadn't seen Fred since I was a little girl; to me he wasn't an old friend – he was a movie star. I felt like I'd walked into one of my mother's old movies. It was magic. I was so surprised to see him I could only gasp, blush, and blurt out like a schoolgirl, "Oh! I . . . I just love you!" I must have sounded like I was about twelve.

Fred smiled that warm, wonderful smile of his and said,

"I love you too, Lorna," and seated himself gracefully beside me in the limo. I was so excited I hardly knew what to say.

The air of glorious unreality continued as I walked into the club on Fred Astaire's arm. It seemed like the evening couldn't possibly get any better, but when we arrived at the party afterward, it did. As Fred ushered me into a beautifully decorated room filled with formal tables, he whispered that he'd asked to be seated by an old friend. He hoped I wouldn't mind? Then, just as Fred pulled out the chair for me, a man seated at the table with his back to me rose, turned toward us, and greeted Fred. It was Gene Kelly. Once again I felt myself flush and started gushing like a schoolgirl: "Oh, Mr. Kelly!" My sister was older and remembered being on sets with these people, but I didn't. On that remarkable night I spent the entire evening seated between Fred Astaire and Gene Kelly, being charmed from either side. It was pure Hollywood magic.

I thought about that evening many years later, when I was walking out of the main post office in Beverly Hills. I was in my thirties by then. The post office looks down on a busy sidewalk, and the steps leading down from the entrance are fairly steep. As I left the building and walked briskly toward the stairs, I saw an elderly man in front of me, poised uncertainly at the top of the steps. I noticed him immediately because of his jacket: it was a beautiful tweed with a velvet collar, the kind you rarely see in Los Angeles. The man held a cane and was hesitating, clearly worried about getting safely down the steps. Seeing his predicament, I walked up behind him and offered my arm, saying, "Can I help you down the steps, sir?"

Turning toward me, he reached for my arm and a familiar voice said, "Thank you, miss. That's very kind of you."

At the sound of his words I looked up, startled, and saw the man's face for the first time. It was Fred Astaire. He didn't recognize me, and I didn't identify myself. I was afraid I might embarrass him.

Choking back tears, I held Fred's arm and carefully helped America's greatest dancer down the steps. He was feeble and had to go very slowly. When we reached the bottom he thanked me again and tipped his hat, still with no sign of recognition, then turned and made his way slowly down the street. I got in my car and drove off to work. I sobbed all the way. I had just helped the epitome of dance down a few stairs.

After Astaire and Kelly, where can life go but straight downhill? Mine certainly did. I didn't know it yet, but my glory days of romance were already fading fast. A few weeks after my evening with Astaire, I met Burt Reynolds. As millions of tabloid readers know, love with Burt is always a disaster waiting to happen.

The irony is that I never wanted to get involved with him in the first place. Half the women in America were in love with him at the time – pretty much everyone but me. My total lack of interest in the beginning should have been a warning.

I first met Burt in 1975. I was still living with Liza and Jack at the time. Burt had just made a truly horrendous movie with Cybill Shepherd called *At Long Last Love* (both of them crooning Cole Porter in the cracks), and as president of Twentieth-Century Fox, Jack was responsible for trying to market this turkey. With the strange logic of Hollywood that says the worse the movie, the bigger the promo, the studio decided to give the film a huge televised premiere. They lined up people to sing Cole Porter songs for this extravaganza, and Jack wanted me to sing "Love of My Life," one of my mom's songs from *The Pirate*, and I agreed. George Rhodes (Sammy Davis's conductor) did the arrangements for me, and I did two numbers, including "I Get a Kick Out of You." I was working only occasionally then, usually club engagements where I sang a lot of Gershwin and Cole Porter tunes. The party was held in a big sound stage all done up in white, with beautiful plants and tables – a real Hollywood A-party. I was blonder than blond by then (my personal rebellion against the family resemblance that had begun to plague me), and I wore a slinky red Halston gown. After my numbers, as I started down the steps from the stage in my long gown, a hand reached out and helped me down the steps. When I arrived at the bottom and turned to say thank you, there was Burt Reynolds, still holding my hand.

Instead of saying you're welcome, Burt said, "When are you coming to Mexico?" He was down there filming *Lucky Lady* with my sister and had just come up for the *At Long Last Love* premiere.

I looked at him blankly and said, "I don't know." I was baffled. I'd never met the man. As a matter of fact, I'd never even seen the guy before – never watched him on television, didn't know any of his movies. So instead of falling down at his feet like most women would have at the time, I just sort of looked at him like "Who are you?"

He introduced himself, I said hello, and that was that as far as I was concerned. For one thing, he was with Dinah Shore that evening, and for another, I wasn't interested. But when I got in the car to go home, Liza said, "Burt Reynolds has gone ga-ga over you."

I said, "He what?"

She said, "You've got to come down to Mexico with me. He wants to go out with you."

I had no interest in going to Mexico. I was having fun partying in L.A. So I said, "Oh, please! I'm not going to Mexico. What am I going to do down there? Stand around on a set with nothing to do but sweat?" End of conversation as far as I was concerned.

I didn't think twice about the meeting, but for Burt, it was apparently love – or at least lust – at first sight. I was twenty years old, still in recovery from Barry, and completely uninterested in a thirty-something actor with a toupee. Burt, though, had other ideas.

My sister had been filming on location in Mexico with Burt for weeks by then. He was ending his affair with Dinah Shore at the time, although the press didn't know it yet, and he'd already become infatuated with me. After weeks of being bugged by Burt, Liza finally called me from Mexico and said,

"You have to come down here and have dinner with Burt." I didn't really want to go, but Liza wouldn't give up, so I finally agreed, as long as it wasn't a real date. After all, I reasoned, how bad could a free trip to Mexico be? Besides, I wasn't really doing anything else. Liza agreed that we'd all have dinner together – me, Liza, Jack, and Burt – at a little restaurant she knew. She sent me a ticket, and I took the plane down.

The first person I met when I got there was a production assistant named Michael Greene who was very cute and very sweet and asked me for a date. I wanted to skip the dinner with Burt and go out with Michael, but Liza would have none of it. She insisted I go to dinner with Burt. "But I don't even like him [Burt]. And besides, he's got beady eyes," I told her.

Liza was horrified. "Are you crazy? Do you know how many women would kill you if they heard that?"

"I don't care," I replied. "I don't want to go."

"You have to," Liza told me. We went. I just wanted to get dinner over with so I could go out with Michael afterward. Liza and Jack and I got there first, and about half an hour later Burt arrived, spilling over with apologies for being late. I looked at him with disbelief. It felt like it was 900 degrees that evening in the Mexican sun, but Burt was dressed from head to toe in brown leather – boots, pants, jacket, everything. He was beet red from heat and nerves, and from the moment he sat down at the table, he began to perspire. By the time the food got there, he was sweating so much I was afraid his toupee would slide off. I kept thinking, "He's going to have a heart attack right here at the table from the heat."

I thought he was very sweet but too old for me and just not my type. His only saving grace that evening was his sense of humor. He knew more clearly than anyone else there how ridiculous he looked, and his self-deprecating jokes were funny and oddly charming. He joked about his toupee and told me, "I hope you're impressed because I'm having heat stroke in all this leather." I couldn't help but like him, but I still had no romantic interest in him. I was relieved when the dinner was over and I could escape with Michael, the cute assistant.

I returned to Los Angeles thinking, "Well, that's over with," and thought that was the last I'd hear from Burt Reynolds. I was sure he'd lose interest. I couldn't have been more wrong. He simply turned the courtship up a notch. I began getting flowers, flattering telegrams, phone calls from Mexico. He wanted me to come down to Mexico again and spend some time with him. His break-up with Dinah had hit the tabloids, so he was apparently unattached. After a few weeks of pressure from Burt, my sister called me and said, "Burt's driving me nuts. You have to come down here and go out with him. Come on, it won't kill you just to go on one date with him."

It's very hard to say no to my sister, and she wouldn't give up. Besides, it was flattering to be wooed by a man so many women wanted. I wasn't interested in Burt romantically, but he was funny and sort of cute. Between Burt's flowers and Liza's phone calls, they wore me down. I finally agreed to just one more date.

Once again, I flew down to Mexico. Upon arrival I discovered I was having dinner alone with Burt, and I begged Liza to come with me. But Liza was sick of playing chaperone, and I ended up going alone. Burt was funny and charming, and I had a pretty good time. After dinner Burt suggested we drive back to his place so we could talk. I wondered privately just what he had in mind, but I knew he wouldn't force me into anything I didn't want to do, and I thought we might as well talk and find out if there was any point in starting a relationship.

I needn't have worried about any sudden moves on his part. As we drove toward the little bungalow the movie company had rented for him, I noticed Burt becoming more and more agitated. Finally he stopped the car in front of the cottage, turned to me, and said, "Promise you won't scream at what's about to happen?"

"What's about to happen?" I asked suspiciously.

"Something is going to happen to me. Promise you won't scream," Burt repeated.

I eyed him carefully and said, "Are you having a panic attack?" He was starting to hyperventilate, gasping for air and turning white. Without first aid, I knew he might pass out.

Burt nodded and told me to open the glove compartment. It was filled with paper bags for him to breathe in, Valium, and hot water for just such occasions. Clearly this wasn't his first panic attack. He came prepared.

So I told him, "I won't scream if you promise not to faint until we get in your house, because you're much too big for me to carry." In reality, I didn't have the slightest impulse to scream. After five years of coping with my mother's seizures, I wasn't likely to get hysterical at the sight of someone fainting.

We stopped in front of his bungalow, and Burt managed to stagger into the house. Once inside I helped him to the couch, got his boots off, gave him two Valium, hot water, and a paper bag to breathe into. The carbon dioxide trapped in a paper bag helps keep the sufferer from hyperventilating. God knows, I knew how to administer sedatives. Burt sucked on the bag for a while, and in no time he'd passed out and was snoring away, still clutching the paper bag. I watched him snoring and thought, "Well, this is lovely, really lovely." Since he seemed to be out cold, I called a cab and left. Back at my sister's bungalow, I said, "Gee, thanks, Liza. You're right. That was real romantic." The next day I took the plane back to L.A.

Incredibly, though, that wasn't the end of it after all. Burt called me in L.A., embarrassed but undeterred by our disastrous first date, and the whole routine started all over again. Flowers, telegrams, letters, messages, on and on and on. Few girls my age could resist that kind of persistent flattery from a man, much less a national heart-throb like Burt, and eventually he just wore me down again. He promised that if I'd come back for one more date, he wouldn't faint. He didn't. The tabloid rumor at the time was that he and Liza were having an affair, but it wasn't true. Liza was playing the beard so Burt could date me without going public. He already had enough bad press from dumping Dinah.

Burt was persistent, he treated me like a queen, and when he was conscious, he could be a lot of fun. I drifted into a relationship with him. When they wrapped *Lucky Lady* and Burt returned to L.A., Liza asked him point blank if he was going to take me to the wrap party, meaning, was he ready to go public with me? We went to the wrap party together at the Scandia restaurant on Sunset, and it was a regular media circus. We tried to sneak out the back door of the restaurant, but it was hopeless. No sooner did we walk out the back door than somebody snapped our picture, and the next day we were on the cover of every tabloid in America: "Burt Dumps Dinah for Twenty-Year-Old," "Garland's Kid Steals Burt from Dinah." It was horrible. I hadn't stolen anybody, and I really liked Dinah. For the first time in my life, I felt what my parents had experienced over and over for so many years. It was humiliating to see my face at every newsstand; I wanted to scream, "But it isn't true! I didn't steal him! I *like* Dinah." I suddenly found myself cast as the evil other woman, the "secret woman" who'd stolen the man of America's sweetheart.

Luckily, Dinah had all the class the tabloids don't have. One day about this time, as I was having lunch with my friend John Hillerman (well-known from *Magnum P.I.*) in Joe Allen's, the actors' hangout, Dinah walked in and saw me. Everyone in the place suddenly became very uncomfortable. But Dinah, who knew the truth of the matter, just walked over to me, gave me a friendly "Hello, how are you?" and we shook hands. Then she said, "I think you have very good taste in men."

I said, "Thank you." And that was that. What a classy lady.

By that time, Burt and I were dating in earnest. I wasn't exactly in love with him, mostly because I couldn't get rid of the feeling that one day the other shoe would drop and he'd dump me the same way he'd dumped so many other women. In spite of my apprehensions, I was fond of him, attracted to his easy charm; and the attention was exhilarating. From the beginning, though, we were terribly mismatched. For starters, Burt never wanted to go out. He was used to staying home with Dinah, who was a great cook and a wonderful homebody, but I didn't want to stay home and take care of any man; I wanted to party. Burt and I never went anywhere. By then Liza was in Rome filming *A Matter of Time* with her father, and Burt was back in Florida filming *Gator*. At first he wanted me to come, but there was nothing for me to do there. I told him, "What am I going to do while you're filming, look at the alligators?" So I stayed in L.A. When *Lucky Lady* premiered, he told me, he'd come back and we could go to the premiere of "our movie" together. The premiere was the special moment we were always talking about.

It was tough. I've never been very good at long-distance relationships, as Philippe and I had learned. Burt still called me several times a day, and he expected me to be there whenever he called, day or night. If I wasn't, the interrogation would begin. "Where were you? Who were you with? What were you doing?" I didn't like the questioning one little bit. I wasn't cheating on him, but I didn't have any intention of sitting home by the phone day in and day out, either. I had parties to go to, people to see. I resented the fact that he expected me to be on call twenty-four hours a day. He, on the other hand, was used to women doting on him. In his relationships, the women's worlds had always revolved around him. He couldn't comprehend my attitude.

Obviously, the relationship was doomed to failure. In spite of my discontent, however, I had grown very attached to Burt and was convinced he was serious about me, maybe even hoped to marry me. He seemed so sweet, and I loved the devoted attention. He fed that illusion, initiating conversations about having children someday and inviting me down for romantic weekends at a beautiful old house in Savannah he always referred to as "our house." I had the impression he planned for us to live there someday and raise theoretical children. I had no idea that he'd invited a long series of women to that same house until Loni Anderson told me so, years later. And he'd told each one of us that it was "our house." So in spite of the long separations I stayed in the relationship, vaguely hoping to live happily ever after.

Meanwhile, I was desperate to get away from my father's management. My dad was driving me crazy, and I was sick and tired of being "Daddy's little girl," especially since Sid seemed to think I should be a bad imitation of my mother onstage. Burt and I talked about it, and shortly afterward Burt set me up with his own business manager, Lee Winkler, who couldn't have been nicer. In no time at all Lee had booked me for the premiere of the TV show *McCloud*, and I got to film the pilot episode. That was just one more reason for me to be grateful to Burt. So by the time the premiere of "our movie" finally arrived, I was looking forward to it with a sentimental glow only increased by the fact that I was now well over twenty-one. Real adulthood – at last.

I'd been booked to open for Sammy Davis, Jr., my mom's old ratpack friend, in Lake Tahoe. Shortly before the movie premiere I made the Reno appearance. When I got back to Los Angeles, my regular driver was waiting to pick me up. I noticed he was acting oddly while he drove me back from the airport. He knew I always liked to see what I'd missed while I was gone, so he always brought the local papers when he came to pick me up. This time, though, there was no paper, and when I asked him about it, he said, "Sorry. I forgot." Except when I looked over at him, I saw he was sitting on a newspaper!

Now unless you've got a bladder control problem, this is very odd, so I demanded he hand me the paper. After trying to talk me out of it, he reluctantly gave it to me. And there it was, splashed all over the paper: "Burt and Dinah, Back Together." There was a picture of them together at a party given by his stunt man, Hal Needham, and to make it worse, the article explained that Burt and Dinah had been seeing each other again for weeks and that Burt had arranged a special screening of *Lucky Lady* at the party so Dinah could see it. Happy birthday to me. I was hurt and angry and humiliated. I kept thinking, "For God's sake, Burt, why couldn't you just tell me? There's this new invention called a spinal column. Grow one!"

The next day I was so miserable that my brother-in-law Jack suggested I go down to the set with him to watch them shoot a TV show he was producing with Mac Davis. Mac Davis had written a series of hits for Elvis Presley before recording in his own right, and had just begun starring in his own musical variety show on television. Ironically, Mac's wife had just run off with Glen Campbell a few days before. This was at the height of Glen Campbell's popularity as a cross-over country singer, and Glen had a television show of his own. When I arrived on Mac Davis's set that day, Mac said to me, "I hear you're having a really shitty day."

I replied, "And I hear you're having a really shitty time, too." So we went out that night after the shooting, got really drunk together, and felt thoroughly sorry for ourselves. By the time I got back to Jack and Liza's house at three in the morning, I was so drunk I could hardly walk straight. And as it turned out, the night wasn't over.

Propped against the front door was a small black jeweler's box and a note with my name on it. When I opened the box there was a ring inside – a big, ugly, man's ring. The note said, "Happy Birthday, Lorna. Love, Burt." I was floored. The man had actually given me an old ring that he had no use for. I was furious. I took a pencil, crossed out the words "Happy Birthday," and wrote "Wrong" instead. The next day I drove over to Burt's place on Miller Drive and put the ring and the note in his mailbox.

I'm a great friend, but I'm a bad enemy. You don't treat me badly and get away with it. A couple of nights later I was on the *Tonight Show* with Gene Hackman, who told me he was flying to Rome with Burt because they had to reshoot the ending of *Lucky Lady*. So I said, "Do me a favor, will you?

When you get on the plane, sit down next to Mr. Reynolds, look at him, and say just one word: 'Wrong.' "

So the next day he got on the plane with Burt and did exactly what I'd asked him to. Burt said, "Oh, Jesus." Then when they arrived in Rome, the first thing my sister said to him was "Wrong." You don't treat Liza's baby sister that way, either. Burt couldn't believe it. No one had ever retaliated like that before. No one had dared. When the reshooting was finished and the movie finally premiered, Jack and Liza and I flew to New York for the opening. Somehow it seemed only fitting that the movie was a total debacle, badly edited and hopelessly flawed. I felt terrible for Liza. She was in tears. Burt was on the plane back to L.A. with us. I was sitting upstairs in the 747, and most of the cast and crew were downstairs, including Burt. We still hadn't spoken to each other. His press guy kept trying to get me to talk to him, and after an endless number of "No, I don't want to's," I finally agreed to talk to Burt. When I got downstairs and sat next to him, Burt said, "I was an asshole."

I didn't say anything. I just kept staring straight ahead. Then he started to tell me how badly he'd treated me, what a schmuck he was, which might have been touching if I hadn't heard him say all the same things on the *Tonight Show* more than once about other women. At some point in all this drivel I couldn't stand it any longer and started humming the *Tonight Show* theme and finished with, "And he—re's Burt!", just like Johnny Carson's famous intro. And I got up and left before it got too deep to walk.

I can't honestly say that Burt broke my heart. I'd never really been in love with him the way I'd been with either Philippe or Barry. The truth is that he'd hurt my feelings and bruised my ego. It didn't help that the story was in all the tabloids, either. "Burt Dumps Lorna, Goes Back to Dinah." And it didn't help that most readers thought I deserved it for "taking Dinah's man away." At twenty-three humiliation is still pretty hard to swallow gracefully.

I have to hand it to Burt, though. In the long run, he turned out to be a friend. Years later I ended up on a plane to New York with Loni Anderson, and she told me she was in love with a wonderful man. When she told me who it was, I said, "Ay!" And I proceeded to trash him. Loni took it all good-naturedly, and after they got married, we laughed about the whole incident.

When times got lean in later years and I wasn't working, Burt even found work for me. He invited me down to his theater and said, "I'm going to find a show for you," and he did. Burt had a dinner theater in rural Florida that served as a training ground for young actors and production people after they graduated from college. Burt made it possible for these young students to get real world experience in a working theater; at the same time Burt brought in his friends in the business to conduct classes for them. Burt is generous in his own way, and he often gave his friends a chance to teach and perform at the theater when they needed work. I've worked at his theater many times over the years; it was Burt who first suggested I teach class. We never talked about what happened between us romantically, but I knew he was truly sorry for the way he had treated me. In his own way, I think he was trying to make things up to me. He and Loni even invited me to their wedding. I couldn't go, but I appreciated his asking. I'd rather have a good friend than an old enemy. Burt's a complicated man. He and Loni had a wonderful relationship, and I was sad when it ended. My tabloid time with Burt was nothing compared to his break-up with Loni. I don't know if he'll ever find lasting happiness with a woman. He's had some of the best. At any rate, I wish him well.

Naturally, I wasn't quite so philosophical at the time. I was hurt and humiliated by the collapse of my relationship with Burt, and when Liza invited me to join her in Italy for a while, I jumped at the chance. Her father, Vincente Minnelli, was directing Liza in what turned out to be the last movie of his life, *A Matter of Time*. We didn't realize it yet, but Vincente was already in the early stages of Alzheimer's disease, and the shoot in Rome was difficult. It was really painful for my sister. There wasn't much knowledge of Alzheimer's at the time, and we didn't understand why Vincente was acting so strange. We kept trying to laugh it off when he made odd mistakes. One day he came into the dressing room and called Liza "Yolanda." She kept saying things like, "Oh, he's just got his mind on the film," but I knew she was worried. We comforted ourselves with the notion that he was getting older, and that he hadn't directed a movie in many years. It was tragic to watch the brilliant man who'd once directed *An American in Paris* struggling just to function.

While my sister was trying to deal with her father's deteriorating health, I was trying to mend a broken heart. I was partying with my girlfriend Manuela while I was in Rome (her mother was the French actress Anouk Aimée from *A Man and a Woman* and other European hits). Like my mother, partying at clubs always seems to be my cure for a broken heart. Liza's movie was constantly being shut down because of a strike (Italy was very big on strikes), so we had all the free time in the world. Liza and Manuela and I would go to a club called Jackie-O's every night, stay till dawn, sleep until three the next afternoon, go to lunch and dinner, and then resume the cycle at Jackie-O's. Every now and then Jack would fly over from California, but most of the time we girls were on our own. That was the era of the "spaghetti westerns," as they called them in the mid-1970s, and I kept meeting these Italian "cowboy" actors. One of them thought he was the next Clint Eastwood, and he introduced himself to me. He told me his name was Fabio Testi, and someone whispered to me that he was the "Italian Burt Reynolds." Talk about the wrong recommendation! Fabio kept asking me out, but I knew we'd never get his ego through the door. I nicknamed him "Fabulous Testicles" and laughed about him with Manuela and Liza. I never wanted to date an actor again. This time I was holding out for my prince.

Funnily enough, my prince actually showed up, right on cue. No kidding, he really was a prince. His name was Stash Klossowski de Rola, and he was descended from royalty in some obscure European country that I'd never heard of.

Our meeting was straight out of the movie *Roman Holiday*. Manuela and I were sightseeing one afternoon about four o'clock, and it was an exceptionally beautiful day. It was that magic time when afternoon is just starting to hint at evening. We had reached the bottom of the Spanish Steps when I looked up, and there he was! An Italian god, straight out of the cinema, and absolutely gorgeous. Six feet tall, long dark hair, and a flowing cape. He smiled at me, and to my infinite joy, it turned out that my friend knew him. She introduced us, and after spending the evening being charmed by him, I went home with him after dinner. I was in the mood to be seduced, and the prince was the guy to do it. He was very good at it (I later learned he'd had lots of practice). We spent a passionate week together, and then he left for some island hundreds of miles away. Liza was afraid I'd be devastated, but I wasn't. I knew it had been what they call "a romantic interlude," not true love. When Liza asked me if I was upset, I just started singing, "Someday My Prince Will Come," and we rolled around on the floor laughing. Stash was just what I needed at the time. I later found out that although his bloodlines were genuine, he wasn't what you'd call a prince of a guy in relationship terms. It didn't matter. He was there when I needed him, and that was all I cared about.

At the time I broke up with Burt, I wondered how I could have let myself become involved in such a miserable relationship. I thought I knew what miserable was, but I was wrong. Then I met Jake Hooker, and I found out.

No one sets out to marry the wrong person. Nobody sits down in a rational moment and says, "Just think, this person will wreck my life. We'll be absolutely miserable together. So I know what I'll do; I'll marry him!" My parents certainly didn't. The Vegas bookies might have bet against my parents' marriage, but Mama and Sid thought they'd live happily ever after. Love is a great deal more complicated than that. I don't think Jake set out to make me miserable. It just worked out that way.

I had first met Jake Hooker when I was only a kid. He was seventeen or eighteen then and living with Lynne Allen, Peter Allen's sister. Liza was married to Peter at the time, and I had just moved to New York with my mom. I must have been about fourteen. I remember being at the Plaza Hotel. Liza was upset about something and said, "I need to talk to Lynne." I was accustomed to running errands for my sister, so she put me in a taxi and sent me over to pick up Lynne and Jake. I didn't think much of it at the time. To me, Jake was just some guy with long hair who was dating Lynne. I remember that my brother Joe and I nicknamed him "Jake the Snake" (because of his snakeskin boots) and "Jake the Rake" (because he liked to play around). That should have been my first hint.

I'd seen Jake off and on while my mother was alive, always very casually, and when I'd opened at the Talk of the Town in London a couple of years before, Jake had looked me up. I was about to fly off to Australia for a show, so I hadn't thought much about seeing him. But then I met him again in 1976, a few months after my break-up with Burt. I'd gone to London to do an appearance at the Palladium with Eddie Fisher. I was first there ten years earlier, when my mom filmed some of her concert scenes for *I Could Go on Singing*, and the theater is filled with memories of my mother. It's a magical place for me. In spite of its size, it's an intimate theater that makes you feel the audience is up on the stage with you.

Jake sent a message backstage after the performance asking to see me. He came by my flat the next day and asked if he could take me out to dinner after my performance that night. I told him okay.

I was in a dangerous state of mind, though of course I didn't know it. I was still smarting from my break-up with Burt a few months before. My fling with Stash had helped, but

I still wasn't back on my feet. Jake and I started dating. Jake played guitar in a rock band called the Arrows at the time. I liked the other band members – I thought the guys were funny and cute – and Jake was very attentive to me. Just like with Burt, the attention never stopped. It was constant. And after a while, just like with Burt, Jake's interest began to wear me down. After all, I liked him, and besides, there was a sense of connection with him because he knew my sister well, and I liked that. I had loved Peter Allen like a brother, and Jake knew Peter, too. So I thought, "This is sort of nice." It was a way of feeling connected to my past without being suffocated by it like I usually was.

I wasn't really in love with Jake, but I liked him, so when it was time for me to leave London and he asked me to come back to England and live with him, it sounded like it might be a good idea. I thought, "This could be interesting. What do I have going for me in L.A. anyway?" England could give me a new career start, away from my father and from my mother's ghost. It could be exciting – I'd always loved England, ever since I'd lived there as a little girl. So I thought, "Why not? Let's do it." I flew home to L.A. and announced to my dad and Patty that I was going back to England again. When they asked me how long I'd be there, I said, "Forever." It was clear that I wasn't going to be talked out of it. My dad had been after me for years to get some focus in my life, to stop partying so much, to concentrate on my career, but all his advice had fallen on deaf ears. What could they say besides "Have a nice time"?

Interestingly, although I was bold enough to move to London with a rock singer and live with him out of wedlock, I wasn't bold enough to tell my father what I was up to. Rather than tell him about Jake, I lied and said I was moving in with two girlfriends there so I could work in England and Europe. I couldn't tell my dad the truth about my rock-and-roll lover any more than Sid had been able to tell me that I was conceived before marriage, or that Patty was sleeping in his bed years before. I couldn't look my father in the eye and tell him the truth. Instead I made something up and took the next plane to London.

Jake was waiting at Heathrow airport with a limousine and a bottle of champagne when I got there. He was nervous and excited, anxious to impress me. I think maybe he'd been worried I wouldn't come. He told me he'd spent the whole week picking out curtains and fixing up his flat really nicely for me, and in the limo he talked nervously about how he hoped I'd like everything. He'd already polished off one bottle of champagne waiting for my plane to land, and he opened a second one as we drove. I sipped a few drops in the limo as the driver took us back to the flat, but I didn't drink often in those days, so Jake finished the second bottle, too. When we got to the flat, he continued drinking vodka and orange juice to steady his nerves. When his nerves were "steady" enough, it was time for bed. We crawled into bed for my first night in our romantic London hideaway; Jake took me in his arms, looked into my eyes, and vomited champagne and orange juice all over the bed. Afterwards, he promptly passed out. I cleaned up the mess as best I could with Jake out cold in the middle of it all, and then I tried to fall asleep as he snored beside me. "Welcome to England," I thought. The next day Jake was embarrassed and apologetic. He told me he'd just been nervous, afraid I'd be disappointed in the flat. So I told him not to worry, that it was okay. I'd had a lifetime of training in thinking it was okay, so I just tried to make him feel better and forgot about it. The whole episode was all too prophetic of our future together, but somehow I missed the point at the time. I've always been strong on hindsight.

Most of the time, though, we had fun. I worked sporadically in Europe, but mostly I just partied and enjoyed my independence. So much for the new career start. Jake and I clubbed with the Rolling Stones, the Who, and other "cool people" in the world of rock, and all of this appealed to my rebellious spirit. It was the 1970s, and I was in the middle of the biggest party in London. The Arrows had their own television show in England at the time, and Jake was a minor celebrity. So I played and enjoyed being what I thought was a grown-up.

Months later, when Jake said, "We're gonna get married," I said, "We are? Okay." I thought, "What a perfect way to really get away from my family. It'll be great." I'd like to say I thought it all through, but I didn't. I just sort of drifted into the marriage without ever realizing what I was doing.

I called my dad and Patty with the news. We were going to get married in London on Valentine's Day, 1977. I flew back to L.A. in January for a wedding shower with my family and old friends, and then I went back to London to get ready for the wedding ceremony. Ceremony? Performance is more like it.

Our wedding made all the London papers. "Judy's Little Girl Marries Rock Star." It wasn't exactly what my mother had envisioned for me when I was little. We got married at St. Bartholomew's Church in London. The ceremony itself was traditionally Anglican. The Reverend Peter Delaney, who had married my mother and Mickey Deans – and officiated at my mother's funeral – years before, performed the ceremony. I wore an outfit designed by Dee Harrington, Rod Stewart's ex-girlfriend. It was an off-the-shoulder tunic and harem trousers made of off-white satin, and I wore flowers in my hair. It was the ultimate rock-and-roll wedding. Everybody who was anybody came. The Stones were there, the great jazz singer Annie Ross, the Who, everybody you could think of who was a hot item at the time.

Everyone but my family. On his only daughter's wedding day, my father was in California with Patty and Joe. None of them could afford to fly to London for the wedding. Sadly, I didn't really miss my dad that day. I was still running away from my past, from being little Lorna, Daddy's girl, still relishing my independence. I was also uncomfortable about having my father see for himself how I was living. Having learned how to use drugs as well as alcohol for what I felt were recreational purposes, I had nonetheless gone to great lengths to conceal what was now my ever-increasing cocaine consumption from him. I knew he would have a fit. From my point of view, Dad just wasn't cool enough to understand the way I lived. It would be another twenty years before Dad got to attend my wedding to Colin Freeman in a beautiful English castle. By the second time around, Dad was a guest of honor.

After the wedding we had a reception at Tramp, the hot London club owned by my friend Johnny Gold. The whole affair was a circus, with thousands of people in the street and press everywhere. It was out of control, and so was I, though I was a long way from facing that yet. I didn't want to think about what I was doing with my life. I didn't want to think about anything.


Ten years before I had watched my parents' marriage fall apart. I'd spent another five years watching my mother rush from one miserable relationship to another. Between them, my parents had ten marriages. What had I learned from all of this? Apparently, absolutely nothing. I was by-God determined to screw up my own life as thoroughly as they had ruined theirs. The apple doesn't fall far from the tree, and a bad marriage was only the beginning for me. Marrying Jake wasn't the problem; it was only a symptom of something much darker and more destructive in my life.

# Chapter Fifteen

# CLUELESS

When I was a little girl, I loved St. Joseph's children's aspirin
– tiny orange tablets with a delicious citrus flavor. I had no
idea they were medicine; as far as I was concerned, they were
just candy, my favorite candy. I didn't understand why I only
got to have one or two at a time. After all, they were so small.
Then one summer afternoon in Hyannis Port, when I was eight
years old, I found the "orange candy" in the bathroom cabinet
and proceeded to take advantage of my good luck by eating
the whole bottle. Fortunately, my mother found out what I'd
done, or I might not be here today. Terrified, she called the
doctor, who told her to induce vomiting immediately. Apparently the doctor instructed her to use milk-soaked bread for
the purpose, so Mama stuffed me with the soggy mess until
she succeeded in making me throw up. After I had seemingly
vomited up my stomach lining, she was so relieved that she
celebrated by giving me the spanking of my life. Unable to see
why she had to spank me after all that vomiting, I cried hysterically as my mother repeated, "Don't you understand? You
could have died! You could have died! Don't you ever do that
again!" That evening, as further punishment, I had to stay
home with a sitter while the rest of the family went to watch
my sister perform at the Tent.

At the time I couldn't understand why Mama was so mad
at me; only years later, as a parent myself, can I appreciate my
mother's terror that afternoon. And only since reading piles of

Al-Anon books can I understand the irony of the fact that my mother, so concerned about my first "overdose," was hospitalized for the same problem that summer – though I seriously doubt she'd swallowed St. Joseph's aspirin. The whole incident made a deep impression on me. I was convinced that if I took a drug, someone would make me throw up, so for years I resisted taking any kind of medication. Unfortunately, however, the lesson didn't last.

It's a funny thing about addictive families. We never recognize our own addictions. We may recognize everyone else's, but never our own. My mother couldn't acknowledge her problem; she justified it to herself by resolutely labeling her drugs "medication." After all, she reasoned, they were prescribed by a doctor. It wasn't like she was in some back alley buying hashish. The fact that most "patients" don't tape their medicine under carpets or sew it into the drapes completely escaped her. I was equally blind to my own behavior. After years of watching my mother deteriorate, I avoided "Mama's medication" like the plague. Prescription drugs? Not me. For most of my adult years I rarely even drank alcohol. I never thought of my mother as an addict; that would have been too harsh a word. I did know, though, that prescription medication had ruined her health and eventually killed her, so I was afraid to take the same pills my mother did. Instead I took the "fun drugs," the party drugs everyone else took – you know, the "harmless" ones that you could smoke or snort at night to enjoy yourself.

Incredible, isn't it? My mother wasn't the only one in denial all those years. I was also a regular rocket scientist, really quick on the uptake.

I guess you could say my first drug was nicotine, the day I stole my first smoke with Katy Sagal behind the bushes in her back yard. But tobacco never really stuck with me. I thought smoking was cool at that age, but at the most, I never smoked more than a pack of cigarettes a week in my life, and even that stopped before I was out of my twenties. My first "real" drug was marijuana. I'd gone to a party with an older friend when I was fourteen, and everyone there was smoking pot, so when they offered me a joint, I took it. I really didn't know what the stuff was, so when I went home, I told my mother what I'd done at the party. I expected her to be as nonchalant about the joint I'd smoked as she'd been when the school caught me smoking in the bathroom. Wrong! Mama had hysterics, yelling at me about how I was going to become a drug addict. Smart aleck teenager that I was, I just thought, "Yeah, right. You should talk." By that age I'd already been educated about "Mama's pills."

I didn't become a drug addict, though – not right away, anyhow. I wasn't interested in smoking another joint. The marijuana had barely affected me, and I've never been attracted to the sedative effect pot can offer. I like a buzz, a good high, and for that you need a stimulant. When the 1970s came along, they brought the ultimate high with them, a little pile of white powder called cocaine. It was the party drug of the decade: expensive, chic, and plentiful. Everywhere you went, the A-crowd was doing cocaine. Not one to be left out of a good party, I happily joined in. After all, everyone else was doing it. What could it hurt?

I did my first line of cocaine when I was about nineteen. I was living in New York then, and I spent every spare minute in the local clubs. The club scene was full of cocaine by 1970, and one night at a restaurant called the Brasserie, a friend of mine named King Curtis offered me a line of coke. King was a brilliant musician, a saxophone player, and we'd gone to the club with friends after a late night to have "breakfast." King offered me some coke, and I really didn't know what it was. Somebody at the table told me how to lay out the powder, roll up a dollar bill, and snort it. I thought, "Oh, okay. Why not? I'll try some." I gave it about as much thought as if someone had said, "Try the curly fries." I took it in the bathroom, laid it out on the sink like they'd told me, rolled up the dollar bill, and snorted it. I got almost as much *on* me as *in* me that first time, so it didn't really affect me much. It made me more dizzy than high. I thought, "Hmmm, this is weird," and that was about it. I thought it was kind of interesting, but not exactly a life-changing experience. I'd do a line with friends every now and then after that, but not often in the beginning. Not long afterward I took my sister into the bathroom at the same restaurant and introduced her to this interesting new experience. Liza likes to remind me that it was her baby sister who first introduced her to coke, not the other way around. She's right. Needless to say, I was clueless about the implications of what I was doing.

It wasn't until I moved to California in 1975 to live with Liza and Jack Haley Jr. that I really got involved with cocaine. It started shortly after I arrived, at Sammy Davis's house. Sammy was an old family friend; he was also one of the most extraordinary performers I've ever known. Apart from my mother, few people could match Sammy's talent as an actor, a singer, and a dancer. He had succeeded in show business against all odds, overcoming racism and a physical handicap to do it. I used to tell him that since he was black, Jewish, and had only one eye, he should have succumbed to the three strikes baseball rule years before – three strikes and you're out of the game. That made him laugh. Sammy's talent and humanity were so enormous that they transcended every obstacle he encountered. He was an extraordinary man.

Sammy had coke parties at his house every night in those days; it seemed like cocaine was coming out of the air conditioners. That sounds shocking now, but it was as if everybody in Hollywood was using in the 1970s, and no one thought there was anything wrong with it. Sammy would never have harmed me intentionally. He was just doing what all his friends were doing. I started going to Sammy's house every night to party, and when Liza was in town, she'd go, too. There would always be a crowd there – Sammy, a whole host of managers, agents, and assorted Hollywood types. Most of us would be up all night doing cocaine and partying our brains out. I loved it. By then I'd learned how to snort coke "properly," and I loved the rush that came along with it. It's like they tell you: when you've experienced that pure, powerful rush once, you spend the rest of your life trying to duplicate it. Only you never really succeed. But you keep trying, and after a while I was hooked on the stuff. I couldn't get enough of it. Sammy's house became my home away from home. When he was working out of town, Sammy would often fly his friends down to wherever he was playing so we could party there. A sort of moveable feast. Soon my life was nothing but one long A-list drug party. Career? What career? I was having too much fun to worry about a little thing like that.

Not that I didn't try to maintain the illusion of a career. Every now and then I'd do a club gig or audition for a part, but it's hard to get much done when you can't make it out of bed until two in the afternoon. I had no real incentive to work that year: living with Liza and Jack, I had no rent to pay, and even the cocaine was free at Sammy's. At twenty-three my life was one long party. I worked once in a while, chiefly to keep my dad off my back and convince myself I wasn't totally wasting my time. Dad was in New York with Patty and Joe, and I wasn't about to tell him I spent my life snorting cocaine and partying. As far as he was concerned, I was in California auditioning for parts in movies and television. I was an adult; why should I have to put up with my dad's complaints about my life?

Besides, Sid had criticized me too much already. Sid became my manager in 1973 or 1974; before that I had been with Liza's manager, Marty Bregman. When Liza and he parted ways I left too, and Dad took over my career. Dad tried to make me into my mother. He wanted me to sing her songs, and even look like her. But it was too painful, and I didn't want to appear as though I was cashing in on her death. Sid put together a night club act for me and brought in a wonderful woman named Miriam Nelson (who had married Gene Nelson, the great dancer) to help me with the show. Sammy Cahn wrote some of the material for us.

We did a big vaudeville piece as part of the act. I would come out as a series of different people in a Broadway-revue format. I would go behind a screen, change costume, and emerge as a new character. For one of the vignettes, I danced with a dummy. The dummy wore a tuxedo, and had a skirt fastened to its waist. The skirt was designed so that I could walk into it, zip it up, put my arms around the dummy, and dance. When we danced, the dummy and I looked like Fred and Ginger.

This gave Miriam an idea, and one day she called a special effects guy she knew in Burbank, California. Juggling was a tradition in vaudeville, and Miriam wanted to know if he could come up with some sort of high-tech prop with dummies that could be used for a juggling act. The dummies would be attached, somehow, to a costume I would wear. She was talking to him on the telephone when I heard her howling with laughter. I asked her, "What's going on?" She said, "I've got a guy on the phone who said he can make a belt that we can put on you, and as you come out on stage, you can pull down on some tabs and four people will inflate out of the belt. There's only one problem. It'll knock you about twelve feet back into the orchestra!"

One night after we finished the act, the stage manager told me that I shouldn't leave the Fred Astaire dummy backstage, as he was afraid it might get stolen. We had to take it with us upstairs to the hotel. We put "Fred" into Miriam's bed. Miriam and I were hungry, so we ordered room service. When the waiter came into the room and saw two women with what looked like a blow-up doll under the covers, God knows what he thought!

I had a great time doing the show and it was a big success, but I certainly chafed under my dad's management. He'd told me what to wear, what to sing, what color to dye my hair. I once told him at a rehearsal that if it were up to him, I'd be sitting on the edge of the stage in a black wig, singing "Over the Rainbow." He told me, "It couldn't hurt." In defiance I dyed my hair platinum and headed for the next party.

I did get a tiny wake-up call during that period – ironically, from Sammy himself. Sammy was playing Reno a few days before my birthday that year, and he gave me the opportunity to open for him. Instead of thinking, "What a great career opportunity," I thought, "Oh, I'll just throw a few of my old numbers together," and headed north with Sammy. Unlike many at the time, Sammy was too much of a professional to do coke when he was performing; he was always clean during his engagements. I, however, thought, "Cool! I don't even have to stop partying." I did drugs and played around for days before my performance and went onstage less than prepared. My performance showed it. One night as I was singing, a woman from the audience yelled out, "Hey! We came to hear Sammy Davis, Jr., not you!" There was a long silence. I didn't know what to do; I'd never been heckled before, and it really hit me hard. Hotel security took the heckler out (it was a woman too drunk to stand) and I decided not to say anything to the audience, just to do my next number.

When I finished, Sammy came on stage and said to the audience with his usual kindness, "You know, I want to thank my opening act for being so terrific." That was all. Everyone applauded. I felt better knowing the audience was on my side. Afterward Sammy came backstage and said, "That asshole," referring to the woman who'd heckled me. Sam never criticized me. He was one of the kindest men I've ever known, and a dear friend to my family. I still miss him.

In spite of Sammy's support, the whole incident made me think a little about what I was doing. I knew I hadn't been giving my best performance. It crossed my mind that I might be partying too much. Unfortunately, the thought didn't stick. I was already in way over my head.

It was only a week later that Burt Reynolds dumped me.

Shortly afterward I flew to Italy to be with Liza, but the change of scene did nothing to change my habit. There was at least as much cocaine in Italy as there was in California, and besides, it was the same old crowd, just relocated. Everywhere I went, someone was doing coke. A guy in Rome named Gil Cagney was organizing parties for the entertainment elite. Cagney didn't provide the cocaine, but I had no trouble finding a source. With Liza's film often hit by strikes, we had plenty of time on our hands. We filled this by shopping all afternoon, going to parties Gil had organized, partying our brains out with coke, sleeping in, nursing a hangover, and then starting all over again. For my sister and me, life became a pleasant, endless haze.

It seemed like everyone we knew was perennially high. The club we went to was always crowded with celebrities who were either drunk or high or both. Marcello Mastroianni was one of the drunkest, or at least one of the most obnoxious. The drunker he got, the ruder he got. One night he started picking on my sister, saying all sorts of nasty things to her, until she lost her temper. Marcello had recently had an affair with Faye Dunaway and been dumped, so Liza finally got up out of her chair and said as loudly as she could, "I have only two words to say to you: Faye Dunaway!" And she stalked out, with everyone in the room laughing at Marcello's expense. When we got back to the hotel, we rolled around on the bed screaming with laughter. It had been worth it just to see Marcello's face when Liza yelled at him.

By then Liza was drinking, too. Jack enjoyed a drink too, although he never acted drunk. When I lived with them in California, I'd sometimes see him mix a drink in the morning; I wondered whether the drinking continued during the day. I know it usually started again when he got home. In Rome things got worse. By that time Jack had left Twentieth-Century Fox, though I didn't know it yet. I also failed to realize that Liza and Jack's marriage was in serious trouble. Liza never talked about it, but how could a marriage survive those kinds of pressures? Not long after, when Liza had left the show *Chicago* and was filming *New York, New York* with Martin Scorsese, the marriage was pretty much over.

As for me, I hadn't started drinking yet – that would come later. In those days I was "just" doing coke. In fact I was having so much fun "just doing it" that when I got a call from Los Angeles to fly back and do the *Tonight Show*, I considered it more of an inconvenience than an opportunity. I did the show, but a part of me resented having to leave the party to do it. Shortly afterward I got a chance to open for Eddie Fisher at the London Palladium, and I did have the common sense to sober up before I went onstage this time. The show was still a disaster, because Eddie Fisher was in considerably worse shape than I was by then. Sobering up for the Palladium barely made a dent in my habit, though, much less my career. Not that I cared, of course.

Meanwhile Jake had entered my life again and suggested I move in with him. Since moving in with Jake meant not going home to my family, it had a lot of appeal for me. Liza was gone by then, and I had run out of excuses to stay in Europe. My father still had no idea I was using drugs, but it was clear to him that I was out of control. Every time we talked he'd end up yelling at me: "What the hell do you think you're doing? What are you doing with your career? With your life?" He worried constantly that I was ruining my life, and jerk that I was at that age, I resented his interference. I decided to deal with the problem by avoiding my family altogether. Instead, I married Jake. Yes indeed, another brilliant decision. If you're a drug user anxious to get away from home, the obvious solution is to marry someone with an alcohol problem.

In a sense, Jake and I were the perfect couple in those days. My cocaine never interfered with his drinking, and his drinking never came between me and my coke. I was soon aware that Jake had a drinking problem – when he vomited on me after two bottles of champagne during our first night in London, I got a hint – and every now and then I'd say to him,

"Jake, I think you have a drinking problem." Of course, I was usually high when I said it. In retrospect, the whole situation was like a moment from the theater of the absurd, but at the time I was oblivious to the irony.

I'd been using cocaine regularly for over a year when Jake and I got married. It wasn't until I began living in London, though, that things got really out of control. Until then I'd used coke simply because it was there, and because it was fun, but it wasn't until 1976 that cocaine became an obsession for me. It was no longer just a way to have fun at a party; it became my life. I had to have it. I didn't realize it yet, but I had become an addict.

I rarely woke up until four in the afternoon, and the first thing on my mind when I did was getting my hands on some coke. When I first got up, I would feel really terrible, but then I'd take a shower and eat something, and as soon as I did, I'd take my first hit of coke. Then it was party time – get together with your friends at somebody's house and get high. Find a place to go for dinner, go back to the party, and do coke all night. At eight or nine the next morning, go home and go to bed. I'd always lay out a line of cocaine on the bedside table before I went to sleep, so it would be ready for me as soon as I woke up. There was nothing in my life by then but my party friends and that white powder. It was all I wanted.

There was a big celebrity coke group in London in those days, and I knew them all. I'd become really good friends with Bill Wyman, the bass player for the Rolling Stones, and his long-time friend and live-in fiancée, Astrid. Whenever the Stones were in town, I was over at Bill and Astrid's house. Bill later wrote about those years in his book, *Stone Alone*.

Bill never did drugs, but Astrid did a lot of coke. She could function, though, so if you didn't actually see her do a line, you might not realize she was stoned. Bill and Astrid were the sane ones in the group I partied with, but most of the rest were barely clinging to reality much of the time. I thought running around London with people like the Stones and the

Who was great fun, and Jake was more than happy to run around with me. Most of us were musicians, but that wasn't what held us together. The common bond for a lot of us in my group was cocaine. Our lives centered on how to get it and where to use it. The minute we woke up in the late afternoon, we'd start calling each other. Who's got some? Where do you want to meet? It was an endless cycle. Every now and then we'd try something else; I used heroin once, but luckily for me, I didn't like the feeling, and I got sick. So for me, it was usually just coke. Never once in any of this did I stop to think about what I was doing, and I certainly never made the connection between my mother's addiction and my own. I didn't have an addiction; I was just having fun.

It was Bill Wyman who first pointed out that what I was doing wasn't just "fun." What I was doing had consequences, serious consequences. Bill had a son named Steven, and he knew that if he were ever caught doing drugs, he'd lose custody of Steven. He wasn't willing to take that risk, so in the middle of the insanity around him, Bill stayed cold sober. He was the only one of us who did. The summer after Jake and I got married, there was a charity event in Cannes, at the Yacht Club, hosted by Grace Robbins, the wife of the novelist Harold Robbins. Bill was involved with the event, and I was invited to perform. I went onstage that night stoned out of my mind. It's the only time in my life I've ever performed while I was completely stoned. I don't think the audience knew it, but Bill did. He was livid. Afterward he came backstage, slammed me against a wall, and said, "What the hell are you doing to yourself?" He shouted right in my face, "I've been around people like you all my life, and I can't stand by and watch you do this to yourself. You're going to come to my house with me, now, and you're going to stay there! I'm not even going to discuss this with you. You're doing it." I started crying. I guess you could say I was shocked sober that night. Bill was as good as his word. He and Astrid put me in a car and took me to their house. He kept me there for two weeks. And for two weeks, he refused to speak to me.

For the first time in two years, I got sober. Completely sober. I was desperate to talk to Bill, and I kept saying, "Why won't you talk to me?" But he wouldn't. He was forcing me to deal with me. I would stand on the balcony and cry for hours, thinking about my life and the mess I was in. With my mind clear, I could no longer avoid the obvious question. What was I doing with my life? I took a good look at myself and saw someone who had completely screwed up, given up on her career, didn't care about anything. It was terrifying. Cocaine is a very evil thing because of its power to delude you. It deludes you into believing that it can't hurt you because it's supposedly not physically addictive the way heroin is. Worse yet, it deludes you into believing that you are better for using it – that you sing better, talk better, feel better, *are* better while you're on it. On that balcony, though, the delusion evaporated, and I was horrified by what I saw. Astrid would try to comfort me: "It's just that Bill really cares about you, and he feels you need to stop using. He just wants you to figure that out for yourself."

I did. At the end of those two weeks, Bill came to me and said, "I want you to know that you are my friend, and that we will always be friends. But it's your choice now." I looked at him in that moment and thought that for the rest of my life, Bill Wyman could run over me with a car and I'd still get up and say thank you, because he helped me save my life. He showed me myself, and I'll thank him for that until the day I die.

I stopped using. I went back to London with Bill and Astrid, and though I still made the rounds of the clubs with my friends, I struggled to stay sober. In a deeply painful irony, however, as I got better, Astrid got worse. She'd been able to hide the cocaine she was using from Bill for a long time, but now she was beginning to fall apart. Making the situation worse was the fact that Bill was cheating on her, but unwilling to admit it. Sober myself, I watched in pain as Astrid disintegrated before our very eyes.

One night we all went to dinner at Trader Vic's. Keith Moon and his long-time girlfriend Anita were with us, too. Afterward when we came home, Astrid walked into the bathroom, locked the door, and slit her wrists. It was horrible. We had to find a doctor who would come in the middle of the night because if we took her to a hospital, it would be all over the press within hours. As it was, whoever came would find the room filled with rock-and-roll royalty. I found a doctor who would come, and I got cash to pay him with. We bound Astrid's wrists until the doctor got there and sewed them up. Afterward I paid his fee and some hush money in cash, warning him not to tell anyone what had happened that night. It was my mother all over again; I was fifteen years old and calling the doctor to come and take care of Miss Garland privately at the hotel. God knows, I knew what to do in a situation like that. At that moment part of me wished I wasn't sober. I wanted something to dull the pain.

Whatever pain I was feeling was nothing compared to Bill's, however. He watched in agony as a sixteen-year relationship crumbled under the pressure of Astrid's addiction, and he felt partly to blame. Bill and Astrid were so much in love; I'd always thought of them as the perfect couple, the two people in all the world who would always be together. The night she slit her wrists, Bill and I went walking through the streets together afterward, and when we came to an alley, Bill just collapsed in sobs, saying, "I don't know what to do anymore. I don't know what to give her, how to make her happy." I put my arms around him, and as he sobbed on my shoulders, I was frightened. This was serious.

A few days later Astrid agreed to go to a clinic, but it didn't work. Once she came out, the cycle started all over again. She was in and out of clinics for a while, and Bill tried to hold onto hope, but the relationship was doomed. It was so painful to watch him struggle to come to grips with the truth.

The man who had rescued me from addiction was helpless to save the woman he loved.

Eventually, the `relationship collapsed, but fortunately Astrid did not. She was able to get sober, with immense strength and courage, and ironically was among the first of her friends to do so. She lives in Los Angeles now, and works with a rehab clinic there. She's happy and in good health. Bill later married Suzanne Costa, and they now live in London with their two beautiful children. Bill eventually quit the Stones. He and Astrid still share a deep affection in spite of the pain they caused each other, and they've remained in contact over the years.

It was about that time that a new neighbor moved into the cottage behind our flat. His name was Christopher Reeve. I'd seen a picture of Chris that the *Superman* producer's wife, my friend Skye Aubrey, had brought over to show me. No one besides a few soap opera fans had heard of Chris until he did the movie, but even in photos he was cute. He was even cuter in the flesh – let alone the spandex. I nicknamed him "Crittifer Reeb." Chris had never been to England and didn't know a soul, so we would invite him over to our house to spend time. I'd watch his dates come in and out of his house as I stood at my kitchen window, and I'd give Chris a "thumbs up" or "thumbs down" rating on his women, which he thought was hilarious. When he brought a girl called Gay home for the first time, now his former lady and the mother of his kids, I gave him the big high sign because I thought she was great. Jake and I spent a lot of time with Chris and Gay. Once shooting wound down on the movie, Chris would be over in my kitchen constantly, eating the spaghetti I'd make him. He'd had to diet throughout the film to look good in those tights, and he could hardly wait to chow down on pasta by then.

Meanwhile, I was having fun running around with the *Superman* crowd. With my career in low gear and drugs off limits for me, there wasn't much to keep me busy during the day. *Superman* provided a pleasant distraction. Richard Donner, an old friend of Jack Haley, Jr.'s and a talented director, was directing the film. I spent a lot of time on the set or with the cast. Dick used to make us all laugh on the set. When it was time for Chris to do a take, Dick would always scream, "Hey, you in the tights! Get over here!" When it came time for Marlon Brando to shoot his part as Superman's father, I was very excited about going to the set to watch. As a child I'd known Marlon Brando as George Englund's friend, when Joe and I hung out in Cloris Leachman's kitchen on Rockingham Drive, but I'd never seen him as an actor, and I looked forward to seeing a screen legend in action. What a disappointment he turned out to be. When it came time for him to shoot, there were cue cards everywhere with his lines on them. He had only about seven lines in the film, but he hadn't even memorized them. Instead he had to read them. I thought it was extraordinary – one of the greats of the American screen reading his lines. Watching Marlon Brando turned out to be a tremendous letdown.

Overall, though, I had a grand time. I became close friends with Valerie Perrine, also of the *Superman* cast, and with her new boyfriend, Dodi Fayed. Dodi was only nineteen at the time, the son of a rich Arab businessman building an empire. Valerie was thirty-three and a little embarrassed about her young boyfriend. She needn't have been; Dodi adored her, and he treated her like a queen. Dodi was sweet, eager to please, and he did everything in his power to woo this glamorous older woman. Every time he came to pick her up, he drove a different car. After a month or so of this, Valerie asked him where he was getting them all from. He took her to the basement of his home in London, and showed her a huge garage, filled with expensive cars of every imaginable type. Valerie was floored.

Dodi then asked her what car she wanted to go out in that night. Looking around the huge showroom, she quickly spotted her choice. "That one," she told him, pointing to a white Rolls-Royce. They climbed in and were off for the evening.

The press have had a field day with Dodi, portraying him as a heartless playboy. That's not the Dodi I knew for twenty years. The man I knew was warm, funny, generous, and a faithful friend to me and several other people within my circle. He was the sort of person you could call on, whatever fix you were in and wherever you were. He never left town without making certain his friends had all of his emergency numbers. I still have them all listed in my organizer, accurate up to the day he died. Valerie enjoyed certainly every moment of their relationship.

One day Jake and Valerie and I went shopping in London. I had my heart set on a very beautiful Yves St. Laurent cape. Jake said he'd buy it for me, but when he saw how much it cost he hesitated. "It's too expensive," he said. I got really upset at him, because I had thought he was going to buy it for me and all of a sudden he was backing out. We left the shop and walked down Bond Street a little way and went into a shoe store, and when we got inside I discovered that my purse was missing. "This is just great," I thought, "my purse is gone, I didn't get the cape, I'm having a wonderful day." I burst into tears. Jake felt so bad, and so guilty, that he took me back to Yves St. Laurent and bought me the cape. As the three of us walked back out, Jake hailed a cab and left to go to a meeting. As Valerie and I stood together at the curb, watching the cab drive away, she leaned over quietly and slipped my purse into my hand. I looked at her in astonishment and said, "You mean you . . ." She had taken my purse and hidden it under the heavy coat she was wearing. Valerie said, "You got your cape, didn't you?" Valerie and I laughed all the way home. I couldn't stop giggling. Jake couldn't figure out what was so funny. The next day Valerie called, and I pretended the police had found my purse. I wasn't about to tell Jake the truth. He'd make me take the cape back.

By the time *Superman* wrapped in 1978, I was getting

awfully homesick for America. After two years, London had begun to wear thin. There had been a lot of in-fighting among the Arrows, and the result was that Jake found himself out of the group. Jake met a guy named Paul Vigrass who had also broken away from a musical group, and the two of them were planning to team up and form a new group, but so far nothing had come of it. My career was stalled, and I didn't see much hope of jumpstarting it in London just then. Jake and I talked it over and decided to go to New York, just to visit and see what was going on there. The plan was for us to stay with Alan and Arlene Lazar in New York for a week or two while we decided what to do next. So we booked a ticket, flew to New York, and moved in temporarily with the Lazars.

The Lazars are my oldest and dearest friends in New York. I'd first met them a few years before, when I was doing *Promises*, at a Hallowe'en party at the Friars' Club. Everyone was in costume, and Alan was dressed up as a mad doctor, which was especially funny since he really is a doctor. He was wearing his white medical jacket with lots of fake blood on it, a lunatic mask, and an amputated rubber hand in his pocket. I was with a wonderful actor friend named Noel Craig, and we hit it off with Alan and Arlene right away. We all started talking, and at the end of the evening, Arlene asked us if we'd like to go to dinner with them the next night. I looked at Noel and said, "What do you think? We haven't actually seen this guy without his mask. No telling what he looks like."

Noel said, "Yeah, why not?"

So we all went to dinner the next night. And the night after that. And the night after that. We had a wonderful time, except for one thing: Alan still hadn't taken off the mask. There he was in his nice suit, still wearing that stupid mask. It was like going out with the Phantom of the Opera. After a while I began to think he was slightly nuts, so I asked him, "What are you doing? Why are you still going around like the mad doctor?"

Alan said, "I am a doctor. No, really. A periodontist." Eventually he did take off the mask, and Arlene explained that the gag was just Alan's quirky sense of humor. Under the mask was a very dear man and a very bright man.

No sooner had Jake and I arrived at the Lazars' apartment from London that winter than Alan asked us if we knew what had been going on in New York. I had no idea what he meant. So he told us that a new club had opened about a month before, and that it was wildest place he'd ever seen in his life. "A guy named Steve Rubell runs it," he told us, "and the man is crazy. I mean, really crazy. The whole place is pandemonium."

"What do you mean, he's crazy?" I asked him.

Alan said, "He only lets certain people in. He's put up a velvet rope and staked the place out with bouncers so he can control who comes in." I was floored. I'd never heard of anybody doing that. Alan continued, "Listen, if I can get this guy on the phone, will you talk to him and convince him it's really you? He knows your sister, and if you talk to him, I'm pretty sure he'll let you in."

Intrigued, I said, "Okay. I guess so."

Alan made some calls, and a few minutes later he handed me the phone and I heard a nasally voice on the other end say, "Lorna, is that really you?" Then Steve said, "If you want to come on down tonight, I'll keep an eye out for you. You can come in." And after a very brief and rather bizarre conversation, he hung up.

I still thought this was the weirdest thing I'd ever heard of, but I was more than a little curious to see the place. Party girl that I was, this newest and hippest of clubs was intriguing. After I got off the phone with Steve Rubell, we all went to dinner and then took a cab to the new club. As we pulled up a block or so away, I got my first glimpse of Studio 54. I was astounded. In the streets surrounding the club stood hundreds of people, blocking off the intersection, all hoping to get into the Studio. It was staggering; I'd never seen anything like it in my life, and I thought I'd seen everything by then. A man Alan identified as Steve Rubell was standing on a platform outside the club, where he could see over the crowd and choose the people to be admitted. Alan grabbed my hand tightly, said, "Here we go," and started pushing forward through the crowd. Jake and Arlene followed close behind. As we neared the platform, Alan began shouting, "Steve! Steve, I've got Lorna! Here she is!" Steve heard the shouting and gave his people orders to let us pass. We shoved our way through the crush to the doors, and someone let us in. For me, walking through those doors was like entering the gates of heaven. I'd reached the Promised Land.

Studio 54 really was a studio – an old sound stage, to be exact. It was huge. The entrance was ornate, like an old theater, and when you went inside, you passed through a lobby and through the main doors into the studio itself. The panorama that greeted me as I walked in that first night took my breath away. The sheer size of the room was overwhelming, a massive space with several levels and banquettes lining the walls. The main bar was on the first level, with hunky bartenders dressed in shorts and vests. The stage itself had been made into a gigantic dance floor, filled with hordes of people. As they danced, neon columns would descend periodically from the ceiling to the dance floor. They were filled with flashing lights and had police sirens on the bottom. A few moments later the columns would disappear again into the darkness above. Upstairs was a balcony with a huge disco booth that ran parallel to it so the DJ could see the dance floor below. The balcony ran all around the dance floor, looking down on it. There were several bars up there and more banquettes, and of course the restrooms. In the basement under the dance floor, I would soon discover, was a "private room" where Steve Rubell would entertain his special guests with an assortment of their favorite designer drugs. The basement was the Holy of Holies; only the very rich and famous, and their relatives and friends, were admitted there. The most astounding thing of all, though, was the special effects. A variety of flying set pieces had been mounted in the dark recesses of the catwalks above, and they would periodically sweep down from above. A sun and moon and stars would appear, accompanied by appropriate special effects. The most remarkable one was the moon. It was a big crescent moon with a face like the man in the moon, and as it came sweeping down across the dance floor, a huge spoon would arc down to meet it from the other side of the room. As the two met in the center, the spoon would go up the moon's nose, and the moon would appear to sniff. Every time it did, the ceiling would explode with white glitter, tons of it, raining down on the dance floor like a snowstorm. The moon was snorting coke. As I watched the spectacle in awe that first night, I thought, "What am I doing in England? This is the wildest thing I've ever seen." It was like my first night in a club all over again, when I was only thirteen years old. I thought I'd died and gone to heaven. I never wanted to leave.

The next night was even more memorable. On that second night in New York, Mother Nature greeted us with the biggest blizzard of the year. I was disappointed because all that snow meant we'd never make it back to the Studio, but Alan said we were going anyway. There was going to be a big party for Fabergé, and we weren't going to miss it. I thought he'd lost his mind. "Nobody's going out on a night like this," I said. "They'll cancel the party."

But Alan just said, "They won't cancel anything. This is New York, and nobody's going to miss a party at Studio 54, snow or not."

The problem was, how to get there? We bundled up and went out onto First Avenue, but it was deserted, a white-out. Not a taxi in sight. We tramped around in the snow for a while looking for a taxi, knowing that even if we found one, it probably wouldn't stop to pick us up. No cab driver would stop in that much snow. We were getting numb by the time we finally spotted a cab. Alan said, "I'm going to make that cab stop if I have to lie down in the street to do it." And he proceeded to do just that. As the taxi approached, Alan walked out and actually lay down in the street in front of it, in the snow, forcing the cabbie to stop. The rest of us piled in the back of the taxi, and as soon as Alan climbed in next to us, we told the cabbie to take us to Studio 54. All the way over, I kept thinking we were going to an awful lot of trouble for nothing. Even if the Studio was open, nobody would be there. Not in this weather.

I had badly underestimated the dedication of Studio regulars. When we finally walked in at about midnight, there were huge numbers of people on the dance floor, a massive disco frenzy in the middle of a blizzard. We joined them and were having the time of our lives when Alan suddenly said, "You know, we're going to have a big, big problem. We have no way to get home." By then it was past three in the morning, and we knew we were in trouble. Alan thought a minute and said, "There's only one thing to do. We've got to find somebody with their own limo. We'll never be able to hire anything." We started looking around the room, and a few minutes later I spotted Huntington Hartford, of the good old A & P supermarket chain, surrounded by a crowd of young girls.

Perfect! He was richer than Croesus, definitely limo material, and I'd met him years before with my mother. So I marched right over to him and said, "Huntington! How are you?" He was quite elderly by then, and full of the party spirit, but he remembered me, and when I asked him for a lift home, he said, "Absolutely." I motioned to Jake and the Lazars, and for the rest of the evening (morning, actually), we all stuck to him like glue until it was time to go. When he got ready to leave about an hour later, we raced along behind him saying, "Oh, thank you, thank you. This is so nice of you to take us home." And it was. We'd have been in a fine fix without him. We all piled into the limo behind him, and the minute the driver pulled away, Huntington passed out on the seat next to me. He did it so suddenly, and so unexpectedly, that I thought he was dead. "Oh God," I thought, "one of the richest guys in America, and he dies on the seat next to me." I could already see the headline in *The New York Post*: "Huntington Hartford Found Dead with Hookers" (me and Jake, of course). The next day, when I found out Huntington was still alive, we all heaved a huge sigh of relief.

After a week of this craziness, there was no question of returning to live in London. We spent every night of our vacation at Studio 54, and when the vacation was over, we returned to England only long enough to pack our things and put the flat up for sale. There was nothing for us in England anymore. Within weeks we were back in New York to stay, first with my old friend Jody, and soon in an apartment of our own. Paul Vigrass, who was still planning to form a new rock group with Jake, was right behind us. He and his wife and kids came over from England, too, and moved into an apartment in our building. I was back in New York to stay.

For me, New York became synonymous with Studio 54. I spent every spare moment there. Liza and I often met at the Studio, but we didn't really spend much time together. We had different circles of friends. The people at the Studio were remarkable, fascinating to me for their sheer variety. Anthony Hayden-Guest's book, *The Last Party*, captures the mood at Studio pretty well. Certainly, some of the people who went there were famous. The clothes designer Halston was there almost every night, usually with my sister. We were nodding acquaintances, but I never really got to know him. God knows he was talented, very talented, but not very approachable. If you were famous, Halston was your friend. If you weren't famous, he wasn't particularly interested in getting to know you. He wasn't nasty, just uninterested. Liza was famous. I wasn't. It was as simple as that. Having a famous sister and mother entitled me to a speaking acquaintance, but that was pretty much it. I didn't mind. I wasn't going to hold his aloofness against him. He was a snob, but a gifted one. Andy Warhol, on the other hand, became my friend.

Andy and I had met years earlier, when I'd been photo-graphed for his *Interview* magazine, and we were soon friendly. I had been asked to do the cover and a four-page photo spread inside. I was excited and honored to be asked to pose, especially since the photographer was the great Francesco Scavullo. I went for the photo session and had a great day. He took some of the most beautiful pictures of me I've ever had taken. However, I didn't make the cover until years later. I found out then that the old editor hadn't wanted to use me for the cover, but Francesco, bless his heart, bought out all of the photos, saved them, and had the new editor put me on the cover.

Andy and I became friends in part because he loved the stories about old Hollywood and the people I'd grown up with. I became very fond of him, and always found him generous to a fault. He often gave me pieces of his work, and Liza commissioned a portrait of me, which naturally I still have.

However, some of the most interesting people at Studio weren't famous at all, at least not until they started going there. Bob Petty was one of them. He was a bartender at the Studio who used to dance and make drinks at the same time, kind of like Tom Cruise in *Cocktail*. He could mix anything you wanted and never miss a beat. And then there were the Studio freaks, the ones who became famous just for being bizarre. There was Rollerena, the male stockbroker who showed up dressed like Cinderella on roller skates every night. There was Disco Sally, a woman in her late seventies who became a disco queen in sneakers. Some people even showed up in see-through clothing or "dressed" only in body paint. Bianca Jagger cele-brated her birthday by showing up as Lady Godiva (in an off-the-shoulder dress), mounted on a white horse and led by an elf green naked man wearing only a painted fig leaf. What made it even more bizarre is that these same people often had alternate identities as conservative business men and women during the day. My friend Nikki Haskell, who achieved con-siderable fame of her own at Studio 54, summed it up nicely. She said, "You'd go to Studio 54 one night, and the next day you would get into an elevator on Wall Street. In front of you would stand a guy in a three-piece, pin-striped suit, looking very conservative and dignified. As you waited for the elevator to reach your floor, you'd look at the back of his head and notice tiny remnants of glitter, still embedded in his hair. And you knew where he'd been the night before." The good part of the Studio was that it was also filled with gay couples, mixed in with the straight people. Gay couples had always had to hide their relationships when in public places, but at Studio 54 they didn't get a second glance.

Out of all the wild nights at Studio 54, Hallowe'en was the best. On Hallowe'en, they would pull out all the stops. That first Hallowe'en, Jake and I celebrated the anniversary of my friendship with the Lazars. Of course, Alan had to dress up in his mask as the mad doctor again, the way he had the night I met him. We went to dinner at Elaine's and then over to Studio for the big party at midnight. It was astounding. God knows, the people there were outrageous on any given night, but Hallowe'en gave people the opportunity to really get into costume. I've seen some pretty strange Hallowe'ens on Santa Monica Boulevard, but Studio 54 made Hallowe'en in Hollywood look like a PTA meeting. The street outside the club was jammed with mobs of people in bizarre costumes. One guy arrived in a real ambulance, siren screaming, and climbed out bandaged head to toe like a mummy. Two people came dressed like drugs – giant Quaaludes. One couple showed up having dinner, literally having dinner. They had chairs and a table set with a lighted candelabrum and a full meal. I didn't bother to dress up; I have to wear costumes for a living, so I just doused myself with glitter and went dripping sparkles. When we walked into Studio that night, the foyer was lined with little sets designed by Ian Schrager, one of the owners of the club with Steve Rubell. Some of the sets were curtained, and when you opened the curtain, there would be a very realistic were-wolf or something equally scary waiting to jump out at you. The most original was a scene labeled "a little dinner." It was a table with a group of midgets sitting around it, eating. "Munchkin leftovers," I thought to myself. My mother would have loved it. Inside, the dance floor was dark, covered with cobwebs and special effects designed to scare you to death. The money they would spend there on Hallowe'en was unbelievable.

In many ways Ian Schrager was the driving force behind Studio 54, but Steve Rubell was the one who drew all the attention. Ian would design the parties, but he'd usually disappear before things really got started, turning the club over to Steve to run for the evening. Steve was a great host, the ultimate life and soul of the party, but there was one problem: Steve had a massive Quaalude habit. By 11 p.m. he'd have taken two and still be relatively coherent, but by the end of the night, he'd be so stoned he was literally foaming at the mouth. He'd walk around chewing on Quaaludes, seven or eight in an evening. He had to have two people with him all the time to keep him from falling down, and to get him home at the end of the night. At one point he actually got a red wagon for his "helpers" to pull him around in, when he got too stoned to walk. It was insane; there was Steve, sitting in his little red wagon, popping pills and refusing to leave. It should have scared me; it should have scared most people, and me more than most, who'd spent all those terrifying nights with my mother's overdoses. But it didn't scare me. Because I was stoned, too.

It didn't take long for me to slip back into my old habits once I started at Studio 54. The place really was drug central. People did drugs there openly in the late 1970s, especially at the private parties, and I soon forgot all about the insights I'd found during those weeks at Bill Wyman's house in the south of France. I was partying again, and this time at the biggest party of all. Something about the place made people throw caution to the winds and forget every restriction and inhibition they'd ever known. It was like Woodstock every night, with different drugs and without the mud. It seemed most of the people at Studio 54 did drugs; it was as much a part of the experience as the music and dancing. Steve would invite the elite, which sometimes included me, to go down to the basement with him and enjoy his private stock of cocaine and other drugs of choice. Sometimes my sister was there with Halston or another of her Studio friends. We'd all snort cocaine together, a regular family affair. By then I was drinking, too. I'd always told everyone I was allergic to alcohol, but the truth was, I'd just never liked the taste. At Studio, though, I invented a drink for myself and called it the Lorna Special. Bob Petty, the main bartender, would whip it up for me. It was a mixture of vodka, gin, orange juice, and champagne, all swirled together. One of them would knock you on your bum. Between the Lorna Specials and the trips to the basement, I was semi-conscious most of the time. I cringe now when I see pictures of myself at the Studio in those days, staring blearily into the camera. I didn't need a little red wagon to get around in, but it was close.

Studio 54 really did change all of our lives. It changed our perceptions of what was normal behavior, and it created a new standard of night life that lingers even today. New York had been through a long drab period in the early 1970s when people didn't go out much, because there was nowhere special to go. Studio 54 changed all that. It was a social phenomenon that came to symbolize all that was unique to the early 1980s. It was the ultimate disco, the place every club is compared to until this day. Studio 54 put New York back on the map. People flew in from all over the world just to go there. I still think of Studio every time I hear my friend Paul Jabarra's disco classic, "Last Dance." We lived to be there; everyone would be on the phone the next day saying, "Did you see this? Did you hear about that?" It was insane, of course, and often dangerous, but there was a strange innocence about it, too. The 1980s would teach us all hard lessons about the price that is paid for chemical addiction and sexual promiscuity, but in those days we hadn't heard of AIDS, and the term "drug abuse" wasn't in our vocabulary. That would come soon enough, for me and for so many others.


It couldn't last. It didn't. Eventually Studio 54 collapsed under the weight of its own excesses. Political pressure began building as the conservative backlash went into full swing and Ronald Reagan's moral majority elected him to office. The New York police had been willing to ignore celebrity excesses in favor of catching real criminals, but that came to an end when the Feds were called in to investigate Studio 54. They found everything. It turned out that Steve Rubell had been stuffing money in the ceiling of the Studio instead of paying taxes, and the Feds found a fortune stashed away, tax-free. They also found drugs, and they found Steve's little black books with the records of who had been using what, complete with little "c's" for "cocaine" next to our names. In short order, they shut the place down. The last party, as it came to be called, was over. For me, the party would soon be over forever.

Chapter Sixteen

# WAKE-UP CALL

There's an old television commercial that says, "It's not nice to fool Mother Nature," accompanied by a large bolt of lightning. I didn't exactly fool Mother Nature, but I ignored her with a vengeance, and the time came when she wouldn't put up with it any longer. The phrase "nature calls" took on a whole new meaning for me. After years of living out the motto "Girls just want to have fun," Mother Nature let me know it was time to start cleaning up – and growing up. Not coincidentally, both things happened at pretty much the same time.

For nearly ten years I had been living my life like it was one long party. To say I hadn't been taking things very seriously is one of the great understatements. I don't altogether know why. Maybe it's because for so many years I was "little Lorna," forced to go to bed while my mother and big sister had all the fun. Maybe it was the fact that I spent my preteen and early teen years with adult responsibilities as caretaker of my mother and vulnerable little brother instead of just going to the school dances like other girls my age. Maybe it was just the time and place I lived in. I don't know. Whatever the reason, as my thirtieth birthday approached, Nature decided to take me into her kind but firm grip. It was time for me to clean up my act.

The first step in my transformation was to rid myself of the drug habit that had controlled my life for so long. For me, the cure turned out to be the hair of the dog that bit me. One night I got really high with a friend from Studio; even for me, it was a lot of cocaine. So much cocaine, in fact, that I was violently ill the next day. And the day after that. And the day after that. After vomiting for three or four days, it began to dawn on me that I really wasn't having a whole lot of fun. As a matter of fact, the thought occurred that I hadn't been having fun on cocaine for quite some time. For weeks I had followed a pattern of doing a line of coke, retching my stomach out, doing another line of coke, and so forth. For years I'd been able to drink, use, fall asleep, and start all over the next day with only a few unpleasant recovery hours at most. Now, though, it was taking me days to recover from a night out, and a night out doing what? Sitting in a basement with a bunch of fellow junkies. Every night for years I'd spend hours doing my hair and make-up just to get dressed up and go sit in the basement at Studio 54 getting stoned. I'm a slow learner, but eventually I do get the point, and as I leaned over the toilet bowl one miserable morning, I said to myself, "What are you doing? Are you nuts? This is definitely not fun."

I'd gotten started on cocaine initially as a party drug. I'd never been the lonely drug user who holed up alone with her drug; on the contrary, I used drugs as a social activity, a way to have fun with friends. Unfortunately, though, unlike some of my friends, I'd always been an all-or-nothing user. Other people could do a line or two of coke at a party and say, "That's enough," but I would keep on using until there was no more to be found. Once I started, I couldn't quit. It was the same with the Lorna Specials I drank; I never drank just one. And to compound the problem, taking too much cocaine left me so high I'd have to take a sedative such as Quaalude to come down again. It was a vicious cycle, and I had to stop. My body was screaming in protest. So I did stop, just like that. I never touched another line of coke.

Physically, it was easy enough. Physically, I felt better the minute I quit. Luckily, cocaine isn't addictive the way heroin is, and it doesn't have the long half-life in your fat cells that was such a problem with the medications my mother took. So physically I did just fine. It was the psychological adjustment that was tough. I really wanted the coke, and I knew that if someone put it within my reach, I'd take it. The only way I knew to handle the craving was to avoid the stuff like the plague, which to me meant simply not being around it. I continued going to Studio 54 when it reopened for a while under new management, but now I limited my activities to the dance floor. No more trips to the basement to share the goodies people had with them. I might still have a Lorna Special at the bar on occasion, but that was easier; it was no trouble to limit my alcohol intake once I no longer needed to balance the cocaine. As for my drug-using friends, I avoided going out with them to places where people would be using, and if they arrived at my house to socialize in the evening with their pockets full of drugs, I'd say, "Sorry, gotta go!" and get out of there as fast as I could. Avoid temptation became my new motto. I'd finally learned my limits.

Sick of the club circuit, I turned to summer stock to jumpstart my career once more. Summer stock is bread and butter for American actors who need work. Revivals of old plays, especially musicals, are its primary stock in trade. Casts filled with former stars and talented second-stringers tour the countryside in the summer time, bringing well-staged professional productions to cities and towns all over America. It's exhausting but fun, and I enjoyed being back on stage, doing what I do best. I'd done *Grease* in summer stock with Gary Sandy, former star of the popular TV series *WKRP in Cincinnati*, and Barry Williams, from *The Brady Bunch*, in 1979. Two years later I did the national tour of *They're Playing Our Song*. I enjoyed the work, I needed it, and the continual touring made it easier for me to stay away from the dangers of the old Studio crowd.

I even quit smoking that year. I'd never been a really heavy smoker, but still, nicotine was just one more stimulant in my body. That little light dawned during a performance of *Grease* one summer in Ohio. I had this tiny little dance number, and at the end I was wheezing so hard I could barely breathe. I thought to myself, "This is ridiculous. I'm huffing and puffing like the Big Bad Wolf from a couple of hops. I have to quit smoking." And I did. It wasn't very hard. I rarely smoked unless I was high, so once I quit getting high, I lost the desire for cigarettes. It was a good thing, too, since I was later diagnosed with asthma and told smoking could be dangerous for me. Once the cigarettes went, for the first time since I was a teenager I was completely free of chemicals. It's a wonder my body, not to mention my friends, didn't die from the shock. I'd like to say that getting sober was a moment of profound revelation for me, but it wasn't. It was really more of a practical necessity. The revelations were coming, but not yet. Not yet.

Along with my newly improved health and state of mind, my career was looking up as well. In 1982 I heard that they were doing a sequel to the movie *Grease* called *Grease 2* with a girl called Michelle Pfeiffer in the Olivia Newton-John role, and I was ready to kill for a part. I went on a crash diet, eating nothing but watermelon three meals a day, and worked hard to get into shape. I flew to California to audition, and I was thrilled when I got the role. It was my first real film role (you can get a quick glimpse of Joey and me on the boat in the Thames scene of *I Could Go On Singing*). We were all disappointed with the movie's poor reception; we'd hoped it would be as big a hit as the original *Grease*. Still, it was a start for me.

Just as *Grease 2* was drawing to an end in 1982 and I was getting worried about another job, one of the dancers in the movie, a girl named Donna King, told me they were holding auditions for the American premiere of Andrew Lloyd Webber's London hit, *Cats*, in New York. I arranged for an audition as soon as I got back to New York, and it went very, very well. I read for the lead role of Grizabella, and Andrew was very impressed with my try-out. I'd never met him before, but we got along well, and he told me he wanted me to work on the show with the musical director for three or four months. I worked with the musical director and dance master every day, at the producer's expense, learning the role.

Andrew returned to London while I rehearsed. He was negotiating to do a movie version of *Evita* at the time (fifteen years before it actually happened), and Liza had done a screen test for the role. A rumor circulated through the tabloids that I was trying out for the same role opposite my sister, but it wasn't true. I never saw myself as Eva Peron, but I desperately wanted the role of Grizabella the Glamour Cat.

Meanwhile, Liza was in London discussing *Evita* with Andrew, who told my sister I had gotten the Grizabella role. Liza called me from London with the news, but said I had to wait for Trevor Nunn, the director, to approve Andrew's choice. As far as Liza and Andrew were concerned, Trevor's approval was just a formality. Four months after my original audition, Trevor came to New York and saw my final version. I had been working very hard to get ready for him, because Grizabella was clearly the role of a lifetime.

The next day it came out in the trades that Betty Buckley had been cast as Grizabella. I was devastated. Trevor Nunn wrote me a very nice note explaining that the decision had nothing to do with my performance; it was just that they'd decided to go with another actress, someone with a different look to mine. The part had originally been intended for Judi Dench in London but was taken over by Elaine Paige at the last minute. Even though both of these actresses certainly had a different look to mine, Trevor's explanation didn't help. Intellectually, I understood his decision, but emotionally it was desolation. My friend John Napier, the set designer for *Cats*, said he'd thought the role was already mine, too. To this day he says I'm the only person who ever sang the role of Grizabella and made him cry.

After a stint onstage as Peppermint Patty in *Snoopy*, the sequel to *You're a Good Man, Charlie Brown*, I was cast in a second film, a remake of the 1960s beach classic, *Where the Boys Are*. No sooner had I finished shooting the movie than I got a wonderful opportunity to star opposite Farrah Fawcett off-Broadway in *Extremities*, a brilliant and harrowing piece about a rapist and his victims. My life was taking a definite turn for the better.

My newly sanitized social life began improving, too. I began going to a little eating place called Café Central after work with the members of the *Extremities* cast. It was a dumpy little place on the West Side with good food and what people refer to as atmosphere. We'd go there after the show for a late dinner or early breakfast. I'd get something to eat and have one drink, but I stayed out of the bathroom. If people were doing drugs in there, I didn't want to know about it. Café Central soon became an actors' hang-out. It was there I first got to know Mickey Rourke and Joe Pesci. The only problem was the bartender at the Café, a guy named Bruce who never seemed to get a drink order right. No matter what I ordered, I got the wrong thing. Fortunately, Bruce turned out to have talent for something other than bartending. A year later I saw him on the TV show *Moonlighting*, and discovered that Bruce the bartender's last name was Willis.

Farrah and I became great friends during this time, too. Farrah has gotten a lot of attention because of her beauty, but she's also one of the best – and most giving – actresses I've ever worked with. *Extremities* was a very demanding show, and neither of us was on a superstar salary, by any means. Farrah and I often sat in the dressing room after matinee and evening performances talking about our futures. One evening as Jake and I were stretched out on the couch watching television, the *Tonight Show* came on, and Johnny began interviewing a Farrah look-alike who had just been cast as the lead in a major television series. Johnny asked her how she'd gotten the part. In a baby-doll voice she said, "It was the strangest thing. I'd never done any acting in my life, but one day I was just coming up the elevator in this building in L.A., and this man came in and handed me his card and said, 'Are you an actress?' I said, no, but I'd like to be. So I called him and now I have this series." I rolled off the couch and screamed, "What elevator?" At which point Jake said to me, "You know whose fault that is? It's your co-star." So the next day I burst into her dressing room and called her "Farrah Forceps." "It's all your fault," I said, "that we're being paid a dollar fifty! It's the hair and the teeth." Then I told her about the show, and she screamed with laughter. All during the performance that night I would mouth to her on stage, "It's all your fault." It was extraordinary that while we were there trying to be real actors, for no money, bimbos were cashing in on Farrah's looks.

Out of all the good things happening in my life during that year, though, by far the best was my decision to have a baby. I'd always expected to have children "someday," but it had been easy to postpone someday under the circumstances. One day early in 1983, shortly after my thirtieth birthday, I found myself standing in front of a store window in New York staring at a display of baby clothes and thinking, "I want to have a baby. *Now*." Almost overnight, I became obsessed with having a child. I really do believe our bodies are programmed to tell us certain things, and my body was telling me that the time had come. I longed for a baby of my own.

I'd had one pregnancy, two or three years before, but that one had been an accident that ended in a miscarriage, a serious one. I didn't even know I was pregnant until I miscarried. I was at Studio 54 one night, and I'd gone into the restroom when a horrific feeling swept over me, and I suddenly started bleeding heavily. I hadn't taken any drugs yet that evening, so I thought I must just be having an unusually bad menstrual period. I sat down and asked an attendant to please bring me up a Coca-Cola to settle my stomach. By then the bleeding was worse, so I had someone track down Jake, and I told him we had to go home. Given my phobia of hospitals, I was hoping I could handle it at home. The bleeding continued to worsen on the way home, and Jake insisted I call a doctor when we got there. I did, and the doctor said it sounded like I was having a miscarriage. I told him that was impossible. He wanted me to come in, but I refused. Instead I lay on the bed, wrapped in towels and ice to slow the bleeding, and checked in with the doctor every hour or so. Finally the doctor said, "You have to come to my office right now. This is serious." By that time it was 5 a.m., and I'd been bleeding for hours. So Jake wrapped me in towels and half-carried me down to a cab and over to the doctor's office.

The doctor took one look at me and told me we were going to the hospital immediately for surgery. I continued to refuse, but he told me I'd pass out soon and have to go anyway. Panic-stricken, I called my godfather, Dr. Lester Coleman, and he told me to go to the hospital and he'd meet me there. By the time we got there, I was taken straight to the operating room, where they put an ether mask on my face before I knew what was happening and performed a D and C to stop the bleeding. When I woke up from surgery, Jake and Lester were there with me. The whole thing was over so quickly that it didn't even seem real to me. I didn't feel like I'd had a miscarriage; I felt like I'd had an operation. I'd never known I was pregnant, so I didn't feel any sense of loss when the pregnancy terminated naturally.

Fortunately, I recovered quickly and completely, so when I decided I wanted a baby two or three years later, there was no problem medically. Jake and I talked it over, and we both agreed it was the right time. Three months later I was pregnant, right on schedule. Once again, I was very fortunate, and with my body clean and healthy, the prospects for a healthy baby were excellent. I'd also gone on the Cambridge diet a few months before, so I was slimmer than I'd been in a long time as well.

I got the news I was pregnant a few weeks into my run in *Extremities*. I was so excited I went straight from the doctor's office to the department store and bought a crib. A friend of mine named Randy Booth, the musical director I knew from my stage tours, helped me paint the spare bedroom for the baby, and Jake and I filled it with furniture and baby clothes

*At work in the recording studio*

*The wrap party after* Trapper John, MD *finished its seven-year run*

*With Vanessa Redgrave in London, 1992 (above)*

*HRH Prince Albert of Monaco congratulating me after singing at the closing of the Special Olympics (below)*

Backstage in Tokyo with one of the great voices, Whitney Houston

In my dressing room with my friend, Whoopi, after a performance
of Guys and Dolls

*Vanessa with her grandfather, Sid (left)*

*Vanessa at three weeks old (below)*

*My beautiful Vanessa (bottom)*

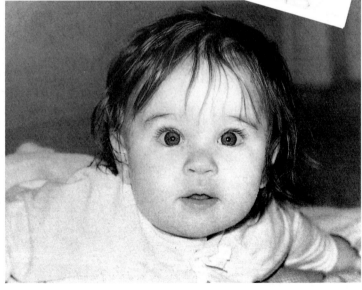

*Joey, me, Vanessa, Liza and Lee Minnelli on Hollywood Boulevard
after Liza received her star on the 'Walk of Fame'*

*Me and Jesse. Jesse is both my son and best friend.*

*Vanessa with a photo of her grandmother (above)*

*My son Jesse. Is this a petulant look, or what? (left)*

*With Vanessa outside the house Mama was born in, Grand Rapids, Minnesota, 1994 (opposite top)*

*With HRH Princess Diana after a charity luncheon at the Mayfair Hotel, London. She made the world a better place. On my left is Colin, my future husband, and in the background is ballet star Wayne Sleep. (opposite)* © RICHARD YOUNG

*Colin and me right after our wedding ceremony,*
*14 September, 1996*

before I was even pregnant enough to show. We painted the room blue with a little nursery-style border, which turned out to be fortunate when the doctor told me shortly afterward I would be having a boy. I was ecstatic. Jake was as excited as I was.

Farrah was excited for me but also worried because *Extremities* is such a physical play, and she was afraid I might get hurt doing the rough-and-tumble blocking. I wasn't worried; I had no morning sickness and felt just fine. It turned out, though, that Farrah's fears weren't unfounded. Not long after I joined the cast, James Russo, who originated the role of the rapist off-Broadway and also did the film, left the show and was replaced by another actor. The new actor's name was Tom Waite, and he was thrown into the very difficult part with little rehearsal time to perfect his scenes. He was even a little too rough for Farrah at times, and she is one of the strongest women I know. He would hurt her unintentionally in the scenes where they struggled.

I'd already taken one fall on stage doing the *They're Playing Our Song* tour. A crew member had forgotten to fill the holes where a door had been removed, and my heel got caught in the hole. I fell and injured a disc in my back. At the time I recovered in a few days, but the injury came back to haunt me. One night while I was doing a scene in *Extremities* with Tom, he had to yank me into the fireplace when I handed him something. He pulled too hard, and I slid and slammed my back against the rear wall of the fireplace. I couldn't move. There I was, wedged into that fireplace onstage, in so much pain I couldn't move. They literally had to stop the show and carry me offstage, put me in a taxi, and take me straight to the hospital. Once we got there, the doctors examined me, but they couldn't x-ray me because I was pregnant. They told me I had a damaged disc and would have to stay off my feet completely because of my pregnancy. So much for doing the play. To complete the fiasco, when I called the producer the next day to tell him they'd have to use my understudy, it turned out

I needn't have worried. My understudy had gone on the night before to finish the performance I'd started, but they'd never finished the play. Apparently, not long after I was carried offstage to the hospital, Tom had accidentally broken Farrah's arm in the next scene. The poor man was devastated by guilt – he'd taken out two actresses in a single performance! That finished off the play; they had to close the production. As a final touch to the entire strange experience, Farrah called me a few days later to say that her arm was feeling better, but guess what? She was pregnant too! She'd just been telling me the week before that she didn't see how I did it; she just didn't think she could deal with her career and a baby at the same time. Surprise! Her son Redmond would be born just a few weeks after my son. Farrah and I had a good laugh over the whole situation. Our lives had apparently turned into a sitcom.

With the play at an abrupt end, I suddenly found myself relegated to the couch with a sore back and a rapidly growing body. Too rapidly. With a license to eat and nothing to do all day, I filled the empty hours with food. You name it, I ate it – entire pizzas, bags of chips, and cookies, box after box of Entermann's chocolate chip. It was astounding. The first month of my pregnancy I gained ten pounds, and by the time the baby was born, I'd gained over seventy-five and waddled like a duck. Jake was worried and so was the doctor, but I looked the doctor in the eye and lied about what I was eating. I wasn't about to give up my cookies. I stocked up on maternity t-shirts with logos that said things like "Under Construction" and pretended my alarming bulk was all baby. Too fat to work, there was nothing to distract me from the refrigerator, and with my system free of chemical stimulants, there was nothing to curb my appetite. Just as with the cocaine, I could never have just one. Late in the pregnancy I went into the recording studio to do a disco version of "Where the Boys Are" with the Village People, and I still laugh at the picture we made: the cop, the cowboy, the construction worker, and the circus fat lady!

Luckily, they were a great bunch of guys who congratulated me on the baby and discreetly avoided mentioning my girth.

It really didn't dawn on me how big I'd gotten until I went to the premiere of *Where the Boys Are* in my ninth month. The posters for the opening showed photographs of my head on another woman's body. By the time they'd done the publicity photos, I'd already put on too much weight to pose. I had to take the doctor with me that night because I was so close to delivering. There I was, waddling into the Ziegfeld Theater with Jake and the doctor riding herd on either side of me. I jammed myself into the theater seat, and once the lights went down, spent the next two hours watching my formerly 98-pound body prancing around in a bikini and a series of skimpy costumes. I looked at the image on the screen and couldn't believe it was me just a year earlier. "Oh God," I thought, "I'll never look like that again." I got so depressed watching the movie that I cried through the whole thing. Afterward Nikki Haskell gave the cast a party, and when it came time to leave, I couldn't get off the couch. I had to have two people pull me to my feet. It was a scene straight out of *I Love Lucy*, before Little Ricky's birth. Jake tried to be supportive, but I still felt very low.

The worst moment of my pregnancy occurred at Bloomingdale's some time in my ninth month. I literally got stuck in a department store. Since I was afraid to go through the revolving door in my condition, I decided to go through the regular door. But I was so big, I got stuck and couldn't move, couldn't go in or get out again either. There I was in all my glory, jammed fast in the door at Bloomingdale's. I had to call for help, and the only way they could get me out was to have someone come over, put his boot on my bum, and shove me firmly until I came free of the door jamb. Talk about humiliation; I kept wishing I could just melt away on the spot.

In between cookies and soap operas, I did manage to squeeze in a baby shower. Liza and Nikki Haskell gave me a shower at a place called Serendipity, on 60th Street. It was an ice cream and soda place, which seemed all too appropriate under the circumstances. Liza and Nikki had rented the top floor, and more than fifty people came. My sister's secretary Ronni Agress made out the guest list and did a lot of the planning, and it really was a wonderful party, what the papers referred to as a "star-studded event." Farrah was there, of course, almost as pregnant but considerably thinner than I was. There were piles of beautiful gifts, and the whole event couldn't have been better.

The baby was due on April 2, but by late April I could hardly walk and was still having only mild labor pains. Finally, early on the morning of April 24, I called the doctor and said I couldn't take one more day of the discomfort. The doctor agreed, so Jake took me in to Mount Sinai Hospital a little after 6 a.m. to have labor induced. They put me on an IV drip with a labor-inducing drug, and I suddenly found myself in labor with a vengeance. Jake and I had done all the Lamaze classes so we'd be ready, but nothing could have prepared us for what lay ahead. It was one of those nightmare labors, the kind you see in the movies that make you afraid to have a baby.

For one thing, the labor seemed endless. A friend from my Lamaze class who was having twins arrived a few hours after I did, had her twins, and was back in her room long before I was ready to deliver. As the hours wore on, I began to beg for pain medication, but my doctor was hesitant to give me anything. Late in the evening, after I'd been in labor for more than sixteen hours, he finally agreed to give me an epidural. The catch was that because of the injured disc in my back, the space they could use to insert the needle in my spine was unusually tiny. And even though I was desperate for relief from the pain, my childhood needle phobia made the procedure nightmarish for me. Because the risk of serious injury to my spinal cord was so high, they had to have two nurses actually sit on me while they slowly inserted the needle. It hurt like hell. When they were finished and my lower body gradually began to numb, the relief was exquisite. By then it was past 10 p.m., and I was exhausted, but I was still having trouble delivering because of the baby's size. Worried I might not be able to deliver normally, they transferred me to an operating room a little before midnight and began to prepare for an emergency Caesarean. I was ready for anything at that point; all I wanted was for someone to get that baby out of me. The doctors decided to try one last time for a normal delivery. The obstetrician already had the forceps around the baby's head, but he still wouldn't come out. In desperation the anaesthesiologist finally folded his arms Indian style, grabbing his elbows with the opposite hand for support, and thrust his arms straight down on my abdomen with all his strength, literally forcing the baby out. And out he came, all nine pounds of him, with a loud popping sound from the force they'd applied, like a cork out of a champagne bottle. The force was so great that the baby's head broke my tail bone as it came free, and I ripped badly in both directions. I cried with joy and pain as they put the baby in my arms. My son peered back at me through swollen eyes. He'd had as bad a day as I had. Black and blue from head to toe, he looked more like a prize fighter than an infant. The nurses joked that he looked like he'd been boxing all the other babies in the nursery. But he was healthy, and he was mine, and I didn't care if he did look like a little Joe Louis. He was my son. Jake was beside himself with excitement.

Meanwhile, the hospital corridor outside the operating room was rapidly turning into a circus. Liza had arrived a few minutes before Jesse's birth, complete with her entourage, insisting they let her come in. What a sight they made – Liza, still made up from her performance that night; Joe Pesci; Liza's bodyguard, a former Hell's Angel; and Gail, Liza's limo driver. When the nurses told Liza they couldn't come in, Liza pulled out eight by ten glossies of herself and began offering to autograph them as bribes for the hospital staff! When Jesse finally did arrive, Jake came out and took Liza and the whole crowd back to my room. We opened a huge bottle of champagne that

Liza and Jack Haley had given us years before for our wedding, and everyone drank a toast to me and Jesse.

By that time, I was in a haze. Afterward the staff kicked everyone out, gave me a blast of pain killers, and left me to fall into an exhausted sleep. The next morning I awoke to a room overflowing with flowers, so many flowers that I didn't know if I'd had a baby or died. There were flowers from Dad, Joe, Liza, my godparents, a whole host of friends. The most remarkable arrangement was from Al Pacino – a huge swan with white flowers actually growing on it. I drifted in and out of consciousness all day, overpowered by medication and the fragrance of all those flowers.

My pleasant daydream came to an abrupt end the night after the delivery. I decided I wanted to keep Jesse in the room with me all night, so I could nurse him and be close by. What a mistake that was. I had the full responsibility for the baby that night, for the first time, and I just wasn't ready yet. Jesse was fussy, but when I got up to feed him, he couldn't really nurse, so I would change his diaper and try to get him back to sleep. Every time I sat up or got out of bed to pick him up, it was pure agony. Between my broken tailbone and the stitches where I'd ripped, I could hardly bear to move. The low point of that endless night came when I went to the small refrigerator across the room, leaned on it as I tried to open the door, and the refrigerator fell over on me, knocking me to the floor. Al Pacino's beautiful flower swan, balanced on the refrigerator's top, landed on me, too. I just lay there for a while, felt sorry for myself, and cried, as Jesse cried with me. The next morning, when the nurse came to take Jesse to the nursery, she asked me when I wanted her to bring him back again. "When he's in college," I moaned, and she chuckled on her way out the door.

I hoped things would get better when they let me take the baby home a few days later. They didn't. Like most new mothers, I had rosy visions of a cozy nest and an adorable infant. Jesse was adorable all right, but life wasn't perfectly rosy. To begin with, I felt terrible. The difficult birth had taken its toll on my body, and I didn't recover overnight. I had a tailbone to knit, stitches to heal, and a whole lot of weight to lose. Worse, I discovered I'd hired the baby nurse from hell. Jake and I had hired someone to help with Jesse during my first weeks home since I didn't have a mother or aunt to do it, and the woman we'd found turned out to be a real nightmare. I nicknamed her Eva Braun; she was an older woman with a thick European accent and a serious attitude problem. She was about as flexible as the average Nazi, and immediately put the baby on a rigid schedule and wouldn't let me interfere. She loved the baby but considered me an unfortunate inconvenience. Nothing I did was right; if I picked up Jesse and he cried, she would tell me it was because he didn't like me to hold him. I was anxious to learn the right way to care for my son, but instead of teaching me, Eva would hardly let me touch my own son. On the other hand, she expected me to meet her needs. By the time she'd been there a few days, I was cooking her meals and going to the kitchen to bring her juice while she rocked my baby. I was sunk in post-partum depression, in tears all the time. I begged Jake to fire her. I should have done it myself, but I was too demoralized. The woman scared me to death. Jake finally gave her notice, but it seemed like forever before we got her out of the house.

The problem then was that I was still exhausted, hurting, and overwhelmed by taking care of Jesse. Jake was wonderful with the baby, playing with him and admiring him for hours on end, but when it came to the practical stuff I was on my own. I did all the feeding, diapering, and getting up several times a night. Furthermore, though Jake was never unkind to me, he wasn't much of a support, either. He expected me to be my old self within days of Jesse's birth. He couldn't understand my continual exhaustion and was frustrated when I didn't want to go out on the town during my first weeks home from the hospital. Bored, he would open a bottle of wine the minute I put Jesse down each evening, and for the rest of the night, he sat and drank while I was dying for companionship.

My friends weren't much better. They'd arrive at our house and head straight for the baby, as though I were invisible. One of the things they don't warn you about is the way you disappear once the baby is born. During the pregnancy everyone makes a fuss over you and pats your stomach, but once the baby arrives, everyone loses interest in the mother. I was lonely and dying for attention and affection, and to make it worse, I was guilty and ashamed of being envious of my own baby. I adored Jesse, but sometimes I wished people would notice me, too. It was like my little brother Joey coming home from the hospital all over again; I would think, "But what about me?" And of course, the minute the thought crossed my mind, I'd guiltily tell myself not to be so selfish. Sid and Joe flew out and stayed for a few days, which was wonderful, but they soon returned to California, and Liza never came by during those early weeks. When I recovered from the birth, I'd take Jesse over to her place, but she'd say, "He's so cute – gotta go!" and be out of there in no time. I'm sure she didn't mean to neglect me; I think being with Jesse was just too painful for her right then. She'd lost a baby herself a year before, a little girl born prematurely at six and a half months. I think the reality of my new baby was just too much for her.

Worse yet was the post-partum depression. No one had prepared me for that, either. My body was going through hormone hell, and the result was a deep depression that overwhelmed me with sadness and guilt. After all, here I had this beautiful baby son, and I was sad and lonely. *What was wrong with me?* I wondered.

And most of all, I missed my mother. I missed her so much during those first weeks that I could hardly stand it. For the first time in years, I was overwhelmed again with the grief and anger of her loss. Where was she when I needed her? I had this wonderful child, her only grandchild, and I wanted desperately to show him to her. All of the pain I'd felt during the first years after her death came back again. "God dammit," I'd think, "why aren't you here? Why can't I pick up the phone and talk to you? Why aren't you ever here when I need you?" I had a million questions I needed to ask her about Jesse, about what I was going through, and I couldn't ask her. I needed a woman to talk to, to share the joy and anxiety and confusion with, and to make sense out of what was happening to me. I needed my mother and she wasn't there.

Eventually, of course, things did get better. Jesse got cuter with every day that passed. Once the bruises and the swelling went away, he turned into a handsome little replica of his father. He was a good baby, too; and within three weeks of his birth, he was actually sleeping through the night most of the time. My body gradually recovered, too. The pain went away as the birth damage healed, and as I began regaining my strength I ate better and my weight started going down. A month after Jesse's birth, in fact, was the best day of my entire adult life – my first Mother's Day. For fifteen years, ever since my mother had died, I'd hated Mother's Day. Each year as it approached, I would get terribly depressed because my mother was gone. But the year Jesse was born, everything changed. As I held my infant son that first Mother's Day, I was flooded with joy. Jesse's birth redeemed the holiday for me. Ever since then, Mother's Day has been my favorite day of the year, better even than my birthday. It is the day I count my blessings. When my daughter was born seven years later, she only confirmed the sense of blessedness I'd already learned from my son.

As important as my son was to me, though, being a full-time mother was out of the question. I had to work again, as soon as possible. As the saying goes, baby needs new shoes, and I was the wage earner in the family. Jake was managing the singer Rick Derringer as well as managing me, but only got a small percentage of Rick's fees. As my husband, he got all of mine, so most of our income came from me. That meant I needed to go back to work as soon as I recovered. Jake had been supportive of the pregnancy, but he was also very anxious for me to work again.

Work had come first in our relationship for a long time by then. Even when I'd had the miscarriage a few years earlier, I'd been back singing and dancing in a club two days later. Jake insisted I keep the engagement. The Lazars actually sat in the front row holding smelling salts in case I fainted onstage because I was still anemic from the loss of blood. By the time Jesse was six weeks old, I was performing again, with my sweet Jamaican housekeeper to take care of Jesse while I did.

I was coming to another major crossroads. I knew I needed someone else to manage my career if my marriage was to survive, so I signed with a successful management firm run by a man named Bob Lamond. Bob suggested Jake and I leave New York and move to California permanently. He thought I'd gone about as far as I could go right then in New York theater, and I would be better off living in L.A. and doing movies and television. Bob told me a move to Los Angeles would mean less traveling, more job security, and a better environment for Jesse.

I was ready for a change. When Bob Lamond suggested I shake the dust of New York from my feet, it sounded pretty good. Jake and I talked it over and agreed that the move to California would be a good thing, both for my career and for our family. We began making arrangements to lease our apartment. If things went well in California, Jake would return to New York and put it up for sale.

# Chapter Seventeen

# LIZA

Ever since I walked onstage in my first professional part, people have been comparing me to my sister. They compare our height, our hair color, our voices, everything. Reviewers debate about which one of us is a better dancer or singer, and which one of us sings more like our mother. Columnists invariably refer to Liza as "Judy's daughter" and me as "Judy's other daughter," as though I were somehow less closely related to my mother than my older sister is. Show business gurus analyze our relative success and speculate about our relationship. Implicit in all of this is the assumption that Liza and I are somehow in competition with each other, consumed by some sort of sibling rivalry that originated in the home and spilled over onto the stage. Also implicit in the comments is the belief that Liza was in competition with my mother onstage. Neither belief could be further from the truth.

The ironic thing about all of these rumors is that the two people who have never shared this public obsession are me and my sister. Liza and I have never felt like we were in competition. I was fiercely proud of my sister when she first achieved professional recognition; my whole family was. Mama and Joey and I were always in the front row cheering, the same way the Gumm Sisters had cheered for each other all those years ago. After my mother was gone, I continued to catch Liza's act whenever I possibly could; I was proud to know that the phenomenon on that stage was my sister. I was thrilled by her work in *Cabaret* and bragged about her to anyone who would listen. I never tried to compare myself to my sister professionally; as far as I was concerned, Liza was in a league of her own. Liza has always been equally supportive of me. When I was first trying to launch a career, Liza was there in the front row cheering for me. We've never felt that each other's success did anything but enhance both of us. From the time Joe and I first began taking refuge in Liza and Peter Allen's apartment during those late night crises, Liza and I have been not only sisters but friends.

Maybe the age difference between us helped us avoid some of the pitfalls of sibling rivalry. I was fiercely, painfully jealous of Joey from the day Mama brought him home from the hospital. Less than three years younger than I am, Joe immediately became a source of competition and displacement in my young life. Liza, on the other hand, seemed light years away in my childhood. With seven years between us, she was in junior high by the time I entered kindergarten, and by the time I started junior high school, she'd been out on her own for more than two years. It would be true to say that although I loved her as a little girl, I didn't really know her. Joe and I lived in a world separate from our older sibling. We were being put to bed in the nursery while she was off at the movies with her friends. It's the same with my two children, who are also seven years apart. Jesse loves his little sister, but at fourteen he has nothing in common with her. He's playing Nintendo while she dresses her Barbie dolls. When people ask me about my memories of my sister when we were kids, I have a hard time thinking of any. I have a thousand memories of Joe as a child, but few of Liza. It wasn't until we grew up that we really got to know each other, and when we did, we became true friends.

Over the years our friendship continued, but in the early 1980s our lives began to take different paths, in part because of Liza's inability to have a child. She desperately wanted a baby of her own, and although she never said so, Jesse's birth – and later Vanessa's – must have been deeply painful for her.

Ironically, the stupendous professional success that made her a world class celebrity also complicated her life tremendously. Wealth and fame are glamorous, seductive, but they don't make life simpler. On the contrary, my mother's life had been destroyed by the very adoration that created the Garland legend. My mother had too much adoration and too little privacy. As a child she inhabited a make-believe world at MGM; as an adult she became trapped by the celluloid image of that same child. Once she became a star, she lost the luxury to make a mistake the way private citizens do.

Liza inherited some of the same problems. As a child her father took her to MGM with him when he was filming. On Vincente's sets, Liza was the little princess in a fairy tale kingdom. Vincente even had costumes made for her by Irene Sharaff and the cream of Hollywood costume designers. My father was a business man at heart, but Liza's father was an artist. In a sense, Liza also grew up in a movie studio. I didn't envy Liza's celebrity; after years of watching the toll fame took on my mother, I had no desire to repeat the pattern. Living in the constant glare of the spotlight, Liza had pressures on her that I never experienced.

While I was busy cleaning up my act and getting my personal life in order, Liza's life had been falling apart. She and second husband Jack Haley hadn't lived together since Liza came back from Europe to do *The Act*, shortly after my wedding to Jake. Legally they remained married, but they lived on different coasts and were deeply estranged.

I sometimes wondered if Liza would ever find happiness again, the way she'd once found it with Peter Allen. On some level I don't think Liza ever got over Peter. She loved him so much, and when their marriage fell apart, it almost destroyed my sister in the process.

When Liza and Peter married, she had no more idea that he was gay than our mother did when she married Mark Herron. When the truth finally came out, Liza was devastated. I vividly remember the day it happened: I was still living in

West Los Angeles with Dad and Patty and Joe at the time. One evening Liza showed up unexpectedly at our front door, sobbing and distraught. When Dad came over to ask her what was the matter, she cried out, "Oh, Poppa Sid!" and threw herself into his arms. As I sat quietly nearby, Liza sobbed out the heartbreaking news about Peter. Her marriage was over, she told us, because Peter was in love with a man. She simply couldn't comprehend it. None of it made sense to her. It didn't make sense to any of us.

Eventually, Peter and Liza became friends again, and in their own way, they loved each other until the day he died. When Peter became so ill with AIDS near the end of his life, Liza helped take care of him. In a sense, Peter really was Liza's true love, and I am saddened by the thought of what might have been in my sister's life.

During the Studio 54 years, after Liza separated from Jack Haley, she tried once again to find happiness in a relationship. She became publicly involved with Mark Gero, the assistant stage manager on *The Act*. Physically and psychologically separated from Jack, she felt the marriage was already over. Jack was angry and humiliated by the rumors and the pictures of Liza and Mark in the tabloids, so he had filed for divorce, saying he "wasn't going to be made a fool of by Liza." By the time her divorce from Jack became final, Liza was already living with Mark, and eventually they got married.

What a wedding it was. Liza's friend Halston designed what had to be the ugliest dresses I've ever seen for me and Liza to wear – straight from my closet to the bin at the Salvation Army. Liza wore a long pastel thing – peach, I think. For me, Halston designed a truly ugly, old lady thing in lavender chiffon. I've always said that dress was his way of letting me know that he really couldn't stand me. But what could I say at the time? When Halston designs you a dress, you can't very well refuse to wear it.

The wedding ceremony was held in St. Bartholomew's Episcopal Church on Park Avenue, in Manhattan. The place was a regular cavern; it was so empty it echoed. Only a few people were there, family and a couple of Liza's closest friends. Her father attended, and Vincente's ladyfriend Lee Anderson came with him. Jake and I were there, and Halston, and Steve Rubell. And that was pretty much it, besides Liza and Mark, of course. I kept wondering why they had chosen such a big church for such a small wedding. Afterward we went to Halston's house, where he gave her a big reception, and then on to Studio 54. The comic point in the evening came when Liza threw the bouquet. Lee really wanted Vincente to marry her, and she was by-God determined to catch that bouquet. The minute Liza let go of that bouquet in the crowd of women at the reception, Lee, a tiny little woman not much bigger than my mom, suddenly turned into a Green Bay Packer. She went flying through the crowd and beat all comers to catch that bouquet. It was hilarious, but I guess it worked, because Vincente did marry her. Lee loved Vincente with all her heart, and all these years after his death she still does.

I wasn't exactly thrilled about Liza's choice of husband the third time around. I didn't like Mark; at the time I was worried that however much he cared about Liza at the beginning of the relationship, in the long run he would be more interested in the money and the fame than my sister herself. I was concerned he wouldn't give her the care she needed.

I blamed Mark for other things, too, then. As a sculptor, he didn't seem to have many real demands on his time, and he spent a lot of his days and nights partying. Liza had the money to support this. The fact that I'd spent my life at the same party until recently somehow still managed to escape my attention. Liza tried to get his sculptures some attention in the art world, but I didn't see anyone interested in his work. The tension between Liza and Mark was visibly growing. The relationship became deeply troubled; stories abounded of their fights. Sick of being "Mr. Liza," Mark retaliated with harsh criticisms of Liza and her life. It was also clear that Liza's drug use was out of control, and I blamed Mark for that, too. Stories were circulating about Liza's drug problems. Hardly a day passed when someone didn't call to tell me about this or that "incident" involving my sister. But what could I say to her? Until recently my own drug use had been so heavy that I was hardly in a position to cast the first stone at Liza. And although rumors reached me constantly, I had never seen any erratic behavior from Liza myself. I couldn't very well tell her I couldn't stand Mark; that kind of thing never goes over very well no matter how troubled the marriage. So I kept my mouth shut, concentrated on my baby, and worried.

It wasn't until Jesse was almost six weeks old that I came face to face with Liza's unhappiness myself. Liza and Jesse were chosen to be knighted by the Knights of Malta, a charitable organization we'd been involved with for years. I had been knighted the year before, and now Jesse was also being knighted in my honor. We had a tiny tux made for Jesse that matched Jake's, and he looked adorable.

We were all supposed to appear together at a special ceremony at a church in Manhattan. Jake and I went by Liza's house to pick up her and Mark, but when we got to her house, Mark wasn't there and Liza was in bad shape, high and out of control. I was angry with Mark for leaving, and worried about Liza getting through the evening in one piece. She made it through the knighting ceremony pretty well, but by the time we got to the reception afterward at a private club, she was starting to go over the edge. She became extremely effusive, hanging all over people and inviting total strangers back to her house, passing out her private phone number to everyone in sight. It was the same thing our mother had done so many years ago, at the end of her life. I kept thinking, "Oh God, this is really bad." I followed her around all evening, "uninviting" people and trying to retrieve her phone number by saying, "Oh no, that's not her number. She got it mixed up with another one." It was the first time I'd been with Liza when she was really stoned and I was completely sober. It was sad and frightening to watch her.

By midnight I was exhausted and well ready to go home to my baby, but when I told Liza it was time to leave, she said, "No, I can't go home. I don't want to be alone." There was panic all over her face. I didn't want to leave her like that, so I told her she could come home with me and Jake to spend the night.

"You can sleep on the nanny's cot, in Jesse's room."

Liza agreed, but when we got back to my house, she was still bouncing off the walls, unable to sleep and afraid to be alone. I kept saying, "Liza, I have to go to sleep, and so do you. You have a show to do tomorrow." After a while she went into Jesse's room and started talking to him, and I drifted off to sleep in the room next door. Two or three hours later I woke up to the sound of the television set. I went in the living room, and there was Liza, curled up in front of the television, sound asleep. It was 3 a.m. I put a blanket over her, made sure the shades and drapes were pulled tight so the dawn wouldn't wake her, and went back to bed. It was so sad – my sister, the big celebrity, scared and lonely there in front of the TV. It was Mama all over again. When Jesse woke up hungry at 7 a.m., I took him into the bedroom to nurse so he wouldn't wake Liza.

At 9 a.m. the phone rang, and all hell broke loose. It was Liza's secretary, Ronni Agress, saying they couldn't find Liza, that she hadn't come home. I told Ronni that Liza was with me, but a second later Mark called to say, "Where the hell is she?" I put Liza on the phone, and she and Mark started screaming at each other. This was the first time I'd witnessed one of their fights. Clearly, Liza's marriage was in trouble.

After that it became a regular pattern. Liza would show up at our house late at night, after her performance on Broadway in *The Rink* with Chita Rivera, and stay over. At first I would ask her what was wrong, but all she would ever say was, "I just don't want to be alone." It was clear she didn't want to go home to Mark, either. After a while I quit asking. I would make up a bed for her on the couch, and she would settle down with the television on. Like my mom, Liza couldn't sleep without a radio or TV on. Most of the time she was high when she arrived, so she'd take two or three pills, presumably sedatives, and eventually she'd fall asleep with the TV on. In the morning I'd ask her if she wanted to take a shower. Usually she'd say no, she'd better just go home, and then she'd gather her things and take a cab to her apartment. She never talked about what was wrong, but she was painfully unhappy. It made me so sad to see her like that. Life was strange; all those years ago Joey and I had taken refuge with her and Peter at their apartment in New York when our mother was out of control, and now Liza was taking refuge with me and Jake. For the first time in our lives, I felt like the older sister instead of the other way around. On the nights she didn't come to our house, friends told me she would sleep in her dressing room rather than go home. It was heartbreaking. Her personal unhappiness was also affecting her performance. She was going onstage with little or no sleep, constantly coming up or down from drugs, sometimes barely able to function. The other actors were running out of patience; their initial sympathy was turning into frustration and anger. This couldn't go on.

That became clear to me one night in a Manhattan restaurant. Jake and I met Liza after her performance for a late dinner with Chita Rivera and her family and several friends. We were talking and having a good time when someone at the table said, "Did you read that funny story in the paper about spontaneous combustion?"

We started to talk about it, but Liza interrupted by saying, "I can't hear this. Stop talking about it."

We looked at Liza, and someone said, "What is your problem?"

Liza repeated, "I can't hear this!" I looked at Chita's face, and she was tense with anger. Liza started to lose it; she jumped to her feet, yelling at us and crying hysterically. Everyone in the restaurant turned around and looked at her. Carrying on at the top of her lungs, she finally ran out into the street, calling for a car. Chita's daughter ran after her and tried to calm her down, to talk to her, but Liza just kept yelling at her. By that time everybody in the street was watching the scene, too; Liza Minnelli, yelling at the top of her lungs in the middle of the street at midnight, has a way of attracting attention. Finally her car came, and she got in and roared away as the other patrons watched in fascination. In the silence that followed her exit, I looked at our friends and said, "Well gee, I guess we better not talk about spontaneous combustion, huh?" Everyone broke up laughing.

Then it all came pouring out. "Do you see what we have to put up with every night?" someone said. Someone else said, "Oh, this is nothing. You should see one of her big scenes." Finally Chita said, "Why doesn't she just get a hold of her goddamned self," or something to that effect. I couldn't believe the anger at that table. Clearly, Liza's friends were fed up. All I could think was, "What was that? What the hell was that?" None of it made sense. Only one thing was clear to me: Liza was in trouble. Real trouble. It was only a matter of time before it all fell apart.

It wasn't long after that night that I got the call. It was Ronni, who is an extraordinary woman, competent and deeply loyal to my sister, way beyond the call of duty. But lately even Ronni had been in over her head with Liza. She had put up with Liza's temper tantrums and the late hours, sometimes staying in Liza's dressing room with her all night. She'd handled every conceivable problem for my sister by then, but the morning she called me, she was at the end of her rope. Very calmly, but with deep concern, Ronni said, "Lorna, I don't know what to do anymore. Your sister's in the hospital."

Shocked, I said, "What?"

Ronni said, "She thinks she has cancer. She's completely out of control. I've already had a car sent to your house to get you. You're next-of-kin; you're going to have to deal with this." She went on to explain that Liza had given a huge party for a group of Cuban and Brazilian people she barely knew the night before, and she had gone out of control. She'd found a mole on her back and become hysterical, thinking she had cancer. One of the party guests, a guy named Barry Landau, had taken Liza to the hospital for the "cancer." "You've got to come now, Lorna," Ronni repeated. "All hell is breaking loose. Get a sitter for the baby and get over here."

I called Arlene Lazar, told her what little I knew, and asked her to come and take care of Jesse for me while I went to the hospital. Jesse was still very small, only four months old, and I didn't want to leave him with a stranger. By the time I'd thrown some clothes on and Arlene had arrived, the car Ronni had sent was waiting for me downstairs. I jumped in the car, and we took off. The driver headed straight for a part of downtown New York I'd never been in before, and pulled up at the emergency entrance to a strange hospital in a rundown neighborhood. What was Liza doing there? Why hadn't she gone to a hospital she knew?

By that time I was a nervous wreck. I had no idea what I'd find when I got inside. What I found was Barry Landau, talking on the phone. He and I had had some personal differences after he'd volunteered to work as my road manager on one tour, so I wasn't particularly thrilled to see him. As a publicist, he was also in contact with the New York gossip columnists. To say he wasn't my favorite person is a real understatement. So when I saw him talking rapidly on the pay phone, the first thing that popped into my mind was, "That son-of-a-bitch! He's calling the *Post*!" It was like waving a red flag in front of a bull. I literally jumped on him, screaming in rage, "You son-of-a-bitch! I'm going to kill you!"

Ronni, who had met me at the entrance, literally had to pull me off Barry. She kept saying, "Let's not do this now. Come with me. We have to see your sister."

I was still shaking with rage, but Allen Eichhorn, Liza's press agent who was there with Ronni, stepped between me and Barry and said, "It's okay. You go to Liza. I'll take care of this guy." Between the two of them, they got me away from

Barry. Sure enough, the next morning a notice about Liza appeared in the *Post*. I never was able to confirm who placed it, but to say the least, I have my suspicions.

Meanwhile a doctor had come out to see what all the noise was about, and I told him I needed to see my sister. They took me down the hall to an examining room, and when I walked in, Liza was lying there on the table. I was shocked by what I saw. She looked like she hadn't been to bed in days, with mascara smeared all over her big eyes, and her face as white as death. She was also out of her mind with whatever she'd taken – pills, coke, liquor – probably all three. But what disturbed me the most was that she didn't know me. When I walked into that room, she looked at me blankly, with no recognition whatsoever. After a moment she said to me, "Who are you?"

Terrified, I stepped close to her and said, "Liza?"

The sound of my voice seemed to snap her out of her confusion for a moment. Her eyes focused, and she said, "Oh, my God, Lorna," and she started to cry and cling to me. She kept saying, "I have cancer, Lorna; I have cancer. I think I'm going to die." She kept holding onto me as tightly as she could, mascara streaming down her face, desperate for reassurance.

I just put my arms around her and kept saying, "No, it'll be okay. They don't think you have cancer. It'll be okay. We're going to deal with this. I'm going to make sure everything's all right."

My mind was racing. I was quite sure Liza didn't have cancer, but I was equally sure it was a life or death situation nonetheless. I told Liza I needed to leave for just a few minutes to talk to the doctor, and I walked back down the hall to where Ronni was waiting. I had already made a decision; it was one of the hardest decisions I'd ever had to make, and one of the fastest. There was no time to wait. I found Ronni in the waiting room and said, "Get me Chen Sam's number." Chen was Elizabeth Taylor's long-time press agent, personal assistant, manager, and gate-keeper. (She was a lovely South African woman who, sadly, died of cancer. She stayed at Elizabeth's house for the last months.) At the very time when Liza was in the hospital, Elizabeth was in the Betty Ford Center, so I knew Chen would have the information I needed. Ronni got me the number. By then it was 10 a.m. in New York, but still early in California, where Chen was. When Chen answered the phone, I said, "Chen, this is Lorna. I'm really in trouble, and I don't know what to do. I need to find out who got Elizabeth into Betty Ford, the name of the doctor, or who to talk to."

Chen said, "What's going on?"

I said, "It's Liza. I'm here at the hospital with her right now. I'm playing Beat the Clock. I've got to keep Liza here, and I have the press on my tail. I need help."

Chen said the doctor's name was Dr. Bill Skinner. It might take a while because it was still early, she said, but she'd track him down for me and get back to Ronni or me at the hospital right away. And she did. Bless her heart, it must have taken considerable legwork on her part.

While I waited for Chen to call back, I still had Liza and the doctors to deal with. They were pressing me to admit Liza to the hospital for a psychiatric evaluation, but I knew that would be disastrous. I told them no, I would have Liza transferred to New York Hospital, where we knew some of the doctors on staff. But when I called New York Hospital, they told me the same thing: if I wanted to have Liza admitted, it would have to be to the psychiatric ward, a locked ward, for a temporary hold and evaluation. They kept telling me Liza was exhibiting psychotic behavior and that legally they had no choice. Once again I refused; I knew the psych ward would terrify Liza, and if the press got a hold of it, there would be hell to pay. My mind was racing; I told Roni to give me the name of a doctor, any doctor, whom Liza had seen in the last six months. She managed to come up with a name from one of Liza's prescription bottles, and I called the doctor up and told him, "You've got to get Liza admitted onto a floor, any floor, just not the psych ward. Please." Thank God, he agreed and made the arrangements.

Meanwhile, Chen had called back with Dr. Skinner's number, and I called him immediately and said, "You have to come to New York, immediately."

He said, "But I can't. I have patients. Maybe in a few days . . ."

I told him, "No, now. You don't understand. This is a life or death situation. If she gets out of here now, she'll die. Elizabeth trusted you, and now I'm appealing to you. Help my sister. Please." He finally agreed to take a plane out the next morning, and he told me he wanted to bring an interventionist with him. Not having the faintest idea what an interventionist was, I said, "Okay."

By that time the press was breathing down our necks. Allen Eichhorn warned me, "The *Post* knows. They're already on their way."

I said, "Just keep them out of the way until we can get Liza out of here." We were all running around at warp speed by then, making complicated arrangements, fielding calls. The ambulance arrived to take Liza to New York Hospital, and we managed to get her out the back, literally as the press was coming in the other door. We made it by a hair's breadth. I pulled the covers over Liza's head as she lay on the stretcher and ducked out the back way into the ambulance with her. It was like the great escape. Once in the ambulance, the situation became truly absurd. I was trying to keep Liza covered up, but she kept thrashing around restlessly, throwing the sheet off her face. There was an attendant in the back with me, and I kept trying to make light conversation, but he was looking at Liza.

About halfway to the other hospital, he said, "You know who your sister looks like?"

I said, "No, who?"

He said, "She looks like Liza, you know, Minnelli."

I just said, "Oh yeah, people are always saying that. Of course, half the drag queens in the city look like Liza."

He just laughed, and we went on chatting. The first chance I got, I pulled the sheet back over Liza's face.

When we got to the hospital, we took her inside, got her admitted under a false name, and had her taken upstairs. Once there, I handed the doctor Liza's purse, with its cache of assorted pills, and said, "Here. I don't know what they are. I imagine she's had some other stuff, too." We got Liza settled, and then it was back to the phones. I had to call Mickey Rudin, Liza's attorney, and have him make financial arrangements for the treatment at the Ford Center. He wasn't too pleased, but he went along with me. Then Ronni and I talked about transportation. We couldn't very well put Liza on a commercial flight to Palm Springs, where the Ford Center is located. We finally decided to call the Sinatras; I knew Frank had a private jet that could make the trip, and I knew he would be discreet. Ronni got a hold of him, and he agreed immediately, no questions asked, and said he'd have his manager, Eliot Weisman, make the arrangements. Eliot was wonderful, a real champion, the Sinatras very supportive, and the plane was ready the next day.

By that time Liza was sound asleep, so I left her at the hospital and went home to finish my calls. Arlene was still with Jesse. By then it was mid-afternoon, but it seemed like weeks since I'd left the house that morning. I gave Arlene a brief explanation, sent her home, nursed Jesse, and got back on the phone to Dr. Skinner. I really didn't know what I had gotten myself or my sister into; I only knew that the Ford Center handled problems like Liza's, and that they were used to dealing with celebrities. I also trusted Elizabeth Taylor's judgment, and I knew Liza did, too – or would, if she were thinking clearly. Dr. Skinner tried to explain to me that we couldn't force Liza to go, that she had to go willingly, and that was why he would need to bring the interventionist with him. I still didn't understand; I understood nothing of my sister's disease, and I'd never heard of an intervention. Baffled, I had no choice but to trust Dr. Skinner and agree. While I tried to deal with him, Ronni and Allen continued to scramble around making arrangements for money, for the press, for Liza's understudy to take over in *The Rink*, and a thousand other details.

Fortunately, we had an ally we could trust staying at Liza's house, an old friend from high school named Pam Reinhardt. Pam and Liza had been friends since they were kids. Pam was as square as you can be, in the nicest possible way, and she truly loved my sister. I knew I could trust her absolutely. Liza had called Pam the week before and asked her to come and stay a while because Liza was depressed over her problems with Mark. Pam, always the staunch friend, had flown out from California and was still at Liza's house. I'd called her to come to New York Hospital and "babysit" Liza while I went home to make calls. Pam had been with Liza all afternoon, watching over her while she slept, and about 9 p.m. Pam called me to say Liza was awake. Pam and I had already agreed that Pam wasn't to tell Liza anything about the plans. By that time Jake had come home, so I handed him the baby and told him I had to go back to the hospital. He didn't ask any questions, and I didn't want to get into it right then.

Once at the hospital, I decided it was time to start preparing Liza for what was about to happen. Pam and Ronni were both there with her, so I said, "Don't you think it would be a good idea if they ran some more tests or something? You might need some, you know . . ."

"Need some what?" Liza asked suspiciously. Her head was beginning to clear.

"Well, look at Elizabeth," I said. "Amazing. She went to the Betty Ford Center, and they say it's really quite an amazing place."

Liza immediately said, "Well, I don't need to do anything like that!" She was starting to feel better, and now she wanted to go home and pretend nothing had happened.

"Fine," I said. "But you know, Elizabeth's coming out soon, and I hear she's looking really great." I looked over Liza's head at Pam and Ronni. Pam's eyes were crossing, and Ronni mouthed, "Oh, my God!" at me. They couldn't believe I was saying it. But somebody had to say it. I was just planting the seeds, giving Liza something to think about.

By the time I got home that night, I was so exhausted, I just fell into bed and went right to sleep. Early the next morning Ronni called to say that she was sending a car; Dr. Skinner had arrived, and we were going to meet him at his hotel. He had given orders for me, Ronni, and Pam to meet him there immediately. We were all to bring yellow legal pads and pencils with us. I turned Jesse over to our Jamaican housekeeper, threw some clothes on, and climbed in the car with Ronni and Pam. The next thing I knew, the three of us were sitting in a hotel room with Dr. Skinner, taking notes on our legal pads like three schoolgirls.

As we took notes, Dr. Skinner and the interventionist, a conservative-looking woman in her mid-forties, explained what an intervention was. "You are going to confront Liza," she told us.

We all looked at each other. "Confront her?" Liza is incredibly scary when she's angry. Her eyes turn dark and snap, just like my mother's did. None of us wanted to confront my sister.

The interventionist continued, "You need to write down all of the times she has hurt or embarrassed you with her behavior while she was using. You can't use hearsay; you can only talk about times she has hurt you personally. Your job is to confront her with the reality of her own behavior, so that she will realize she does have a problem and will accept help. She must be convinced that she needs help." She and Dr. Skinner continued, explaining that they would be with us throughout the intervention, to monitor the situation and keep it under control. He also explained Liza's state of mind; he made it clear that as the drugs left her system and she started feeling better, she would think she was fine and just want to go back home. We must not let that happen. If we were lucky, he said, she'd see the problem and want to go to the center.

But if not . . . well, it was up to us. We might not get another chance. Liza might not get another chance.

I looked at Ronni. I had never respected her as much as I did at that moment. Ronni had everything to lose by doing this: her job, her friendship with Liza, her whole way of life. But she never wavered. She just nodded. Pam was frightened, too, afraid it would be the end of a lifelong friendship. Of the three of us, I had the least to lose. After all, you can't fire your sister. But still . . .

After a moment's silence, I said, "We're doing this to save Liza's life." We were. So we started writing, each of us making a list on our yellow legal pads. Mine was the shortest, for Liza had hidden much of her worst behavior from me. Mostly I wrote about how sad I was when I looked at her, how sad I felt when she slept on my couch at night. The whole time I was writing, I kept thinking about my own drug use and saying to myself, "Who are you to talk?" I was also scared to death about confronting her. I kept thinking, "God, I hope this doesn't happen. I pray this doesn't happen. Please, please, don't make us have to do this." But most of all, I thought, "I lost my mother to drugs. I'm not going to lose my sister. I don't care what it takes. I'm not going to lose my sister."

Our lists completed, Dr. Skinner gave us final instructions. We were to prepare to depart for Palm Springs immediately, because if Liza said yes, with or without an intervention, we would have to leave right away. That meant we wouldn't even have time to go home. Pam was to go to Liza's apartment and pack bags for both herself and Liza. Under no circumstances was Liza to be allowed to return home. She would have to go straight from the hospital to the plane. Ronni was to pack a bag as well, and to make sure the Sinatras' plane had arrived and was gassed up and ready to go. Ronni was also to finalize the business arrangements and make sure Liza's driver was ready with the car. I was to go home, make arrangements for someone to care for Jesse for at least a week, and pack a bag for myself. And that was it. We doublechecked our orders and went home to wait for the night, like soldiers about to be sent to the Front on D-Day. I don't think we'd have been more frightened if we'd been facing a firing squad.

At home I called Jake and told him briefly what was going on. He asked few questions. Then I checked on Jesse, made a few last-minute arrangements, and sat down quietly for the first time in more than twenty-four hours. And finally, sitting there on the couch, I just fell apart. Ever since Ronni's emergency call the morning before, I'd been in Superman mode, pumped up on adrenaline and fear, functioning in overdrive. I'd reverted back to the little girl who'd run around taking care of things when my mom went out of control. But now, for the first time in the whole ordeal, it all hit me. I started sobbing. I cried out of frustration, and out of fear, and out of hope – hope that somehow my sister would still be all right. "Maybe this is good," Dr. Skinner had told me. "She's bottomed out. That can be a blessing." Maybe Liza would be all right after all. But then I thought of what we were about to do, of taking Liza to this strange place in the California desert, and most of all, I thought of what we'd do if Liza just got up and bolted out of the hospital and down the street. For an hour or two I sat there, crying with fear and exhaustion.

It was about 6 p.m. when the phone rang. It was Pam, from the hospital where she was sitting with Liza. She sounded hysterical, giddy, and she kept saying, "She's going to go! She's going to go! She saw Elizabeth Taylor on the news, coming out of the Ford Center, and she's going to go!" Pam was laughing and crying at the same time.

I couldn't believe it. What an incredible stroke of luck. None of us had known Elizabeth was coming out of the hospital that very day. "Thank God, thank God," I kept thinking, dizzy with relief as I called Ronni, and then Dr. Skinner. As soon as the sun came up the next morning, Roni arrived in Liza's car, and we went straight to the hospital to get my sister. With Dr. Skinner and the interventionist, we sneaked Liza and Pam out a side door, sidestepping the press, and whisked her away in the limo, toward the airport. Gail, Liza's faithful driver, was in on the secret. She'd been told not to stop for any reason without orders from me or Dr. Skinner, so the minute Liza stepped into the car, Gail hit the gas pedal, and we went roaring out of there.

What a ride! I'll never forget it. The whole thing was like a ridiculous movie plot. Liza was wedged in between me and Gail, and reality was beginning to dawn on her as we sped toward the private airport where the Sinatras' plane was waiting. All of a sudden she yelled, "I want a hot dog!"

I said, "You don't need a hot dog. We'll eat on the plane."

Liza yelled, "I want a fucking hot dog!" You do not want to be in a car with my sister when she's yelling.

I shouted at Gail, "Keep driving!"

Gail began to shake. Liza was still yelling at the top of her lungs, and Gail kept saying, "I don't see any. I can't find a hot dog stand. It's too early." All the while she was saying this, Gail kept pushing harder on the accelerator. By then we're roaring through the streets of New York at eighty miles an hour, with everybody's eyes bugging. When my sister is angry, she's scary.

Liza continued to yell for a hot dog, and I finally said, spotting a hot dog stand, "Stop, Gail! I'll get it!" Gail hit the brakes, and before Liza could move, I leaped out of the limo and ran to the hot dog vendor, shoving money at him. Pam and Ronni somehow managed to keep Liza in the car until I got back and shoved the hot dog into Liza's hands. It worked. She finally shut up for a few minutes and gobbled down her hot dog.

Meanwhile we'd arrived at the airport where the Sinatras' plane was waiting. As we all piled out of the car, Gail said to Liza, "Go and be healthy," and burst into tears. Liza was really touched. She put her arms around Gail and started to cry, too.

"I'll be all right," Liza told her. "Don't worry."

We said goodbye to Gail and went inside while the baggage was being put on the plane. We were so relieved to have made it that we all collapsed into chairs in the small waiting area. There we sat, catching our breath, when Pam suddenly said, "Where'd Liza go?" We all sat bolt upright and looked around. Liza was nowhere to be seen. Our hair went on end. "Oh God. Oh God, oh God, oh God . . ." And we were off. It was like the Marx Brothers. Everybody took off at top speed, scattering in all directions. I ran to the limo, where they were still unloading the luggage. Gail said, "She's not here!" I raced back inside the terminal, where the others were frantically searching. We looked everywhere – the cleaning closets, the ladies' room, lying on our stomachs to peek in the stalls. We were grabbing everyone in sight, saying, "Have you seen a short woman with dark hair?" We threw open one door, and it turned out to be a conference room filled with businessmen. As the startled faces in suits turned to look at us, I said, "Have you seen . . . oh, never mind," and shut the door.

We went panting back to the waiting area, in a blind panic, staring hysterically in every direction, when we suddenly heard a voice say, "What's the matter?" It was Liza. She had reappeared, from God knows where, as if by magic. We all looked at each other blankly.

"Uh, nothing," somebody said, and we all sat down simultaneously and tried to look casual.

At last someone came out and said, "Time to board." We jumped up like we'd been shot and tried discreetly to hustle Liza onto the plane. Once there we sat down, buckled our seat belts, and got ready for take-off. I'm absolutely terrified of airplanes, and the Sinatras' plane was a little Learjet, which is even worse. I kept thinking, "I can't let Liza see I'm scared. I can't let Liza see I'm scared." So I sat there pretending to be calm, making casual conversation, while every nerve in my body was shrinking in terror. I looked at Liza's purse, filled with that little pharmacy of hers that would be emptied at Betty Ford. I felt a sudden impulse to leap on it and swallow every capsule I could find. "Calm, Lorna, be calm now. Calm . . ." The plane took off. Liza had begun chatting with

Dr. Skinner. Pam and Ronni and I looked at each other. All three of us were still wearing our sunglasses, big dark lenses. We looked like three bugs, all in a row. We each whispered, "You okay?"

"Yeah. You okay?"

"Yeah." We were in the air by now, several thousand feet above the ground. Liza couldn't escape now. We were safe. Six hours later, we landed in Palm Springs, California, and drove to the Ford Center.

I helped Liza check in. She was upset to find there was no TV – she can't go to sleep without one – but all in all, she took the whole procedure calmly. They asked her a list of routine medical questions. When asked if she took any medications, she said, "Occasionally. On weekends. Prescription drugs." I didn't say a word. They knew what they were dealing with. The paperwork completed, Liza signed some forms and was told she would be going to the Eisenhower Center first thing the next morning, for a round of medical tests. And that was it. Ronni and Pam came in to say goodbye, and we all hugged her and cried. I still remember how small she looked as they led her away – tiny and vulnerable and scared. My big sister.

Afterward we checked into the hotel and made the necessary phone calls. I asked Liza's press agent to say she had been hospitalized but not to give the location or the reason, though they would find out soon enough. I called Jake, and I called Elizabeth. Then I called my father in Los Angeles, and finally I called Liza's father. That was the hardest. Vincente understood all too well what was happening to Liza; he had gone through it forty years earlier with my mother. He started to cry, and I had to keep reassuring him that Liza was going to be all right, that it was a very fine hospital. He was elderly by then, and the news must have been very hard for him to absorb. He hadn't realized what bad shape Liza was in. Finally he seemed to feel better, and he thanked me for helping save his little girl. I was touched, but I told him I'd just done what I had to do, what anyone who loved Liza would do. By the time I got off the phone, I was drained.

Only three days had passed since Ronni had called me that morning to say, "I need help." It had been the longest seventy-two hours of my life. By the time Pam and Ronni and I finished our calls and regrouped in Ronni's room, we were beyond exhaustion, mentally and physically. We all looked at each other, and then somebody said, "Where's the bar?" Oblivious to the irony of the situation, we headed straight downstairs to the cocktail lounge and ordered three huge margaritas with extra ice. As we sat there sipping our drinks in that blissfully cool lounge, Ronni suddenly said, "I want a hot dog!" We all cracked up. We laughed until we were sick from laughing, the margaritas running out our noses. And then we started crying from sheer relief until someone else said, "But I really do need a hot dog. I need one *now*." And we'd burst out laughing all over again. I don't know how long we sat there together, alternately laughing and crying, until they started closing up the place, and we made our way upstairs and fell asleep.

Chapter Eighteen

# THE MAGIC LAMP

These days the Betty Ford Center is almost a rite of passage for celebrities. In the decade of *Oprah* and *Sally Jesse Raphael*, it's hard to believe that just fifteen years ago, the word "addiction" was only applied to junkies in back alleys, and if a family member had a "problem," the best you could hope for was a quiet month or two in a medical clinic. These days there's a rehab facility in every city in America.

In 1982, when it was established, the Ford Center was revolutionary. Like an oasis in the California desert, the Center, established by and named after Betty Ford, was the first place "respectable" people could go to get help. The day that the former First Lady publicly said, "I am an alcoholic with an addiction to prescription drugs," she changed the face of America with her courage. And the day Elizabeth Taylor picked up the gauntlet Betty Ford had thrown down and checked herself into the Ford Center for chemical dependency, she transformed herself from a glamor icon to a role model millions of Americans could identify with. We owe these courageous women a tremendous debt of gratitude. I knew that when I took my sister to the Ford Center on that remarkable morning fourteen years ago, I was giving her a chance to save her life. What I didn't know that day was that I was saving my own life, too.

With Liza safely tucked away in Palm Springs, I returned to Jake and my baby, satisfied that I'd done my job. I knew I'd be overwhelmed with questions from friends and strangers alike, but I was prepared for that. I avoided people as much as possible, talked with the close friends who called to express their concern, and tried to go about my business. I ignored Liza's husband Mark; he didn't ask, and I didn't volunteer anything.

Meanwhile, Jake and I went about making plans for the move to California. Bob Lamond, my manager, wanted to make sure I was there for the pilot season in the fall to audition for upcoming television roles. I had lost most of the weight I'd gained with Jesse by then and wasn't working in New York, so we agreed I'd move to L.A. in September. It was already summer, so Jake set about making arrangements to lease out our New York apartment until we were ready to sell.

Things were moving along right on schedule when I got a message that the Ford Center was trying to get in touch with me. I called them, thinking it must be about Liza, but instead they told me they wanted me to come to the Center for the Family Program. I had no idea what they were talking about. When they explained that I needed to come back to California and spend some time at the Center myself, I objected. I couldn't possibly go right then, I told them; I have a baby, and I'm getting ready to move. Privately I thought, "What are you bothering me for? Liza's the one with the problem. I've been clean for over a year." I thought I was fine. Problem? I didn't have a problem. As far as I was concerned, that was that, but the Ford Center didn't give up that easily. They kept calling and calling, telling me it was very important that I attend the sessions at the Center for the families. I continued to say no until they finally gave up and called Ronni. Ronni felt very uncomfortable about going since she's not a family member, and she urged me to reconsider. Finally I gave into the pressure and thought, "Okay, what the hell. I'm moving out there in a month anyway. I'll get a sitter for Jesse and just take him with me." Then I called my friend Liz Derringer, so she could watch Jesse while I was at the sessions. "We'll get a really nice hotel, and I'll pay for everything. It'll be sort of like a paid vacation." Liz agreed. Jake and I packed up the rest of our possessions and made plans for him to follow in two weeks and set up our living quarters in Los Angeles. Early in August I said goodbye to New York, flew to Palm Springs with Jesse, and checked into the same hotel I'd stayed in when we'd first brought Liza to the Center. Liz would join me in a couple of days. But before she did, I had someone I needed to see first.

From the day I'd made the first call to get Liza to Betty Ford, I'd been besieged by people's opinions about what I was doing. Some, like Gail and Ronni, had put themselves on the line to help me. But others weren't so supportive. I had gone out on a very big limb by getting Liza admitted to the Ford Center. In my heart I believed I was doing the right thing for my sister, but I needed reassurance from someone I could trust, someone with more experience than I had in dealing with the family crisis. Who better than Elizabeth Taylor herself? She was an old friend of my mother's from their MGM days. Elizabeth was a few years younger than my mother, but they'd been there during the same era. I'd seen Elizabeth socially over the years, usually at some celebrity event, but I didn't know her well. I did know her to be a kind person. She had just finished the program at the Ford Center, so I called to ask if I could come by and see her at her home.

I still remember watching her walk into the living room that afternoon. The first words that went through my mind were, "What an extraordinary woman she is." She was amazingly beautiful, in a way that took my breath away. I'd always seen Elizabeth at formal occasions, fully made up and dressed to the nines; but at home, with just the two of us, it was a completely different thing. She was simply dressed in a white top and pants, and she wore no make-up. Somehow that clean-skinned simplicity made her beauty even more striking. As she gave me a hug and sat down on the couch across from me, I looked into those famous violet eyes and thought, "My God. You're amazing."

More important for me that day, though, Elizabeth carefully listened as I poured my heart out about Liza and my fears for my sister. The first thing I said was, "I'm here because I don't know what to do when my sister gets out of the Center. I'm scared." Most people would have said, "There, there. She'll be fine. It will all work out." But Elizabeth didn't. She recognized the gravity of the situation, and she took me seriously. She truly cared about my sister – about the addiction, the current crisis, what Liza had already been through, and the press, already circling like sharks who smelled blood. She never gave me any glib, easy answers; she replied to all my questions thoughtfully, with real honesty.

Most of all, I needed reassurance from Elizabeth that I'd done the right thing for Liza. She gave me the validation I needed. And she warned me that it wouldn't be easy. She told me, "Liza may hate you for doing this. She may resent you for it. She'll be going through a lot of changes. She may resent the fact that you're clean and sober, and that you have a child. That she can't be like you. She may have many painful feelings about you." I kept saying, no, no, that would never happen. Liza wouldn't feel like that. I was sure she wouldn't.

I will be grateful to Elizabeth for the rest of my life for what she shared with me that afternoon. She was extraordinarily helpful, an invaluable source of information and support. People love to say nasty things about her, but she has always been kind and gracious to me. I didn't go to her because she was a friend of my mother's; I didn't even go to her as a mother figure. But still, because of the generational difference, I felt like I had validation from my mother's age group, someone with so much more wisdom than I had. At the end I cried, and I thanked her for just being there for me. I left her house that day deeply reassured.

I needed the reassurance. Although most people had been wonderfully supportive of my decision to take Liza to the Ford Center, I knew it was a risky decision, and I had taken some criticism for doing it. The chief critic was Mickey Rudin, my sister's attorney. Mickey was the Sinatras' attorney for years, and he has a well-deserved reputation as an attack dog; he's smart and efficient, but ruthless. He's a powerful man, one to be reckoned with. When I'd first checked Liza into Betty Ford, he had called my hotel to say he wanted to see me in Los Angeles before I returned east. Ronni and Pam and I had driven down together to his office, expecting him to want an update on Liza and to tell us he was glad all had gone well. We couldn't have been more wrong. No sooner had we sat down in his office than he proceeded to chastise us like school-children. "I can't believe you did this," he told us. "When I heard you had taken Liza to Betty Ford, I thought to myself, 'The inmates have taken over the asylum.' Do you know what this could do to Liza's career? Thank God she knows I had nothing to do with this. I made that very clear to her." I just sat there, appalled at what he was saying. Aside from the fact that I resented being treated like a child, I was deeply upset by his attitude toward my sister. I'd always known that first and foremost he was concerned with business matters, but Liza trusted him, and I'd assumed he was genuinely concerned with Liza's best interest. Sitting there that day, though, hearing him talk about canceled performances and bad press, I realized our ideas about her "best intentions" differed radically. I thought, "He doesn't care one little bit about my sister. All he cares about is her career." I was disillusioned and angry. I left his office that day feeling disgusted.

The Center had been in contact with me in the interval. The Family Program would last ten days, they'd told me. I picked up Liz Derringer at the airport and got her settled into the hotel in an adjoining suite. I would need to be there at 8:30 the first morning for orientation and be prepared to spend the whole day. Early the next morning I arrived at the Center. Walking into the room they directed me to, I found myself surrounded by several dozen strangers – and my sister's husband, Mark. I was floored. He was the last person I'd expected to see there. I hadn't spoken to him since Liza entered Betty Ford. Diplomat that I am, I said, "What are *you* doing here?" He explained that he'd thought seriously about his life since Liza had left, and that he'd made some big decisions. He'd realized he, too, had a problem and that he needed help. I was surprised, but I told him I was glad he'd realized it. I respected his decision, but I felt uncomfortable with him, and I was relieved when we were assigned to different groups. Mark completed the Family Program on his own, got help for his alcohol problems, and has continued to live responsibly. He and my sister have been divorced for a long time now, but I've come to admire and respect Mark for the changes he made in his life. I now know that Mark wasn't to blame for my sister's problems.

It soon became clear that the Family Program was hard work. Classes started every morning at nine and didn't end until 5 p.m., with a break for lunch. We were given an agenda and a pile of reading material – books, pamphlets, and articles. We even had homework to take home at the end of the day. There were large group meetings, small group meetings, seminars, movies, discussions, everything you could name. We were being given a crash course in the realities of chemical dependency and the role families play in the process. It was the most intense educational experience I've ever had. It was, for me, revolutionary. It was as if I had rubbed a magic lamp, and a genie had popped out and said, "You know all those questions you've had since you were a little girl on Rockingham Drive, Lorna? Well, here are the answers."

It was a revelation to me. I sat there enthralled, soaking it all up. They explained that an "alcoholic" is their term for anyone with an ongoing chemical dependency, whether the chemical is alcohol or something else. The dynamics and the behavior are the same, no matter which chemical the addict is using. When they explained that the "alcoholic" may actually be dependent on pills, I made the connection with my mother immediately. Mama never really drank much, so I'd always objected to her being called an alcoholic, but with the new definition I was being given, it made perfect sense. My mother's "alcohol" was prescription medicine. And then when they said that "98 per cent of adult children of alcoholics marry an alcoholic," it was like a light bulb went on in my head. Bingo! That was me, me exactly. Suddenly it all came together: Mama, Liza, me, Jake, and, as I would soon discover, my brother Joe – all of us were bound together in an ongoing, destructive family pattern that I had never recognized. I had simply never made the connection. It had never occurred to me that all of these things were interrelated.

What really brought it home to me was listening to the stories of the people around me. In my mind, I guess all the drugs and the craziness I had witnessed were tied up with the insane celebrity lifestyle I had known since I was a kid, but the people in that room with me couldn't have been further from celebrities. They were just regular people from all parts of America, all lifestyles – mothers, fathers, brothers, sisters, teenagers and people in their early twenties, who had made tremendous sacrifices to place their loved ones at the Ford Center. In most respects their lives couldn't have been more different from mine. Yet in the essential sense, our lives were exactly alike. They might never have been to Europe or Studio 54, but it didn't matter; under the surface, we were all the same. We'd all done the same things, reacted the same ways, told the same lies, to ourselves and to those around us. It was funny and scary and mind-blowing all at the same time. Over and over again someone would share something, and I'd think, "I did that. I said that. That exact same thing." And when the counselors told us how families like mine act, it was unnerving. I thought, "God, how did he know I did that?" I was over-whelmed. Instead of dreading the classes, I soaked up every word they said to me. Sometimes I didn't even want to leave at the end of the day. It was all so new to me, and I wanted to learn more and more. I was starved for it. At the end of the day I'd rush back to the hotel to tell Liz Derringer what I'd learned. A close member of Liz's family had a severe addiction problem, too, and she was blown away by what I was sharing with her. Soon she was reading the pamphlets when I was finished with them. It was intense but wonderful.

For the first time since childhood, I didn't feel alone. From the day I'd stood in that doorway in Hawaii and watched my mother overcome with rage and chemicals, I'd been keeping a terrible secret in my heart, a secret I could never share with anyone. But there in that room in Palm Springs, I found out that it didn't really matter that my mother was Judy Garland, the legendary singer and screen icon. It didn't matter who your mother was; every one of us in that room had told the same lies, struggled with the same shame. As I listened to the stories from the people around me, I kept thinking how alike we all were. The stories were funny and sad and tragic, but they all had a common thread. Every one of us was an accomplished liar. "Miss Garland isn't feeling well tonight. She has the flu. My sister is just tired. She'll be all right for tonight's perform-ance. Jake can't go to work this morning. He has food poisoning. Oh no, I don't have a drug problem. I just like to have fun at parties with my friends." And on and on and on. I thought about all the lies we'd told my mother, Sid and Joe and I. We don't want to hurt Mama's feelings. We don't want to make Mama mad. And later it became, Jake isn't an alcoholic. Of course not. I don't have a problem. Don't be silly. Once you start lying, you never stop. It takes over your whole life. I wasn't the only actor in that room; we were all actors, and our lives were one long performance.

I also began acquiring a whole new vocabulary at the Center. It was there I learned what words like "intervention," "co-dependent," and "enabler" meant. The counselors carefully and clearly explained the part that each family member plays in the addictive cycle. I really resisted the concept that by my behavior, I was enabling family members to continue their addiction. There are so many ways we enable those around us to keep using. One is to cover up for them, protect them from the consequences of their own actions. I'd done that for my mother, and I was still doing it for Jake. Another way is to scream and yell at them constantly for what they're doing. It only makes them want to use more, and it sets up a conflict that makes solving the problem impossible. That had become the story of my life with Jake. And finally, you can enable an alcoholic to keep using by simply pretending the problem doesn't exist. Problem? What problem? That was what I'd been doing with Liza. She could be bouncing off the ceiling with cocaine or popping pills on my couch, but I'd never said a word. I'd just gone about my business as if nothing was happening.

Difficult as it was to accept the concept of enabling, accepting the idea of "detachment" was even harder. The counselors explained to us that when we were talking to an alcoholic under the influence, we weren't talking to a person at all; we were talking to a chemical. We were having a conversation with a bottle of gin or a line of cocaine, not a human being. Reasoning with a chemical was out of the question. Trying to "fix" a chemical was equally impossible. The result, they told us, was that it was our responsibility to "detach" from a loved one in that condition until they were sober again. In other words, if your loved one comes home dead drunk, don't undress them and put them to bed. Let them pass out on the couch, and leave them there. If they vomit and pass out on the bed, don't clean it up. Let them wake up in it. Sleep in the other room. Turn on the television. Step over them and go to a movie with a friend. Let the *alcoholic* deal with it. We were only responsible to take care of ourselves, and that was what we should do, just as it was the alcoholic's responsibility to take care of himself. I was stunned by this piece of advice. What do you mean, step over him and go to a movie? What happened when he woke up and was furious about the mess left behind? What happened when he got fired? Sick? Run over? One woman in my group expressed exactly what I was feeling: "What do you mean, don't pay my son's rent? He'll get *evicted*." When the counselor replied, "Let him," she looked at him like he'd lost his mind.

That was the hardest part for me, the concept of letting go. I simply couldn't comprehend it. Over and over I would ask about my sister: "What should I do when she gets out? What should I do if she starts using again? How can I stop her if she gets out of control?" And over and over the counselors kept saying to me, "It's not your responsibility. It's her responsibility. Don't do anything. Don't help her. Let her help herself." I couldn't get that. It was incomprehensible to me. I finally voiced what all of us were thinking: "But she could *die*." When the counselor said that was her choice, I thought he was insane. Didn't he understand? I couldn't let that happen. I had to prevent it. It was my responsibility, just as it had been my responsibility to take care of my mother. From the day my father had taught me to monitor my mother's pill intake, I had been taking care of an alcoholic. I was very good at it; I knew where to look for the pills, what lies to tell other people, how to get medical help discreetly, how to administer first aid if they needed it. I was an expert. How could this counselor look me in the face and tell me just to walk away?

I'd walked away from my mother. That last year, I'd walked away and left her to take care of herself. And she'd died. She'd goddam died. *Didn't they understand that?*

That's what I wrestled with the hardest that week. For sixteen years my mother's ghost had haunted me, the ghost of my own guilt. I could have saved her, I'd thought over and over again. I could have saved her. I should have stayed with her at the end. But there in that conference room in Palm Springs, I finally confronted that ghost. The counselor looked me in the eye and said, "Do you really believe that, Lorna? Your mother died. Do you honestly believe you could have saved her?" That night, and for several nights after that, I lay awake and asked myself that question: could I really have saved her? Countless books and articles have been written about my mother, about how she could have been saved if someone had really cared enough. I believed it myself. But there in that hotel room, I finally faced the hard truth: there was nothing I could have done to save her. There was nothing anybody could have done. It wasn't my fault. It wasn't even Mickey Deans' fault. If she hadn't overdosed that night, it would have been the next. Or the one after that. Sooner or later it would have happened, and none of us could have stopped it. I would lie there and cry for my mother, and for all those other mothers and fathers and grandparents who had died because nobody understood the disease that had taken them. I saw the pain in the faces of the people surrounding me there at the Center, and I knew it was the same pain I'd carried for so many years. I wondered how different my mother's life might have been if they had understood addiction when she was young, if there had been a Betty Ford Center to send her to during those last, agonizing years. And for the first time I truly understood that what had taken my mother from me was a disease, and for the first time, I was able to forgive her – forgive her for the pain in our home, forgive her for the anger and the terror, and most of all, forgive her for dying and leaving me all alone when I needed her so much. And I looked at my baby son sleeping there next to me and thought, thank God. Thank God it doesn't have to go on another generation.

As my ten days at the Center drew to a close, I received a message saying Liza had requested a meeting with me before I left at the end of the program. I'd seen her two or three times already since the day we checked her in. She was allowed a limited number of visitors; her father had been to see her, my father had been, and a couple of her closest friends had been there, too. When I'd been to see her earlier, I'd already told her that I'd seen Elizabeth Taylor, and that she had been wonderfully helpful. Liza's reaction had startled me. Her head had whipped around, and she'd said, "What? What do you mean, you saw her?" There was a great deal of anger and resentment on her face as she said it, and I remember a little bell had gone off in my head. Uh oh. Maybe this was what Elizabeth had meant. But my sister has always been very possessive about her friends, and I thought maybe she considered Elizabeth her friend, not mine. I chalked it up to possessiveness and didn't connect it with her stay at the Center.

So when I walked into the one-on-one counseling session at the end of the Family Program, I had no expectation that anything unpleasant would occur. I was still overwhelmed by the power of the new discoveries I'd been making day by day. But the minute I sat down, it was clear that Liza was angry with me. She began to pour out her resentment about all kinds of things I'd never known she even thought about. There were two areas she talked about the most; one was what she called my judgemental attitude. She thought I was constantly judging her and her friends, looking down on their behavior. Things that I thought of as expressions of caring and concern, she thought of as criticism. The other source of her resentment was Mark. She was very angry about my obvious dislike of Mark. When I tried to tell her that I didn't like him because I thought he didn't care for her properly and because I didn't like his lifestyle, she told me it was none of my business. I was very surprised by the way she felt, and very hurt. I tried to explain why I'd acted as I had, but it didn't seem to make any difference to her. She was too filled with resentment to care about my point of view. I was stunned. I hadn't expected her reaction. I should have, especially after my conversation with Elizabeth Taylor, but I didn't.

Then I got angry. When the counselor asked me what I wanted to say to Liza, I told her I was very unhappy with her behavior, too – all the insanity, all the deception. I told her that the thing I resented the most about her was the constant lying. She could never seem to tell me the truth about anything; either she'd avoid the subject or make something up to get herself off the hook. Even when I called, she'd often pretend not to be there or have someone say, "She's in the shower." I'd think, "God, how clean must she be by now? The woman takes more showers than anyone I've heard of." I told her I'd rather she just said it was a bad time, that she'd call me back when she could. Instead I always ended up feeling stupid, like the dumb little sister, and I wouldn't want to call her the next time. "Why do you have to lie to me about everything?" I asked her. By then I was in tears of anger and pain. She didn't seem to have anything good to say to me, even about getting her help. I didn't want credit, from her or anyone else; I just wanted her to understand that I'd taken a big risk because I loved her.

By the time it was all over, we were both in tears. Everybody said the right things, and the session ended in a friendly manner. But I was deeply disturbed by what had happened. Even when we hugged at the end, I thought to myself, "I wonder if this is for real, or if it's just another performance." Like our mother, Liza didn't get that Academy Award for nothing. The whole experience reminded me of moments with my mom years before. I couldn't be sure whether Liza was expressing her real feelings or just giving another performance. I was beginning to think that the lying was so deeply ingrained in her that I wasn't sure she could quit. I understood that; all of us – me, Liza, Joey, and Sid – had become expert liars as a way to survive with my mother, who was only willing to hear what she wanted us to say. Joe and I had struggled long and hard to develop honest relationships with people. But with Liza, it went much deeper. The line between truth and performance had blurred with her as it had with our mother, and the question that disturbed me the most was whether Liza, though finally sober, was still doing it. It had been different with my mom; Mama's "performances" were a product of her advancing disease, of the chemicals working on her mind. Liza, on the other hand, was now stone cold sober and had just finished a lengthy process of education and introspection. If the Ford Center hadn't changed her, what would? I wrestled with my doubts all night after my conference with her, and for a long time after that I continued to struggle. Was Liza well now? I just didn't know.

Two weeks after the Family Program ended, Liza came out of the Ford Center. She rented a house in Beverly Hills and started giving interviews. The press agents were all over her for a statement. She gave a long interview to *People* magazine about her time at Betty Ford, and for a long time the press was flooded with articles about her experiences. Her story was always the same: she'd realized she had a problem and decided to check herself into the Ford Center because they had such an excellent program there. In all the interviews she gave the impression that she had taken the initiative herself every step of the way. She never mentioned her mental disintegration in the hospital in New York, and she certainly never mentioned the role the people around her had played in virtually kidnapping her to get her to the Center where she could be helped. On the contrary, she presented herself as if the entire program had been her own idea from the start. People close to the situation would come to me and say, "She never mentions you, all you went through to get her there. Doesn't that bother you?" It really didn't. I knew what I'd done, but I also knew it was just Liza's style to dramatize things and make herself the center of attention. It was her coping mechanism, a way to protect herself from the humiliation she would have felt in telling the press what had really happened. I didn't mind that she didn't mention me. She hadn't mentioned Ronni or anyone else who'd helped her, either. The important thing was that she was healthy and sober and alive. I'd come too close to losing her to worry about who got the credit for her recovery.

Besides, I had my own family to worry about. With a three-month-old baby and a career change in the works, it was time to turn my attention back to my own life. I left the Ford Center Family Program excited, rejuvenated, brimming over with new information that I hoped to carry into my daily life. But first things first. For one thing, I needed to find a place to live.

By this time Jake had packed up the rest of our belongings

in New York, leased our apartment, and flown out to California to meet me and Jesse. We needed a place to stay, so Jack Haley offered to let us stay with him until we could find a place of our own. I had remained on good terms with Jack after Liza's divorce and still considered him a friend, so Jake and I moved in for a few weeks as Jack's houseguests. Jack was happy about what I had done in getting Liza to the Ford Center, and he was very kind to us. He still drank socially himself, so I'd talk about what I'd learned at the Center, and he'd express his warm support while sipping a drink, oblivious to the irony of the situation.

Jake located a house for us to lease in Studio City, a small city nestled against the Hollywood Hills just minutes from the Burbank television studios. It was a very cute little house, and we got a cute little dog to go with our cute little baby. With no work to occupy my time, my life had gotten so cute it was nauseating. I was trying to live a normal, sober life, but the problem was that I didn't know what normal was; I hadn't had a "normal" day since I was seven years old. I started going on auditions for television work, but had little success in the beginning. I would get very close to a part, but at the last minute the deal always fell apart. I didn't know why, and it bothered me. Finally my manager, Bob Lamond, told me he wanted me to work with an acting coach named Jered Barkley to see if he could figure out what was wrong.

I liked Jered immediately. It didn't take long for him to find the problem. I had arrived in L.A. after a career in New York, and I thought and behaved like a New York theater person. Like so many New York actors, I had an attitude about L.A. I thought the television people in Los Angeles were all slightly nuts, and I looked down on them. It was the old New York/L.A. feud that has been going on in the acting community for years. What I didn't realize was that I was taking that attitude into meetings with me.

Jered sat me down and said, "Look, it's like this. In New York, they sit you down and say, 'Let's play Monopoly,' so you play Monopoly. But in L.A. they say, 'Let's play a game, but we're not going to tell you what the game is.' The game is Bullshit, and you're going to have to learn how to play it."

When I protested that I hated all the bullshitting that when on in Hollywood, and I didn't want to do it, he said, "Then you will never work here. You might as well pack up your baby and go back to New York, because you will never get a job in L.A."

"But if I do what you're asking, I'll be just like all the rest of them. I don't want to be like that."

And then Jered gave me a great piece of advice. "You don't have to be like that all the time. You only have to be that way while you're standing in those offices. Think of it like this: Pretend it's a piece of luggage. Call it your 'full-of-shit' bag. When you go to the meetings, you're going to pick up your shit bag and carry it to work with you like a briefcase. As long as you're in that office, you're going to clutch that shit bag. You're going to be Dorothy Adorable, act like everything they say is brilliant, and charm everyone in the place. The minute you leave the office, you're going to put the shit bag in the car, go home, take a shower, and become a normal person again. As long as you don't take it home with you, you'll be fine. And you'll get a job. I guarantee it."

I took his words to heart. The next time I had a meeting, I packed up my little bag and took it with me. I was charming and adorable. One week later I landed a part in the television series *Trapper John, M.D.*, a spin-off of the *M.A.S.H.* series, set in a U.S. hospital after the characters return from the Korean War. I was offered an ongoing, supporting role as a staff nurse.

I loved doing *Trapper John*; the cast was great, and it was wonderful to settle into the steady routine a television series provides. Since I didn't have to tour anymore, I could be home with Jesse on evenings and weekends. I found a wonderful nurse for him named Maria, and with the money from the series we were able to buy a house in Beverly Hills. I'd come full circle. I was back in my childhood neighborhood, just up Sunset Boulevard from Mapleton Drive, except now I was the mom, and the baby boy in the next room was my son. My dad lived less than five miles away, and my brother Joe was just on the other side of the Hollywood Hills from us. I was determined to make a success of my new life.

Jake was happy with the situation, too. Money had always been very important to him, and he relished the things my salary could provide for us. Along with the new house came a new Mercedes for Jake and a relatively posh lifestyle. Jake still traveled sometimes as Rick Derringer's manager, but most of the time he was home with us in California. He loved the glamor of Hollywood, all the trappings, the glitter and the glitz. We attended a lot of the premieres, always dressed to the nines. "Stop," Jake would say as I was walking along. "Have your picture taken." And we'd pose for the camera. Jake always saw to it that I looked glamorous in public; he wouldn't let me leave the house unless I was nicely dressed and fully made up. "You have an image to maintain," he would tell me over and over. He was intensely aware not only of my own career, but of my identity as Judy Garland's daughter and Liza's sister. It was very important to him that I promote a glamorous image for myself.

I began to settle into our new life, and to form a personal and professional network. The most important of these relationships was with Bob Lamond and his partner, Lois Zetter. They became not only my agents, but important sources of friendship. Bob and Lois had formed a highly successful management team called Lamond/Zetter. They had a stable of the most beautiful men in Hollywood. It was a standing joke; if you saw a really gorgeous guy, someone would crack, "He must be managed by Bob Lamond." Bob managed John Travolta among many others, and it was through Bob and Lois that I first got to know Johnnie. Bob was the one with the artistic sense, and Lois was the one with the business sense who provided the nuts and bolts of the operation. Bob would pick out your headshots and plan your look; Lois would call to tell you if you got the job. They were a perfect team, each balancing the other's gifts. I'd first met them through my friend Maxine Messenger, the columnist from the *Houston Chronicle* who'd helped me out of the jam with Danny Thomas years before. After going on tour with *They're Playing Our Song* a couple of years before, I'd felt my career – and my marriage – both needed a boost, so I'd signed with Bob and Lois to manage me. Jake wasn't exactly crazy about the arrangement, and he certainly didn't like Bob and Lois personally, but he also recognized it was a good career move. Lamond/Zetter was highly respected in the business, with good connections to all the networks, and as long as they were getting me work (and they were), Jake was willing to put up with the arrangement. Bob had a reputation as a starmaker, and Jake wanted me to be a star.

Life wasn't perfect, but it was, as they say, "good enough." I had a wonderful little son, a nice home, people to love, and work I enjoyed. My marriage wasn't the kind of thing they write songs about, but then whose was? My two magical weeks at the Ford Center Family Program were rapidly fading into a memory as the demands of everyday life took over. I had found a measure of understanding and peace in Palm Springs that summer, and if I wasn't really applying my new knowledge to my relationships with those around me, at least I was staying sober myself. I told myself that was enough, and tried not to think too much about it. I had faced about as much truth as I could take for the time being. What I didn't yet understand was that once you take the first steps on the long journey to health, there's really no going back. One way or another, life will force you to make choices you never wanted to make.

# Chapter Nineteen

# MY OWN BACK YARD

It's remarkable how patterns repeat in families without our even knowing it. That had become very clear to me at Betty Ford. All three of my mother's children had developed serious addiction problems. In spite of what we experienced as children, or more accurately because of it, we had each followed a similar path. For me and Liza, it was cocaine and alcohol, and in Liza's case, pills as well. For Joe it was primarily alcohol. Yet none of us realized we were repeating a pattern. I never once made the connection between my coke use and my mother's medication until I went to the Ford Center. Unfortunately, addiction wasn't the only destructive pattern that ran in the family.

I had unknowingly repeated my family's pattern in marriage as well. In marrying Jake, I had chosen someone with a problem, someone who needed a partner with the training I'd received during those years on Rockingham Drive. I was an expert co-dependent. I knew how to put Jake to bed, how to deal with his abusive moods, how to cover up for his excesses, how to lie to myself about the reality of our mutual addictions. I had married Jake because I felt comfortable in the role of enabler. It was what I did best. Compounding the difficulty, I had also repeated my grandparents' pattern of mixing business with family, and with the same dismal results. The relationship between my mother and my grandmother had been destroyed when Grandma Ethel became more of a manager than a parent to my mom. And even though my mom had been desperate to escape her mother's control, she had made my father into her manager because it was what she felt comfortable with. She was frightened to make her own decisions; she wanted a man who would take over the role her mother had played in her formative years. I did exactly the same thing. Bitterly as I'd resented my father's attempts to manage my career, I had broken free of my dad by marrying a man who took my father's place professionally. Being my mother's daughter, I had repeated her mistake. And as the years went by, that mistake gradually eroded my relationship with my husband.

Somewhere along the line Jake had stopped being my husband and become my manager instead. I felt like his client, not his wife. He was obsessed with making me a star, and to do so, he tried to control every aspect of my life. If I left the house when he wasn't there, I had to call him and tell him where I was going. If I wasn't on the set or at home, he had to know exactly where I was at all times. If he disapproved of my plans, it meant either an argument or canceling my plans. It was like being a teenager with a strict parent. He kept a careful eye on my weight and insisted I diet if I put on a few pounds. He was also concerned about my make-up and my hair. He oversaw what I wore, onstage and off; his image of me was a glamor queen, and he liked me to attend premieres with plenty of sequins and a flashy look. He even insisted I dress up to go to the grocery store. Our evenings out together were always photo opportunities in Jake's mind; we could never just relax and have a good time. We constantly had to position ourselves so we'd appear in the press the next day, and Jake always made sure he was in the frame with me, the starmaker husband. Watching me on screen, he critiqued every aspect of my performance. Most of his comments were critical; I was never good enough. I still remember seeing the first screening of *Grease 2*, and as all of us in the cast walked out together, excited about seeing the finished film, Jake's only comment was, "You acted too tough. You should have played it softer." I felt completely deflated. He never seemed to have a word of praise for me. Auditions, career moves; these became the only topic of conversation in our home. He dreamed of me becoming a big star, a one-name celebrity like my mother and sister – "JUDY," "LIZA," and finally "LORNA." No last name required. I think he was deeply disappointed that I never seemed to attain the legendary status he was hoping for. During the last years of our marriage, we rarely discussed anything but business.

By the time we moved to California, there really was no marriage in the usual sense of the word. I switched to Bob Lamond's management primarily because I didn't think my marriage could survive much more of Jake's management, even if my career could. Since Lois had all my checks mailed directly to Jake, he could still control the money, and that was what mattered most to him. He never allowed me to see the accounts, to use a credit card, or even have a checkbook. He said I couldn't be trusted with money. The remarkable thing is, I accepted the role of child-wife in the marriage. I had grown up watching other people, including my father, manage my mother's money for her. I'd always been surrounded by business people who handled money for the performers in the family. The fact that my mother had gone broke that way never quite registered with me. I'd like to blame Jake for the whole situation, but the truth is, I let him do it. What I was thinking, I don't know.

I was resigned to the professional relationship, but it was getting harder and harder to ignore Jake's drinking. The problem with getting sober yourself is that you begin to notice that half the people around you are stoned or drunk much of the time. With my new understanding, and with a small son in our home, using was no longer an acceptable way of life for me. I was still in denial about many things in my life, but even I couldn't ignore the fact that Jake had a serious drinking problem. Ever since my time in the Ford Family Program, I had been acutely aware that I had followed the family pattern in marrying an alcoholic. But I hadn't yet faced the fact that I was continuing in the same old patterns myself, not as a drug user, but as an enabler for my husband. I kept trying to think of ways to control the situation, ways I could change Jake and make everything okay. I had completely missed the part about letting the alcoholic take responsibility for his own actions. I had also missed the part about attending a support group and continuing to practice day by day the new behavior I'd been taught. I hadn't attended a single Al-Anon meeting since the Family Program. So who was I to criticize Jake? I didn't want to change, either.

In some respects, though, my life was changing. Since the move to California, I had become close to many of the people at the Lamond Zetter Agency. Two of them had picked up on the fact that I was in an unhealthy family situation, and one day they invited me to go to an Al-Anon meeting with them. I was very surprised; I had no idea they were involved with Al-Anon. They generously shared that information with me. Fool that I was, I told them, "Thanks, but no, really, I'm fine." They knew that wasn't true, of course, but they just told me that if I ever needed to talk, they were there for me.

Things were changing in my professional life, too. A year and a half after I joined the cast, *Trapper John* was cancelled. The timing was really bad for me, because the television industry was right in the middle of a terrible writers' strike, which had already lasted for months. With the writers on strike there were no scripts, and without any scripts, there wasn't any work for actors. For nearly an entire television season, American stations ran nothing but reruns and old movies. What made things even worse was that Jake and I had just bought the house in Beverly Hills, and I had hefty mortgage payments to worry about. So I put some numbers together and set up some singing dates, mostly in town. I didn't want to go back on the road again with Jesse so small. Thank God I can sing, I thought; many of my fellow actors really suffered when the work just disappeared. It was a tough time in the profession.

It was soon to get much tougher, but that had nothing to do with the writers' strike. It was about this time that I began to notice that Bob Lamond was rarely in the office. After a while he stopped coming in completely. The odd thing was that nobody was talking about it. Things still ran smoothly at the agency; Lois brought in people to make sure it did, but I missed Bob and wondered what had happened to him. When I asked Lois, she would make up excuses, but after a while it became clear that he was sick. As time went on, I grew increasingly worried, but the few people who knew what was wrong with Bob kept stonewalling me. After a while I quit asking what was wrong and just started asking, "Is Bob okay?" I could read the answer in people's faces. Bob wasn't okay.

Finally one day Lois called me into the office and said, "Lorna, Bob won't be coming back to work." When I asked her why, she simply said, "Bob's very sick."

"Does he have AIDS?" The words fairly flew out of my mouth. It was the mid-1980s, and I had already lost several loved ones to AIDS.

Lois simply replied, "Bob is very sick," and left me to draw my own conclusions. I later found out that Bob was hospitalized by then, in the late stages of cancer. I was grief-stricken; we all were. I badly wanted to see him, but he was refusing all visitors. He didn't want his friends to see him in the last stages of disease. The word did spread to John Travolta, and Johnnie completely came apart when he heard. Somehow Johnnie found out what hospital Bob was in and went to see him. It was a painful but deeply healing reunion; Bob and Johnnie had suffered a breach some time before, and John didn't want Bob to die without their reaching an understanding. The rest of Bob's clients, those of us who didn't get to see him, banded together as the end drew near. We all loved him, and we turned to each other for support. We needed each other.

About this time I got a call to do a cabaret slot on a cruise to Alaska. I didn't really want to go; I knew Bob could die any day. I had to, though, as jobs were scarce right then. Jake stayed home with Jesse, and I didn't want to go alone, so I asked Liz Derringer to go along with me for emotional support. I also left my shipboard number at the agency, telling them to call me immediately if there was any change in Bob's condition. We left the port, and shortly after the first show, I received the wire I'd been dreading. Bob had died. I was overwhelmed by the news. In spite of the fact I'd been expecting it, losing Bob was incredibly painful. He'd not only given me a sense of security professionally; he'd been my friend, never judging me, always there to listen when I needed to talk. That night on the ship, Liz and I got a bottle of champagne and a big plate full of every dessert they had on board. Bob always loved dessert more than life itself. So we took it all to the stern of the ship, toasted Bob, saying, "This is for you, Bob," and threw the whole thing into the ocean. Then we just stood there together and cried.

Goodbye, Bob. I still miss you.

In a strange way, losing Bob was the beginning of the end of my marriage. The pain of that time brought home to me how alone I really was in the relationship. Emotionally, Jake simply wasn't there. That's one of the things alcohol does to you; it erodes your ability to feel, to share yourself with other people. It's terribly isolating. During the weeks before Bob's death, I felt painfully alone. I couldn't talk to Jake about what was happening to me because he simply didn't care. One night, after I put Jesse to bed, I was sitting alone in the bedroom crying when Jake walked in and asked me what I was crying about. "What is the matter with you?" he asked impatiently.

"It's Bob," I told him.

"What about him?"

"Don't you understand? Bob, my manager, my friend, he's dying."

"Oh, get over it," Jake snapped irritably, and went in the

other room. I just sat there crying wordlessly, feeling completely alone.

With its guiding light gone, the agency rapidly began losing clients – rats off a sinking ship, as they say. For Jake, this was a golden opportunity to take over as my manager again, which I knew he'd been wanting to do for some time. I stayed with Lois for several months after Bob's death, and the whole time Jake kept saying, "What are you still doing there? Lois isn't doing anything for you." Eventually I gave in to the pressure. Lois was very understanding about it. She didn't like Jake any more than he liked her, and she knew what was going on. I'm sure it was no surprise to her when I told her I was leaving. She'd probably been expecting it.

So once again, it was just me and Jake, and with every day that went by, things got harder. Once again Jake was the salesman, and I was the product. I went out on the road again, on cruises, anything to get a booking. Sometimes I felt like Jake would sell me to anyone who had a few bucks. Eventually he got me a good booking, at the Cine Grill in the Roosevelt Hotel in L.A. I put together a show I really liked with my musical director, Larry Blank, and the reviews were very good. Opening night was a real star-studded event. The only problem was Jake; that night started the pattern of him being drunk on opening night. He would get nervous when I opened, and his way of coping was to drink non-stop all day long. By the time I came offstage at the end of my act, he would be falling down drunk, his words slurring together and his eyes half-shut. The result was that no matter how well a show went, I never got to celebrate opening night. I always had to keep Jake on his feet and get him out of there before he fell down or caused a scene.

It hadn't always been like that. When we were younger, Jake had drunk mainly at home, or at a party where the main activity was taking drugs. His usual pattern would be to start drinking after dinner and eventually fall asleep, usually at home. For years his drinking came and went in spells, usually two or three weeks at a time, so it took me a while to realize how addicted he was. Looking back, of course, it's clear to me that he was an alcoholic when I married him. He was already dependent on alcohol as a coping mechanism. The fact that he drank two bottles of champagne with vodka and threw up on me our first night together should have been a hint. Besides, I wasn't exactly clear-headed myself. But the difference was that Jake needed alcohol as an emotional crutch; he used it to kill the pain of things he didn't want to deal with. And he had a lot of pain.

Jake is Jewish, though he hasn't told many people. He was born in Israel to East European parents who were survivors of Nazi concentration camps. Jake was harshly treated as a child, and he never got over it. He did everything he could to put his past behind him, to pretend it never existed. He even changed his name three or four times because he didn't want people to know where he came from. It was just too painful for him. These were things I learned gradually, in the early years of our marriage, because Jake never really talked about it, and I didn't dare bring it up. That was really the heart of Jake's problem: he couldn't talk about the pain, so he tried to drink it away. And of course, it didn't work. The alcohol dulled it for a while, but it just kept coming back.

I wasn't the only one trapped in a destructive family pattern. So was Jake. He never developed the coping skills he needed for a good relationship with me, although he was a good parent, so things got hard. As the years went by, his anger grew, and he became harder and harder to handle. One of the worst nights I ever spent with him, and one of the most frightening nights of my life, was at the wrap party for *Trapper John*. It was held at a Chinese restaurant on Wilshire Boulevard in Santa Monica. The whole cast was there, Tim Busfield and Pernell Roberts and dear, wonderful Madge Sinclair, and we were all so sad because we knew it was our last time together as a cast. Jake was with me, and he drank non-stop from the moment we arrived. I wanted so much to have this last evening with my friends, but Jake got so loaded that I had to leave early and take him home. I was furious with him, and we got into a big argument about his drinking on the way to the car. Jake always denied being drunk, and when I accused him of it, he said, "I'm fine. You're the one with the problem. I don't know what you're talking about. You're insane."

By the time we got to the car, we were screaming at each other, and things only got worse when I didn't want to let him drive. He shoved me in the passenger side and got behind the wheel himself, and as we were weaving down Wilshire Boulevard, I kept trying to get him to stop. He was furious, and when I continued yelling at him, he turned toward me and hit me so hard that I slammed against the door and fell out of the car onto the street. I was still clinging to the door handle as I fell, but instead of trying to pull myself back into the car, I let go and rolled. I was scared to death. I staggered to my feet and went running right down the street, crying hysterically. I was afraid Jake would pull me back in that car and hurt me worse. He'd hurt me before, but this was the first time he'd actually hit me like that, and I didn't know what he might do next. Thankfully, Jake roared off in the car, and I found the nearest phone box and called my girlfriend Julie Stein, who lived nearby. She came to get me, and I spent the night at her house.

It was a long night. My face was sore and discolored, and I ached all over, but the emotional pain was the worst. Julie kept saying, "Lorna, don't go back. You can't go back. This is terrible." I didn't know what to do. Early the next morning Jake sobered up and went to my father's house looking for me. Not long afterward I called my dad, too, and told him only that Jake and I had had a fight. I didn't tell him what had really happened.

Sid just tried to be diplomatic, saying, "Well, now, these things happen. It'll be all right." It made me feel better just hearing his voice. I told him where I was, but I made him promise not to tell Jake. I needed some time to think.

I sat with Julie most of the day. Finally I said, "I have to go home, Julie. I have a son. I can't just leave Jesse there."

I called Jake at the office, and he was depressed and very, very apologetic. He kept saying, "I'm sorry. It'll never happen again. Please come home." I did. I thought I had to. I had a husband; I had a baby; what else could I do? Jake brought me flowers and took me out to dinner and treated me like a queen for a while. He continued to promise that his drinking days were over, that he'd never do that again. And he didn't – until the next time. It would start with "just one" glass of wine with dinner ("I can have this. One won't hurt me"). But of course, it wouldn't be just one, and soon he'd be drinking two bottles of wine after dinner at night and growing more belligerent with every glass. Sometimes I'd come home and my dear Spanish housekeeper, Maria, would say, "Mr. Jake come home drunk again, with very black eyes." There was never any explanation for the black and blue marks on his face. He was afraid to beat me, but it was clear that he'd been in a fight with somebody else.

I continued to ignore what I'd learned at Betty Ford about my own part in the family cycle; instead I pulled on my Superman suit every day and went back to work like I always had. Rick Derringer had parted company from Jake by then, so Jake had even more time to concentrate on my career. The pressure was building. There were never enough jobs, never enough money. We had a house in Beverly Hills, but Jake wanted a bigger house. He had to have a new Mercedes every year. We were perennially house poor, with our mortgage taking up all the money I made. It was a constant struggle to keep up the appearances Jake felt were necessary to people in "our position." I was a constant disappointment to Jake, professionally and personally. "When are you going to get another job?" became the never-ending question at home. Sometimes I felt so desperate that I would light green candles (somebody had told me they brought good luck) and pray for a television series so I would have enough money to leave Jake and support Jesse on my own. I would look in the mirror sometimes and remember my mother's advice to me when I told her I wanted to go into show business: "Look at me. Look at this face. Do you want to look like this when you're forty?" Forty was no longer that far away, and it scared me.

Meanwhile, my sister had turned forty, and she decided to celebrate with a big party in London. She flew me over for the occasion, along with other family and friends, and we had the time of our lives. Whatever resentments the Ford Center had caused seemed to be over, and Liza looked healthier than ever. It gave me great joy to see my sister happy again. When I turned thirty-five, Liza decided we should celebrate in Paris. We flew to New York and took the Concorde to Paris for a four-day holiday. My first love and former fiancé, Philippe Lavot, met us at the airport for the occasion. He and I had kept in touch off and on over the years, and he was delighted to join in the celebration. For four days the three of us and a friend of Liza's traveled around France together and had the vacation of a lifetime. The press didn't bother us, so we got to do whatever we wanted. Liza and I were both cold sober, and it was good to find out we could have as much fun as ever without taking anything to give us a buzz. When it was all over, I hated to come home. But I had a baby boy waiting for me, and I wasn't about to leave him behind.

Those were the best years of my life with my sister. I think they were some of the best years of her life, too. What I didn't know was that the disease that had nearly destroyed her before was already rearing its head again. She had come out of the Ford Center ready to take on the world, but it hadn't lasted long. I had gone to an opening to see her and Elizabeth Taylor, and she seemed fine to me, but only two days later Liza called me, crying, and said she was at a place called Hazelden in Minnesota. It was a rehab center, with a much tougher program than the Ford Center. It turned out that her friends had caught her using the night I'd seen her at the opening, and done an intervention. Her manager, Eliot Weisman, had the guts to cancel her remaining shows and take her on the next plane to Minnesota. Hazelden or, as Liza called it, "the Big House," has a prison-like atmosphere where they take addiction problems very seriously. She was going to be there for six weeks this time, and part of the therapy was to call your family one by one and tell them what you'd done. By the time she called me, she was practically hysterical.

It was a terrible conversation. She just kept saying, "I'm sorry, I'm sorry," and crying. I did exactly the wrong thing – I personalized it.

Instead of thinking of my sister, I felt hurt, betrayed. "I've been lied to again," I kept thinking. "All this time she's been deceiving me. How could she do this to *me*?" It was a self-centered response. I didn't say all those things to my sister, but I was thinking them, and I know she must have felt it. The time at the Ford Center hadn't only been wasted on Liza. It had been wasted on me, too.

It seemed like all around me, my family was falling apart. My brother Joe had been living with friends in the San Fernando Valley for years, and I knew he still struggled with the emotional fall-out of our childhood. He's such a sweet man, but I was beginning to suspect that some of the oddities in his behavior were symptoms of an abuse problem of his own. I should have expected it, but as usual, I hadn't. Not Joey. My dad wasn't in the best of shape, either. His marriage to Patty had fallen apart some time before. I was sorry; I liked Patty, and she had struggled mightily to survive life with a difficult man and at least one impossible stepchild (me, as a teenager). But even Patty couldn't survive life with a ghost, and it was clear that the other woman in Patty's marriage was my mother. She was still alive to my father. Her photos filled his house, and he felt her presence every day of his life. He couldn't let her go. How do you compete with a dead woman? After a while, Patty left my father alone with his memories.

It's a funny thing about the past. If you don't watch out, it will become the present.

\*

One thing about children. They have a way of forcing you back into the present moment. My son was nearly six years old by now, the emotional center of my life, and I was about to get one of life's unexpected bonuses. Shortly after Jesse turned six years old, I found out I was pregnant. I couldn't have been more surprised. I wasn't sorry to be pregnant. On the contrary, I had wanted another baby for a long time, but Jake had always said no, a baby would be bad for my career. Fortunately, Mother Nature stepped in and took a hand once again.

Jake wasn't thrilled with the news. He wasn't sure he wanted another child (although he was delighted when she was born). "How will we afford it?" he kept saying. "What about your career? You can't work if you're pregnant."

I just told him I didn't care, that I was having this baby, even if I had to have it alone, and there was nothing Jake could do but give in. His response was to get a bigger house for the new baby, and since with Jake everything has to be "bigger and better," that meant a million dollar house in the Hollywood Hills. "Great," I thought. "We can't afford a baby, but we can afford a zillion dollar home." I was glad for the extra space, though, and if it made Jake more content with the situation, it was worth it.

As I nurtured the new life inside me, I was about to learn a new lesson about how precious the life of a child really is. The child who would teach me that lesson was Ryan White.

I had first met Ryan when he was twelve. I had become involved with an organization called Athletes and Entertainers for Kids, and our goal was to put together an AIDS awareness program for children struggling with the disease. I'd read about Ryan in the newspaper, and the organization flew him out here for a few days to see what we could do to help. I met him at the airport, and he spent about five days in Los Angeles along with his mother, Jeanne, and Ryan's grandparents. I'd been deeply touched by Ryan's story on the news, and we became really good friends during his visit. Afterward we kept in touch.

He'd visit me when he could, and he came to see my show when I did *Girl Crazy*. From the beginning it was a special relationship. Ryan had that effect on people. I still carry his school pictures in my wallet.

Ryan was one of the most remarkable human beings I've ever known. He had absolutely no malice in his soul. He'd been treated so badly when he'd contracted HIV – he'd even been spat on in public places – but he had no bitterness about it. Instead he just enjoyed the good things life offered him. He was no plaster saint; he and his sister fought like cats and dogs, but he was truly good in a way you seldom see. His mother was heroic. She loved Ryan enough to let him be who he was. Whenever Ryan came to visit, he wanted to go to every surf shop in town. He'd bring a list of places he'd found in his surfer magazines and make me drive him all over the county, buying every surf T-shirt on the planet. One day I said to him, "Forget the disease. If I have to drive you to one more surf shop, I'm going to strangle you right here and now." He thought that was hilarious, and just broke up laughing. We went to Disneyland together, too, and had the time of our lives.

Only one time did I see Ryan really lose control. The press wanted to do an interview with him, and he agreed. He was thirteen at the time. He wanted me to stay with him, so I did, and everything was going fine when one of the women reporters said, "So how does it feel to know you can never have sex?" Ryan just lost it. He started to cry, and I went ballistic. I threw the press out of the room, and Ryan grabbed onto me, and I sat there holding him while he cried. I was so angry that all I could think about was punching that reporter right in the face, and I pictured myself being hauled off to prison for hitting a photographer. But I didn't say any of that. I just comforted Ryan, telling him the lady had done a terrible, hurtful thing, and that in the future he would need to make it clear that *he* was the one who made the rules about what was asked. Meanwhile his mother came in, and when she found out what had happened, she went after the reporters. I could hear her screaming at them from the other room, "How DARE you do this to my son?" I thought, "Go, Jeannie. Maybe you can punch them out."

I was several months pregnant with Vanessa when Ryan died. We'd all known it was coming. I was on tour in the East when Elton John's secretary called me with the news. I flew home immediately after the show and made arrangements to fly to Indianapolis for the funeral. I asked Jake to come with me. Jesse wanted to go, too. He adored Ryan, and he was grief-stricken at losing his friend, but I thought Jesse was too young at six to get through the grueling trip and media frenzy at the funeral. I remembered the hysteria at my mother's funeral all too well, and I didn't want him to go through that. The trip was complicated, with no direct flights and several stop-overs to change planes, and it soon turned into a nightmare. We were flying over Denver when the pilot announced we were going to make an emergency landing at Denver airport because of a mechanical problem. Once we landed, we couldn't make the necessary connecting flights. We finally got a flight into Chicago that night, and from there we had to drive all night to get to Indiana. We arrived at 6 a.m. with no sleep and no luggage. With only four hours until the funeral, we slept for two hours, drove to a department store and bought everything from shoes to hats, and drove to the funeral.

It was a remarkable occasion. So many people were there, celebrities and dignitaries: Barbara Bush, Phil Donahue, and Marlo Thomas, and of course Elton John. I was okay until I saw Ryan. He was lying there in that little casket wearing his coolest sunglasses and his favorite surfer shirt. There he was, that sweet boy, just lying there in that little shirt. His schoolfriends wanted to do something for him, so they all gathered around Ryan and sang, "That's What Friends Are For." It was one of the most touching things I've ever seen, and it was then that I started sobbing. I think everyone did. Afterward somebody came and took me to the family room where Jeannie was, and Elton was there, and Ryan's family. It was really good to be with them. Jeannie patted my stomach and said, "How's our little girl?" I was so touched. There I was, with this new life inside me, and Jeannie had just lost her son. To this day, whenever Jeannie calls, she says, "How's my Vanessa?" If I ever have another child, boy or girl, the baby's middle name will be Ryan.

Ryan's death made my daughter's birth even more significant for me. Vanessa's birth was a turning point in so many ways. It had been a difficult pregnancy. My obstetrician had diagnosed me early on with gestational diabetes. It turned out that I'd had the same problem with Jesse, but it hadn't been diagnosed at the time. That was why I had craved food so much, and gained such a huge amount of weight; that was also why Jesse had been so big. The doctor impressed on me that I had to monitor my blood sugar and diet carefully, or both the baby and I could suffer serious consequences. I followed his instructions religiously, even overcoming my fear of needles to test my own blood every day. I kept my weight under control this time around, and overall I did remarkably well. The doctor kept telling me he wasn't going to let this baby go full term, because given Jesse's size at birth, this second child could weigh eleven pounds. Eleven pounds! I remembered my broken tailbone at Jesse's birth and tried not to think about it.

Six months into my pregnancy, Jake had scheduled a singing date for me in Bermuda. It was for quite a lot of money, so I was planning to keep the date. But a few days before I was scheduled to leave, I suddenly went into labor. I told Jake to get me to the hospital, right away. It was too soon to have this baby. Jake took me to the hospital, and they put me on an IV drip for several hours to stop the labor. Finally they sent me home, with orders to stay in bed for several days. But as soon as we got home, Jake started saying, "You can't stay in bed all week. What about Bermuda? You've got to go to work."

I didn't know what to say to him, but he just kept saying, "You can't back out of this date. It's too much money. You've got to go to Bermuda." Finally I told him to call Ed Liu, my doctor, and talk to him. He did.

A few minutes later I could hear them arguing over the phone. Jake hung up, and then Ed called me. "Stay in bed," he told me. Dr. Ed Liu, my mild-mannered obstetrician and gynecologist, had said, "Jake, you care more about the fucking money than you do about Lorna and the baby!" Then Ed said to me, "You stay put."

I did, for a few days. And then I packed up my son and I flew to Bermuda. I rested as much as I could, and I checked in with a Bermudian doctor every day, but I went. I was just too weak and intimidated to say no to Jake's bullying. I was desperate to get away from him by that point, but I just didn't have the strength.

Three months later, the doctor put me in Cedars Sinai Hospital and induced labor. For three days I lay there soaking up medicine, and nothing happened. But on the third day, just as the doctor was about to give up and do a Caesarean section, I went into labor. No sooner did the real pain hit than they gave me an epidural, and shortly after that, Vanessa just popped out. Compared to Jesse's birth, it was easy, clean, and painless. Vanessa weighed eight pounds, pink and healthy, with big blue eyes and dark hair with blond frosting. She was beautiful, and I was thrilled. Jesse had his baby sister, and I had my little girl.

Why do we always expect a new baby to solve all of life's problems? They never do, of course. All through my pregnancy with Vanessa, I kept hoping that somehow, mystically, this new child would bring new life to our marriage. Of course, she didn't. No child could. The inevitable ending of our relationship was rapidly approaching.

Things had come to a head once again several months before Vanessa's birth. One evening Jake had gone to a friend's house to watch a boxing match on TV, and I had fallen asleep early. When I woke up at 6 the next morning, Jake wasn't home. When I went to check for him, I saw the Mercedes he'd taken the night before parked haphazardly in front of the house, and I noticed my Jeep was gone. Apparently Jake had taken it.

I panicked. I began calling around, but nobody knew where he was. I was scared to death; I didn't know if he was in a hospital, or dead, or what. He'd always come home by morning. I had to be on the set by 10 a.m. to shoot a segment of *Murder, She Wrote*, but when I got there, I was a wreck. I called a friend of mine, who was an Al-Anon member, and bless her, she said, "Get down on your knees right this minute and say the Serenity Prayer. You know it; I told you about it. And then you go straight to an Al-Anon meeting. There will be one on the lot somewhere. Ask around. Someone will know." Then she asked if I was okay to drive to work.

I said, "Yeah, I'm okay."

Then she told me that if Jake hadn't shown up by that afternoon, I should call the police. She reassured me once again. I hung up, told Maria, "Please, just stay with Jesse," and went to work. When I got there, I went into the make-up trailer, and the artist said, "Are you all right?" She could see I'd been crying. I burst into tears and went into my trailer. The actor who'd been in the chair next to me followed me in and asked what was wrong. I said, "My husband's missing. He's an alcoholic."

The actor just walked over to me, took my hands, and said, "So am I. I've been in the program for twenty-five years. Let me take you to a meeting." I was stunned. It was like a little miracle. I'd taken my first tiny step forward, and here was this man standing in front of me, an answer to prayer. At the lunch break, he took me to my first Al-Anon meeting, right there on the Universal Lot. It was, as they say, one small step for Lorna, but one huge step in our lives. That meeting changed my life. It was the first of many.

Shortly after we got back from the meeting, the phone rang. It was Jake. My dad had been calling over looking for him, and Jake had turned out to be in jail. They'd just released him. The police had found him weaving all over Sunset

Boulevard in my car and arrested him. They'd thrown him in the drunk tank with all the other drunks Jake said he wasn't like. In Jake's mind, he wore an Armani jacket; they didn't. So he wasn't like them. With my hand shaking so hard I could barely hold the phone, I said, "You call everyone and tell them. You have to call my sister, and my dad, and all our friends. They're worried about you. Tell them where you've been. I'm not doing it for you anymore."

Jake said, "I think I have a problem. I think I'm an alcoholic." It was the first time he'd said it. It was a beginning.

For Jake, it didn't last. He went to meetings for a while, and he behaved himself because he wanted his driver's license back. But I kept going to those meetings. All the things they'd told me at the Ford Center six years before were finally beginning to sink in.

It was so hard. How do you unlearn a lifetime of responses? How do you contain all that anger, that frustration, that embarrassment? Most of all, how do you let go? How do you stop trying to save someone you love? How do you walk away and leave them with that terrible disease? Liza didn't think I had the strength to do it. Neither did anyone else. Neither did I. But I was trying.

Before I could let go, though, there would be one last battle with an old enemy. Jake hadn't drunk in front of me for weeks, but I knew something was wrong. I could sense it in his behavior. He wasn't drunk, but he wasn't sober, either. There was something familiar about it all. It was then it began to dawn on me. Of course. It was my mother all over again. And like the well-qualified little detective I was, I swung into action. I knew exactly how to search. I began systematically to go through the house – the drawers, the closets, the hems of his pants, the seams. I knew that he wouldn't keep it at the office, so it had to be in the house. Then I started on the bathroom, and I found his toiletry bag under the sink. I emptied out the contents; nothing; but then I noticed something on the bottom, and I turned the bag over. On the bottom, beneath the zipper compartment, I reached under and found a hidden compartment inside. I ripped it open. There it was: a whole cache of tranquilizers.

I hit the ceiling. The minute Jake walked in the door, I confronted him. "Tell me if you're using." He swore he wasn't using anything. Then I did something really horrible. Shaking with rage, I said, "Swear on Jesse's life." He swore on Jesse's life. The minute he did, I pulled out the leather bag, opened it, and threw the pills at him, screaming, "Then what the fuck are these?" And I continued to scream at him. It was exactly the wrong thing to do, and I knew it, but I was out of control. Jake, cornered, stayed relatively calm and continued to invent excuses for the pills, saying I was making something out of nothing, that the pills barely affected him. When it was all over, I'd only made things worse. As I lay in bed sleepless that night, I kept thinking, "What am I going to do? I've got a baby and a seven-year-old son. What am I going to do?"

In recovery they tell you that if you stay in a relationship with an alcoholic too long, you'll be consumed by three things: resentment, revenge, and the desire to retaliate. For years I had been obsessed by all three things. Jake was so controlled by his addiction that he wasn't able to be the husband I needed, or that he wanted to be. There was so much anger and distrust between us by then that even if Jake had been able to give up alcohol overnight, it would have been too late. I was hollow inside, beaten and bloodied by years of abusing myself and letting others abuse me. I wanted to be happy and healthy again. I'd left both of those things behind in the house on Mapleton Drive thirty years before. I wanted healthy, happy lives for my children, free of the sickness that addiction breeds. In my heart I knew it was no longer possible to find happiness with Jake.

For every camel, there's a last straw. There was for me. I was doing my night club act in Reno, Nevada, a few weeks later, and I had to fly home at 4 a.m. to pack, pick up Jake and Vanessa, and catch a flight to London. I was exhausted by the time I got there, and upset because Jesse was in tears at being left behind. Jake didn't want Jesse to miss school, but from Jesse's point of view, his whole family was going off and leaving him with the housekeeper. As we drove back toward the airport, I couldn't get Jesse's tearful face at our front door out of my mind. I was still struggling with the baby and the luggage when Jake said he'd meet me at the departure gate. By the time I reached the gate, I realized that Jake had managed to stop at one of the lounges along the way and have a drink. It had been only ten minutes, but I knew immediately. I could always tell. I said to Jake, "What have you been doing?"

He said, "Nothing," and I dropped it.

A few minutes later we boarded the plane. I noticed that by take-off there were still two empty seats a couple of rows behind us, so I decided to take Vanessa back there so I could feed her and put her down. As soon as the plane took off, they served dinner, so I just stayed put while I ate. Two rows in front of me, Jake was eating dinner, too. I finished feeding Vanessa, and she fell asleep on the seat next to me. I looked over the heads of the people in front of me, and I could see Jake still sitting there. He had a blanket over his head, one of those little flight blankets the stewardesses give you. I got out of my seat, walked down to the aisle to him, and pulled the blanket off his head. There he sat, bleary-eyed, with a full glass of red wine in his hand.

I just looked at him and said quietly, "Now tell me again that you're not drinking. There's nobody sitting next to you, so you can't be holding that glass for anybody else. Just look me in the eye and tell me again that you're not drinking."

I was perfectly calm. Jake launched into his usual explanation, beginning with, "I can have a drink now and then if I want one. You're being ridiculous . . ." But it didn't matter what he said. I wasn't listening. His words were already fading into the blue.

They talk about seeing the light. That day, that moment, standing in the aisle of that 747, I finally got it. I looked at

Jake and thought, "I didn't cause this. I can't stop this. I can't cure him. I never will. And that's okay. Take your children, and walk away."

And I did. My marriage ended in that moment. I got off the plane with my baby in London, and I went to an Al-Anon meeting the next day. Jake returned to Los Angeles. A few days later, I called him in California and told him that our marriage was over. I didn't know what would happen next, but for the first time since I was a little girl, I wasn't afraid anymore. I would be all right. I had finally let go, and when I did, there were caring people waiting to catch me. I felt I had finally come home.

# EPILOGUE

It has taken me twenty-eight years to come to terms with the fact that the mother I loved so much left me too soon, taken by a disease that I did not understand. It's hard for me to put into words the irony of being unable to escape my mother's presence while feeling her absence so painfully. In one sense, she's everywhere I turn, but in another, her absence has been agonizing. It hasn't been easy at times, but if there's one thing I learned at the Betty Ford Center, it's that it doesn't matter whether or not your mother is a Hollywood legend. The pain of having a parent held captive by prescription drugs or alcohol is the same for everyone. That knowledge has proven deeply healing for me. It has allowed me to let go of the pain and finally move on with my life.

I'd like to tell you that Jake and I had a very civilized divorce and went on to become best friends in later years, but it simply isn't true. Our separation was as painful as the marriage had become. By the time our attorneys were through, we ended up with joint custody of our children and a fiercely contested financial settlement. Jake still manages performers, but except where the children are involved, I try to stay out of his life.

In most respects now, my life is very happy. I got remarried in 1996 to Colin Freeman, the young English musical director I met on tour shortly after I separated from Jake. Colin and I have been through a lot together; he has survived the assaults of the tabloid press, all of them claiming he broke up my marriage to Jake. He also endures a mother-in-law who seems to be an on-going, if invisible, part of our home. I have two beautiful, healthy children who have come through the rigors of divorce and custody disputes with remarkably level heads and cheerful dispositions. I am grateful for them every day of my life. The seven of us – me and Colin, Jesse and Vanessa, two Dalmatian dogs, and one long-suffering cat – inhabit a happy, if sometimes mobile, home. The thing I hate the most about my career is the constant traveling. Somehow, though, we all manage to adapt. I share custody with their father, and the children can stay in the same school year round. Unlike me, they won't have attended seventeen schools each by the time they graduate from high school. Instead, they'll be able to settle down and lead happy and more normal lives. Not that I count on that, of course. My family is still long on performers and short on more traditional occupations. When they grow up, my children may choose to carry on the family tradition. If they do, I'll be in the front row cheering, like my parents and grandparents before me. Meanwhile, though, my children's only job is to have a happy childhood. The important thing is that they know they have choices.

My father is now in his eighties. His health is good for his age, and he is as irritating and charming as he ever was. His emotions about this project have run from lukewarm to ice cold. He has always acted as if he were the sole guardian of my mother's memory, but I hope when he reads this book he will understand how much I love them both. He still keeps a beautiful framed portrait of two-year-old Frances "Baby" Gumm on the large glass coffee table in his living room.

My brother Joe still lives on the other side of the Holly-wood Hills from me, with the Smiths who have become his second family. Joe has found in them the stable, traditional home he needs. He never married, though he's come close once or twice. Joe continues to battle the effects of my mother's medication intake during her pregnancy. He has suffered some damage that makes life a little harder for him than for me. Like me, he has struggled with addiction. For some time now, however, he has been winning that struggle – one day at a time. I admire his courage and perseverance. Unlike the rest of us, Joe didn't choose performing as a way of life, and he relishes his comparative anonymity. He has a little less hair than he used to, but he still bears the scar of my attack in his crib when he was a baby. Of the three of us, he still looks the most like my mother. Joe has her small frame and pixie face. He's also kept the gentle nature he had as a boy. I cannot imagine my life without the brother I once wanted to send back to the stork.

In 1997 my sister Liza turned fifty-one, just as our mother would have been seventy-five. Liza, of course, is in the tabloids almost as often as our mother was. Her personal disaster in *Victor/Victoria* and a string of canceled concerts have an eerily familiar ring. Liza, like me and Joe, has struggled with her own ghosts and shadows. Sadly, Liza and I have not spoken to each other for a while. Those of us who love her confronted Liza two years ago with our concerns about how she was living her life. I believe she is not yet willing to take responsibility for her life, or to leave the hangers-on who encourage and enable her self-destructive behaviour. Since I feel she has made a choice I cannot support, I have chosen to live my life without her for now. I hope and pray that one day she will make better choices so that I can welcome her back into my life. I truly hope that those who surround my sister will search their consciences and take her best interest to heart.

Some people say my life has been a matter of survival. I object to that word. Survivors are people who, like my former in-laws, emerge from the horrors of Auschwitz and somehow manage to live beyond them. My life bears no comparison to that kind of experience. I choose to think of my life not as surviving, but as coping. Sometimes it's been difficult, and sometimes it's been glorious. Either way, I've coped. And I've learned from it, which may be the most important thing of all.

I was never very good at school, and I've been a slow learner in life's school sometimes, too. But the important thing is that, eventually, I did get the point. I understand, and that understanding has changed my life, and I hope and pray it will change the lives of my children. There are some family traditions I don't want my children to carry on. My mother would be the first to agree with me.

Meanwhile, I count my blessings. I have a healthy body, free of the chemicals that once controlled it, and a wonderful group of people who help me keep that commitment. I have a husband who is able to love me for who I am, and who doesn't try to make me someone I can never be. I have a teenage son with a wonderful smile, his father's face, and his uncle Joe's sweet disposition. And I have a beautiful little girl with my blue eyes, my mother's face, and a voice like an angel.

My Al-Anon book, *Twelve Steps & Twelve Traditions*, lies on the table beside me. Each day I read the passage given to me, and I remember that the blessings of that day are enough. It's all that any of us can ask.

> *God grant me the serenity*
> *To accept the things I cannot change,*
> *Courage to change the things I can,*
> *And wisdom to know the difference.*

# INDEX

*The Act* 319–20

Adam's Apple, New York 231

addiction 150, 180, 357

addictive families 155, 273

Aghayan, Ray 121, 123

Agress, Ronni (Liza's secretary)
    310, 323, 325–32, 334–5,
    337–8, 340–1, 343, 352

AIDS awareness program 370

Aimée, Anouk 265

Al-Anon 273, 360, 374–5, 378

Alaska, cabaret cruise 361–2

"Alexander's Ragtime Band" 5

Allen, Gracie 55

Allen, Lynne 217, 267

Allen, Nancy 172

Allen, Peter 11
    Liza 157, 166–7, 171,
        181–2, 212, 234, 267–8,
        318–20, 324

Alrae Hotel, New York 188–9

Alves, Vern 49–50, 51, 82, 171
    Judy 97, 145, 167
    Lorna 55–9, 187

*An American in Paris* 265

Anderson, Lee 321

Anderson, Loni 261, 264

Anita (Keith Moon's girlfriend)
    284

*Annie Get Your Gun* 36

*Antelope Valley Ledger-
    Gazette* 10

Antonio (London cook) 94

Aquarius Theater, Los Angeles
    226

Arlen, Harold 170

Arnaz, Desi 234

The Arrows 268, 270, 288

Arthur's night club, New York
    172–3, 205

"As Long As He Needs Me"
    126

Astaire, Fred 252–4, 277

Astrid (Bill Wyman's fiancée)
    281–5

*At Long Last Love* 254–5

Athletes and Entertainers for
    Kids 370

Atlantic City, Steel Pier 236–9

Aubrey, Skye 285

*Babes in Arms* 28
Bacall, Betty (Lauren Bogart)
    75, 77–9, 88, 100, 163–4
Bacharach, Burt 232
Ball, Lucille 63
*A Ball of String* 105
barbiturates 69, 84–5, 97, 111,
    145
  see also Seconal; Tuinal;
    Valium
Barbizon Hotel for Women
    226–7, 230
Barkley, Jered 353–4
Bari, Lynn 45, 54
Barry, John 226, 228
Barstow, Dick 170
Bart, Lionel 91
Bartholomew, Freddie 24
Bay of Pigs 103
Beatles 160, 162–4, 173
Bellevue Hospital, New York
    188–9
Bennett, Michael 234–5
Bennett, Tony 175
Benzedrine 29–31, 54, 69,
    84–5, 97, 146
Berenson, Marisa 241
Bergen, Candice 77
Berghof Studio, New York
    229–30, 246–7
Berle, Milton 72
Bermuda, singing date 373
Betty Ford Center 34, 339,
    345, 349
  Family Program 340,
    343–50, 352–3, 356–7,
    359–60, 366–7, 375

Liza 33, 328, 330, 332, 334,
    339, 341–4, 350–51–3,
    367–8
  Taylor, Elizabeth 328,
    331–2, 334–5, 339, 341
Beverly Hills 72–3, 225–6,
    253, 352, 355, 360, 367
  Hotel 85, 110
  see also Mapleton Drive
B.H. [Beverly Hills] Brats 75
Billy Reed's Little Club 41
Blackwell, Charlie 233
Blank, Larry 363
Bloomingdale's 178, 309
*Blue Hawaii* 136–7, 139
"Bob White" 170
Bogart, Humphrey 40–1, 43–4,
    62, 75, 78–9, 88
Bogart, Leslie 62, 73, 77–8,
    88, 100, 105–6, 163–4
Bogart, Steve 62, 78, 100
Bolger, Ray 39
*Bonanza* 122
Booth, Randy 306–7
Boston concerts 176–8, 196
Brando, Marlon 286
Bregman, Marty 166, 235, 276
"Bridget" see Hill, Mariana
Broadway, New York 232–3,
    235
Brown, Georgia 91, 93, 126
Bruce, Lenny 92
Bubbles, John 170
Buckley, Betty 303
Burbank television studios 353
Burnett, Carol 121
Burns, George 55

Burton, Sybil 172
Busfield, Tim 364
Bush, Barbara 371
Butler, Michael 226

Cabaret 229, 241, 317–18
Caesar's Palace 178
Café Central, New York 304
Cagney, Gil 279
Cahn, Sammy, kids 62, 73
California 109–11, 316
Campbell, Glen 262
Cannes, Yacht Club 282
Cantor, Gail 248
Capobianco, Tito 226
Carlyle, John 165
Carmichael, Hoagy 22
Carnegie Hall 107, 217
Carson, Johnny 263, 304
Cats 302–3
CBS
  President Kennedy's funeral
    124–5
  special 109–10
Cedars Sinai Hospital 56, 69,
  373
Champion, Gower 231–2
Chapman, Mrs. 132–3, 135,
  149–50, 152–4
  departure 153–4
  Hong Kong report 203, 207
Chelsea Naval Hospital,
  Boston 176–7
chemical addiction 37, 151,
  201, 205, 298, 308, 344
Chicago 280
Chicago 241–3, 372

A Child Is Waiting 109–10
child stars 84
A Chorus Line 234
Cinderella 91
Clark, Petula 170
cocaine 297
  see also under Luft, Lorna;
    Minnelli, Liza
Cochran, Charlie 165, 206
Cocktail 294
Coleman, Dr Lester 111, 195,
  215–16, 233, 306
Coleman, Felicia 215, 233
Colledge, Mrs. Elizabeth Ann
  114–18
Company 234
Congdon, James 235
Cooke, Alistair 240
Costa, Suzanne 285
Craig, Noel 288
Crawford, Christina 76
Cronkite, Walter 124
Crosby, Bing 47
Cruise, Tom, Cocktail 294
Cuban missile crisis 103
Curtis, King 274

Dali, Salvador 173
Dallas 243–5
David, Hal 232
Davis, Alouise 252, 276
Davis, Mac 262
Davis, Sammy Jr. 252, 261,
  275–6, 278
Day, Doris 30
de Rola, Stash Klossowski 266,
  267

Deans, Mickey 165–6, 205–6, 270
  Judy's death 208–12, 216–18, 343, 349
Delaney, Reverend (Father) Peter 214, 270
Delon, Alain 246
Dench, Judi 303
Denver airport 371–2
Derringer, Liz 340–1, 343–4, 346, 362
Derringer, Rick 315, 355, 366
Desmond, Norma 38
Diana, Princess of Wales 19, 222
*The Diary of Anne Frank* 106
Dietrich, Dr. 55
Disneyland 84, 134, 371
Divine Miss M 248
Donahue, Phil 239, 371
Donner, Richard 286
"Don't Cry Out Loud" 248
"Don't Sleep in the Subway, Darling" 170
Douglas, Mike 234
Dr. Seuss books 105
Dunaway, Faye 279
Duncan Sisters 6
Durbin, Deanna 24
Durgom, Bullets 117

*Easter Parade* 9, 35, 42, 131
Eddy, Nelson, movie 42
Edens, Roger 25–7, 33, 45, 55, 74–6, 194
Egyptian tumblers (Yehad and Yaheed) 81–2

Eichhorn, Allen 326, 329, 331
Eisenhower Center 337
El Morocco, New York 171
"Eli, Eli" 23
Elizabeth II, Queen, doctor 91–2
Englund, Brian 153, 159, 246
Englund, Cloris 152–3, 199, 286
Englund, George 152–3, 286
European tour 59
*Evita* 15, 303
*Extremities* 304, 306–7

Fabergé 291
family
  patterns 357
  photos 128
*The Fantasticks* 247
Farrow, Mia 77, 173
Fawcett, Farrah 304–5, 307–8, 310
Fawcett, Redmond 308
Fayed, Dodi 222, 286–7
FBI 46–7, 49, 326
FDA 38
Fields, Freddie and David Begelman 95–6, 101, 111, 148
Filiberti, Ray 179
Filiberti, Sharon 179–80
Finklehoffe, Carolyn and Freddie 93–4
Fisher, Eddie 267, 280
Florida 103
*Follies* 234
Forest Hill, concert 109, 172

Fran (David Merrick's office)
    232
Frank E. Campbell Funeral
    Chapel 212
Freeman, Colin 17, 58, 248,
    251, 271
Frey, Leonard 228
Friars Club, New York 288
Frost, David 234
*Funny Girl* 251

Gail (Liza's limo driver) 311,
    334–6, 341
Gale, Clark 27
Gardner, Rita 247
Garland Freaks 191–2
Garland, Judy 46–7
    Academy Award nomination
        69–70, 351
    agents 22, 189
        Luft, Sid 17, 83, 223,
            358–9
        mother 14, 67
    autopsy 208, 210
    biography 216–17
    birthday 206
    bodyguards 112–13
    books about 349
    Boston call for help 199–200
    boyfriends 157
    calls to Los Angeles 204
    children
        control of 112–13
        departure 205
        kidnapping 133–5
    clubbing 205

concerts 48, 74, 82, 198,
    205
    cancelled 179, 189
    New York 111
    tours 89, 96–7, 149
contract 23
crises 195–6, 220
death 13, 184, 202–19
debts 189–90
disasters 185
drugs
    amphetamines 38, 84–5,
        97, 180
    anti-psychotics 150
    barbiturates 84–5, 145
    Benzedrine 182
    brain damage 198, 200–1
    chemical addiction 37,
        151, 201, 205
    medications 84–5, 111,
        147, 149, 161–2, 300,
        357
    monitoring 84, 111, 146,
        173–4, 210–11, 348
    overdoses 159, 193, 210,
        273, 349
    paraldehyde injections 84,
        150
    prescription drugs 69, 87,
        120, 148, 273, 345
    problems 96, 145–6
    Ritalin 111, 127, 165–6,
        182
    Seconal 206, 210–11
    sleeping pills 54, 79–80,
        145
    stimulants 97, 206

Thorazine injections 84, 150, 206
England 111
facts of life lesson 161
family love 185
funeral 125, 208–9, 211–12, 214–15, 220, 243, 343
  "The Battle Hymn of the Republic" 125, 215
gay men 193–4
health
  care 187, 196, 198
  hospitals 111, 115, 176, 196–7
  nervous collapse 31
  nervous system 148–9
  post-partum depression 34, 60, 145
  problems 84, 86–7, 111, 133, 149–50, 161, 193
  sick spells 127–8, 147, 160, 168–84, 206
hotels 190–1
husbands *see* Deans, Mickey; Green, Tom; Herron, Mark; Luft, Sid
jewellery 188
"Juvenile Oscar" 31, 69
last two years 168
life style 189–90
Liza 317
Lorna 1, 18, 20, 105, 160
MGM 319, 341
name 22
night
  raids 149, 182–4, 186, 207

  support 191–2
obituaries 185
pregnancies 52, 54–6, 69
press agent 86
public appearances 108–9
records 89
sense of fun 164–5
stage debut 7–8
suicide attempts 36–7, 60, 145, 190, 209
support system 192–3
touring 132
vaudeville to film change 21
voice 42
"The Garland Sisters" 21
*Gator* 260
gay
  couples 295
  men 193–4
Gero, Mark 34, 320–3, 331, 344, 346, 350
Gershwin tunes 235, 254
Gerst, Lee 250
Gilmore, Will 11
*Girl Crazy* 26, 370
*The Godfather* 242
Gold, Johnny 271
*Golden Boy* 58
*The Good Old Summertime* 4
gossip columnists 85
Goulet, Robert 240
Graham, Sheila 76
Grand Rapids 5–6, 8, 10–12, 57, 88
*Grease* 301–2
*Grease 2* 302, 358

Green, Tom 156–7, 164–5,
    171, 188–9
Greene, Michael 256–7
Greenwich Village
  Downstairs at the Upstairs
    248
  New York 225
  Salvation 173
Grossman, Larry 235
guard dogs (Whitey and Saber)
    116–17
Gumm
  family 5, 8–9, 26
  grandparents (Ethel and
    Frank)
      marriage 10–12, 15, 17,
        88
      vaudeville act 4–5, 8–9,
        12, 20–1, 171, 236
Gumm, Baby Frances 6–10,
    13–15, 18, 20–2, 31, 83,
    210, 244
  see also Garland, Judy
Gumm, Ethel Marion Milner
    (grandmother) 245
  accompanist 3–4, 21
  children 3–8, 10–11, 22–3,
    161
  death 60
  Judy's manager/agent 14, 17,
    26, 28–30, 32, 357
  Los Angeles 12
  Rabwin, Marc 155
  suicide attempt 145–6
Gumm, Frank (grandfather)
    2–5, 7–12, 14–18, 20,
    22–3, 26, 57, 194, 210

Gumm, Jimmy (aunt Virginia)
    1–2, 5–7, 9, 13, 20, 25,
    29, 30, 38, 45, 83
  Dallas 243–5
  Las Vegas 116
Gumm, Mary 2–3
Gumm Sisters 8–9, 12–3, 20–1,
    48, 51, 116, 236, 244–5,
    317
Gumm, Susie (aunt) 5, 7, 13,
    20, 116, 244
  suicide 145–6
Gypsy 101, 170

Hackaday, Hal 235
Hackman, Gene 263
Hagen, Uta 230
Hair 226
Haley, Jack Jr. 286, 353
  alcohol 279–80
  Minnelli, Liza 252, 254,
    256, 262–3, 280, 319–20
  Twentieth-Century Fox 254,
    280
Haley, Jack Sr. 39
Hallowe'en 295–6
Halston (designer) 293–4, 297,
    320–1
Hamilton, George 107
Hamilton, Margaret 39
Hardy, Andy 222
The Harlettes 248–9
Harrington, Dee 270
Harrison, George 163
Harrods 89–91
Harry, Prince 19, 222
Hartford, Huntington 292–3

Haskell, Nikki 294, 309–10
"Have yourself a merry little
    Christmas" 175
Hawaii 138–9, 142, 149, 174,
    185, 346
Hayden-Guest, Anthony 293
Hazelden, Minnesota 367
Helen (blind girl) 106, 110
Hemingway, Patricia (Patty)
    220–1, 223–5
  Luft, Sid 171, 178–9, 197,
    203–5, 268–71, 320, 369
  New York 234, 276
Henderson, Jody 207
Henderson, Mrs. 207–8
"Here's to Us" 126
Herman, Jerry 174
Herron, Mark 135–40, 142,
    146–51, 156, 205
  clothes fire 143–4
  sexual orientation 147, 157,
    319
Hill, Mariana (Bridget) 136–7,
    163
Hillerman, John 259
Hippopotamus Club, New
    York 230–1, 237
Holiday, Joy and Ron 237–8
Hollywood 33, 76, 259
  Bowl, Beatles concerts 163
Hollywood Hills, house
    369–70
Hong Kong 149–50, 203, 207
Hooker, Jake 17, 305–9, 311,
    313, 339–40
  alcohol 281, 359, 362–6,
    374–8

Derringer, Rick 315–16
  father 306–9, 311, 313, 331
  jail 375
  Liza 322–4, 337
  London 269–71
  Lorna 267–71, 280–2, 285,
    287–90, 292–3, 295, 297,
    319, 334, 357, 359–60,
    362, 369, 371, 378
  Los Angeles move 339–41,
    353, 355–6, 359
  manager 358–9, 367, 373
Hooker, Jesse (son) see
    Richards
Hooker, Vanessa (daughter) see
    Richards
Hoover, J. Edgar 47
Houston 236
Houston Chronicle 240, 356
Hutton, Betty 36
Hyannis Port 98–100, 124,
    196, 272

"I am a rock; I am an island"
    222
I Could Go On Singing 111,
    115, 267, 302
"I Get a Kick Out of You" 254
I Love Lucy 1, 17, 309
interventionist 332–3, 335
Interview magazine 294
IRS 189

Jabarra, Paul, "Last Dance"
    297
"Jack and Virginia Lee" 4–5, 9,
    12, 20–1, 171, 236

Jackie-O's club, Rome 265
Jagger, Bianca 294
Jagger, Mick 173
Jamaican housekeeper 316, 332
Jessel, George 21–2
"Jingle Bells" 7–8, 50, 83
Joe Allen's 259
John, Elton 371
Johnson, Van 4
Jolson, Al 2
Judalein (cousin) 29, 245
*Judgement at Nuremburg* 98, 107, 222
Judy *see* Garland, Judy
"Judy", Carmichael, Hoagy 22
Judy Garland, Theaters 205–6
*The Judy Garland Show* 22, 121–2, 125–6, 174–5, 244
  "The Battle Hymn of the Republic" 125

Kelly, Gene 34, 36, 181, 253–4
Kennedy, Bobby 98, 100, 124, 196
Kennedy, Caroline 98–100, 123
Kennedy Compound 98–100
Kennedy, Ethel 99, 196
Kennedy, Eunice 99
Kennedy, Jacqueline 99–100, 103, 124, 231
Kennedy, John 98–100, 123
Kennedy, President John F. (Jack) 47, 95, 100, 103
  assassination 123–6, 196, 215
  funeral 124–5
Khan, Aly 49
King, Donna 302
Knights of Malta 322

Lady Eden school, London 89–90, 104, 131
Lahr, Bert 39–40, 178
Lake Tahoe 261
Lamarr, Hedy 44
Lamaze classes 310
Lamond, Bob 316, 340, 353, 355, 361–3
Lamond Zetter Agency 355–6, 359–60, 363
Lancaster, Burt 109
Lancaster, California 10, 12, 18, 88
Landau, Barry 326
Las Vegas
  hotels 81–2, 116, 118, 239–41
  ranch 116–20, 204
*The Last Party* 293
*Laugh In* 196
Lavot, Philippe 246–50, 260, 263, 367
Lawford, Chris 99, 123
Lawford, Peter 131–2, 151
Lazar, Alan 288–93, 295, 316
Lazar, Arlene 288–93, 295, 316, 326, 330
Lazar, Irving ("Swifty") 43, 76
Leachman, Cloris 152–3, 199, 286, *see also* Englund family
*Leave It to Beaver* 1, 221

Lee, Joan 199
Lee, Mrs 199–200
Lennon, John 164
Lerner, Alan Jay 226, 228
Liff, Samuel "Biff" 232
Lindsey, Mort 121
Lionel (butler) 151–2, 154, 159–60, 165
*Little Me* 126
Liu, Ed 373
Liza *see* Minnelli, Liza
Lloyd Webber, Andew 302–3
*Lolita* 226–8, 230–1, 233, 246
London 87–95, 113–14
  cabbie 202
  Dominion 89
  Guy Fawkes Night 93–4
  Hyde Park 90
  King's Road, Chelsea 89–95
  Lady Eden school 89–90, 104, 131
  Palladium 48–50, 87, 91, 267, 280
  St. Bartholomew's Church 270
  Savoy Hotel 114–15
  Talk of the Town 205, 267
  Trader Vic's 284
  Tramp club 271
  vacation invitation 206
Long Island 199, 217–18
"Lorna" 121
Lorna *see* Luft, Lorna
Los Angeles 144
  Aquarius Theater 226
  Brentwood Elementary School 123

Holmby Hills Park 66
lessons and audition 11
Loew's State Theater 12–13, 16
Malibu 120
Meglin School of Dance 12
Mrs. Lawlor's Academy 24
Orpheus 15
Palisades High school 220, 225
Paramount 13
Rialto 15–16
Roosevelt Hotel 363
schools 120
Studio City 353
Studio One 252–3
Warner's Hollywood 13
West, University High school 225–6
*see also* Rockingham Drive
"Love of My Life" 254
*Lucky Lady* 255–6, 259–60, 262
Luft, Aunt Perry 64
Luft (grandparents) 64
Luft, Joey 38–9, 62–3, 198
  alcohol 357
  birth and childhood 69–80, 83, 85–6, 145, 314, 318
  Boston concerts 176–8, 196
  California 197, 320
  childhood 368–9
  dog poisoned 126
  drums 169
  Europe 111
  film debut 115
  Florida 103

Garland Freaks 191–2
guard dog bite 116
*Gypsy* 101
Hooker, Jake 267
hotel moves 188–91
Hyannis Port 98–9
Judy
  attack 197–8
  death 208–19
Las Vegas 81–2, 116–20, 204
learning disability 105
London 89, 93–5, 113–15, 271
Lorna's fall 186
Los Angeles 144, 200, 353
Luft, Sid 198
Madison Square Gardens, Christmas week show 174–5
measles 103–4
New England summer concerts 169–70
New York 97–8, 100–1, 104, 234, 276, 318
Palace Theater 170–1
Rockingham Drive 286
Scarsdale 106–9
twelfth birthday 188
*West Side Story* 91, 99
"Where Is Love" 121
*The Wizard of Oz* 38–9
Luft, Johnny 54, 68
Luft, Leonora (grandmother) 63–6, 70, 151
Luft, Lorna
  alcohol 280, 300, 347

beatings 133
birth 56–7
boys 159–60
Cambridge diet 306
"Don't Sleep in the Subway, Darling" 170
drugs 273–4, 278, 280, 296–7, 299, 322, 333
  addictions 159
  chemical stimulants 302, 308
  cocaine 271, 274–5, 279–81, 283, 297, 300–1, 308, 357
  marijuana 274
dyslexic 105
England 268
film parts 115, 302
growing up 157–64
health
  appendicitis 91–5, 194–6
  broken arm 130–1
  check-up 162
  exhaustion 185–6
  gestation diabetes 372
  hospital stay 186–7
  measles 104
  tonsil operation 194–5
husbands *see* Freeman, Colin; Hooker, Jake
Judy's care 147, 155, 196, 198, 200, 204, 299, 348
junior high school career 163–4
management firm 316

managers
  Hooker, Jake 358–9, 367,
    373
  Luft, Sid 276–8, 357
  "Me and My Shadow"
    170
nicotine 273–4
night clubs 173, 221, 236,
  243, 276–7
performing skills 225
post-partum depression
  313–14
pregnancies 305–11, 314–5,
  369, 371, 373–4
"Santa Claus Is Coming to
  Town" 121
"Senior Prom" invitation
  160–1
singing career 17
"Singing in the Rain" 170
smoking 32, 157–8, 301
teaching class 264
tenth birthday 117
Luft, Michael S. 53
Luft, Norbert (grandfather)
  63–5
Luft, Sid 17, 31, 37, 40–8,
  51–3, 55, 60
  Boston concerts 176–8
  "Bridget" 136–7, 163
  California debts 98
  Christmas 134
  debts 189
  Egyptian tumblers 82, 85
  Fields, Freddie and David
    Begelman 96, 101
  Hair 226

health problems 198, 200
health-consciousness 66
hotels 186–7, 195–6, 198
Joey and Lorna 197–8
Judy
  assistance 144–5, 192
  Christmas week show
    174–5, 178
  concert series 167
  death 207–19
  management 261
  manager 17, 83, 223,
    358–9
  marriage 53, 83
  monitoring medication
    84, 111, 146, 173, 348
  New England summer
    concerts 169–70
  parties 74–7
  protector 50
  reunited 107
Las Vegas ranch incident
  117–20
Lee, Joan 199
letters 115
lifestyle 148
Liza 54, 166, 337, 349
Lolita 228–30
London 49, 87–9, 91–5, 115
Lorna 57–9
  and Joey 112–13, 132
  manager 276–8, 357
Los Angeles 142, 200,
  220–6, 320, 355
Mapleton Drive 62–3, 72–4,
  79–83, 86–8, 146
New York 104, 234, 276

Patty *see* Hemingway,
  Patricia
pilot 104
racing 59
Rockingham Drive 126–7
stereo system 96, 104

*McCalls* magazine 62
McCartney, Paul 164
*McCloud* 261
McDowall, Roddy 172
McGruter, Mr. (music teacher)
  225–6
McQueen, Steve 139, 143–4
Mackie, Bob 121
*Madeline* 93
Madison Square Gardens,
  Christmas week show
  174–5, 178
Madonna, *Evita* 15
Mafia 242
*Make Room for Daddy* 241
*Mame* 174
*A Man and a Woman* 265
Manchester, Melissa 248–9
Manilow, Barry 17, 249–52,
  255, 263
Mankiewicz, Joe 32
Mankiewicz, Tom 32
Manuela (daughter of Anouk
  Aimée) 265–6
Mapleton Drive 53, 56, 59,
  61–83, 85–8, 96, 184, 377
  debts 82–3, 98, 147–8
  disasters 79–80, 86
  guards 134
  Los Angeles 355

Luft, Sid 62–3, 72–4, 79–83,
  86–8, 146
  Sam (dog) 79–80
  staff 86
Maria (Spanish housekeeper)
  355, 366, 374
*Married with Children* 157
Martin, Dean 47, 73, 109
Martin, Gaill 77
*M.A.S.H.* 354
Mason, James 214
Mastroianni, Marcello 279
*A Matter of Time* 260, 264
Mayer, Louis B. 23, 25, 28,
  37–8, 83
*Meet Me in St. Louis* 34, 42,
  175
*Meglin Kiddies Show* 12, 15
Memorial Day weekend (1972)
  236–9
Mercer, Johnny 121–2
Merman, Ethel 26–7, 100–1
Merrick, David 232, 234
*Merv Griffin Show* 225–6
Messenger, Maxine 240, 356
Metro 22–4, 27, 37, 82
Mexico 255–7
MGM 25–6, 29, 31–3, 35,
  37–8, 40
  contract 26–7, 35–6, 41, 47
  days 36, 48, 50–2, 68, 82,
  231
  debt to 37, 49
  make-over artists 24
  musicals 205
  promotional tours 48, 109
  star 174

studio police 38
studio system 23, 83
*The Wizard of Oz* 28
Miami 103–4
Midler, Bette 248–50
"Midnight Blue" 248
Miller, Merle 248
*The Million Dollar Movie* 223
Milner, Eva (great-
    grandmother) 4, 7
Milner, John (Grandmother's
    brother) 4
Milner, Norma
    (Grandmother's sister) 4
"Milord" 93
Minnelli, Frances Gumm 53
    *see also* Garland, Judy
Minnelli, Liza 35–6, 39, 155,
    236, 368
  Academy Award 351
  Arnaz, Desi 234
  Betty Ford Center 33, 328,
    330, 332, 334, 339,
    341–4, 350–3, 367–8
  Beverly Hills 62, 68, 74–8,
    80, 85
  birth 34, 56
  *Cabaret* 229, 241, 317–18
  cancer scare 325–8
  Chicago 241–3
  *Chicago* 280, 319–20
  childlessness 318, 342
  Christmas 134–5
  drugs 321–38
    cocaine 275–6, 279, 357
    prescription drugs 337
  *Evita* 303

  fortieth birthday 367–8
  gay men 194
  hospital 325–6
  husbands *see* Allen, Peter;
    Gero, Mark; Haley, Jack
  Hyannis Port 98, 272
  Italy 279
  Judy 53–4, 208–19
  London 92–4, 113–14
    Palladium 89, 171
  Lorna's birth 58
  Los Angeles 252
  *Lucky Lady* 255–7, 259
  *A Matter of Time* 260, 264
  MGM 319
  New York 225, 230, 293,
    309–10, 320
  Paris 241
  *The Rink* 323–4, 331
  Rome 263, 266
  singing career 17
  Taylor, Elizabeth 329–32,
    334–5, 337, 341, 349–50
  *The Diary of Anne Frank*
    106–7
  *The Judy Garland Show* 121
  Vincente 53–4, 78, 166, 319,
    321, 337–8, 349
Minnelli, Vincente 34–6, 40,
    43, 47, 49, 53–4, 78, 181
  *An American in Paris* 265
  Judy 34–6, 40, 43, 47, 49,
    85
  Liza 53–4, 78, 166, 319,
    321, 337–8, 349
  *A Matter of Time* 260, 265
  *The Pirate* 181

*Mommie Dearest* 77
Monroe, Marilyn 231
Moon, Keith 284
*Moonlighting* 304
Morris, William 230, 233
Mother's Day 315
Mount Sinai Hospital, New
    York 310
Mrs. Lawlor's Academy 24
*Murder, She Wrote* 374
musicians 17

Nabokov, *Lolita* 226–7, 246
Napier, John 303
Needham, Hal 262
Nelson, Gene 277
Nelson, Miriam 277
Nelson, Rick 203
Nelson, Tracy 203
Neville, John 228
New England summer concerts
    169–70, 172
New Jersey 236
New York 97–8
    A-crowd 172–3
    Adam's Apple 231
    Alrae Hotel 188–9
    Arthur's night club 172–3,
        205
    Barbizon Hotel for Women
        226–7, 230
    Bellevue Hospital 188–9
    Berghof Studio 229–30
    Billy Reed's Little Club 41
    Bloomingdale's 178, 309
    the Brasserie 274
    Broadway 232–33, 235

Café Central 304
Central Park 112
Christmas 133–5, 178–9
Dakota 100–1, 104
El Morocco 171
Friars Club 288
Garland, Judy 206
Greenwich Village 173, 225,
    248
Hippopotamus Club 230–1,
    237
Hospital 328–31, 352
Minnelli, Liza 166–7, 225,
    230
Mount Sinai Hospital 310
new school 111
night life 230–1
Palace Theater 51, 170–1,
    233
Plaza hotel 112–13, 115,
    179, 189, 267
Professional Children's
    School 171–2, 199
P.S.6. (local public school)
    104–6
St. Bartholomew's Episcopal
    Church 320–1
St. Moritz hotel 183, 188
Shubert Theater 232
sixty second Street 168–84,
    187–8
Splendiferous dress shop
    169, 171
Studio 54 192, 290–301,
    305–6, 320, 326, 345
summer stock 301
Yellow Fingers 246

Ziegfeld Theatre 309
*The New York Post* 293
Newton John, Olivia 302
Nitti, Nick 242
Nixon, Richard 95
Nunn, Trevor 303

O'Brien, Margaret (*Meet Me in St. Louis*) 175
Odets, Clifford 58
Ohio 301
"The Old Gray Mare" 13
*Oliver!* 91, 121, 126, 232
Onassis, Arisotle 231
*Oprah* 339
Oswald, Lee Harvey 125
"Over the Rainbow" 27–8, 91, 170, 278

Pacific Ocean Park 136
Pacino, Al 312
Paige, Elaine 303
Palace theater, New York 51, 170–1, 233
Palisades High school, Los Angeles 220, 225
Palladium, London 48–50, 87, 89, 91, 267
Palm Springs 333, 337, 341, 346, 348
    see also Betty Ford Center
Palumbo, Gene 22, 176, 244–5
parents
    custody disputes 127–8, 132, 155
    debts 189
    divorce 115, 127, 146

fights 126
financial problems 96
marriage 267, 271
    breakup 85–6, 95–7, 101–2, 110–12
New York 38
reconciliation attempts 120
White House visit 103
Paris 107, 241, 367–8
Parsons, Louella 53, 56–7
*People* magazine 352
Perrine, Valerie 286–8
Pesci, Joe 304, 311
Petty, Bob 294, 297
*Peyton Place* 157
Pfeiffer, Michelle 302
phenobarbital 29
Philadelphia Safety Patrol 238
*The Pirate* 34, 107, 181, 254
Plaza Hotel, New York 112–13, 115, 179, 189, 267
Ponedel, Dottie 49
Porter, Cole 235, 254
Potts, Patricia 171, *see also* Hemingway, Patricia (Patty)
Powell, Eleanor 45
prescription drugs 84, 273, 337
    see also under Garland, Judy
Presley, Elvis 136–7, 139, 162, 262
Professional Children's School 171–2, 199
*Promises, Promises* 232–5, 248–50, 288

psychological torture 129–32

Quaaludes (sedative) 295–6, 300

Rabwin, Dr. Marc 11, 37, 49, 155
Rabwin, Marcella 37
Rat Pack 76
Reagan, Ronald 298
Reed, Sir Carol 89
Reeve, Christopher 285–6
Reeve, Gay 285
Reinhardt, Pam 331–8, 343
Reno, Nevada 261, 278, 376
Reynolds, Burt 254–68, 278
Rhodes, George 254
Richards, Jesse 15, 251, 254, 318, 339, 369, 371
early years 245, 311–16, 322–3, 326, 332, 334, 340–1, 360, 366–7, 374
Richards, Vanessa 2, 7, 15–16, 19, 40, 67, 315, 318
birth 372, 374
Ringo Starr 164
The Rink 323–4, 331
Ritalin 97, 165–6
Rivera, Chita 252, 323–5
Robbins, Grace 282
Robbins, Harold 282
Roberts, Pernell 364
Rockingham Drive, Los Angeles 120–33, 148, 152–3, 157, 164, 167, 199, 203, 286, 344, 357
bodyguard 134

Gumm, Susie suicide 145–6
night raids 181
Snowy 150–2
Rolling Stones 173, 269, 279, 281–2
Roman Holiday 266
Rome 263, 265–6
Rooney, Mickey 24, 28, 32, 84, 122, 197, 214, 227
Roosevelt Hotel, Los Angeles 363
Rose, David 32, 34
Ross, Annie 271
Rourke, Mickey 304
Royal Hawaiian Hotel 139, 142
Rubell, Steve 289–91, 296–8, 321
Ruby, Jack 125
Rudin, Mickey 330, 342–3
Russell, Jody 237
Russo, James 307

Sagal, Katy 157–8, 273–4
Sagal, Mrs. 158
St. Bartholomew's Church, London 270
Episcopal Church, New York 320–1
St. John's Hospital, Santa Monica 56–7, 59
St. Joseph's aspirin 272–3
St. Jude's Children's Hospital 239
St. Laurent, Yves 287
St. Moritz hotel, New York 183, 188

Sales, Tony 172
*Sally Jesse Raphael* 339
Salvation, Greenwich Village
     173
Sam, Chen 327–9
Sandy, Gary 301
Santa Anita Racetrack 63
Santa Monica 365
   St. John's Hospital 56–7, 59
Savannah 261
Scandia restaurant, Hollywood
     259
Scarsdale 106–9
Scavullo, Francesco 294
Schlatter, George 122
Schrager, Ian 296
Seconal (barbiturate) 84, 111,
     206, 210–11
Secret Service 100
Sewanee Military Academy 2
sex
   orientations 147, 157, 193
   promiscuity 298
Sharaff, Irene 319
Shaw, George Bernard 89
Shepherd, Cybill 254
Shore, Dinah 255–7, 259–62,
     264
Shriver, Maria 98–9
Shubert Theater, New York
     232
Simon and Garfunkel lyric 222
Simon, Neil 232
Sinatra, Frank 69, 75–6, 162,
     173, 251, 343
   Judy 47, 56, 109
   private jet 330, 334–7

Sinclair, Madge 364
Sirhan, Sirhan 196
Skinner, Dr. Bill 328–35, 337
*Snoopy* 303
Snowda-Wu (Snowy) 149–52
*Some Like It Hot* 231
"Someday My Prince Will
     Come" 266
Stack, Robert 63
*A Star Is Born* 51, 67, 69, 98,
     170, 214
Steel Pier, Atlantic City 236–9
Stein, Julie 365–6
Stewart, Rod 270
Stigwood, Robert 303
*Stone Alone* 281
Studio 54, New York 192,
     289–301, 305–6, 320,
     326, 345
Studio One, Los Angeles 252–3
*Sugar* 231
suicide, family history 145–6
*Summer Stock* 36
Superior, Winsconsin 3
*Superman* 285–6, 288
"Swannee" 89

Talk of the Town, London 205,
     267
Taylor, Elizabeth 84, 368
   Betty Ford Center 328,
     331–2, 334–5, 339, 341
   Liza 329–32, 334–5, 337,
     341, 349–50
Taylor, Rip 170
Temple, Shirley 12
Terry, Ellen 89

Testi, Fabio 265–6
*That Girl* 233
"That's What Friends Are For" 372
"The Battle Hymn of the Republic" 125, 215
*They're Playing Our Song* 301, 307–8, 356
Thomas, Danny 239–41, 356
Thomas, Marlo 239, 371
Thompson, John 244–5
Thompson, Kay 32, 74, 208–9, 212, 215
Tierney, Gene 44–5
"Together" 170
*Tonight Show* 262, 280, 304
*The Towering Inferno* 143
Trader Vic's, London 284
Tramp club, London 271
Transcona Enterprises 51–2
*Trapper John, M.D.* 354–5, 360, 364
Travolta, John 355, 361
Tuinal (barbiturate) 84, 111
Turner, Lana 31
Twain, Norman 226–7
Twentieth-Century Fox 254, 280
*The Twilight Zone* 124

*United States* 88
Universal Lot 375
University High school, West Los Angeles 225–6
University of the South 3
*The Untouchables* 242

Valium (barbiturate) 111, 258
*Valley of the Dolls* 166
Vandow, Steve 236–9
vaudeville days 48
Vernon, Jackie 170
Vigrass, Paul 288, 293
Village People 308

Waikiki, Diamond Head 139–44
Waite, Tom 307–8
Wanda the Wonder Horse 237–8
Wards of High Court of Britain 114
Warhol, Andy 294
Warner, Jack 51, 60
Warner Brothers 51
Washington, suicide attempt 145
*Weep No More, My Lady* 216
Weisman, Eliot 330, 367
*West Side Story* 91, 99
*Where the Boys Are* 303, 309
"Where the Boys Are" 308
White, Jeannie 369–72
White, Ryan 370–2
The Who 269–70, 282
William Morris agency 236, 239–40
William, Prince 19, 222
Williams, Andy 174
Williams, Barry 301
Willis, Bruce 304
Winkler, Lee 261
*The Wizard of Oz* 16, 22, 29, 31, 38, 104–5, 109

Academy Award nomination
  69–70, 351
Dorothy 28, 219
Lion 178
Lorna and Joey viewing
  38–9
Luft, Joey 38–9
memorabilia 19
tributes 217
WKRP in Cincinnai 301
World's Fair, Chicago (1934)
  21

Wyman, Bill 281–5, 296
Wyman, Steven 282

Yellow Fingers, New York 246
Young Rascals 207
You're a Good Man, Charlie
  Brown 303

Zetter, Lois 355–6, 359, 361,
  363
Ziegfeld Theatre, New York
  309